Strategic Planning: Development and Implementation

Strategic Planning: Development and Implementation

Dr. Bonita H. Melcher
and Dr. Harold Kerzner

TAB Professional and Reference Books

Division of TAB BOOKS Inc.

Blue Ridge Summit, PA

FIRST EDITION
FIRST PRINTING

Library of Congress Cataloging in Publication Data

Melcher, Bonita H.
Strategic planning : development and implementation / by Bonita H.
Melcher and Harold Kerzner.
p.   cm.
Includes index.
ISBN 0-8306-9310-6
1. Strategic planning.   I. Kerzner, Harold.   II. Title.
HD30.28.M437   1988
658.4′012—dc19   88-15954
                                                                                    CIP

Questions regarding the content of this book
should be addressed to:

Reader Inquiry Branch
TAB BOOKS Inc.
Blue Ridge Summit, PA 17294-0214

Contents

Preface

The importance of strategic planning as a management function will increase dramatically in the next decade. This book was developed to provide a hands-on approach towards learning the necessary analytical tools and techniques of strategic planning. It is intended for the generalist who wants to learn how to develop an integrated system of planning activities to ensure the efficiency and effectiveness of the firm. Because of this emphasis, our book focuses more on the implementation processes than on the formulation processes. There are many excellent texts which develop the formulation processes in great detail, and it is not our intent to improve upon those approaches, but rather to draw upon them to build a base for defining what strategic planning is. We have kept the formulation processes at a simple, manageable level. Our intent is to focus on the "how-to" of strategic planning.

The general framework has been tested with hundreds of our MBA and undergraduate business students. We find the framework is very effective for students and managers who desire an overall perspective of how the organization fits together as an integrated system of activities. The many helpful comments of students and managers of companies who have graciously permitted their firms to be studied have been used to revise the manuscript. Special acknowledgement is given Kenneth Smith for his work contributed for Chapter 10.

Special mention should be given to President Neal Malicky; Vice President and Dean Mark Collier; and Chairman of the Division of Business Administration,

Ronald Ehresman, for their continuous support and encouragement. We would be lost without the efforts of Marcia Turify and Pat Ray who typed the many revisions of the manuscript. Finally, a special thanks to our families and friends who supplied emotional support throughout the effort by believing we could do it.

Bonita H. Melcher
Harold Kerzner
Baldwin-Wallace College
Berea, Ohio

Introduction

The significance of strategic planning for the survival of the firm emerged from the demands of the turbulent environment of the '60s and '70s. Many firms were caught by surprise as rapid environmental changes went unnoticed or unheeded. The study of environmental changes and their impact on the firm becomes the most significant area of management study in the '80s. The '90s, with a globally defined environment, will make strategic planning even more important. The United States will enter the 1990s with increased foreign competition, increasing scarcity of natural resources, and a continuation of flattened growth rates. The future requires trained strategic planners who recognize changes and adapt. No longer will a CEO have the luxury of saying, "We don't see the need for change."

As a field of formalized study, strategic planning is now required as the capstone course in all major schools of business, at both the undergraduate and graduate levels. This emphasis represents a maturation of the field of business study, both from the standpoint of integrating the basic business functions of marketing, finance, manufacturing/operations, and R&D into a unified whole and from the standpoint of moving management from an art to a science.

We have been through a long period of specialized study on how to run successful businesses, and each of the business functions has enjoyed its emphasis as the driving force of a business entity's success. Business colleges encourage or even require students to major in a specialized function, but the increasing environmental demands of the '80s and '90s require a shift in focus to a more generalized approach. We now need to understand how all the functional areas work together as a system to effect the survival of the firm. The need for this type of understanding was recognized in the '60s; developing an understanding has been in process for over 25 years.

A great deal of research effort has been devoted to the refinement and development of the *strategy formulation* process. Development in this area has moved from descriptive case studies to theoretical conceptualizations. With increasing research to test models and theories, the concepts which emerged in the '70s and '80s have more of the attributes of a true science. Formulation consists of analyzing the company's environment and assessing its resources to arrive at strategic fits between opportunities and threats, and strengths and weaknesses. Strategic planning has been defined and the basic variables have been identified. The next step is to develop a theory of implementation.

Our text builds on the wealth of theory development to this point. We have devoted an entire chapter to the evolution of strategic management and its function, strategic planning, and have attempted to integrate the best of these conceptualizations into our text.

Much of our book focuses on the development of the implementation process. Knowledge of implementation has been slow to develop due to limited vision caused by overspecialization in business education. To understand the implementation process, we must develop a systems theory of how business functions operate as a unified whole. This is a difficult endeavor. The risk exists of oversimplifying business functions in an effort to explore and develop the interface points within and between functions. Some activities of a functional area are critical to an effective interface; others are not. We devote an entire chapter in an attempt to identify these critical interfaces.

This book is drawn from our collective experience of teaching in the MBA and Executive MBA programs at Baldwin-Wallace College, the undergraduate strategy and policy course, a multitude of consulting experiences with industry, and many years of research.

At the undergraduate level, our book is appropriate for the senior level business strategy and policy course. This market is currently dominated by books which combine the theoretical development of the formulation process with case material. The case material in these books ages rapidly, requiring faculty who use these books to adopt new ones or find, at least, new cases. Our book is easily used with any of the excellent case books now available, such as *Cases in Strategic Management* by Mescon and Vozikis.[1]

The book is also appropriate for the advanced course in a management major where the focus is on the planning process from the top of the organization. Critical factors of all the basic functions are developed in enough detail to give the generalist an appreciation of the functions and how they interface.

Conceptual books without cases are generally written for the graduate level student. These include Michael Porter's *Competitive Advantage*[2] and Igor Ansoff's *Implanting Strategic Management*.[3] These texts presume a prior exposure to specialized functions and some knowledge of the strategy area. Our text is written for those who do not have a prior exposure to the strategic process. And, because of this, our text is appropriate as the capstone course in an MBA program, concentrating on a general management curriculum for students without business undergraduate degrees.

Chapter 1 presents an overview of strategic planning defining the formulation and implementation processes; the ever-increasing need for strategic planning in a complex business world is highlighted. Chapter 2 takes the reader through the evolution of the conceptual modeling process with illustrations of dominant strategy formulation models. The best of these conceptualizations are integrated into a comprehensive framework to be used throughout the rest of the text. The integrated framework is presented in Chapter 3.

The next four chapters begin the development of the implementation process. Four functional area strategies are presented in depth: finance, marketing, manufacturing/operations, and R&D, each with a summary of the critical interface activities. Chapter 8 discusses how these functional areas are integrated into a unified whole for achieving corporate and business level goals. Chapter 9 develops the unique perspective of strategic planning for the small business. In Chapter 10, the process is applied to multinational business planning. Finally, Chapters 11 and 12 deal specifically with the problems of developing strategic managers and using project management as a technique for implementing strategy.

Our book is intended for practitioners, as well as students of strategy. The practitioner may choose to skip Chapter 2 on the evolution of strategic theory.

Strategic planning is more than a current management fad. It is an area of study vitally important to the student of business and the current practicing manager who must wrestle with an ever more uncertain future and an increasingly complex environment.

ENDNOTES—Introduction

1. Mescon and Vozikis, *Cases in Strategic Management* (Harper & Row, 1988).
2. Michael Porter, *Competitive Advantage* (The Free Press, 1980).
3. Igor Ansoff, *Implanting Strategic Management* (Prentice-Hall International, 1984).

Chapter 1

The Role of Strategic Planning in the Survival of the Organization

1.0 WHAT IS STRATEGIC PLANNING?

trategic planning is the process of formulating and implementing decisions about an organization's future direction. This process is vital to every organization's survival, because it is the process by which the organization adapts to its ever-changing environment and is applicable to all levels and types of organizations. The formulation process is the process of deciding where you want to go, what decisions must be made, and when they must be made in order to get there. It is the process of defining and understanding the business you are in. The outcome of this process results in the organization doing the right thing by producing goods or services for which there is a demand or need in the external environment. When this occurs, we say the organization has been effective as measured by market response, such as sales and market shares. All organizations must be effective or responsive to their environments to survive in the long run.

The formulation process is performed at the top levels of the organization. Here, top management values provide the ultimate decision template for directing the course of the firm.

Formulation:
- Scans the external environment and industry environment for changing conditions.
- Interprets the changing environment in terms of opportunities or threats.

- Analyzes the firm's resource base for asset strengths and weaknesses.
- Defines the mission of the business by matching environmental opportunities and threats with resource strengths and weaknesses.
- Sets goals for pursuing the mission based on top management values and sense of responsibility.

Implementation translates the formulated plan into policies and procedures for achieving the grand decision and involves all levels of management in moving the organization toward its mission. The process seeks to create a fit between the organization's's formulated goal and its on-going activities. Because it involves all levels of the organization, it results in the integration of all aspects of the firm's functioning. Middle- and lower-level managers spend most of their time on implementation activities. Effective implementation results in stated objectives, action plans, timetables, policies and procedures, and results in the organization moving efficiently towards its mission.

Strategy must be executed to be effective. Tom Peters reports that the secret to the success of the firms that he and Waterman studied was "Almost invariably mundane execution."[1]

Implementation:
- Translates mission into specific measurable objectives.
- Acquires needed resources.
- Allocates resources to required activities.
- Directs required activities.
- Uses control to assure activities achieve objectives.
- Creates and changes activities as necessary.

Strategic planning consists of two processes (see Fig. 1-1): formulating strategy and implementing strategy.

The concept of strategy is not new. Military leaders have used the process for centuries. The application of strategy to the relationship between an organ-

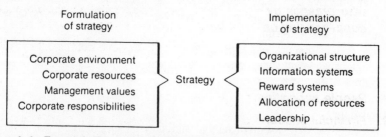

Fig. 1-1. Formulation and implementation of strategy.
Source: Norman A. Berg, General Management, Irwin, 1984, p. 30.

ization and its environment, however, is a relatively new application. Steiner, Miner, and Gray have developed a list of 17 elements showing the change from recent past to future managerial practices (Table 1-1). The current and future practices on this list highlight the need for strategic education of current managers.

Table 1-1. Recent Past Versus Current and Future Managerial Practices
Source: George A. Steiner, John B. Miner, Edmund R. Gray, Management Policy and Strategy, MacMillan, 1982, p. 75.

Recent Past Toward	Current and Future
1. *Assumption that a business manager's sole responsibility is to optimize stockholder wealth; operational management dominant*	*Profit still dominant but modified by the assumption that a business manager has other social responsibilities; strategic management dominant*
2. *Business performances measured only by economic standards*	*Application of both an economic and social measure of performance*
3. *Emphasis on quantity of production*	*Emphasis on quantity and quality*
4. *Authoritarian management*	*Permissive/democratic management*
5. *Short-term intuitive planning*	*Long-range comprehensive structured planning*
6. *Entrepreneural managers who prosper by concentrating on exploiting*	*Renaissance managers who have the capability of entrepreneurs but how also understand political, technical, social human and other forces influencing their organizations*
7. *People subordinate*	*People dominant*
8. *Financial accounting*	*Financial, human resources, and social accounting*
9. *Caveat emptor*	*Ombudsman*

Table 1-1. (continued)

Recent Past Toward	Current and Future
10. Centralized decision making	Decentralized and small group decision making
11. Dominance of solely economic forecasts in decision making	Major use of social, technical, and political forecasts as well as economic forecasts
12. Business ideology calls for aloofness from government	Business-government cooperation and convergence of planning
13. Business has little concern for social costs of production	Increasing concern for internalizing social costs of production
14. Managerial emphasis on internal efficiency	Emphasis on devising strategy to adapt to turbulent environment plus internal efficiency
15. Decisions based on assumption of price stability	Assumption of continuing inflation
16. Decisions based on assumptions of cheap and abundant energy	Expensive and uncertain energy supplies
17. Most companies not involved in foreign trade and international competition	Many multinational corporations facing stiff foreign competition.

1.1 THE ADVANTAGES OF STRATEGIC PLANNING

Research indicates a strong relationship between strategic planning and the survival of the firm.[2] Although findings are still uncertain about the relationship with levels of performance, there appears to be a positive relationship. As more sophisticated methodological techniques are applied to strategy research, this finding is certain to be verified. Planners have the winning edge.

Although strategy does not guarantee improved profits, it does improve the chances of improved profits and success. Continuous monitoring of the environment provides an awareness of the need for change.

One primary advantage of planning is that it provides a firm with consistency of action. As the numbers of interrelated units in organizations have increased, so have the benefits from the integrating direction afforded by the implementation process. Without this process, subunits tend to drift off in their own direction without regard to their role as a subsystem in a larger system of goals and objectives. The goal-setting of the formulation process and the integrating of the implementation process assure that all the parts of an organization are moving toward the same common objective. Strategy gives direction to diverse activities.

Another advantage of strategic planning is that it provides a vehicle for the communication of overall goals to all levels of management in the organization. It affords the potential of a vertical feedback loop from top to bottom and bottom to top. The process of communication and its resultant understanding helps reduce resistance to change. It is extremely difficult to achieve commitment to change when employees do not understand its purpose. The strategic planning

FUNCTIONAL RESPONSIBILITY

Planning Activities	Corporate		Divisional		
	Top Management	Corporate Planning Department	Divisional General Management	Divisional Staff Groups	Intermediary Planning Groups
Phase					
Establish corporate goals and objectives	▲				
Establish corporate goals and objectives	●	●			
Set planning horizon	●		●		
Organize and co-ordinate planning effort		●			●
Make environmental assumptions					
Make environmental assumptions	▲	●	▲	●	
Collect information and forecast					
Forecast sales	▲		▲	●	
Assess firm's stregths and weaknesses			▲	●	
Evaluate competitive environment			▲	●	
Establish divisional goals and objectives					
Establish divisional goals and objectives	▲		▲	●	▲
Develop divisional plans	▲	O	▲		▲
Formulate alternative strategies		O			
Select alternative strategies		O	●	●	
Evaluate and select projects			▲	●	
Develop tactics			▲	●	
Revise objectives and plans if objectives are not met	▲				
Integrate plans		●			
Allocate resources	▲				
Review progress against the plan	●		●		
Evaluate plan's effectiveness		●			

Key   ▲ Approves   O Reviews, evaluates and counsels   ● Does the work

Fig. 1-2. Functional responsibility relationship in strategic planning.
Source: Ronald J. Kudla, "Elements of Effective Corporate Planning"
Long Range Planning, August 1976, p. 89.

process gives all levels an opportunity to participate, thus reducing the fear of the unknown and eliminating resistance. Figure 1-2 illustrates the involvement of all levels in the planning process.

The final and perhaps the most important advantage is the thinking process required. Planning is a rational, logically ordered function. Many managers caught up in the day-to-day action of operations will appreciate the order afforded by a logical thinking process.

The advantages of strategic planning are multifold:

* Survival of the firm.
* Chance of improved profitability.
* Consistency of action.
* Vehicle for communication.
* Vertical feedback loop.
* Reduced resistance to change.
* Ordered thinking process.

1.2 WHY IS IT NECESSARY?

All organizations have strategy, but not all organizations have explicit strategy. If strategy is not explicitly formulated, it can be deduced by observing the pattern of activities the firm pursues. Usually these activities result in a strategy to simply react to unanticipated events as they occur in a storming fashion. If this *storming strategy* is pursued, then events control the destiny of the firm rather than the firm controlling the destiny of events. Rationalizing strategy and making it explicit increases the firm's control over its own destiny. The firm becomes *proactive* rather than *reactive*. The activity of planning itself begins to shape the course of events.

In the absence of explicit strategy formulation and implementation, decisions are made incrementally. A response to the crisis of the moment may result in a choice which is unrelated and perhaps inconsistent with the choice made in the previous moment of crisis. Discontinuous choices serve to keep the organization from moving forward. Contradictory choices are a disservice to the organization and cause its demise. These discontinuous and contradictory choices occur when decisions are made independently to achieve different objectives. When the strategy formulation process is made explicit, however, goals, missions, and policies become visible guidelines which produce logically consistent decisions.

A well-known example of this type of logical inconsistency is Sears and Roebuck's offering high fashion designer clothes and discounted appliances. These strategies serve different missions. The actions necessary to market designer fashions would drive away the customers who seek discounted appliances and vice versa. This example of contradictory choices has resulted in a decline of Sear's retailing operations.[3]

The planning process helps the firm anticipate the effects of environmental change on the operations of the firm. While it is not always possible to eliminate the occurrence of unanticipated events, an explicit framework for tracking changes can greatly reduce unanticipated changes.

Anticipating change gives the firm longer lead times for commitments. The longer the lead time, the greater the opportunity to minimize cost and improve quality. The firm has the luxury of thinking through alternative forms of financing, competitive bids on raw materials, and cost-out alternative designs. Reacting to unanticipated events always puts the firm at a cost disadvantage. Research is full of examples of organizations who failed to see the changes in their environments and failed to plan for these changes. W. T. Grant, AMC, U.S. Steel, and Amtrack are a few obvious examples. One spectacular example is the takeover attempt of Goodyear. Management failed to buffer the threat their undervalued stock presented them in a permissive environment for takeover attempts. They did not anticipate the effects of letting the stock become undervalued.

Once the planning process is made explicit, it provides a system of continuous review and analysis. It imposes a discipline on the firm to continually monitor the goals for achievement, to reevaluate goals based on environmental changes, and to continually seek more efficient ways to implement strategy.

We have progressed past the point where a firm that has financial capital can hope to be successful by investing in unrelated businesses for purposes of financial synergy. Today's organizations have a need for a logical planning base which will provide the guideline for strategic choices.

Strategic planning is necessary in today's organization because its application:

- Increases control over destiny.
- Shapes the course of events.
- Provides visible goals.
- Allows for long lead time.
- Demands continuous review and analysis.

1.3 THE ELEMENTS OF STRATEGY

Strategies may be classified according to their scope, specifications, and deployment. *Scope* broadly defines what business the company is in. It will identify the products to be produced, the customers to be served, the location of operations, and the overall competitive emphasis of the firm. Top management determines the scope as part of the firm's strategy formulation.

The second element of strategy is *specifications*. Specifications are the standards used to measure the present strategic position of the firm. They answer the question, "How are we doing?" and "How would we like to do in the future?" Every firm can be specified according to:

- Present size and rate of growth.
- Market share.
- Profitability.
- ROI, ROE.
- Life expectancy.

By measuring our current position on our specified benchmarks, we gain information on how we are doing at a point in time. Comparing these levels with past levels enables us to specify the rate of growth or decline over time. Strategy is adaption to change. Answering the question "How are we doing?" determines if the adaption processes have been effective.

Market share measured by the percent of total sales is another specification. Both the current level and change in the percent are important determinants of how we are doing relative to the competition.

Profitability is the most widely used measure of organizational performance. Firms seek to at least maintain and at best increase their profitability. Specifying an increase in profitability requires formulating and implementing strategies to meet the new level desired.

Return on investment (ROI) and *return on equity* (ROE) are commonly used specifications. Both current levels and changes are important measures. Return on investment tells us how well assets are being deployed and return on equity measures the return on shareholder's contribution.

Life expectancy is a measure of "staying power." It's useful for management to assess how long a particular strategic advantage will last.

Specifications define how well we are doing compared to our past performance and provides a benchmark for determining what our prospects are for doing well in the future.

The third element of strategy is *deployment*. Deployment is the relative allocation of funds, facilities, equipment, and manpower to the various activities of the firm. Deployment answers the question "What are we doing?" It is the essential element in the implementation of strategy. Activities ultimately determine the direction in which company moves. Deployment indicates the true emphasis of the firm. Effective deployment is essential to the firm's meeting its stated goals.

By identifying and describing the scope of operations, specifications for performance, and deployment of resources, the present strategy of the firm can be profiled. This is an essential part of evaluating strategy, because many firms think they are going in one direction while actually deploying resources for activities which move them in a different direction. Thus, the firm needs to know if it is going where they think they are.

The basic elements of corporate strategy are defining scope, setting specifications, and deploying resources. Scope and specifications are outcomes of the formulation process. Deployments are outcomes of the implementation process.

1.4 LEVELS AND KINDS OF STRATEGIES

At the highest level in the organization, strategy focuses on the entire organization and the time horizon is long-range. Strategy formulated at this level is referred to as *corporate* or *grand strategy*. The outcome defines the scope and specifications for the entire set of organizational activities.

The appropriate grand strategy will depend on the mission, the growth rates of related markets, and the company's competitive position. Depending on changes in the environment, the firm's corporate strategy will be adapted for the appropriate response.

Strategies which affect a single business unit are called *business strategies*. As companies grow and mature, the number and type of product lines, services, and markets will increase to the point where strategic planning may become overly complex. To promote coordination and gain better control over the diverse business units, an additional layer of management may be necessary. Divisions with similar interests are then clustered into *strategic business units* (SBUs), where each SBU is strategically autonomous from other SBUs. For example, General Electric restructured 48 divisions into six SBUs.

The characteristics of SBUs are as follows:

- Each SBU establishes its own profitability and accountability channels.
- Each SBU should be oriented to the external environment and have direct control over those resources and key factors necessary for success.
- Each SBU should have customers/markets that are distinct from other SBUs.

Shown below are the characteristics of an SBU at General Electric:

- A statement of the SBU's mission.
- Environmental assumptions including external environment and its opportunities and threats.
- Assumptions about key competitors.

- Inside and outside constraints.
- Objectives that are sought.
- Strategy to be followed in achieving objectives.
- Development and investment programs critical to strategy.
- Specific time-phased events that must be met to attain objectives.
- Resources required to implement strategy.
- Contingency plans.
- Statement of financial plans that integrate the strategic and operational plans.

SBUs can drastically improve the company's ability to perform strategic planning. However, there are disadvantages such as the need for an additional layer of management, role conflict, ambiguity at the senior levels, and conflict over control of critical corporate resources. The scope of business strategy is narrower than corporate strategy. Business strategies are usually formulated by business-level managers in cooperation with corporate managers. Business unit strategy flows from corporate level strategy.

Functional strategy, the third level of strategy, deals with the setting of objectives and deployment of resources for the activities of the functional areas of the firm. Functional strategies are narrow in scope and are generally for a one-year time span. Functional strategies deal with "how to" questions and are the starting point of the implementation phase of the strategic planning process. Functional strategies must be carefully integrated with each other and with business unit and corporate strategies to assure that the firm actually moves in the desired direction. Figure 1-3 shows the nature and relationship of the three levels of strategy.

	Corporate	*Business*	*Functional*
Level of management responsibility	Top: corporate-level managers	Upper middle: business- or division-level managers; or top, in a single-business or -product company	Operating: functional-level managers
Scope	Entire organization	SBU or single-business or -product company	Functional area, geographic area, product area, customer area
Time span	Long range (0–5 years)	Intermediate range (1–3 years)	Short range (0–1 year)
Specificity	General statements of direction and intent	Concrete and operationally oriented	Action and implementation oriented

Fig. 1-3. Characteristics of corporate-, business-, and functional-level strategies.
Source: Leslie W. Rue, Phyllis G. Holland, Strategic Management, McGraw Hill, 1968, p. 12.

1.5 NEED FOR DECISION-MAKING MODELS

To be effective, strategic planning must be founded on a systematic and logical base, a framework for guiding decisions. Because it requires vision into an uncertain future, strategic planning will always be a process of logic and creativity. If the base of logic is missing, it is highly unlikely that creativity alone will result in success. Logical decision models lay the base on which to build creativity, judgment, and common sense. Logic and creativity enhance the strategic planning process.

Most of the complex and interrelated changes occurring within the environment today are beyond the thinking capacity of a single individual and demand the use of multivariate *decision models* as an aid to analyzing and formulating strategy. Figure 1-4 shows the starting point for developing a decision model for formal strategic planning.

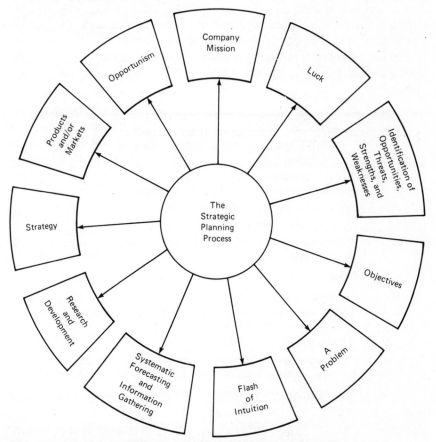

Fig. 1-4. Starting points for formal strategic planning.

As strategic planning has evolved into a recognized field of management study, many competing decision models have emerged. Essentially, all of these frameworks include the same basic components of the strategy formulation process. These components are:

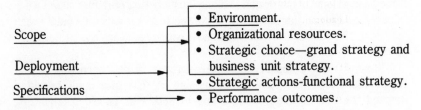

Scope

Deployment

Specifications

- Environment.
- Organizational resources.
- Strategic choice—grand strategy and business unit strategy.
- Strategic actions-functional strategy.
- Performance outcomes.

1.6 THE ROLE OF POLICIES—IMPLEMENTING STRATEGIES

Policies provide specific guidelines for directing the thinking, decisions, and actions of managers in implementing strategy. Policies contribute to the on-going implementation of strategy by standardizing many routine decisions and controlling the discretion of managers and subordinates in implementing strategies. Tables 1-2 and 1-3 show the issues involved in formulating and implementing policies.

Table 1-2. Issues Involved in Formulating Strategic Policies
Source: Strategic Management *by Boseman, Phatak and Schellenberger, John Wiley, 1986, p. 53.*

Scope of the corporation's business—defining the product(s) of the corporation and the market segment(s) served.

Criteria for entering or existing in a business or industry.

Geographical scope of company activities.

Nature of technology utilized in production process.

Channels of distribution.

Product quality.

Company image.

Fundamental organizational objectives—growth, stability, retrenchment, turnaround, divestment, liquidation.

Dominant method of competition.

Social responsibility of corporation.

Role of corporation in society.

Philosophy regarding management style and organizational climate.

Organization structure.

Corporation orientation—marketing vs. production.

Table 1-3. Issues Involved in Formulating Implementation Policies
Source: **Strategic Management** *by Boseman, Phatak and*
Schellenberger, John Wiley, 1986, p. 53.

Type of organization structure—divisional vs. functional.

Leadership styles—authoritarian, democratic, participative.

Motivation systems—incentive programs, reward system.

Staffing practices—matching executives to job requirements.

Coordination techniques—quality circles, project teams.

Information needs of managers and systems to meet those needs.

Promoting entrepreneurship in managerial behavior.

Employee's career paths and promotion methods.

Performance evaluation systems.

Measures for evaluation of total organization performance.

Policies achieve the following purposes:

- Provide control over decision discretion of lower level managers.
- Provide consistency in handling of similar decisions.
- Provide quicker decisions by routining regularly occurring activities.
- Provide clarity of strategy and reduce uncertainty at lower levels.

To be effective, policies should be written. Many firms refrain from making policies explicit because of the need for competitive secrecy.

1.7 WHY DOES STRATEGIC PLANNING FAIL?

We have developed a strong case in earlier sections of this chapter for the benefits of strategic planning. Knowledge about the process is continually growing, and new information is disseminating rapidly. Why, then, does the strategic planning process fail?

Following are some of the problems which occur in the application of the process. Each of these pitfalls must be carefully avoided if the process is to be effective:

- Failure to reexamine. Strategic planning is not a one-shot process. It is a dynamic, continual process. Outcomes are linked directly back to a reexamination of mission, goals and objectives, and activities. The system must be structured for continuous feedback control.

- Extrapolation of present performance into the future. This is long-range planning. As an example, a company with an annual growth rate of 10 percent for 1983-1987 might extrapolate this growth rate into 1990 and come up with a projected sales volume of $300 million. But, what if management wants the sales volume to be $350 million in 1990? What decisions does the company have to make today and tomorrow in order to arrive at the desired objective? The latter is strategic planning. Extrapolation assumes the future will be like the past; strategic planning anticipates changes in the environment and then simulates what the effect of these changes will be on future performance. Extrapolation only helps an organization repeat the mistakes it made in the past.

- Overoptimism and/or complacency. Overoptimism occurs when the firm overestimates which variables over which it has control. Complacency sets in when efforts do not translate into immediate results. In the overoptimistic state, the organization becomes manic, hyperactive, and burns itself out. Management allows the strategic planning process to overstimulate the organization. With complacency, the organization is understimulated. The process occurs too infrequently or with such lack of enthusiasm that no one really believes it works.

- Blinded by success. In periods of phenomenal growth of profits, it is easy to believe the "everything we do is great" and "we can do no wrong, so there is no need to plan." Strategic planning is hard work. It is a disciplined process. It is not a lot of fun, and as soon as things are going wonderfully, it is easy to believe you do not need to do it.

- Overresponsiveness to industry trends. Too many changes in too short a time frame cause a firm to overextend and spread too thin. Strategic planning is the careful selection of which trends to follow and which to ignore.

Strategic planning is successful if the pitfalls are avoided. The process must be structured for continual reexamination. Forecasts must flow from perceived changes in the environment and not mirror past performance. The process must be correctly balanced to avoid overoptimism and complacency. Success should not be interpreted as a time to rest from planning, and management should carefully select which changes to which it will respond. Table 1-4 lists the pitfalls of strategic corporate planning identified by Steiner, Miner, and Gray. This list encompasses and expands upon those mentioned above.

Unfortunately, too many managers deveolp a short-term strategy which improves profitability to appease shareholders. The process may ultimately erode

Table 1-4. Major Current Pitfalls in Corporate Strategic Planning
Source: George A. Steiner, John B. Miner, Edmund R. Gray,
Management Policy and Strategy, MacMillan, 1982, p. 195.

1. *Failure to develop throughout the company an understanding of what strategic planning really is, how it is to be done in the company, and the degree of commitment of top management to doing it well.*

2. *Failure to accept and balance interrelationships among intuition, judgement, managerial values, and the formality of the planning system.*

3. *Failure to encourage managers to do effective strategic planning by basing performance appraisal and rewards solely on short-range performance measures.*

4. *Failure to tailor and design the strategic planning system to the unique characteristics of the company and its management.*

5. *Top management becomes so engrossed in current problems that it spends insufficient time on the strategic planning process, and the process becomes discredited among other managers and staff.*

6. *Failure to mesh properly the process of management and strategic planning, from the highest levels of management and planning through tactical planning and its complete implementation.*

7. *Failure to modify the strategic planning system as conditions within the company change.*

8. *Failure to keep the planning system simple and to weigh constantly the cost/benefit balance.*

9. *Confusing the extrapolation of financial and/or economic projections with strategic planning.*

10. *Management's failure to understand the analytical tools used in different parts of the planning process and thereby becoming captive to staff experts.*

11. *Failure to secure in the company a climate for strategic planning that is necessary for its success.*

Table 1-4. (continued)

12. *Failure to balance and link appropriately the major elements of the strategic planning and implementation process.*

13. *Failure by managers to understand the importance of implementation of strategy and how to make that process efficient and effective.*

14. *Blame strategic planning for failures in other managerial and staff procedures.*

---

the very resources necessary to improve sales. Although it is true that costs need to be cut to match declining sales, managerial efforts need to be focused on improving sales. If top management shifts its focus to managing operating variables that determine internal efficiency, the firm has no one managing the strategic variables that determine external effectiveness. This is, unfortunately, the story of many U.S. firms today. For this reason, it is very important that the strategic manager has a clear understanding of his/her role in the firm.

1.8 THE ROLE OF THE STRATEGIC MANAGER

The strategic manager is an objective thinker who uses systems thinking to develop decision frameworks for formulating strategy. A strategic manager is:

- An objective thinker.
- A decision model builder.
- A systems processor.
- An alternative generator.
- A choice maker.
- An action implementor.
- A feedback monitor.

Figure 1-5 shows the level of strategic thinking required based upon the manager's level in the organization.

Strategic planning is far more likely to succeed if the CEO initiates the strategic planning process and provides his/her general endorsement. The final responsibility for developing the organization's philosophy and mission statement rests with top management. Because strategic decisions require large commitments of resources, top management must be the starting point of the process.

Level in the Hierarchy	Objectives	Constraints and Policies	Plans and Goals
Corporate Managers	Stated in terms for: stockholders, other identifiable constituencies, society at large. Examples: Financial performance of the corporation, Corporate citizenship and "personality" characteristics	Financial policies (debt structure, dividends, diversity of risk, etc.). Specific industries to be in, or characteristics of appropriate industries. Criteria for approving new resource commitments to businesses.	Prospective magnitude of discretionary resources to be utilized by the corporation. Prospective distribution of resources in order to affect the future mix of businesses. Performance expectations for the corporation and for each business over the next 5-10 years.
Business Managers	Stated in terms for: corporate management. Examples: Financial performance of the business, Position of the business in the industry	Definition of niche in the industry; relative importance of, and interrelationships between, each activity. Priorities for changing the relative contribution from each activity.	Prospective patterns of resource allocation intended to affect the future contribution from each activity. Performance expectations for the business and for each activity over the next 3-7 years.
Activity Managers	Stated in terms for: business management. Examples: Contribution of the activity to the business, Position of the activity in the industry	Delineation of limits on the scope of the entire activity. Criteria for optimizing the use of resources available to the activity.	Prospective sequence of resource utilization intended to affect the future contribution from the activity. Performance expectations for the activity and for each subactivity over the next 1-3 years.

Fig. 1-5. Elements of strategy in hierarchical organization.
Source: Peter Lorange, Richard F. Vancil, Strategic Planning Systems, Prentice-Hall 1977, p. 12.

Table 1-5. Role of the Executive in Small Versus Large Companies
Source: George A. Steiner, John B. Miner, Edmund R. Gray, Management Policy and Strategy, MacMillan, 1982, p. 190.

Small Company	Large Company
1. Chief executive is basically an entrepreneur	1. Chief executive is a team leader and skilled at conflict resolution.
2. Most important decisions made at top.	2. Exceptional decisions made at top. Many important decisions and routine decisions made at lower levels.
3. Workers and top managers in frequent and close contact.	3. Middle managers stand between top and lower level managers and workers. Middle managers not often bypassed.
4. Lines of authority and responsibility loosely defined. Titles mean little. All top managers participate freely in decision making.	4. Generally, authority flows from title, not personality. Jobs have defined responsibilities and duties.
5. Communications largely face to face, oral, and unspecified	5. Communications more frequently in writing. Standard procedures are followed.
6. Few explicit policies and rules.	6. Many explicit policies and rules governing subordinate actions and freedom.
7. Staff functions are weak and poorly defined.	7. Staff function expanded and expertise respected.
8. Top managers personally check employee performance. Few statistical controls.	8. Formal, impersonal statistical controls established and used.
9. Operations not too complex.	9. Very complex operations.
10. No or little money to hire staff help.	10. Financially able to hire staff experts.

Strategic planning in a large corporation will obviously differ from strategic planning in a small company. Likewise, the role of the executive in the process will also be different. These differences have been identified by Steiner, Miner, and Gray and are shown in Table 1-5.

1.9 SUMMARY

Strategic management is the formulation and implementation of actions for achieving the organization's mission. Organizations which plan strategically clearly have the winning edge on long-term survival. The major benefit is an integrative framework for directing the decision process at the corporate business unit and functional units of the corporation. The commonly defined elements of strategy, scope, specification, and deployment are developed into a decision-making model, which is applied when following the basic steps of corporate planning. The strategic planning process differs in large versus small companies, but the involvement, commitment, and responsibility of top management has the same critical significance.

ENDNOTES—Chapter 1

1. Thomas J. Peters, "Strategy Follows Structure: Developing Distinctive Skills," *California Management Review*, Vol. XXVI, No. 3. (1983).

2. H. I. Ansoff, R. J. Brandenburg, F. E. Porter, and H. R. Rodosevich. *Acquisition: Behavior of U.S. Manufacturing Firms, 1946-1965* (Nashville, TN: Vanderbilt, 1971). D. W. Karger and Z. A. Malik, "Long Range Planning and Organizational Performance," Long Range Planning 8(6):60-64 (1975). D. R. Wood., Jr.; and R. L. LaForge, "The Impact of Comprehensive Planning on Financial Performance," *Academy of Management Journal*, 22:516-26 (1979).

3. Carol J. Loomis, "The Leaning Tower of Sears," *Fortune*, July 2, 1979, pp. 78-85.

Chapter 2

The Theory of
Strategic Planning

2.0 EVOLUTION OF
STRATEGIC PLANNING THEORY

The beginnings of strategic management can be traced to the Harvard Business School in 1933, when "the top management point of view" was added to the business policy course.[1] From its inception in 1911, to 1933, the business policy course at Harvard was primarily concerned with the general management process of coordinating the internal operations of the firm. By incorporating the "view from the top," the emphasis shifted to integrating the firm's external environment with its internal operations. Further impetus for the development of strategic planning theory came with reports sponsored by the Ford Foundation and the Carnegie Corporation of New York in 1959. Both reports sponsored the evaluation of course content in schools of business, and both recommended a capstone course in "business policy." This course would pull together all of the functional specialties of business for the purpose of solving complex business problems, while considering the external environment and questions of social responsibility.[2] Working with a base of empirical case studies, theorists at Harvard pulled together the now famous body of knowledge comprising business policy. Pieces of the framework appeared earlier[3], but in 1965 Learned, Christensen, Andrews, and Guth published their *Business Policy Text and Cases,*[4] which is now in its sixth edition. This was followed by Andrews in 1971 with the *Concept of Corporate Strategy*[5], and Uyterhoeven in 1973 with *Strategy and Organization*[6], all of Harvard.

The work of these early strategic theorists was highly influenced by Alfred Chandler's historical research of 100 firms, *Strategy and Structure*[7], published in 1962. Chandler demonstrated beyond a doubt that firms who change product lines and internal structures to meet the changing needs of consumers not only survive but become leaders in the industry. Thus, the case was made for the importance of the need to adapt the firm to the changing external environment.

It was John Child[8] who identified and introduced the concept of strategic choice of products and markets as the most critical factor in the theory of organizations. He defined the process as the system by which strategists conceptualize, visualize, or otherwise determine the products to be produced and the markets to be served. In his view, it is the central variable that determines the internal organization structure; thus, the evolution of the thesis that structure must follow strategy for the firm to be effective.

Business policy evolved to business policy and strategy. The process of aligning the organization's product or service with the demands of the environment was identified as strategy formulation. The development of this process dominated one strand of strategy literature, while implementation and its management processes continued from its earlier beginnings to dominate another strand of literature. The focus of much of this literature was on integrating plans throughout the firm. The movement of this strand toward the strategy strand is exemplified by Steiner and Miner's *Management Policy and Strategy*.[9] The two strands, policy and strategy, are now merged into the concept of strategic planning.

Survival as the ultimate outcome of the alignment process traces its theoretical beginning all the way back to Darwin's *The Origin of Species* and Spencer's applications of Darwin's concepts to social organizations. From these theorists we learned the following principles of organization survival:

- All organizations are based in a natural environment.
- Organizations act out the vital process of variation.
- They experiment in a constant effort to find a combination of outputs and resources that will match the environment.
- They abandon those experiments that do not fit the outside world.
- They retain their distinctive competencies, products, and services that turn out to be effective and the internal resources that turn out to be efficient.
- For organizations that survive and grow, the process can be viewed as mutation.

Thus, the basic strategic problem of long-term alignment between the organization and its outside environment has been the topic of theoretical pursuit for over a century. Most of the earlier models from sociology, zoology, ecology, and even economics are deterministic in nature; that is, they assume the organization has no choice but to react to changes in the environment. Strategic planning theory evolving from the '60s views the process as proactive. Top management, CEOs, can make choices which determine the destiny of the company. By planning and implementing decisions concerning mission, an organization can affect predictable environmental changes. Being able to predict and react to environmental changes is *sufficient* for survival; being able to control the environment is *necessary* for survival. This is one of the major ways in which man differs from animals. Through planning, we can shape the environment. We can control our own destiny.

Theories emerge to explain why "things happen." The theory of strategic planning seeks to understand and explain why and how organizations survive. If we can discover the answer to "why," then we can predict the "if," or better yet we can prescribe "what" organizations need to do to survive. This is the purpose of science, to be able to predict and control outcomes.

Science has been defined as:

> " . . . a classified and systematized body of knowledge . . . organized around one or more central theories and a number of general principles . . . usually expressed in quantitative terms . . . knowledge which permits the prediction and, under some circumstances, the control of future events."[10]

A discipline becomes a science when a "central theory" or paradigm emerges that is accepted by scientists working in the area. For example, we now accept chemistry as a science. It is defined as the "science of substances—their structure, their properties, and the reactions that change them into other substances."[11]

Thus, science involves:

- A distinct subject matter and the description and classification of that subject matter.
- The presumption that underlying the subject matter are uniformities and regularities that science seeks to discover.

In its present stage of development, strategic planning is still involved with the process of identifying subject matter and describing and classifying that subject matter. Theories or paradigms are beginning to emerge. Some of these are highly specified, others more loosely contrived. In some instances, the components of theory are confused with the process of applying the theory. Nevertheless, there is evidence that strategic planning is beginning to evolve as a theory as several paradigms with similar underlying uniformities and regularities emerge.

2.1 EMERGING THEORIES

Several emerging theories have gained popularity in the field of strategic planning, as evidenced by their staying power. It is useful to trace the emergence and development of theory in these popular paradigms, which have survived several revisions. One of the more popular is Glueck's paradigm[12], first published in 1972 and revised as recently as 1984 by Jauch (Fig. 2-1).[13] The variables identified by Glueck's latest edition, which are similar with other theories, are:

- Environment.
- Internal competitive advantages.
- Alternative strategies.
- Resources.
- Structure.
- Policies.
- Objectives.
- Strategists.

Glueck specifies the analytical properties of the external environment component and the competitive environment component as opportunities and threats, and strengths and weaknesses. These same analytical properties appear almost uniformly across the emerging paradigms, indicating a common agreement among theorists.

Some of the relationships among the components have been specified. These are:

- There is an interaction between strategists, objectives, and the environment.
- There is an interaction between functional policies, administrative style, and strategy.

    Although there appears to be convergence on common components and the general properties of these components, the area of interactions is still divergent. Empirical research is still needed to help sort out all the complex interactions among components.

Glueck and Jauch also developed the process to follow in applying their model and offer the following steps:

- Analysis and diagnosis.
- Choice.
- Implementation.
- Evaluation.

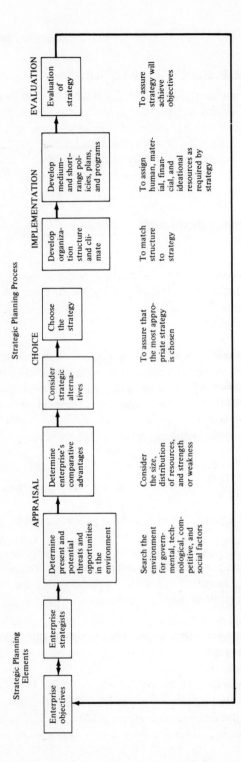

Fig. 2-1. A model of strategic planning.
Source: William F. Glueck, Business Policy: Strategy Formulation and Management Action, Second Edition,
McGraw-Hill Book Company, 1976, p. 5.

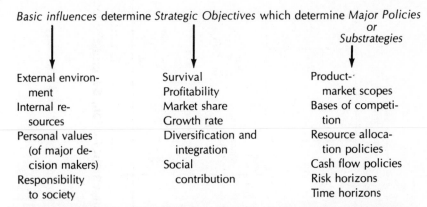

Basic influences determine *Strategic Objectives* which determine *Major Policies*
or
Substrategies

External environment	Survival	Product-
Internal resources	Profitability	market scopes
Personal values	Market share	Bases of competi-
(of major de-	Growth rate	tion
cision makers)	Diversification and	Resource alloca-
Responsibility	integration	tion policies
to society	Social	Cash flow policies
	contribution	Risk horizons
		Time horizons

Fig. 2-2. Major elements of organizational and business strategy.
Source: Daniel J. McCarthy, Robert J. Minichiello, Joseph R. Curran,
Business Policy and Strategy: Concepts and Readings, Revised
Edition, Richard D. Irwin, Inc., 1975, p. 14.

Thus, they differentiate between the common elements or substance of the theory and the process of applying the theory. This is a major developmental change from Glueck's first edition.

Another early conceptualization that has survived several revisions is the McCarthy, Minichello, and Curran paradigm (Fig. 2-2)[14]. The basic elements of this model are:

- Basic influences.
- Strategic objectives.
- Major policies or substrategies.

Under basic influence, the common elements are external environment, internal resources, personal values, and responsibility to society. Under objectives, we see survival, profitability, market share, growth rate, diversification and integration, and social contribution. Under policies, we see the beginnings of the development of functional strategies with product market scopes, bases of competition, resource allocation policies, risk horizons, and time horizons.

The richness of this model lies in its explanation of the causal relationships among the elements. Basic influences *determine* strategic objectives, which determine major policies and substrategies. Here we have substance plus an explanation of the relationship among the elements.

The fourth edition of this theory, published in 1987, reveals the degree of theory development in strategic planning during the last dozen years. While the authors maintain their basic elements approach, they introduce a process model (Fig. 2-3), which includes the implementation of strategy. Their earlier

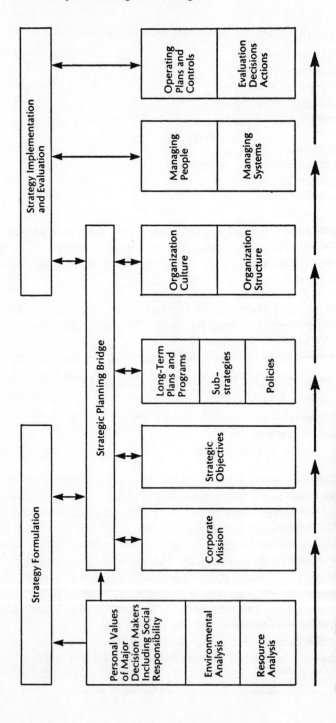

Fig. 2-3. The strategic management process.
Source: Daniel J. McCarthy, Robert J. Minichiello, Joseph R. Curran, Business Policy and Strategy: Concepts and Strategy, Fourth Edition, Richard D. Irwin, Inc., 1987, p. 6.

conceptualization forms the basis of strategy formulation. They add the concept of mission and long-term plans to the basic influences, and diversification and integration become corporate strategies rather than objectives.

Another popular framework with staying power is the Thompson and Strickland paradigm[15] which first emerged in 1978. The elements of their third edition framework are illustrated in Fig. 2-4.

- Performance.
- Current objectives and strategies.
- External environment.
- Internal environment.
- Strategic options.
- Personal values of managers.
- Societal values.
- Regulatory constraints.

Some analytical properties are identified:

- Market opportunities and external threats.
- Feasible strategic options.
- Internal strengths and weaknesses.

The relationships identified in the flow of the elements of the model actually illustrate the analytical application of the model to the strategic planning process rather than causal relationships among the variables. Thus, the flow depicts the steps to follow in applying the process:

- Pressure for performance.
- Describe current objectives.
- Assess external environment.
- Assess internal environment.
- Identify options.
- Fit options with environments.
- Evaluate options with personal/societal constraints.
- Select plan.
- Revise objectives.

Thus, Thompson and Strickland do not clearly differentiate between the elements of their theory and the process of applying their theory. In the fourth edition, published in 1987, they depart radically from their earlier framework and incorporate the defensive strategies developed by Porter in *Competitive Strategy*.

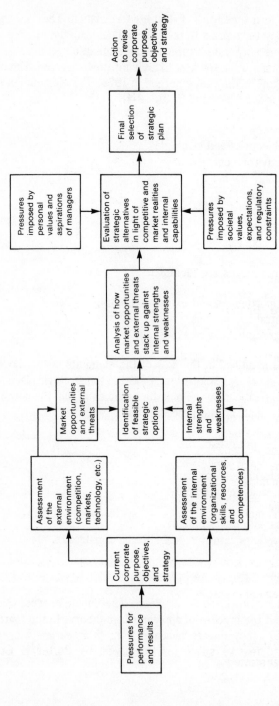

Fig. 2-4. A simple model of the primary factors which shape strategy.
Source: Arthur A. Thompson, Jr., A. J. Stickland, III, Strategic Management: Concepts and Cases, Third Edition, Business Publications, Inc., 1984 , p. 72.

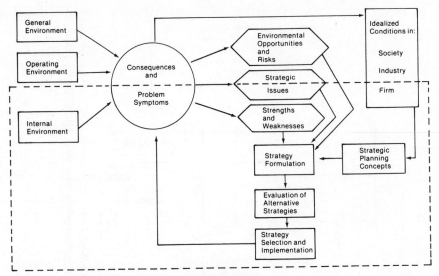

Fig. 2-5. Strategic planning framework.
Source: John H. Grant, William R. King, The Logic of Strategic
Planning, *Little, Brown and Company, 1982, p. 9.*

Conceptualization of both elements and relationships developed more
sophistication in the 80s. In 1982, Grant and King published *The Logic of Strategic Planning* (Fig. 2-5).[16] Their paradigm identified elements, outcomes, and
relationships. The properties of the external environment, opportunities and
threats, internal environment, and strengths and weaknesses are now
conceptualized as the determinants of strategy. Consequences and problem
symptoms are the outcomes of the strategic planning process; they are also
the input for the next round of strategy formulation. The Grant and King
conceptualization depicts the process as a systems model with feedback loops.
The theory now becomes dynamic, and the continuous process flow is
conceptualized. A more detailed development of Grant and King's elements of
formulating strategy is presented in Fig. 2-6 for a single market firm and in Fig.
2-7 for a multiple market firm.

Another dynamic systems model emerged in 1982, with the Pearce and
Robinson paradigm[17] (Fig. 2-8), and was revised in 1985. This model included
the following elements of strategy:

- Mission.
- Grand strategy.
- Functional strategies.

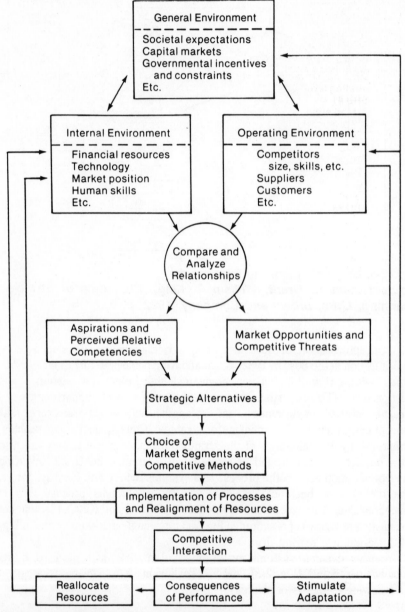

Fig. 2-6. Strategic planning process in a single market firm.
Source: John H. Grant, William R. King, The Logic of Strategic
Planning, Little, Brown, and Company, 1982, p. 24.

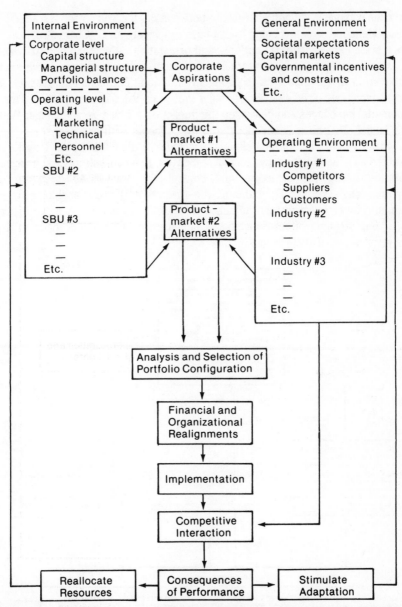

Fig. 2-7. *Corporate-level strategic planning process in a multiple market firm.*
Source: *John H. Grant, William R. King, The Logic of Strategic Planning, Little, Brown, and Company, 1982, p. 31.*

Previous paradigms did not differentiate between mission and objectives. Mission is now identified as determining "what business we are in." "Characteristically, it is a statement of attitude, outlook, and orientation rather than of details and measurable targets."[18] The external environment and company profile are seen as having a major impact on the company mission. The company mission, in turn, is conceptualized as having a major impact on the company profile. Thus, this model introduces and describes the impact of two-way relationships. With this model, we see a closer integration of concepts with processes.

Strategy formulation is defined to include all elements up to long-term objectives and grand strategy. Annual objectives, functional strategies, policies, institutionalizing the strategy, and control are defined as elements of implementing strategy. They identify the strength of the relationship between elements by categorizing the influence as a major impact or a minor impact. By adding strength of relationships, a significant contribution is made to the analytical value of their model.

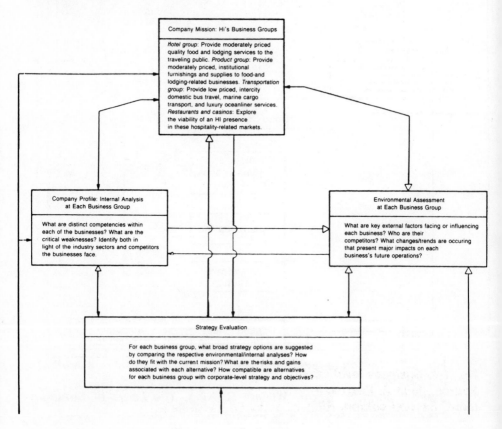

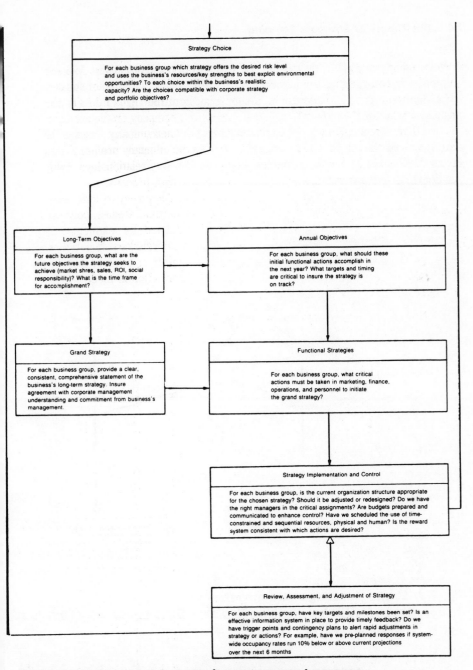

Strategy Choice

For each business group which strategy offers the desired risk level and uses the business's resources/key strengths to best exploit environmental opportunities? To each choice within the business's realistic capacity? Are the choices compatible with corporate strategy and portfolio objectives?

Long-Term Objectives

For each business group, what are the future objectives the strategy seeks to achieve (market shres, sales, ROI, social responsibility)? What is the time frame for accomplishment?

Annual Objectives

For each business group, what should these initial functional actions accomplish in the next year? What targets and timing are critical to insure the strategy is on track?

Grand Strategy

For each business group, provide a clear, consistent, comprehensive statement of the business's long-term strategy. Insure agreement with corporate management understanding and commitment from business's management.

Functional Strategies

For each business group, what critical actions must be taken in marketing, finance, operations, and personnel to initiate the grand strategy?

Strategy Implementation and Control

For each business group, is the current organization structure appropriate for the chosen strategy? Should it be adjusted or redesigned? Do we have the right managers in the critical assignments? Are budgets prepared and communicated to enhance control? Have we scheduled the use of time-constrained and sequential resources, physical and human? Is the reward system consistent with which actions are desired?

Review, Assessment, and Adjustment of Strategy

For each business group, have key targets and milestones been set? Is an effective information system in place to provide timely feedback? Do we have trigger points and contingency plans to alert rapid adjustments in strategy or actions? For example, have we pre-planned responses if system-wide occupancy rates run 10% below or above current projections over the next 6 months

Fig. 2-8. Business level strategic management process.
Source: John A. Pearce, II, Richard B. Robinson, Jr., Strategic Management, Second edition, Richard D. Irwin, 1982, p. 78.

implementing strategy. They identify the strength of the relationship between elements by categorizing the influence as a major impact or a minor impact. By adding strength of relationships, a significant contribution is made to the analytical value of their model.

Further development of the relationship between mission, corporate strategies and objectives, and functional strategies and objectives is presented in the McGlashan & Singleton model (Fig. 2-9). Directionality and two-way relationships are presented.

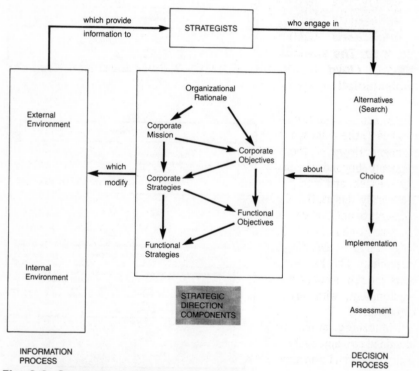

Fig. 2-9. Strategic management model.
Source: Robert McGlashan, Timothy Singleton, Strategic Management,
Merrill Publishing, 1987, p. 28.

Some paradigms focus solely on the process. Byars model[19] (Fig. 2-10) is a step-by-step model of how to apply the strategic management process. By focusing on process, Byars assumes a central theory of strategic planning with agreement on common elements.

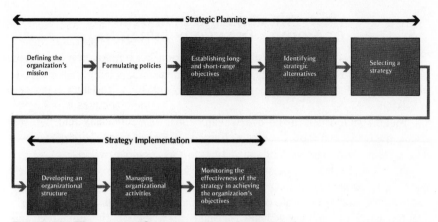

Fig. 2-10. The strategic management process.
Source: Lloyd L. Byars, Strategic Management: Planning and Implementation, Harper & Row, Publishers, 1984, p. 4.

As can be seen from the foregoing discussion, strategic planning theory has evolved to the point where there seems to be general agreement on the basic elements. However, there has been little development of the properties of these elements beyond the nature of opportunities and threats, strengths and weaknesses, and high growth and low growth. Measures for these properties are mainly descriptive in nature, but a specification of relationships among elements is beginning to emerge. Influence, impact, and two-way relationships have been identified.[20] Michael Porter's *Competitive Strategy*, published in 1980, has had a major impact on the development of the dynamics of competitive interaction. This has been integrated in many of the latest editions of strategy texts and represents a definitive specification of the elements of the competitive environment, with directionality and degree of impact included among the elements.

Mintzberg, in his article, "Policy as a Field of Management Theory,"[21] identified two approaches to the development of theory in the area of business policy, the grand plan approach and the empirical approach. He defines the grand plan approach as a prescriptive, which focuses on the development of strategic planning procedures and results in normative models. There is a pervasive tendency in some of the early theories to move prematurely to normative models. The empirical approach, by contrast, seeks to develop descriptive theory. It is this thrust for descriptive theory that has spurred the further development of the concepts of strategy. What we currently have are very highly developed normative models and struggling conceptualizations of descriptive theory. To quote Mintzburg, "Prescription becomes useful only when it is grounded in sophisticated description."[22]

2.2 THE USES AND PURPOSES
OF MODELS IN THEORY BUILDING

Theory building is the process of abstracting and simplifying reality into a coherent whole. The abstraction is usually illustrated by a visual schematic called a model. The purpose of models in theory building is to simplify, visualize, and provide consistency.

Models give order to the overwhelming load of data. By simplifying, we enable the decision maker to impose a framework that orders the set of choices. The classification process lends structure to the cognitive world.

A model enables us to visualize the various classifications of the variables and the relationships among the variables. It helps us to clearly identify consequences and to separate consequences and symptoms from causes. Models are the basis of problem solving, because they lead to the definition and identification of causes and possible solutions. All effective decision makers use implicit if not explicit models to aid their processes. Choice requires that the implications of many courses of action be visualized and compared.

Models provide consistency of thought and action. Because they provide structure and order to seemingly disordered events, they force a pattern on the analytical decision-making process. This pattern assures consistency. Thus, models guide the gathering of data, prioritize and order the data into conceptual categories, and develop integrated conceptualizations.

2.3 THE CONCEPTUAL FRAMEWORK

The model presented in Fig. 2-11 is an attempt to synthesize and integrate the emerging elements of the theory of strategic planning. Strategy formulation consists of:

- Situation analysis.
- Definition of the business.

The situation analysis includes an assessment of:

- The macro environment.
- The competitive environment.
- Internal resource capabilities.

Conditions which exist in the macro environment and competitive environment pose opportunities or threats for the firm. Internal resource capabilities pose strengths and weaknesses. The matching of opportunities and threats with strengths and weaknesses results in a list of strategic alternatives which contribute to a definition of the business.

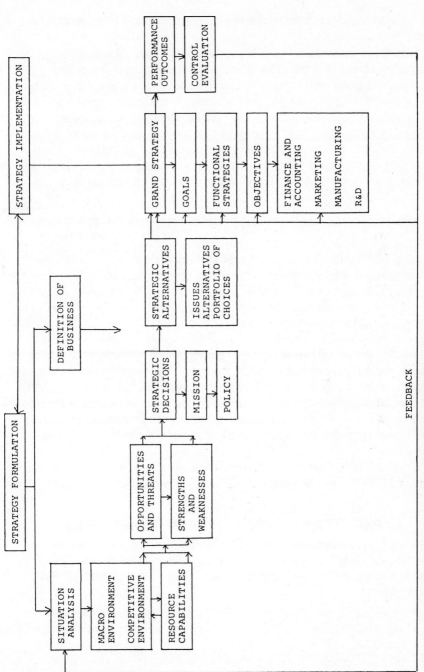

Fig. 2-11. A theory of strategic management planning.

Strategic choices from the portfolio of alternatives result in the identification of mission and policy.

The implementation process begins with the choice of a grand strategy alternative which fulfills the mission within the constraints of the policies chosen. Once the grand strategy is determined, a specific goal statement is written and functional objectives are set. The next step in the implementation process is to integrate functional objectives with each other and with the grand strategy. Performance outcomes occur. The outcomes are evaluated for deviation from the set goals and objectives. If deviation occurs, then the control process begins a problem diagnosis and corrective action via a feedback loop. This loop may cycle back to a reassessment of the situation, triggering a reiteration of the entire process.

2.3-1 ENVIRONMENT—OPPORTUNITIES AND THREATS

Because the planning process requires ordered thinking, it is necessary to conceptualize the firm as part of a larger system. Analysis of the environment and its changes results in the assessment of opportunities and threats facing the firm. This component is generally broken down into two subcomponents for purposes of analysis: the macro environment and the competitive environment. The *macro environment* has an indirect impact on the firm's strategic choices and actions. Changes in demographic variables, economic indicators, technology, and societal attitudes about corporate behavior affect the industry and the market first before they affect the firm. The *competitive environment* has a more direct impact and includes such elements as customers, suppliers, and competitors. The competitive environment can serve to diminish or enhance the effect of changes from the macro environment. Environmental analysis identifies opportunities the organization might pursue and threats it should defend against.

Table 2-1 identifies an environmental analysis checklist that can be used to monitor environmental changes and identify opportunities and threats.

2.3-2 RESOURCES
CAPABILITIES—STRENGTHS AND WEAKNESSES

An analysis of the organization's resources profiles its strengths and weaknesses in pursuing environmental opportunities and defending against threats. Resource components are assets which the firm uses in the pursuit of strategy. These assets include:

- Financial.
- Physical.
- Personnel.
- Information/technology.
- Image/reputation.

Table 2-1. Environmental Variables Checklist
*Source: Danial J. Powers, Martin J. Gannon, Michael A. McGinnis,
David M. Schweiger,* **Strategic Management Skills,** *Addison-Wesley,*
1986, p. 38.

1. Societal Changes

Y N Changing Customer Preferences --- Impacting Product Demand or Design
Y N Population Trends --- Impacting Distribution, Product Demand or Design

2. Governmental Changes

Y N New Legislation --- Impacting Product Costs
Y N New Enforcement Priorities --- Impacting Investments, Products, Demand

3. Economic Changes

Y N Interest Rates --- Impacting Expansion, Debt Costs
Y N Exchange Rates --- Impacting Domestic and Overseas Demand, Profits
Y N Real Personal Income Changes --- Impacting Demand

4. Competitive Changes

Y N Adoption of New Technologies --- Impacting Cost Position, Product Quality
Y N New Competitors --- Impacting Prices, Market Share, Contribution Margin
Y N Price Changes --- Impacting Market Share, Contribution Margin
Y N New Products --- Impacting Demand, Advertising Expenditures

5. Supplier Changes

Y N Changes in Input Costs --- Impacting Prices, Demand, Contribution Margin
Y N Supply Changes --- Impacting Production Processes, Investment Requirements
Y N Changes in Number of Suppliers --- Impacting Costs, Availability

6. Market Changes

Y N New Uses of Products --- Impacting Demand, Capacity Utilization
Y N New Markets --- Impacting Distribution Channels, Demand, Capacity Utilization
Y N Product Obsolescence --- Impacting Prices, Demand, Capacity Utilization

---

Resource assessment results in identifying operating constraints by answering the question, "What can we do?" Table 2-2 indicates a typical strength and weakness checklist that can be used for resource analysis.

2.3-3 MISSION—DEFINITION OF THE BUSINESS

The matching of opportunities and threats with strengths and weaknesses results in the assessment of what the firm should do and leads to a strategic choice of corporate mission. Mission is a statement of purpose which differentiates the

Table 2-2. Strengths and Weaknesses Checklist
Source: Daniel J. Powers, Martin J. Gannon, Michael A. McGinnis, David M. Schweiger, Strategic Management Skills, Addison-Wesley, *1986, p. 37.*

1. **Marketing**

Y N Product Quality
Y N Number of Product Lines
Y N Product Differentiation
Y N Market Share
Y N Pricing Policies
Y N Distribution Channels
Y N Promotional Programs
Y N Customer Service
Y N Marketing Research
Y N Advertising
Y N Sales Force

2. **Research and Development**

Y N Product R&D Capabilities
Y N Process R&D Capabilities
Y N Pilot Plant Capabilities

3. **Management Information System**

Y N Speed and Responsiveness
Y N Quality of Current Information
Y N Expandability
Y N User Oriented System

4. **Management Team**

Y N Skills
Y N Value Congruence
Y N Team Spirit
Y N Experience
Y N Coordination of Effort

5. **Operations**

Y N Control of Raw Materials
Y N Production Capacity
Y N Production Cost Structure
Y N Facilities and Equipment
Y N Inventory Control
Y N Quality Control
Y N Energy Efficiency

6. **Finance**

Y N Financial Leverage
Y N Operating Leverage
Y N Balance Sheet Ratios
Y N Stockholder Relations
Y N Tax Situation

7. **Human Resources**

Y N Employee Capabilities
Y N Personnel Systems
Y N Employee Turnover
Y N Employee Morale
Y N Employee Development

firm from all the organizations serving the same need for goods and services in a society. It identifies the scope of operations in terms of product market, company philosophy, and image.

Every organization has one and only strategic force around which its mission is focused. Tregoe and Zimmerman[23] have categorized the nine strategic focus elements as follows:

CATEGORY	STRATEGIC FOCUS
Products/market	Products offered
Products/market	Market needs
Capabilities	Technology
Capabilities	Production capability
Capabilities	Method of sale
Capabilities	Method of distribution
Capabilities	Natural resources
Results	Size growth
Results	Return/profit

A definition of each strategic focus element[24] follows:

Products Offered. Products are whatever an organization offers to the market it serves, including ongoing support and maintenance. A product may be defined individually or as a line or grouping of products or subproducts. Products are defined on the basis of common characteristics, such as functions performed, customer needs satisfied, size or form, durability, etc.

Market Needs. A market is a group of current or potential buyers or end users who share common needs. Market groupings could be formed on the basis of age, income, sex, education, ethnic background, occupation, industry, etc. These groupings may be formed or limited geographically.

Technology. A technology is a learned body of knowledge which is reproducible and subject to frequent update and extension. This would include the skills and knowledge possessed by those within the discipline, science, or profession involved. It also includes the necessary systems, equipment, and support facilities such as laboratories, libraries, and the like.

Production Capability. Production capability includes the production know-how, processes, systems, and equipment required to make specific products, and the capability to improve those processes. In a service organization, the production capability includes those processes and skills required to provide the service(s) and any necessary support materials, procedures, programs, etc.

Method of Sale. The method of sale is the primary way an organization convinces current or potential customers or users to buy its products. This method of sale may be directed to both its customers and the end user, if different from its customer. This primary method of sale may be supported in a number of ways, such as advertising, display, direct mail, etc.

Method of Distribution. The method of distribution is the way products reach the customer, including field or in-route storage. This includes significant know-how, systems, and equipment to support the method of distribution. This *does not* include how the potential customer is persuaded to buy the product. For example, a rack display would be part of the method of sale. The method of distribution may be directed to both the customer and the end user, if different from the customer.

Natural Resources. Natural resources are those actual and potential forms of wealth supplied by nature. These would include coal, oil, metals, wood, water, usable land, etc. They would not include human resources or resources produced by man, such as money, processed foodstuffs, etc.

Size/Growth. The size/growth of an organization is defined as its overall size and/or rate of growth as measured by the most appropriate indexes. For some organizations, size is most important and rate of growth is how it gets there. For other organizations, rate of growth is most important and size is only the result.

Return/Profit. Return/profit is the financial result of an organization's effort. This result may be measured in a variety of ways, such as a percent of sales, return on assets, or return on equity. In nonprofit organizations, measures of return may be in terms of cost/benefit ratio, budgetary control, or in quality of degree of services rendered.

2.3-4 IMPLEMENTATION—STRATEGIC ALTERNATIVES—GRAND STRATEGY

Once the focus of the mission's grand strategy is decided upon, a set of alternative actions is evaluated and selected for achieving the mission. The outcome of this process results in the selection of a *grand strategy.*

Grand strategies tend to fall into recognizable patterns of activity which have been identified and categorized as either low growth or forced growth.

Low growth strategies fall into three categories of response:

- No change or stability.
- Retreat.
- Focus.

Stability is the appropriate strategy when the firm is satisfied with its current performance. Under this strategy, the firm continues with the same set of activities. The scope of operations, products, and markets remains the same. Deployments are carried out as in the past. Analysis in the formulation stage points to low prospects for growth but good opportunities for being able to maintain the present position. Stability strategies are typically pursued by large dominant firms in mature industries, small privately held companies, and firms whose growth is regulated by law.

Retreat strategies are employed to turn around a negative trend or to overcome a crisis or problem. These are generally short-term strategies based on an analysis of internal or external threats. Internally, the company may be having financial problems. Thus, it may reduce activities in an attempt to improve cash flows, or the firm may see the need for divesting a current production service in order to redefine its business. Another reason for retreat could be the perception of an environment so threatening that there is insufficient resources and time to respond. Retreat is used in times of crisis. Moderate crisis can be met with cutbacks which increase cash flow, layoffs, reduce R&D, reduce marketing research, factoring accounts receivable, etc. Severe crises require divestiture of some divisions or units. The ultimate in retreat is liquidation. In hopeless situations, liquidation is preferred to bankruptcy. Being able to recognize when a firm can take advantage of liquidation is not always easy, particularly when the emotion of failure is associated with the analytical process.

The third low growth strategy is to focus on a particular market segment. A firm pursues this strategy when the opportunity exists to serve this segment better than the competition who serve a broader market.

The second major category of corporate strategy is *forced growth*, which includes acquisition, vertical integration, geographical expansion, and diversification.

One strategy of forced growth is the acquisition of a competitor. An acquisition occurs when one company purchases the assets of another and absorbs them into its own business. One company loses its identity. Acquisition of a competitor is a much quicker way to gain market share than through internal growth strategies, and it also helps eliminate barriers to entry. On the negative side, acquisition is more risky than internal growth, because it requires a large cash commitment. Acquisition is the appropriate strategy when the opportunity exists to acquire a firm which will increase the buyer's growth rate. Mergers may also be considered under this category. In mergers, assets and liabilities are combined to form a new company; both companies lose their identity.

Vertical integration occurs when a firm moves forward in the value-added chain toward the customer or backward toward the supplier. The primary reason for backward integration is to gain control over supplies. Backward integration is an appropriate strategy if the firm is threatened by variations in either the availability, quality, or cost of supplies. In a high growth market, lack of availability of supplies could be a strategic disadvantage. Another reason for backward integration is to gain control over cost of supplies. One reason for forward integration is to gain profit potential by eliminating one or more steps in the value-added chain. Another reason is to gain control over the quality of the final product. Successful integration is often difficult. It means moving into an area of business with which the firm is often unfamiliar and lacking in managerial talent. It is often difficult to match the output supply in backward integration with the firm's exact needs. An excess of supply means having to sell to competitors. Too little output means buying the extra needed, usually at a cost disadvantage.

Geographic expansion is growth through expanding the same product or service into new geographic areas. Many U.S. based firms sought growth by expansion into international markets. For example, Coca-Cola is now developing a market in China. The reasons for geographic expansion are obvious; opportunities exist to create growth through new demand in previously unpenetrated markets.

Diversification occurs when a firm moves into businesses or products that are quite different from its core business. Firms in mature and declining industries seek growth by diversifying away from the products and services that have plateaued. Resource-rich firms seek to diversify to find growth opportunities. Diversification can also be a strategy of risk prevention. It follows the old axiom of "don't put all your eggs in one basket." Thus, firms diversify their portfolio in an attempt to balance risk. Ironically, it turns out that growth through diversification is quite risky. Conglomerate diversifications, such as Litton and ITT, have turned out badly. *Concentric diversification* can be profitable, because it allows the firm to build on an area of expertise, at least in one functional area. Coca-Cola's purchase of Minute Maid allowed the firm to capitalize on its market expertise with consumer beverages. Concentric diversification employs the concepts of synergy with one or more of the firm's functional strategies.

2.3-5 IMPLEMENTATION—GOALS—FUNCTION OBJECTIVES

Once the grand strategy is selected, a specific set of goals can be written to direct the activities of the functional areas of the business. Specific objectives are necessary if successful implementation is going to occur. They answer the necessary questions of:

- What will be accomplished?
- How will it be accomplished?
- Where will it be accomplished?
- When will it be accomplished?
- Why will it be accomplished?

What will be accomplished:	Measurable performance criteria
How will it be accomplished:	Division of objective into tasks and
Where will it be accomplished:	assignment of responsibility for the tasks
When will it be accomplished:	Coordination of task activities to achieve objective
Why will it be accomplished:	Rational consistency check of task with goal achievement

Objectives guide implementation by converting mission into short-term ends. They direct the process of converting mission into a list of *"how to activities."* Table 2-3 presents a list of objectives with examples of how to operationalize objectives for measurable performance specifications.

Table 2-3. Operationalizing Measurable Annual Objectives
Source: Laurence G. Hrebiniak, William F. Joyce, Implementing Strategy, (New York, Macmillan, 1984), p. 116.

Examples of deficient annual objectives	*Examples of annual objectives with measurable criteria for performance*
To improve morale in the divisions (plant, department, etc.).	To reduce turnover (absenteeism, number of rejects, etc.) among sales managers, by 10 percent by January 1, 1987.
	Assumption: Morale is related to measurable outcomes (i.e., high and low morale are associated with different results.)
To improve support of the sales effort.	To reduce the time lapse between order date and delivery by 8 percent (two days) by June 1, 1987.
	To reduce the cost of goods produced by 6 percent to support a product price decrease of 2 percent by December 1, 1987.
	To increase the rate of before- or on-schedule delivery by 5 percent by June 1, 1987.
To develop a terminal version of the SAP computer program.	To develop a terminal version of SAP capable of processing X bits of information in time Y at cost not to exceed Z per 1,000 bits by December 1, 1987.
	Assumption: There virtually is an infinite number of "terminal" or operational versions. Greater detail or specificity defines the objective more precisely.
To enhance or improve the training effort.	To increase the number of individuals capable of performing X operation in manufacturing by 20 percent by April 15, 1987.
	To increase the number of functional heads capable of assuming general management responsibility at the division level by 10 percent by July 15, 1987.
	To provide sales training to X number of individuals, resulting in an average increase in sales of 4 percent within six months after the training session.
To improve the business's image.	To conduct a public opinion poll using random samples in the five largest U.S. metropolitan markets and determine average scores on 10 dimensions of corporate responsibility by May 15, 1987.
	To increase our score on those 10 items by an average of 7.5 percent by May 1, 1988.

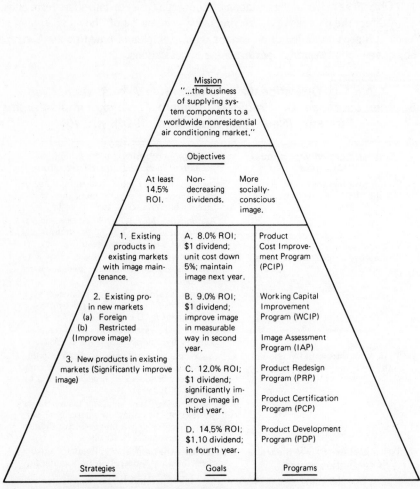

Fig. 2-12. Illustrative strategic choice elements.
Source: William Richard King, David I. Cleland, Strategic Planning and Policy, Van Nostrand, 1978, p. 135.

Figure 2-12 illustrates the translation of corporate mission into functional level objectives for the areas of finance, marketing, manufacturing, operations, and R&D.

Activities within a functional area must be coordinated to move that function in the direction of the chosen grand strategy. The process of checking actions within a functional area is part of the internal consistency check necessary to

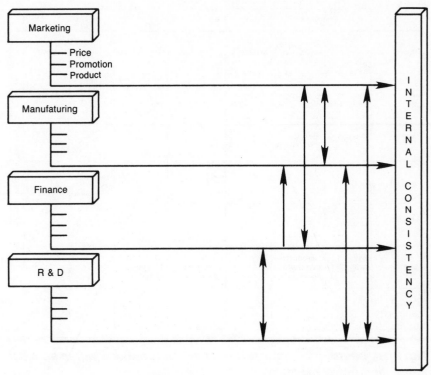

Fig. 2-13. Integrating strategies.

integrate strategies (Fig. 2-13). Actions must be coordinated across functions as well. Figure 2-14 illustrates the across-function consistency check. Not only must the activities within a function all be consistent and moving in the same direction, but the marketing and finance function must be consistent with each other and with each of the other functions. Priorities of the marketing function can easily conflict with manufacturing/operations or finance. Manufacturing seeking to maximize efficiency would prefer long production runs and plant warehousing. Marketing seeking to maximize market response would prefer short production runs and field warehousing. Checking back to the grand strategy helps determine which of these activities are correct. If the goal is to increase market share, then field warehousing is the correct activity. If the objective is to be the low pricer, then centralized warehousing would be the correct action. Figure 2-15 illustrates the types of conflicts that can occur at the functional strategy level.

	Finance	Marketing	R&D	Manufacturing	Human Resources	Materials	External Relations	
Finance	/////	can reduce accounts receivable	not applicable				executive leadership yields investor confidence	
Marketing	cannot support advertising	/////	improve warranty experience		sales incentives attract skilled professionals			Complementing Relationships
R&D	most projects are over budget	late with new products	/////					
Manufacturing				/////		new sources ease scheduling		
Human Resources					/////			
Materials	not applicable	less customer appeal	not applicable	more frequent breakage	often fail OSHA standards	/////		
External Relations			engineers dislike our image				/////	
				Detracting Relationships				

Fig. 2-14. Interdependency review chart for functions within an SBU: some illustrative examples.
Source: John H. Grant, William R. King, The Logic of Strategic Planning, *Little, Brown and Company, 1982, p. 105.*

2.3-6 PERFORMANCE OUTCOMES

The ultimate outcome of the strategic process is the survival of the firm. To survive, a firm must be externally effective and internally efficient. A firm can survive in the short-run without being efficient as long as it provides a good or service for which there is a demand. In the long-run, as the industry matures and competition increases, the firm must be both efficient and effective to survive.

We measure the outcome of the strategy implementation process by measuring where we are on our performance specifications at a point in time. If we fall short of where we planned to be, we know we need to check our implementation process and maybe the formulation process as well.

Effectiveness is measured in terms of sales, sales volume, and market share. The number of units sold is the ultimate test of whether the firm is adapting to market needs and desires. A firm does not have to necessarily increase the number of units sold to be effective. It may increase sales dollars by being able

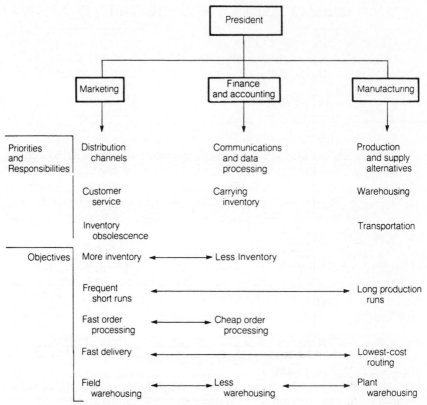

Fig. 2-15. Functional level conflicts.
Source: John F. Stolle, "How to Manage Physical Distribution," Harvard Business Review, July-August 1967, p. 95.

to increase prices. This happens when efficient companies have squeezed out inefficient competitors in declining markets. The successful company is left with a stable market share, very few competitors, and the opportunity to raise prices. Market share is also a measure of effectiveness, but it translates into increased revenues only when demand is high and expanding. Loss of market share is the first warning sign of survival problems in a competitive market. Once market share is lost, it is very difficult to regain. U.S. auto makers fight for survival in the face of Toyota's 33% market share. Why has Japan surpassed us? Lack of effectiveness or, to quote Henry Ford, II, "We've made an awful lot of lousy cars." Effectiveness is absolutely necessary for survival. The firm must be producing a good or service that society wants.

Internal efficiency is measured in terms of costs and productivity:

* Cost of goods sold (COGS).
* Selling and administrative expenses.
* Labor productivity ratios.
* Plant utilization.
* Input/output ratios.

As profits attract competition, it becomes necessary to develop the lowest cost curve in the industry. Price is a very powerful variable for effectiveness, and the price a firm can charge and continue to survive is dependent on its cost structure and productivity ratios. Thus, in the long run, a firm must be efficient in order to be effective. Efficiency by itself does not result in survival. You can be the most efficient producer of buggy whips, but with no customers to purchase them, you won't survive.

The most commonly used measure of survival is profitability. Profitability is actually a combination measure of both effectiveness and efficiency. Increasing profits can be an outcome of increasing sales, if the cost of goods sold does not increase proportionately. Reducing cost of goods sold while holding sales constant can also result in increasing profit. Table 2-4 classifies three changing

Table 2-4. The Effects of Changes in Profitability on the Efficiency and Effectiveness of the Firm

Cogs	SALES		
	Increasing	Decreasing	No Change
Increasing	Effective Efficiency determined by relative rates of change	Ineffective and Inefficient	Inefficient
Decreasing	Effective and efficient	Ineffective Efficiency determined by relative rates of change	Efficient
No change	Effective and efficient	Ineffective and inefficient	No change

conditions of the sales and COGS components of profitability and the resulting impact on effectiveness and efficiency.

If COGS in cell 11 increase faster than sales, then the firm will show decreased profitability. This type of situation can occur when a firm experiences high demand and gears up to meet the demand. The expansion process can result in cost inefficiencies that are later corrected. If COGS decrease faster than sales in cell 22, the firm can actually have a higher percentage of profit. This, of course, points to short-run efficiencies. Such efficiencies could cut into the very life-blood of the firm and render it ineffective permanently. Measures of profitability, while easy to use for comparison purposes, simply do not reveal useful information about the company's survival condition.

Many U.S. firms, in the middle 1980s, focused their entire survival strategies on cutting costs and improving internal efficiencies to the long-term detriment of effectiveness. Cost cutting activities as a means of increasing profit are short-term strategies. There are decreasing marginal returns to activities focused solely on cutting costs.

2.4 STEPS TO FOLLOW IN APPLYING THE CONCEPTUAL MODEL

Once the conceptual model is defined, it is necessary to spell out the logical procedure to follow in applying the model to the process of strategy formulation and implementation.

Step 1—Where are we now?

- Analyze current performance on objective criteria.
- Are there deviations from planned outcomes?

Step 2—What should we do?

- Analyze situation: macro environment, competitive environment (opportunities and threats), and resource capabilities (strengths and weaknesses).

Step 3—What would we like to do?

- Definition of the business mission and policy.

Step 4—What should we do?

- Grand strategy.
- Goals.

- Functional strategies.
- Integration.

Step 5—Are we doing it?

- Go back to Step 1.

2.5 SUMMARY

In this Chapter, we have discussed the development of strategic planning theory. Emerging paradigms were presented with a focus on commonalities and uniformities. A model is presented, for use in this text, which attempts to synthesize and integrate the salient elements, relationships, and interactions of currently popular frameworks. Finally, the steps to follow in applying the model to the process of strategy formulation and implementation are presented.

ENDNOTES—Chapter 2

1. C. E. Summer, *Strategic Behavior in Business and Government* (Little Brown, 1980), pp. 76.

2. Robert A. Gordon and James E. Howell, *Higher Education for Business* (New York: Columbia University Press), 1959.

3. Edward C. Burst and D. G. Fenn, *Planning the Future Strategy of Your Business* (Harvard Press, 1955).

4. E. P. Learned, C. R. Christensen, K. R. Andrews, W. D. Guth, *Business Policy* (Irwin, 1965).

5. K. R. Andrews, *The Concept of Corporate Strategy* (Dow Jones, Irwin, 1971).

6. Hugo Uyterhoenen, R. W. Ackerman, and J. W. Rosenbaum, *Strategy and Organization Text and Cases in General Management* (Irwin, 1973).

7. Alfred Chandler, *Strategy and Structure* (Mass. Institute of Technology Press, 1962).

8. John Child, "Organizational Structure, Environment and Performance: The Role of Strategic Choice," *Sociology* 6:1, January, 1972

9. George A. Steiner and John B. Miner, *Management Policy and Strategy* (Macmillan, 1977, 1982).

10. Robert D. Buzzel, "Is Marketing a Science?" *Harvard Business Review*, Vol. 41 (January - February, 1963), pp. 37.

11. Linus Pauling, *College Chemistry* (San Francisco: W. H. Freman & Co., 1956), pp. 15.

12. William F. Glueck, *Business Policy: Strategy Formulation and Management Action* (McGraw-Hill Book Company, 1972).

13. William F. Glueck and Lawrence R. Jauch, *Business Policy and Strategic Management* (McGraw-Hill, 4th edition, 1984).

14. Daniel J. McCarthy, Robert J. Minichello, and Joseph R. Curran, *Business Policy and Strategy: Concepts and Readings* (Richard P. Irwin Publishers, 1975).

15. Arthur A. Thompson, Jr., and A. J. Strickland, III, *Strategic Management: Concepts and Cases, 3rd edition* (Business Publications, Inc., 1984).

16. John H. Grant and William R. King, *The Logic of Strategic Planning* (Little Brown and Company, 1982).

17. John A. Pearce, II, and Richard B. Robinson, Jr., *Strategic Management, 2nd edition* (Richard D. Irwin, 1985).

18. *Ibid*, pp. 78.

19. Robert McGlashan and Timothy Singleton, *Stratigic Management* (Mervill Publishing, 1987).

20. Lloyd L. Byars, *Strategic Management: Planning and Implementation* (Harper and Row, 1984).

21. Arlyn J. Melcher and Bonita H. Melcher, "Towards a Systems Theory of Policy Analysis: Static Versus Dynamic Analysis," *Management Review*, Vol. 5, No. 2, 1980, pp. 235-247.

22. Henry Mintzberg, "Policy as a Field of Management Theory," *Academy of Management Review*, Jan., 1977, pp. 88-103.

23. *Ibid*, pp. 93.

24. Benjamin B. Tregoe and John W. Zimmerman, *Top Management Strategy* (Simon and Schuster, 1980), pp. 43.

25. *Ibid*, pp. 45-53.

Chapter 3

Formulating Strategy

3.0 UNDERSTANDING THE BUSINESS

There exist numerous companies that provide merely "lip service" to strategic planning. Unfortunately, such companies usually operate with "seat-of-the-pants" management and may not fully understand the business that they are in. The 1960s were characterized by rapid growth through mergers and acquisitions, whereas the 1970s and 1980s were characterized by divestitures. Why the change? Companies simply did not understand their own business, the newly acquired business, nor how to manage them, and had to divest in order to reduce long- and short-term debt.

Today, companies appear to be taking more of a systematic approach to strategic planning, such as shown in Fig. 3-1. The first two boxes in Fig. 3-1 are the definition of the business. This includes identification of the company's target goals and objectives, today and in the future, and a situational analysis of the environment, competition, and resource capabilities. The situational analysis box can be further subdivided as shown in Fig. 3-2.

For an introductory course in strategic planning, understanding the business can be divided into two areas:

- What would we like to do?
- What can we do?

The first question requires identification of the opportunities and threats within the macroenvironment and the competitive environment. This can be seen

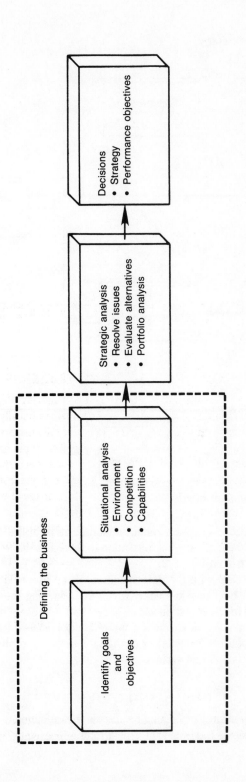

Fig. 3-1. Strategy formulation process.

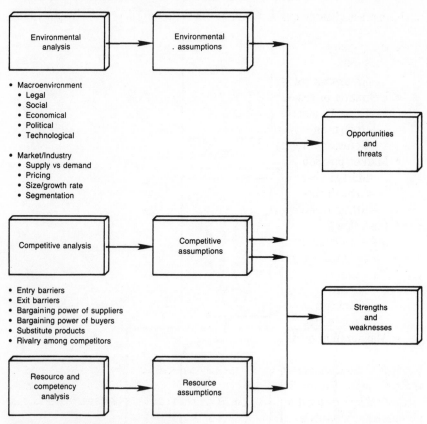

Fig. 3-2. Situational analysis.

in Fig. 3-2. The second question requires identification of the strengths and weaknesses within the company but in relation to the competitive environment. This is also evident from Fig. 3-2.

Both questions deal with the determination of the proper objectives, and the selection of the best possible alternatives for achieving these objectives. Proper analysis and implementation will either make the present business more effective, or identify ways of extending the ongoing business to capitalize on strengths and competitive changes, or change the direction of the business by identifying limitations and constraints.

3.1 GOALS AND OBJECTIVES

The first step in any strategic planning process is the definition of the goals and objectives of the business today and in the near future. These goals and objectives can be expressed either quantitatively or qualitatively. A typical list might include:

- Profitability.
  —Profits
  —Return on sales
- Utilization of resources.
  —Capacity utilization
  —Return on investment
  —Return on net assets
- Market position.
  —Market share
  —Growth rate
  —Attractiveness
- Cash flow.
- Value to customers.
  —Competitive price
  —Quality
  —Service
  —Reliability
  —Value added
- Minimization of risks.

It is not uncommon for strategists to select goals that are totally absurd and look more like a "blue sky approach." Therefore, there should be an established criteria for the measurement of goals and objectives. A typical criteria checklist might include:

- Feasible.
- Specific.
- Not overly complex.
- Measurable.
- Tangible.
- Verifiable.
- Appropriate to the level of the organization.
- Realistic and attainable.
- Specific resource bounds.
- Consistent with resources available or anticipated.
- Consistent with organizational plans, policies, procedures.
- Acceptable to management.

These goals and objectives are needed to accurately conduct a situational analysis.

Executives are paid to define objectives, set corporate direction, and take risks, and this includes strategic planning. Unfortunately, executives may not agree on exactly which risks to take or in what direction to go and, if dissension in the executive ranks becomes apparent, then lower level employees may become disenchanted and no support will be given. Such was the case with a Fortune 500 company, where the Chairman of the Board "delegated" the strategic planning function to the president and vice-presidents. The chairman was under the impression that the company was following the conservative strategic planning philosophy of slow and methodical growth. After reading the corporation's annual report, the chairman realized that the strategic plan was stressing an aggressive penetration into the high-tech arena, a drastic departure from the chairman's way of thinking.

Some strategic plans require years and a great drain of cash before success or failure can be determined and the objectives achieved. An example of this would be Sohio's purchase of Kennicott Copper, which may not show a profit until 1990. Fortunately, Sohio has cash reserves and unused borrowing power, which acts as a partial cushion toward absorbing some of these risks.

3.2 CORPORATE OPPORTUNITIES AND THREATS

All businesses have market opportunities that can enhance the company's growth and survivability. These opportunities can come from trend analyses, such as product life-cycle analysis, or from actual changes in demographics, distribution channels, market structure, and competitive position. The resulting opportunities might be new products, diversification, forward integration, or simply unserved market segments and niches. These opportunities provide the company with the basic idea for "what the company would like to do."

Companies that maintain large market shares often find it possible to develop new market niches even if the market is regarded as "mature." Campbell Soup Company, for example, successfully introduced 42 new products in 1983 to support their 80 percent share of the soup market. This continuous stream of new products was designed to either capture or create and capture new niches due to America's changing tastes and supermarket shopping habits.

Likewise, there exist threats that can prevent growth. Identification of opportunities and threats becomes the basis for evaluating the strategic planning goals and objectives, whereas the strengths and weaknesses relate to implementing the necessary plans to achieve the goals and objectives.

Tables 3-1 and 3-2 identify typical opportunities and threats. Opportunities and threats are identified moreso in qualitative terms than by the quantitative terms used for strengths and weaknesses. Opportunities and threats can be classified into categories, as in the Porter Model shown in Fig. 3-3, which can provide the basis for determining the company's competitive position in the

Table 3-1. Typical Opportunities

- *Improved strategic planning capability*
- *Reorganization for cost control and quality*
- *Low cost manufacturing*
- *Better distribution channels*
- *Increased sales*
- *Lower inventory costs*
- *Hire more talented personnel*
- *Reduce risks*
- *Mergers/acquisitions*
- *Vertical integration*
- *Diversification into related areas*
- *Penetrate new markets (especially global)*
- *Improved credit terms*

Table 3-2. Typical Threats

- *Small company within a large industry*
- *Vigorous competition*
- *Regulatory requirements*
- *Rising gas prices*
- *Mercy of suppliers*
- *Increased operating margins*
- *Political conflicts (internal to company)*
- *Poor cash flow*
- *Seasonality of products/services*
- *Heavy reliance on large customers*
- *Too many product lines*

marketplace.[1] A less sophisticated method would be the opportunity grid shown in Fig. 3-4. The risks increase as one moves clockwise from Quadrant 1 to Quadrant 4.

Although most companies prefer to deal with opportunities rather than threats, it is quite common for companies to develop both opportunity screening

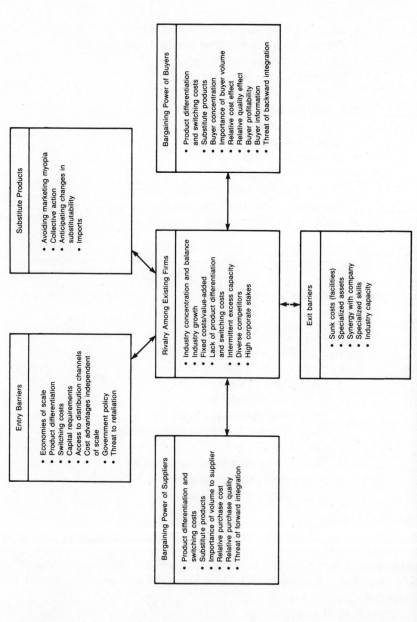

Fig. 3-3. **Factors to analyze in identifying industry characteristics.**
Source: Michael Porter, Competitive Strategy, Free Press, 1980, p. 4.

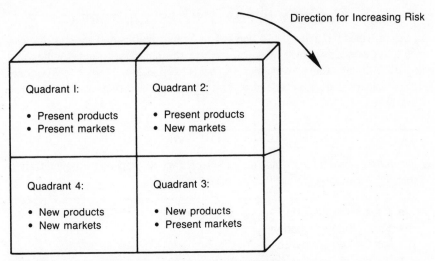

Fig. 3-4. The opportunity grid-basic options.

and threat analysis checklists to evaluate potential opportunities. Typical elements of such checklists might include:

- Does the opportunity fit the company's mission?
- Identification of market needs.
- Identification of size/nature of markets served.
- Relationship with current markets served.
- Available functional resources to support opportunity.
- Evaluating competitors' reactions.
- Ability to penetrate market.
- Profit expectations. When? How much?
- Identification of market threats.
- Evaluation of risks.
- Risks of product displacement.

If the opportunities outweigh the risks, then the opportunity turns into a "product evaluation and screening" project. Realistic milestones for such an opportunity evaluation project might include:

- Market research and analysis, product definition and specifications.
- Preliminary technical analysis, including level of difficulty, rough time/cost analysis, and survey of available resources.
- Detailed competitive analysis.
- Financial analysis.
- Go/NoGo decision.

3.3 INDUSTRY OPPORTUNITIES AND THREATS

In the previous sections, we discussed the opportunities and threats that can affect the company. Here, we will analyze the industry's opportunities and threats. Although there are numerous topics to be included (see Fig. 3-3), only three topics will be covered here: entry barriers, exit barriers, and vertical integration.

Entry Barriers

Entry barriers are forces which tend to discourage a company from penetrating a particular industry. Typical entry barriers include:

- Economies of scale.
- Product differentiation.
- Capital requirements.
- Switching costs.
- Access to distribution channels.
- Government policies.
- Cost disadvantages independent of scale.
- Age of physical plant and equipment.
- Balance of labor industry.
- Excess capacity.

The actual threat of entry into a market is dependent upon two factors; the magnitude of the existing barriers and the anticipated retaliation by the competitors. It is far less likely that competitors will enter new markets if either the barriers to entry are great or if competitive retaliation is expected. Retaliation can be expected from firms with either sufficient resources to retaliate or with firms that have previous "track records" of vigorous retaliation.

Entry barriers are costly to overcome and, therefore, most companies must consider long-term strategies for the profit margins to materialize. Yet, in some mature industries, such as the steel industry, there exist high capital cost barriers but only marginal profits at best. Unused plant capacity can strengthen the entry barriers but reduce profitability.

Exit Barriers

Exit barriers are forces which tend to prevent a company from exiting a business. Typical exit barriers may include:

- Specialized assets.
- One-time costs of exit, labor agreements, or settlement costs.

- Business interrelationships, shared assets.
- Emotional barriers, management fear or pride, corporate image, turf battles.
- Government and social restrictions.

There are several ways that a company can lower its own exit barriers.[2] These include:

- Accounting: establish reserves to offset the cost of writeoff losses.
- Technological: trade off highly specialized assets for flexible assets.
- Financial: lease rather than purchase.
- Multinational: move assets on a scheduled basis and reevaluate.

There are also ways that a firm can lower competitors' exit barriers:[3]

- Acquire their physical plant or assets.
- Offer to serve their customers.
- If a supplier appears eager to help a competitor, offer to purchase more from the supplier.
- Alert regulatory agencies to the competitor's transgressions; i.e., pollution control.
- Start a price war.
- Go public in plea for their exit.

In any case, the company must develop an appropriate "end-game" strategy for exiting a business. Typical strategies might be to milk the investment, allow it to shrink selectively, or simply divest now.

Vertical Integration

Vertical integration is an attempt to improve the efficiency and effectiveness of existing products/services through either forward integration, backward integration, or both. Forward integration involves the controlling of the output (the channels of distribution for the product/services), whereas backward integration involves the controlling of the input (the sources of raw materials, supplier, etc.).

Several industries lend themselves to vertical integration because of improved marketing opportunities, technological intelligence, and an improved ability to forecast changes. Furthermore, integration economies can produce large cost savings by eliminating duplication (i.e. overhead) and bypassing time-consuming steps.

Vertical integration is a risky business because of the amount of assets that are exposed. Therefore, a company should consider transferring some of the risk of vertical integration to outside parties. The key to successful use of vertical integration is timing; at a particular point in time, how broadly should the company be integrated?

The benefits of vertical integration are numerous:

* Economies of combined operations.
* Economies of internal control and coordination.
* Economies of information.
* Economies of avoiding the market.
* Economies of stable relationships.
* Tap into technology.
* Assure supply and/or demand.
* Enhance ability to differentiation.
* Elevate entry and mobility barriers.
* Enter a higher return business.
* Defend against foreclosure.

Vertical integration may also have its disadvantages, the most common one being cost. Some typical costs include:

* Cost of overcoming mobility barriers.
* Increased operating leverage.
* Reduced flexibility to change partners.
* Higher overall exit barriers.
* Capital investment requirements.
* Maintaining balance.
* Dulled incentives.
* Differing managerial requirements.

Because of the costs, vertical integration requires a well thought-out strategy. Typical vertical integration strategies might include:

* Non-integrated strategies. No internal transfers and no ownership is at stake. Customer designed services may be purchased.
* Quasi-integrated strategies. Consume or distribute all or none or some of the inputs and outputs.
* Taper-integrated strategies. Produce or distribute a portion of the requirements internally, but purchase or sell the remainder through specialized suppliers, distributors, or competitors.
* Full integrated strategies. Firms buy or sell all of their materials and/or services internally. Units are normally fully owned subsidiaries, capable of capturing more profit.

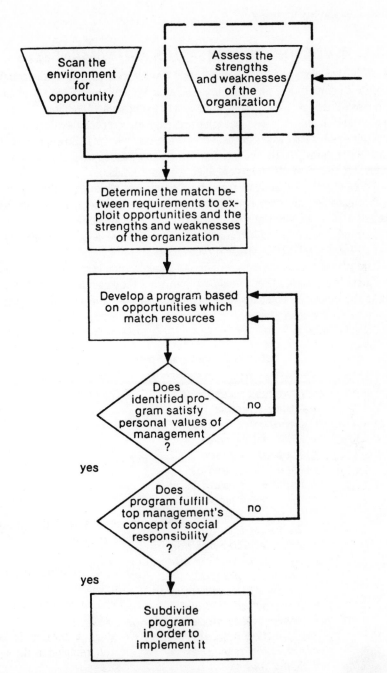

Fig. 3-5. *A process model of strategy formulation.*
Source: "Defining Corporate Strengths and Weaknesses," Sloan
Management Review, *Spring, 1976, p. 53, Howard H. Stevenson.*

3.4 CORPORATE STRENGTHS AND WEAKNESSES

All businesses have corporate competencies and resources that distinguish them from their competitors. These competencies and resources are usually identified in terms of a company's strengths and weaknesses. Deciding "what the corporation should do" can be achieved only after proper evaluation of the strengths and weaknesses to assess "what can we do." Strengths support management's ability to execute the necessary tasks, whereas weaknesses inhibit the ability to meet target objectives and goals.

Strengths and weaknesses can be identified at all levels of management. Senior management may have a clearer picture of the overall company's strengths and weaknesses in the external environment (position in the marketplace) whereas middle management may have a better grasp on the internal (functional) strengths and weaknesses.

Unfortunately, most managers do not think in such terms and, as a result, think more about what they should do than what they can do. It is not unusual to find the objective assessment of strengths and weaknesses high on the list of required activities to be conducted as part of the strategic planning process. This can be seen in Fig. 3-5.[4]

Table 3-3. Typical Strengths

- *Increases sales/profits*
- *Industry leader*
- *Geographic location*
- *Financial reserves*
- *Successful image*
- *Technology leader*
- *Reduced product liability*
- *Fulfilling objectives*
- *Good management team*
- *Customer loyalty*
- *Good industry position*
- *Successful vertical integration*
- *Favorable financial ratios*
- *Successful cost reduction*
- *Modernized facilities*
- *Heavy facility modernization investment*
- *Expanding markets (global)*
- *Access to resources*
- *Brand name*
- *Low personnel turnover*
- *Solid past performance*

Tables 3-3 and 3-4 identify typical organizational strengths and weaknesses. Needless to say, what may be one company's strength may be another company's weakness. Strengths and weaknesses differ from opportunities and threats in that strengths and weaknesses can be measured and assigned quantitative values. Stevenson[5] has carried this analysis further by classifying the strengths and weaknesses into five categories as follows:

General Category	Includes These Attributes
Organization	Organizational form and structure. Top management interest and skill. Standard operating procedures. The control system. The planning system.
Personnel	Employee attitude. Technical skills. Experience. Number of employees.
Marketing	Sales force. Knowledge of the customer's needs. Breadth of the product line. Product quality. Reputation. Customer service.
Technical	Production facilities. Production techniques. Product development. Basic research.
Finance	Financial size. Price-earnings ratio. Growth pattern.

Stevenson further concluded that these attributes are neither mutually exclusive nor collectively exhaustive in partitioning each of the general categories. Furthermore, it must be understood that members of the same management team may not agree precisely on their company's strengths and weaknesses.

Stevenson's research also provides us with a framework of steps which can be used to assess strengths and weaknesses. This can be seen in Table 3-5.[6]

Table 3-4. Typical Weaknesses

- *Overemphasized growth*
- *Lack of business sense*
- *Lack of drive*
- *Strained budgets*
- *Poor cash flow*
- *Identity crisis*
- *Lack of management ability*
- *Poor pricing practice*
- *Declining sales*
- *Lack of modernization*
- *Quality control problems*
- *Too rapid expansion*
- *Unreliable service/warranty*
- *Ethical problems*
- *Stockholder pressure*
- *Limited range of product skills*
- *Eroding dealer relations*
- *Fragmented dealers*
- *Poor organizational structure*
- *Financial pressure*
- *Poor profits*
- *Budget cuts*
- *Interpersonal problems*
- *Lack of self-confidence*

3.5 PORTFOLIO PLANNING AND EVALUATION PARAMETERS

Today's companies have become so complex that it is physically impossible to have strategic planning performed at only one level of management. Below is shown a typical strategic planning culture:

- Corporate level: portfolio planning.
- SBU level: strategic planning.
- Functional level: strategic programming.

Strategic planning within most large, complex organizations is conducted at the SBU level, with the detail execution plans at the functional levels. The SBU level has the responsibility for the identification of the threats, opportunities, strengths, and weaknesses of the SBU.

Table 3-5. Steps in the Process of Assessing Strengths and Weaknesses

Which attributes can be examined?	What organizational entity is the manager concerned with?	What types of measurements can the manager make?	What criteria are applicable to judge a strength or a weakness?	How can the manager get the information to make these assessments?
Organizational structure	The corporation	Measure the existence of an attribute	Historical experience of the company	Personal observation
Major policies				Customer contacts
Top manager's skills	Groups	Measure an attribute's efficiency	Intracompany competition	Experience
Top manager's experience				Control system documents
	Divisions			Meetings
Information system		Measure an attribute's effectiveness	Direct competitors	Planning system
Operation procedures	Departments			documents
Planning system			Other companies	Employees
Employee attitudes	Individual employees			Subordinate managers
Manager's attitudes			Consultants' opinions	Superordinate managers
Union agreements				
Technical skills			Normative judgments based on management's understanding of literature	Peers
Research skills				Published documents
New product ideas				Competitive intelligence
Production facilities				
Demographic characteristics of personnel			Personal opinions	Board members
Distribution network				Consultants
Sales force's skill			Specific targets of accomplishment such as budgets, etc.	Journals
Breadth of product line				Books
Quality control procedures				Magazines
Stock market reputation				Professional meetings
Knowledge of customer's needs				Government economic indicators
Market domination				

What, therefore, is the role of the corporate level? Corporate is responsible for *portfolio planning*. No company can afford to do everything. Activities require the consumption of valuable resources. Therefore, the ultimate goal of a portfolio strategic planning system should be to allocate the available, limited resources to those activities with the greatest potential.

Portfolio planning requires an evaluation of *all* of the company's strengths, weaknesses, opportunities, and threats such that the proper strategic thrust can be determined.

There are three portfolio planning/evaluation parameters: the experience curve; the growth-share matrix; and the business position/industry attractiveness grid. Each of these will be discussed below:

The Experience Curve

The first element of portfolio planning is the experience curve, which states that as more units are produced, productivity and efficiency will increase such that the cost per unit will decline. The experience curve applies not only to manufacturing, but also to sales, marketing, engineering, and so on. (A more detailed analysis of experience curves will be presented in Section 7.11.)

A typical experience curve is shown in Fig. 3-5. The experience curve shows that each time the accumulated production doubles, the average total cost per unit decreases by a fixed amount.

Learning curves provide a company with a strong barrier to entry. Companies with more experience can have lower costs, therefore, it may be best to allocate critical resources early to accumulate experience on a given product line than to enter new "uncharted" waters. Conversely, competing with a company that already has the advantage of the experience curves may be a futile waste of resources. In this situation, the company will eventually become marginally profitable to the point where divestment may be necessary.

The Growth-Share Matrix

The growth-share matrix is an outgrowth of the experience curve. Companies with the highest market shares generally accumulate the most experience and thus have lower total costs. As a result, such companies can generate the necessary cash to finance growth in other areas through new plants, equipment, and facilities.

Figure 3-6 illustrates the growth-share matrix. The four quadrants can be characterized as follows:

- Cash cows. Products with low growth rates and high market shares are *cash cows*. These products generate a large cash flow. Because the product or market has a low growth rate, the cash can be used to finance other activities rather than to reinvest for expansion or possibly idle capacity.
- Stars. Products with high growth rates and high market share might appear to be cash cows, but require heavy investment in order to sustain growth. These products are referred as *stars* and may even consume all of their profits to finance growth. Heavy investment must be made so as to maintain or increase their current market position.
- Question marks. Products with a high growth rate but a low market share are called *questions marks, wildcatters,* or *problem children.* These products have marginal profitability at best, and do not generate much cash. Therefore, it is a critical decision for the company as to whether or not to invest other capital to increase market share or to take a passive role. Question marks become either stars or dogs. Companies can afford to invest heavily in only a limited number of question marks.
- Dogs. Products with low growth and low market share are called *dogs.*

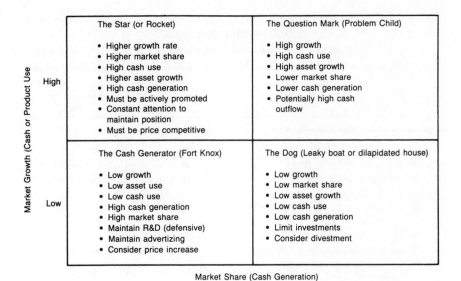

Fig 3-6. Growth-share matrix.

These products both use and generate very little cash. Divestment may be the best approach here, or moderate investment for applications engineering to find new customers for an existing product.

These four quadrants can be related to the product life-cycle analysis normally covered in most marketing courses. Simply stated, any analysis of strengths, weaknesses, opportunities, and threats must be related to the product life-cycle phase for the alternative being considered.

The Business Position/Industry Attractiveness Grid

The business position/industry attractiveness grid is similar to the growth share matrix. The industry attractiveness axis includes essentially the same elements together with quality, technological position, and reputation. Table 3-6 identifies typical factors contributing to market attractiveness and competitive position.

The grid is shown in Fig. 3-7. As a result of the product's placement in the grid, appropriate strategies can be selected such as to build market share, hold present position, or harvest. This can be shown as in Fig. 3-8.

The total portfolio matrix can now be seen as in Fig. 3-9. This figure shows the relationship between the strengths, weaknesses, opportunities, and threats, and the attractiveness/competitive position grid.

Table 3-6. *Factors Contributing to Market Attractiveness and Competitive Position*
Source: Abell and Hammond, 1979.

ATTRACTIVENESS OF YOUR BUSINESS	STRENGTH OF YOUR COMPETITIVE POSITION
● Market Factors	● Market Position
● size (dollars, units)	● relative share of market
● size of product market	● rate of change of share
● market growth rate	● variability of share across segments
● stage in life cycle	● perceived differentiation of quality/price/service
● diversity of market (potential for differentiation)	● breadth of product
● price elasticity	● company image
● bargaining power of customers	● Economic and Technological Position
● cyclicality/seasonality of demand	● relative cost position
● Economic and Technological Factors	● capacity utilization
● investment intensity	● technological position
● nature of investment (facilities, working capital, leases)	● patented technology, product, or process
● ability to pass through effects of inflation	● Capabilities
● industry capacity	● management strength and depth
● level and maturity of technology utilization	● marketing strength
● barriers to entry/exit	● distribution system
● access to raw materials	● labor relations
● Competitive Factors	● relationships with regulators
● types of competitors	
● structure of competition	
● substitution threats	
● perceived differentiation among competitors	
● Environmental Factors	
● regulatory climate	
● degree of social acceptance	
● human factors such as unionization	

MARKET ATTRACTIVENESS	strong	medium	weak
high	**Protect Position: star** • Invest to grow at maximum digestible rate • Concentrate effort on maintaining strength • Expand core business	**Invest to Build: go-go** • Challenge for leadership • Build selectively on strengths • Reinforce vulnerable areas • Expand core business	**Build selectively: wildcatter** • Specialize around limited strengths • Seek ways to overcome weaknesses • Withdraw if indications of sustainable growth are lacking • Expand core business
medium	**Build selectively: blue-chip** • Invest heavily in most attractive segments • Build up ability to counter competition • Emphasize profitability by raising productivity • Expand or maintain core business	**Selectivity/manage for earnings: dark horse** • Protect existing program • Concentrate investments in segments where profitability is good and risk is relatively low	**Limited expansion or harvest: gambler** • Look for ways to expand without high risk otherwise, minimize investment and rationalize operations • Expand or withdraw from core business
low	**Protect and refocus: cash cow** • Manage for current earnings • Concentrate on attractive segments • Defend strengths • Maintain or milk core business	**Manage for earnings: plodder** • Protect position in most profitable segments • Upgrade product line • Minimize investment • Milk or withdraw from core business	**Divest: loser** • Sell at time that will maximize cash value • Cut fixed costs and avoid investment meanwhile • Withdraw from core business

COMPETITIVE POSITION

Fig. 3-7. Strategic options.
Source: George Day, Strategic Market Planning, West Publishing, 1984, p. 121.

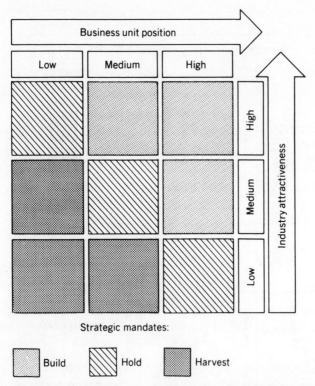

Fig. 3-8. Strategic mandates: Company position/industry attractiveness.
Source: Richard G. Hamermech, Making Strategy Work, John Wiley, 1986, p. 16.

3.6 CLASSIFICATION OF THE VARIABLES

The identification and classification of the company's strategic variables is necessary to establish relative emphasis, priorities, and selectivity among alternatives, to anticipate the unexpected, and to determine the restraints and limitations. Universal systems for the classification process are nonexistent because of the varied nature of organizations, although many professors prefer strengths, opportunities, weaknesses, and strengths. General guidelines, however, can be developed for the variable classification process.

Katz[7] has developed a set of seven variables for strategic planning:

- The market segments to be pursued.
- Products and services to be developed, offered, or discontinued.

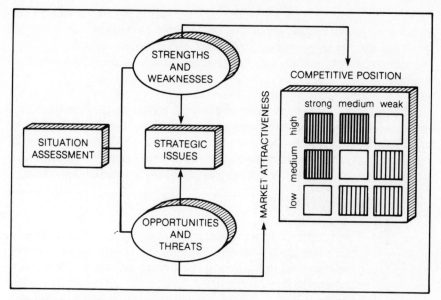

Fig. 3-9. Portfolio classification matrix.
Source: George S. Day, **Strategic Market Planning,** *West Publishing,*
1984, p. 125.

- Channels of distribution and promotion to be utilized.
- Pricing policies and quality/price tradeoffs followed.
- Investment policy and capital expenditures.
- Means of financing and spending constraints.
- The key people required by strategy.

Each of the variables represents a broad spectrum of possible cases. In order to simplify the process somewhat, we can simply classify variables as intra-company and extra-company.

Intra-company variables include such topics as wages and salaries, government freezes on jobs, hiring of minority groups, and lay-offs. *Extra-company* variables normally fall into three categories. The first extra-company variable is technology, such as in computers and electronics. Keeping up with the technology of the competition is a costly process, especially if competitive bidding is included.

The second variable is the social or political nature of the environment. Changes in government, both national and international, can produce major system changes due to imports of raw materials or exports of finished goods. Labor unions and availability of the work force must also be included.

The third variable is the economic characteristics of the environment. This includes per capita income and output as measured by national indicators like gross national product, consumer price index, and prime interest rate. To show the difference between internal and external variable analysis, consider the example below.

Company Z is a manufacturer of chemical cooling towers for industrial applications. The company considers itself a member of the chemical industry and deals primarily with cooling-water efficiency applications. Company Z maintains less than 5 percent of the market share. The industry leader maintains a 30 percent market share. The following factors were identified by the company.

I. EXTERNAL FACTORS
   A. Gnp growth
       This variable provides a measurement of real growth, and an idea of how inflation is behaving. A look at customer industries for this year compared to last year gives a rough indication of how much sales should increase.
   B. Industry trends
       This variable indicates what type of cooling equipment will be required. For instance, would a chemical treatment be preferred over a hardware device?
   C. Legislative trends
       This would include EPA actions. For instance, Company Z uses chromate in 8 percent of its products. Chromate has been used in cooling systems for the last 30 years, but recently it is considered a dirty word. As a result, Company Z is changing its chemical formulas to contain low amounts of chromate.
   D. Political situation
       The political relationship between the United States and Rhodesia (Rhodesia is raw material supplier of chromate). This relationship is important for any foreign supplier.
II. INTERNAL FACTORS
   A. Growth by product
       It is important to know what product is growing in order to anticipate future resource needs. Product growth is important for financial forecasting.
   B. Expansion rate
       Industry bankruptcy is primarily caused by overexpansion. Company Z has been growing at 30 to 40 percent annually for the last three years. Maintaining a stable rate of growth is important for capital expenditures, financing, and acquisitions.

C. Sales effectiveness
Company Z looks at competitors only from the viewpoint of maintaining market shares. The sales force is the major aim of the company, so salesman training is important. A lead time of 1½ years is typical until a salesman becomes profitable, because he must be competent in both the sales and technical areas. This time also allows for a buildup of customer confidence.

It is not our intent to request students to categorize all the possible combinations of strategic variables for all industries. The purpose of the remaining sections is to identify certain categories of strategic variables, which are more readily apparent in a variety of industries.

The ability to identify strategic variables is not an easy task. The identification process requires forethought, timeliness, and an ability to perceive the total system from all points of view. A survey was conducted to determine what variables were considered to be "key" in the success of a company. The survey was conducted at both systems-oriented and nonsystems-oriented companies. The following results were obtained:

- Top management considered fewer variables as being strategic than did middle managers.
- Middle-management and top-management, in systems-oriented companies, had better agreement on strategic variable identification than did managers in nonsystems-oriented companies.
- Top executives within the same industry differed on the identification of strategic variables, even within companies having almost identical business bases.
- Very little attempt was made by top management to quantify the risks involved with each strategic variable.

Strategic variables differ from company to company and from industry to industry. In the following sections, we have attempted to identify the strategic planning variables for a variety of industries. A brief discussion appears at the beginning of several of the sections to identify industry characteristics with which the reader may not be familiar. The cases that follow attempt to identify industry-related strategic variables, not necessarily for system-oriented companies.

3.7 INTERNATIONAL ENGINEERING/CONSTRUCTION INDUSTRY

The international engineering/construction industry is characterized by a large corporate headquarters with multiple divisions, most often with worldwide locations. All divisions normally operate on the systems approach to management. Strategic variables are established at the corporate level; divisions then set their own strategic variables and objectives in relation to corporate plans. The variables are essentially the same within contractors, with only the magnitude of the dollar volume varying.

The basic product-policy variable is to provide engineering, procurement, and/or construction services. The customer-policy variable defines to whom these services are offered. For instance, one large corporation offers the above services to owner/operations in heavy industries such as industry-chemical, steel, nonferrous metals, and foods. Within each area, specific fields are defined such as chlorine/caustic plants, silicone plants, cat-crackers and reformers.

The marketing areas are worldwide. The engineer/contractor has very little, if any, input on plant location, so construction site and project value are uncontrolled variables. However, the location of the plant can determine where engineering and procurement are performed. An example would be a projected plant site in Latin America. The engineering could be done in the United States, Mexico, or Argentina, depending on expertise required, customer preference, and major supplier locations.

Most members of this industry depend upon reputation and sales force effort as their promotion policy. Regardless of justifications from the marketing personnel, reputation is the key, and this includes technical and financial qualifications.

Expertise in a given field is the competitive emphasis. Each engineer/contractor has expertise in several key areas like polymers processing, blast furnace design, and reformers. This then establishes what specific customer policies apply to the promotion policy.

Efforts are continually made to increase the technical base to meet market demands and penetrate new markets. One large contractor is presently expanding its technical base in polymer science and coal gasification. This results from answering the customer-policy question, "Where are our major market opportunities?"

The major pricing variable is contract-related, including cost-plus, fixed fee, and/or lump sum contracts. The type of contract is dependent upon the market. Cost-plus contracts are preferred, because this reduces risks. The actual fee is determined relative to the size of the project.

All strategic variables within this industry are interrelated; one variable cannot be established without looking at the others. The location of a plant may determine where work is performed; the type of plant and its size will determine the level of competitive advantage; and the market, customer, and work level with respect to capacity will determine the type of contract. Below is a brief summary of the strategic variables for the industry.

Capital Expenditures on New Plant by the Major Petroleum and Chemical Companies. This industry acts as a service firm. It provides engineering construction services to firms contemplating new plants or additions to existing ones. The magnitude of such plants reflects in their capital expenditure allocations and, in turn, the volume of business dependent upon it.

Customer or Client Requirements. Clients, in sending out job inquiries for an overseas project, will often require that the successful contractor have previous experience at completing a job in that specific country. Similarly, the client may require that a certain process be incorporated in his plant's design. Contractor's success in securing work, then, also depends on the ability to satisfy these types of customer requirements.

Availability of Both Quantity and Quality of Labor. Many projects today are quite complex and massive in scale. The ability to handle a job of this magnitude, while concurrently allowing for the manning of other jobs, demands sufficient numbers of people. Likewise, the technical expertise must be present to handle different types of plants or those employing special processes. Obviously, this availability of manpower widens the number of jobs the firm can bid on and possibly obtain. (Note also the relationship to the item above.)

Location of Offices in Relation to Those of the Client. In situations where the contractor has an office near a client's existing or proposed plant site, a distinct advantage over the competition exists. The reasons are obvious: travel costs are minimized, communications maximized, and problems solved in a shorter time span, because the necessary decision-makers are located in the same area. Similarly, having an office located near the headquarters of major oil and chemical firms allows numerous conferences with a minimum of expense. Such considerations play a major role in decisions to relocate overseas headquarters in London, England, for example. Nearly all the Arabian oil companies, as well as many U.S. firms, have major offices in London.

Types of Jobs Available. The reference here is to whether lump-sum or cost-plus contracts are available. The firm seeks to minimize the amount of work it bids on a lump-sum basis; but, of course, the market ultimately governs such decisions. A glut of available lump-sum work, let us say, would force the contractor to re-evaluate some of its internal procedures as well as sharpen its pricing arrangement to meet competition. The risks involved with lump-sum work are greater than those associated with the cost-plus variety, and so the risks in profit-making are increased as well. Very definitely then, the type of jobs available on the market could greatly influence the company's financial performance.

3.8 THE CHEMICAL INDUSTRY

Strategic planning in the chemical industry differs drastically from company to company because of such key factors as research and development, product line, and dollar volume. In order to simplify the analysis, only two categories of companies will be discussed: the large corporation with multiple product lines and large R&D, and the smaller firm with limited product lines. Both companies generally maintain project management structures.

The most important variable in strategic planning for large chemical corporations is R&D (research and development). This is a result of the economic competitiveness of the chemical processes in the industry. Whichever company comes up with a new useful chemical will make gains in the market place. This R&D takes the form of searching for new products, improved products, new uses for existing products, new ways of marketing products, and new lower-cost processes. The latter can be accomplished by finding ways to change to a cheaper raw material base, ways to eliminate co-products or costly separations, or ways to reduce the number of reaction steps required. Companies practice a policy of independent R&D under the belief that if too much attention were given to what competitors were doing, they would become imitators and not innovators.

Because the chemical industry is a high investment business, sources of capital and the selection of investments are the next most important variables in strategic planning. The chemical industry is the highest in terms of capital investment per production worker. New plans for expansion are continuously being made. There is a great deal of sophistication required in selecting these investments because of increased competition in cross-industries.

The cost of production is extremely vital to planning. Not only is it important to have access to low-cost raw material, but it is also important that plants operate at or near capacity in order that economies of scale be realized. This refers back to the expansion mentioned above: the unit cost of producing a chemical decreases markedly as the size of the plant producing it is increased, providing that the plant can be operated near capacity.

An important variable in strategic planning is employee safety. If it is determined that a plant, a process, or a product is unsafe, plans will be made immediately to change or eliminate the operation. Equally important is product safety to the consumer. All products are thoroughly tested before they are released to the public. An example of this is the controversy over aerosol-propelled products that may have an adverse effect on the ozone layer of our atmosphere.

A recent variable that has gained a new emphasis is energy. Much greater efforts are being made at energy conservation despite the fact that many a company has been the main supplier to itself of much of its utilities.

The general economic forecast of each country in which the company operates is another variable in strategic planning. This data provides management with information leading to projected production and sales.

Over the past decade, many smaller companies have matured into leaders in the chemical industry. This growth was accomplished partly through their success in strategic planning. The typical strategic plan for a smaller company would have the following parts:

- Planning phase.
- Statement of corporate objectives and strategies that provide the broad goals and policy guidance for the corporation.
- Forecast of the U.S. economy through 1990 (broad economic basis for all business).
- A description of the planning process and procedures to be used for that year.
- Financial analysis on the level of capital currently employed by units and divisions.

Based on the above information, particularly the economic analysis, this type of plan required several variable determinants. A determination of future product and market growth rates had to be made. (This serves as the key to the investment decision.) Also, future demand trends had to be specified.

The broadest possible number of investment options had to be explored and then investments allocated to those projects which best meet corporate goals and strategies.

Each division of a company must reassess its current strategies and make necessary changes for the next three years. (Any approval of money and manpower is based on the corporation's agreement of the divisional strategy.)

As the economy changes, so do markets. Therefore, the divisions are responsible for identifying candidates for divestiture. In addition, flexibility in spending and manpower due to economic uncertainty are mandatory.

Of the aforementioned variables, one company places much of its emphasis on economic trends. In their strategic plan, the following economic factors were considered:

- Continued above-normal rate of inflation.
- Continued rate of unemployment.
- Continued federal government deficits.
- Continued problems in monetary growth and capital markets.
- Continued lack of national energy program, requiring dependence on foreign sources of energy.
- Growing influence of government intervention and regulation. (Government accounts for more than 39 percent of GNP). Policy making geared mostly to short-term problem solving.

- Real GNP only 3 percent.
- No recession or boom period foreseen.
- Lack of consumer buying mood.
- General growth slow-down abroad.

The above variables are probably typical of most successful U.S. corporations. To see where corporations in the chemical industry differ, one must look at the divisional level. It is at this level that competitive differences occur. Here we find the following strategic planning variables:

- Growth rates of present and potential customers by end use.
- Evaluate competitor strengths and weaknesses, taking into consideration both present size and intended expansions.
- Energy-intensive end uses of their products.
- Logistics of shipping.
    —Distribution patterns
    —Package size and availability
    —Terminal and plant locations

The most consistently used variable is market or customer definition. All companies seek to identify major market opportunities.

One company concentrates its planning on market expansion, whether through geographic expansion in the commodity chemicals fields or through acquisitions in specialty chemicals areas. Their goals are increasing market share and a higher sales/capital ratio. Another emphasizes planning for market requirements to *maintain* its share. It is heavily committed to a highly specialized product line where growth has hit a plateau. A third is identifying its market in proprietary, high technology, specialty chemicals. This marks a major market shift (over a period of years) away from the manufacture of commodity chemicals. Market identification in areas where the company can be a significant factor, when coupled with cost control and investment plans, is expected to bring a greater return on investment.

Another company also emphasizes market planning as the key variable. In the half of their business which is distribution of chemicals purchased in bulk from other companies, concentration is on targeting market expansion on a geographic basis. Planning for manufactured chemicals is more detailed, but the key is still heavily product/customer-oriented in terms of strategic plans.

The strategic planning variable discussed centered on the situation analysis area, and the assumption made is that for strategic plans to be effective, the company must continue to formulate specific objectives.

3.9 SNACK FOOD INDUSTRY

Strategic planning for smaller dollar-volume industries like the snack food industry follows the same rules and regulations as larger industries. The major strategic variables in this industry are seasonality, economic conditions, employment rate, raw materials availability, energy availability, competition, and leisure time availability.

Seasonality. The very nature of the products lend themselves to definite seasonal patterns. Spring, summer, and holiday times are high volume periods, while fall and winter are not particularly high. As a result, this variance must be taken into account and plans made to pay particular attention to the low points to even out demand. Without this, production facilities would not operate optimally, and manpower and equipment requirements would fluctuate constantly.

Economic conditions. As with all industry, the economy plays a very important role in business stability. This is particularly true of the snack food industry. Eating is a necessity, but the demand pattern of snack foods is elastic. No one needs to eat potato chips. Therefore, sound economic forecasts are required and must be monitored in order to make accurate planning decisions.

Employment rate. As the rate of employment decreases (unemployment rises) the snack food industry does more business, because people have more leisure time and therefore, spend more money on snack food. Therefore, this must be monitored to control production levels and manpower requirements.

Raw material availability and quality. Key ingredients to this particular company are potatoes, corn, and oil. Natural disasters such as droughts, floods, and extreme cold or heat all have different effects on crops. Large sales to foreign countries may also effect availability on these items. Therefore, this variable must be monitored to insure availability of quality products to meet demands.

Energy availability. All products manufactured by this company are fried. Therefore, gas or fuel oil are required. If these items become scarce, the business might not function.

Competition. Competition enters the market daily. The product line must be kept diverse enough to meet new challenges yet be controllable. This is accomplished by sticking with basic products and varying the package prices, quantity, etc., in various zones to meet competition.

Leisure time. The more leisure time people have, the more snack foods they purchase. This has direct impact on demand. It is, therefore, good business to keep up with developments in union contracts to know how long and when people will work. If one loses sight of this, customers may be lost.

3.10 ELECTRICAL EQUIPMENT MANUFACTURING

The electrical equipment manufacturing industry is international in scope. Large companies, such as General Electric, have as many as 50 plant locations and divisions and produce a wide range of industrial and consumer equipment for generation, transmission, distribution, control, and utilization of electric power.

The strategic variables of each group are generally established at the division level but must conform with overall corporate objectives and strategies. As an example, consider Company X, which has 50 divisions located throughout the world. Corporate strategies are established in general terms and then related to composite and financial objectives from which each operational division must determine the strategic variables most likely to affect these financial objectives. This procedure is shown below.

BASIC STRATEGY 1978-1987

- Develop expertise in related technologies.
- Develop new and better products to broaden markets and command higher-than-average profit margins.
- Grow by acquisition of infields closely related to the basic business.
- Increase investments in new product development.
- Attract talented managers to convert technological expertise and business strategy into above-average profits and growth.

COMPOSITE FINANCIAL & MARKET GOALS

	Present	Goal
Return on net assets	13.6%	16%
Profit before tax	8.2%	7%
Market share - growth	15.3%	12%
Financial stability (debt/equity)	45%	34%

STRATEGIC VARIABLES

- Cost and availability of acquisition money (common thread).
- Demand for energy-related products.
- Cost of raw materials.
- Cost of labor.
- Availability of government contracts.
- Technical capability (R&D).
- Economic indicators.
- Competitive costs.
- Acquisition of top management people.

Most often, each operational division or group establishes its own strategic planning document. As an example, the Control Products Division of a large electrical equipment manufacturer is shown below:

CONTROL PRODUCTS DIVISION

I. BUSINESS ANALYSIS

A. Historical Performance

(1) Historical performance would include a synopsis of Historical performance and the factors that affected it, including such things as market growth patterns, market share, results of previous plans and programs, etc.

(2) Identification of the division's position today as it reflects a base for future growth planning.

B. Recent Performance

(1) This section includes the analysis of the 1976 performance against objectives. It also includes a discussion of significant events which affected performance, reviewing causes and effects for variances favorable and unfavorable.

(2) The identification of accomplishments/progress made in the implementation of the 1977 thru 1982 strategic plan.

C. Backlog/Overdue Status

(1) This section describes the historical pattern of the division's backlog situation and current situation, and what could be considered as the "optimum" condition.

D. Market Structure

(1) This section includes the identification of major industrial segments that represent the high opportunity growth segments for the division and its subsidiaries.

(2) This also includes the identification of major product line groupings and how they relate to the key industries/markets of the division.

E. Present Division Market/Industry Position

(1) This section identifies the division's positioning today as it reflects a base for future growth planning. This includes a discussion of key factors and/or organization(s) segments and explains the current domestic and overseas marketing situation.

F. Competitor Analysis and/or Assumptions

(1) Comment in this section reflects the overall impact of competitors on the future of the division. It includes the assessment of the following items:

(a) Major strengths and weaknesses.

(b) Major limitations.

(c) Assumptions about present and future strengths with regard to sales effort, distributions, services, cost reduction, acquisitions, etc.

(d) What particular resources or unique capabilities does the competitor have to carry out these strategies?

(e) The identification of products in the competitor's line which are in the division's charter but are not presently being produced by the division.

(2) This section also covers a detailed discussion of all the various competitors by the market segment.

G. Competitor Performance History

(1) This section would include the comparison of product performance vs. key competitors with regard to such items as sales billed, ROI, investment, number of employees, sales billed per employee, etc.

H. Competitor Acquisitions

(1) This section includes the identification of historical acquisitions within the domestic market.

(2) This section also includes nondomestic competitors acquisitions into the domestic market.

I. Key Environmental Assumptions

(1)This section lists the strategic variables needed to identify major opportunities for profitable growth or threats. This includes the following areas:

Market growth.

Availability of capital.

Corporate policy re-investment, operating managed cost, strategic managed cost.

Competitor strategies.

Product mix.

"Up," "down," "developing" indicators.

Technology.

Capacity.

Distribution.

Inflation.

Wages/welfare benefits costs.

Availability of key materials.

Cost of key materials.

Price increases/realization.

New material availability.

Foreign competition.

New domestic competition.

Legal liability.

Energy cost and availability.

Metrification.

Government regulation.
—Wage-price controls
—Consumer protection
—OSHA
—EPA
—EEO
—GATT
—Import/export regulations and taxes
—Tax incentives

Standards.

Safety.

Demographic.

Social.

What changes are anticipated in the techniques of marketing, manufacturing, engineering in the next five years...10 years?

Competitor strategic/actions/changes.

J. International/Export Markets

(1) This section describes the current business attitude toward international business, including investments offshore, license development, technical assistance, exports, etc.

K. Division Strengths

(1) This includes the present and anticipated strengths over the planning period.

L. Division Limitations/Weaknesses

(1) In this section, an attempt is made to determine the present and anticipated weaknesses and to *identify corrective actions* required. These include such areas as listed below:

—Product characteristics, completeness of line and cost
—Adequacy of selling effort
—Knowledge of competitors
—Adequacy of distribution
—Negotiation and quotation service
—Customer service
—Physical resources ⎫
—Manpower resources ⎬ Manufacturing, Engineering, Marketing, etc.
—Financial resources ⎭
—Image
—Communications

M. Key Factors Affecting Growth
  (1) *Favorable trends.* This section includes a discussion of the favorable trends that will occur immediately or over a marketing period, which will represent offensive opportunities to exploit.
  (2) *Unfavorable trends.* This section includes a discussion of the unfavorable trends in the immediate period or over the planning period, which represents threats requiring defensive action.
  (3) *Constraints.* This section discusses the constraints that would possibly restrict implementation of the division plans and programs. These constraints would include such things as capabilities, facilities, managed or strategic cost considerations.
II. STRATEGIC OBJECTIVES AND GOALS
  A. Group strategies and objectives.
  In this particular section the objective, the goal and the strategy are given which would have reflected previously to make it variables.
  B. Division strategies.
  These would be the same as Group Strategies only expand to (b) Division levels.
III. CONTINGENCIES AND ALTERNATE STRATEGIES
  A. Contingencies and risk identifications.
  In this particular section the discussion concerns the "What if" and the analysis and the contingency summaries which result in that "What if" statement.
  B. Alternate Strategies
  This section is intended to explain the alternate and contingency strategies required to effectively manage the contingencies outlined above.

The following sections deal in a further breakdown of the previously noted sections under the heading of "business analysis." Each goes into further depth for each of the sub-sections, with charts and graphs being required for display of pertinent information. The use of historical data has been derived through government sources and also through the use of Data Research Institute. The objective is to have 80 percent of the total cost covered by strategic planning, with a plus or minus 2 percent variance in the outcome. This planning occurs for a period of 5 years into the future and is updated periodically for a period of 5 years into the future.

Division Strategic Plan Guidelines
- Objective. A statement of desired future position or destination.
- Goal. Time-based points of measurement along the road to the objective.
- Strategy. The broad course of action to be taken, leading to the desired future position or destination.

- Mission. A statement about the division, describing what it is, why it exists, and the unique contributions it can make to the company.
- Key environmental assumptions. Statements about the future environment in which division assumes it will be operating.
- Key competitor assumptions. Statements of future actions which it is assumed will be taken by a division's major competitors.
- Competitor analysis. Making key competitor assumptions and a most likely strategy for each division's major competitors.
- Constraints. Forces from either inside or outside the company which may limit the division's choice of actions.
- Programs. Development, investment, or other programmed activities that are critical to the pursuit of the division's strategy.
- Resources. Cash, manpower, equipment, licenses, and so on, that are critical to the pursuit of the division's strategy.
- Resource analysis. Assessing the strengths and limitations of a division in terms of its resources, relative to its competitors.
- Opportunity. In a division's external environment, a combination of time, place, and circumstances which offers potentially favorable results for the business.
- Threat. In a division's external environment, a combination of time, place, and circumstances which could have a negative impact on the division's future performance.
- Strengths. Resource capabilities of a division, which can result in competitive advantages.
- Limitations. Resource capabilities of a division, which can result in competitive disadvantages.
- Possible strategy. One way of applying resources to capitalize on an opportunity or to minimize a threat which, while not necessarily optimal nor complete, is nevertheless possible for the division.
- "What-if" analysis. A process by which contingency plans can be developed for a division.

3.11 PAPER CARTON INDUSTRY

Quite often, smaller industries require a more intensive strategic planning process than larger companies, because the cost of failure is greater. The paper carton industry is one such example. The variables shown below are listed but not described. The descriptions are the same as in the previous sections.

The following items are the industry related variables required for strategic planning:

- General economic conditions.
- Inflation.

- Projected wage settlements.
- Material costs, which may affect marketability of the whole commodity.
- Customers coming into, or going out of the territory.
- Current or prospective customers' potential, as a result of the following evaluations:
  - The current carton (or any product) requirements of the account.
  - The status of this customer as a company, chances of success, or even continuing at the current level.
  - The chance that the market for this product to be one of an expanding nature.
- Specific market conditions, which may necessitate either a shift in concentration, or a total change of direction.
- Projected volume available within the organization.
- Changes in consumer requirements due to technological advances in either equipment or consumer usage.

The last five items require additional comment. The paper carton industry is unique in that they can operate only in a certain geographical area, because the costs of shipping items any great distance would result in a noncompetitive position for the company. It therefore behooves the company to take a vested interest in those companies within their own geographical area, in respect to in-and-out movement of industry.

3.12 MACHINE TOOL INDUSTRY

The sector of the machine tool industry discussed below primarily includes the metal-cutting machine group. This comprises manufacturers of machinery such as turret lathes, milling machines, drill presses, boring machines, and gear cutters. This will exclude specialized machinery such as transfer machines, injection molding machines, and forming machines. Characteristically, the products of the machine tool industry will have an extremely high selling price, a useful life generally exceeding 20 years, and a technical complexity far greater than the average industrial product.

The following variables are identified as being important in strategic planning for the industry:

Business Markets and Business Cycles. Traditionally, the main thrust of machine tool marketing has been in nurturing the domestic market. During the last few years, however, there has been increased emphasis in cultivating the international market, due to the fact that the greatest untapped potential for large volume sales lies in overseas markets where either a major retooling is underway, or (in third-world countries, such as in South America) where the GNP is growing at a staggering rate.

Another attraction to the international market is the severe business cycle. Traditionally, the busy periods in domestic machine tool sales occur during the periods for which foreign sales remain healthy. Such a broadened marketing territory would greatly increase sales stability.

Labor Force Skills and Availability. In order to efficiently produce a quality product of great technical complexity, it is quite important to have access to a sufficient pool of competently trained labor. As many other local industries with stronger union shops have a higher wage structure, however, it frequently becomes difficult for machine shops to retain their skilled labor. Out of this unfortunate economic inequality has arisen a very profitable marketing opportunity. As many customers for machine tools have an identical problem in attracting and retaining skilled labor, a market has opened up to supply machine tools which require a lower skill level for machinists. To meet this demand, the highly profitable product line of numerically controlled machines has been developed.

Product Characteristics. One of the major differences between various machine tool manufacturers lies in the degree to which customized machines will be designed and built to meet a customer's specifications. At one extreme, some manufacturers will produce only a standard product. This yields a greater unit margin, but lowers sales volume. At the other extreme, manufacturers will engineer, manufacture, and service a version of their machine customized per customer. This may even go to the extreme of incorporating into the design specialized components for which there is no existing supplier! This strategy of producing customized machines attracts a higher sales volume, but decreases unit margins.

Technological Change. Technological change may impact the machine tool industry in a number of ways and merits constant monitoring and assessment. For instance, a new process such as laser machining may threaten to make obsolete existing mechanical methods of metal removal. Other less sudden changes can be exemplified by the gradual transition from an entirely mechanical to a highly electronic machine tool. These changes introduce a number of critical make vs. buy decisions which affect competitive posture and manufacturing flexibility.

Customer Organizational Restructuring. There has been a major shift in the nature of the industry's customers. In recent years, prominent small independent job shops have been absorbed into large conglomerates. Such a change has major implications regarding the formality of capital equipment justifications. For instance, justification is now more oriented toward industrial engineering considerations as opposed to the experience of the shop foreman, who was a tremendous asset to the marketing effort, once he was satisfied with the performance of previous machines.

Pricing and Promotion Policy. There are two primary modes through which machine tools are promoted to potential customers. Frequently, larger manufacturers will maintain an extensive marketing staff to develop and pursue potential customers. Such a staff is quite expensive, but often pays off handsomely through higher sales due to increased technical competence and product dedication. The alternative to this direct sales approach encompasses the use of existing local machine tool dealers as an outlet for the product. Such an arrangement creates lower sales emphasis when a potential customer is approached but is often worthwhile due to the sharply decreased cost of supporting such a marketing organization.

A company's pricing policy also becomes crucial in attaining sufficient sales volume. Alternatives that must be considered include whether firm prices are to be quoted in all cases or whether original quotations will be negotiable. Similarly, the financing terms of the sale become important, because many customers demand lengthy credit or leasing arrangements.

Although the strategy variables discussed here represent the spectrum of considerations for the machine tool industry, an integrated approach to implementing such policies may take different forms depending upon a company's inherent goals, objectives, and philosophy.

ENDNOTES—Chapter 3

1. Adapted from Michael Porter, *Competitive Strategy* (The Free Press, 1980), p. 40.

2. Kathryn Rudie Harrigan, *Strategic Flexibility* (Lexington, MS: Lexington Books, 1985), p. 179.

3. *Ibid.*

4. Howard H. Stevenson, "Defining Corporate Strengths and Weaknesses," *Sloan Management Review,* Spring 1976, p. 53.

5. *Ibid,* p. 55.

6. *Ibid,* p. 54.

7. Robert L. Katz, *Cases and Concepts in Corporate Strategy* (Prentice Hall, 1970).

Chapter 4

The Role of Finance

4.0 THE FINANCE FUNCTION

Functional strategies are different than grand strategies or business level strategies in that they are more specific, time-oriented, and are developed by specialists within the functional areas. Grand strategies provide a general direction, while functional strategies provide specific annual objectives for each area. These objectives are set with the participation of the functional area manager. Figure 4-1 shows how corporate or grand strategy flows for the General Cinema Corporation into business level strategy for their movie theater business and then into specific functional objectives and strategies. Notice that at the corporate level, cash flow from soft-drink bottling and Sunkist products is being allocated to a diversification into leisure-oriented, consumer-oriented product/service businesses. Within the movie theater business, the strategy is to maintain the current level with selective growth.

With this chapter, we begin a series of four chapters dealing with specific functional strategies, finance and accounting, marketing, manufacturing, and R&D. Finally, Chapter 8 presents the overall process of integrating functional strategies.

Financial planning for Chrysler Corporation nicely highlights the significance of financial strategies. In 1979, Chrysler was near bankruptcy. Huge losses in 1979 and 1980 caused severe cash-flow problems. Because of the losses, Chrysler was totally dependent on the use of external funds to turn the company around. Suppliers were asked to extend payments on accounts payable. Extensions were sought on bank loans, and finally, a long-term debt of $1.2 billion was acquired by U.S. Government guarantee. By 1983, Chrysler's

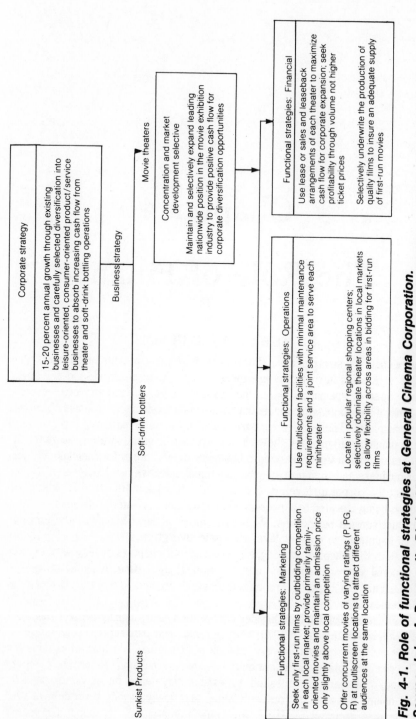

Fig. 4-1. Role of functional strategies at General Cinema Corporation.
Source: John A. Pearce, II., Richard B. Robinson, Jr., Strategic Management - Strategy Formulation and Implementation, Second Edition, Richard D. Irwin, Inc., 1985, p. 300.

Corporate strategy

15-20 percent annual growth through existing businesses and carefully selected diversification into leisure-oriented, consumer-oriented product/service businesses to absorb increasing cash flow from theater and soft-drink bottling operations

Business strategy

Sunkist Products

Soft-drink bottlers

Movie theaters

Concentration and market development selective

Maintain and selectively expand leading nationwide position in the movie exhibition industry to provide positive cash flow for corporate diversification opportunities

Functional strategies: Marketing

Seek only first-run films by outbidding competition in each local market; provide primarily family-oriented movies and maintain an admission price only slightly above local competition

Offer concurrent movies of varying ratings (P, PG, R) at multiscreen locations to attract different audiences at the same location

Functional strategies: Operations

Use multiscreen facilities with minimal maintenance requirements and a joint service area to serve each minitheater

Locate in popular regional shopping centers; selectively dominate theater locations in local markets to allow flexibility across areas in bidding for first-run films

Functional strategies: Financial

Use lease or sales and leaseback arrangements of each theater to maximize cash flow for corporate expansion; seek profitability through volume not higher ticket prices

Selectively underwrite the production of quality films to insure an adequate supply of first-run movies common stock had reached a level making it possible to raise external funds by the sale of common stock. Steering Chrysler clear of this crisis required careful forecasting of the needs for funds and ability to seek available external sources. By 1987, Chrysler was healthy enough to allocate cash resources for the acquisition of AMC, providing Chrysler with the capital assets now needed for growth.

The objective of the finance function is to provide maximum benefit for the owners.[1] This means choosing the sources and allocation of funds that maximize the wealth of the firm. Financial decisions are made to support the overall goals of the firm. It is generally assumed that top management's objective is to develop and allocate resources as efficiently as possible within the constraints of the larger objectives of the firm.

In this chapter, we deal with financial and accounting strategies, but the objectives of each of these areas are different. Accounting strategies are primarily concerned with maximizing short-run profit, while financial strategies are concerned with maximizing the wealth of the firm for the long-run. The key differences in these two strategies are the timing of returns, the distribution of returns, and risk.

Accounting strategies are short-term in focus. Their emphasis is to account for the firm's resources in such a fashion as to maximize the return to the firm in the short-run. Thus, a firm may choose an inventory evaluation method which shows inventory to be expensed at the lowest cost possible, producing the highest possible profit. If a firm followed an accounting strategy only, it would purchase inexpensive, low quality machinery, perform maintenance only when necessary, use the cheapest raw materials, and use cheap, unskilled labor. These activities would result in high profits in the short-run due to their emphasis on maximizing profits by minimizing costs. Another example of short-run accounting strategies is to forego expenditures for R&D, because these expenditures are treated as an expense in the year they are incurred.

Finance strategies, unlike accounting strategies, consider the time value of money. Returns received in earlier years have higher present value than those received in later years. Finance strategies also take risk into consideration. The higher the risk incurred, the higher the expected returns. Accounting strategies, by contrast, focus on return without regard to risk assessment. The finance function is also responsible for monitoring the firm's performance to see if actual performance is consistent with short- and long-range objectives. This monitoring function is performed with the assistance of financial ratio analysis.

4.1 WORKING CAPITAL

Anticipating the need for cash and developing strategies for managing liquidity is the most important function of the financial specialty. Because of this, the management of working capital consumes a great deal of the financial manager's time. The goal of managing working capital is to achieve returns that maximize the value of the firm. Current assets must be available for the support of on-going operations, and current liabilities must be obtained at minimum cost with maximum flexibility. The consequences of effective working capital have major impact on profits, cash flow, and risk. Some analysts point to cash flow as the most significant variable to track. There is evidence to suggest that cash flow problems are the early warning signs of much larger, significant problems. Cash flow problems are hard to turn around, and the consequences of the turn-around actions themselves create greater long-term problems.

To anticipate the need for funds, cash flows must be forecasted. Every event that leads to cash entering the firm or leaving the firm must be anticipated. These forecasting activities are essential to managing the liquidity of the firm. The cash budget, a detailed analysis of the cash flows by month, forecasts the need for cash. The finance area must interface with marketing, accounting, personnel, and production as the cash flow budget is constructed from planning documents prepared in each of these areas: sales budget, collections budget, wages-and-salary budget, purchases budget, and capital budget.

The difficulty with anticipating the cash flow budget is that the outflows are not matched with the inflows. Figure 4-2 shows the operating cycle of a typical manufacturing firm with mismatched flows. To further compound this problem, growth creates tremendous needs for cash at a time when little is coming in as a result of operations. This is particularly true of a new company selling on credit. Capital becomes tied up in accounts receivable. It doesn't have to be a new company for a firm to find itself in this type of cash flow bind. The now classic case of Grant's illustrates the point. A corporate strategy decision to

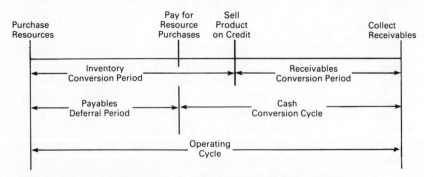

Fig. 4-2. Operating cycle of a typical manufacturing firm.
Source: R. Charles Moyer, James R. McGuigan, William J. Kretlow,
Contemporary Financial Management, Second Edition, West
Publishing Co., 1984, p. 563.

enter the white goods market required extending credit terms and carrying customers. Grant's greatly underestimated how much of their financial resources would be tied up in accounts receivable. Many of Grant's customers were not credit-worthy, and accounts were slow, if not impossible, to collect. Grant's had financed their inventory of white goods with bank loans, thus incurring a high level of risk by using financial leverage. The bank loans came due, but cash flows from sales of white goods did not arrive. The banks became concerned and started calling their loans. Soon Grant's was in an irreversible cash crisis. Although the finger of blame in cash-crisis situations often points to the finance function, in the case of Grant's the blame should also be shared by marketing for not understanding the profile of their typical customer. Nevertheless, borrowing money to finance accounts receivables requires a good understanding of credit collections, an area of expertise that Grant's did not have nor did they anticipate.

The essence of financial planning is the long- and short-term forecasting of cash flows. Although accounting earnings report after-the-fact, it is cash flow that is the heartbeat of the firm. Kolb makes this distinction in the following excerpt:[2]

Net working capital consists of current assets minus current liabilities. Thus, the amount of working capital available is a function of the amount of resources tied up in current assets such as cash, marketable securities, accounts receivable, and inventory. If resources are committed in large sums to these accounts, then the total return of the firm is affected. Short-term assets do not return the high levels that long-term capital profits do. The firm is, however, safer and more secure from sensitivity to volatile revenue flows. If too little is committed to current operations, then shortages will affect operations. The costs of "running short," such as borrowing short-term cash or ordering small quantities of raw materials or running out of finished goods, can easily eliminate profits, if not cripple the survival of the firm.

Net working capital is a measure of absolute liquidity. The current ratio is a complementary measure and indicates relative liquidity. We use the current ratio when comparing firms within an industry or a single firm overtime.

WORKING CAPITAL POSITION
NET WORKING CAPITAL = CURRENT ASSETS − CURRENT LIABILITIES

$$\text{CURRENT RATIO} = \frac{\text{CURRENT ASSETS}}{\text{CURRENT LIABILITIES}}$$

The general rule of thumb for manufacturing firms is a current ratio of 2:1. Statistics from the Federal Trade Commission's *Quarterly Financial Report* [3] indicate that in 1983, manufacturing firms devoted 41 percent of total resources to current assets. Their current liabilities averaged 25 percent of total debt and equity. Thus, manufacturing firms have been reducing their holdings of current assets and increasing financing with short-term debt. These reduced holdings will result in increased profitability (short-term) but at an increased risk to long-term returns. Chapter 7 will discuss the short-term manufacturing strategies pursued by firms such as GM. Financial evidence suggests that finance strategies have followed manufacturing strategy in these firms.

The optimum level of working capital depends on the needs of the industry and stage of growth. Table 4-1 shows the different levels of working capital by industry type. Wholesalers have substantial portions of current assets invested in inventory and accounts receivables, while the petroleum industry has very little need to tie resources up in current assets.

Stage of growth also affects working capital needs. As sales revenues grow, the needs for working capital grow. Despite the fact that most introductory finance texts assume this relationship to be linear for purposes of calculating working capital needs, in practice the relationship is quite different. In the early stages of growth, the needs for working capital increase at an increasing rate. If financial managers use a linear proportion, they greatly underestimate the level of need for current assets. In later stages of growth, the needs do follow a linear relationship and then begin to decline, as sheer size or economies of scale take affect. In later stages, firms may unknowingly find themselves with excesses of working capital and become a take-over target for a cash hungry firm.

Working capital strategies range from aggressive or risky to conservative and safe. The leaner the investment in current assets, the greater the profitability but at the risk of causing cash flow problems. The manipulation of working capital to increase profitability exposes the firm to greater risk. Thus, the financial manager must carefully consider this trade-off.

The firm's management must evaluate its risk position versus the trade-off between expected profitability and the risk that it will be unable to meet its obligations and thus create a cash flow crisis and maybe even risk bankruptcy. A conservative risk orientation dictates that the firm will hold a large proportion of its assets in the form of current assets. Because the rate of return on current assets is less than on fixed assets, this policy results in lower profitability as measured by the rate of return on the firm's total assets. An aggressive risk orientation dictates that the firm will hold only a small proportion of its total assets in the form of current assets. This policy results in a higher expected return on the firm's total assets. Figure 4-3 shows the three approaches to working capital levels and the amount of investment tied up in current assets. Table 4-2 illustrates the risk return trade-off. As the current ratio decreases to 1.75 for Ohio Engineering due to the aggressive policy on holding current assets, the firm's return increases to 15.38 percent. The higher risk position will affect the firm's ability to borrow funds. Thus, if the 1.75 current ratio is considered

Table 4-1. Industry Variations in Current Assets and Current Liabilities; 1981 Averages

Source: Federal Trade Commission, Quarterly Financial Report: Manufacturing, Mining and Trade Corporations, (Washington, D.C.: U.S. Government Printing Office, 3d quarter, 1983).

	Drugs	Nondurable Manufacturing	Petroleum and Coal Products	Nonferrous Metals	Electrical Equipment	Aircraft and Aerospace Manufacturing	Mining	Wholesale Trade
CURRENT ASSETS								
Cash	1.5%	2.1%	.8%	2.5%	3.8%	2.0%	2.4%	3.5%
Marketable securities	2.6	2.6	2.1	.9	4.1	1.8	2.2	4.2
Accounts receivable	14.2	13.7	8.4	14.4	20.7	12.4	8.5	25.3
Inventories	14.0	13.0	6.0	15.2	24.0	49.5	4.1	27.9
Prepaids and other	4.1	3.0	1.9	1.9	4.5	1.1	2.0	4.1
Total current assets	36.4%	34.4%	19.2%	34.9%	57.1%	66.8%	19.2%	65.0%
CURRENT LIABILITIES								
Notes payable and current maturities	6.1%	3.0%	1.3%	3.8%	4.2%	1.6%	2.7%	17.6%
Accounts payable	4.0	8.6	8.7	7.4	8.5	8.4	5.7	20.4
Accrued taxes	2.8	1.8	1.9	1.3	1.5	5.2	.3	.6
Accruals and other	9.9	8.4	5.8	7.4	20.3	38.5	6.8	8.5
Total current liabilities	22.8%	21.8%	17.7%	19.9%	34.5%	53.7%	15.5%	47.1%
Current ratio	1.59	1.58	1.08	1.76	1.66	1.24	1.24	1.38

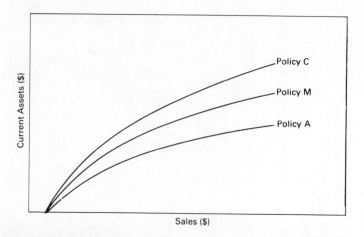

Fig. 4-3. Three alternative working capital investment policies.
Source: R. Charles Moyer, James R. McGuigan, William J. Kretlow,
Contemporary Financial Management, Second Edition, West
Publishing Co., 1984, p. 566.

to be significantly out of line with the industry, the firm's credit rating will drop. The effect of the lowered credit rating will mean more costly short-term borrowing if the firm should have to borrow short-term funds. The increased risk also affects the cost of long-term capital.

The optimal level of working capital depends on the variability of sales and cash flows and also the degree of leverage employed by the firm, as well as the risk orientation of its management. Thus, there are no hard and fast rules for the optimal level a firm should hold.

4.2 FINANCING WORKING CAPITAL

Once the level of working capital is decided upon, financial managers must make choices on how to finance these needs. Unless the firm chooses all equity financing, the proportion of short- versus long-term debt must be decided upon.

In general, the cost of long-term debt is greater than short-term debt. Even when short-term rates are equal to or greater than long-term rates, the effective cost of long-term debt is greater, because the payments must be made even when the firm has no need for the funds. With short-term debt, the funds can be paid off when they are not needed.

For the firm, there is more risk associated with incurring short-term debt. First, there is the risk that the firm will be unable to refund short-term debt when it is due. Uncertainty of events such as strikes, natural disasters, or

Table 4-2. Profitability and Risk of Alternative Working Capital Investment Policies for the Ohio Engineering Company (In Millions of Dollars)
Source: R. Charles Moyer, James R. McGuigan, William Kretlow, Contemporary Financial Management, Second Edition, West Publishing Co., 1984, p. 567.

	Aggressive	Moderate	Conservative
	Relatively Small Investment in Current Assets	Moderate Investment in Current Assets	Relatively Large Investment in Current Assets
Current assets (C/A)	$ 35	$ 40	$ 45
Fixed assets (F/A)	30	30	30
Total assets (T/A)	$ 65	$ 70	$ 75
Current liabilities (C/L)	$ 20	$ 20	$ 20
Forecasted sales	$100	$100	$100
Expected EBIT	$ 10	$ 10	$ 10
Expected rate of return on total assets (EBIT ÷ T/A)	15.38%	14.29%	13.33%
Net working capital position (C/A − C/L)	$ 15	$ 20	$ 25
Current ratio (C/A ÷ C/L)	1.75	2.0	2.25

recessions can cause sales and cash flows to decline on a temporary basis. Second, short-term interest rates fluctuate more over time, which will cause the expenses of borrowing to vary and thus have an impact on the variability of earnings.

The need for financing is equal to the sum of fixed and current assets. Current assets consist of two types: permanent and fluctuating. Fluctuating current assets are affected by the seasonal or cyclical nature of demand. Permanent current assets are held to meet a minimum long-term need. Figure 4-4 illustrates the relationship between fixed assets, permanent current assets, and fluctuating assets.

A conservative approach to meeting these financing needs is to use a relatively high proportion of long-term debt. This reduces the risk of not being able to refund debt and reduces the risk of fluctuating short-term interest rates. Because the cost of long-term debt is greater, this approach reduces the expected returns to stockholders.

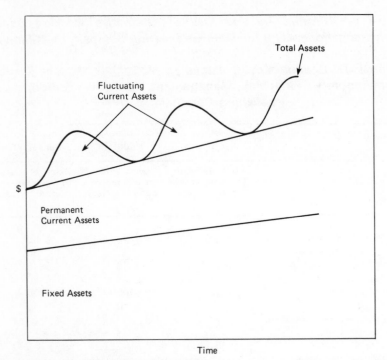

Time

Fig. 4-4. Financing needs over time.
Source: R. Charles Moyer, James R. McGuigan, William J. Kretlow,
Contemporary Financial Management, Second Edition, West
Publishing Co., 1984, p. 570.

An aggressive approach would use a high proportion of short-term debt. This approach increases risk due to inability to refund the debt and short-term rate fluctuations. Because short-term financing is lower cost, the after-tax earnings of the firm will be increased. Table 4-3 illustrates this risk/return trade-off, again using the Ohio Engineering Company as an example. The moderate approach illustrates the middle-of-the-road position. The optimal levels of short- versus long-term debt used for financing assets will depend on the variability of sales and cash flows, as well as the risk orientation of management.

4.3 DEBT VERSUS EQUITY FINANCING

Once the need for financial resources is determined, the financial manager is responsible for acquiring the resources. Policy must be set regarding the use of debt financing versus equity financing. The choice of short-term and long-term debt, plus the degree of equity financing, determines the capital structure of the firm. The ability to borrow depends on the level of perceived risk on the

Table 4-3. Profitability and Risk Alternative Financing Policies for the Ohio Engineering Company (In Millions of Dollars)
Source: R. Charles Moyer, James R. McGuigan, William Kretlow, Contemporary Financial Management, Second Edition, West Publishing Co., 1984, p. 573.

	Aggressive	Moderate	Conservative
	Relatively Large Amount of Short-Term Debt	Moderate Amount of Short-Term Debt	Relatively Small Amount of Short-Term Debt
Current assets (C/A)	$ 40	$ 40	$ 40
Fixed assets (F/A)	30	30	30
Total assets (T/A)	$ 70	$ 70	$ 70
Current liabilities (STD)(C/L) (interest rate, 8%)	$ 30	$ 20	$ 10
Long-term liabilities (LTD) (interest rate, 10%)	12	22	32
Total liabilities (60% of T/A)	$ 42	$ 42	$ 42
Common equity	28	28	28
Total liabilities and common equity	$ 70	$ 70	$ 70
Forecasted sales	$100	$100	$100
Expected EBIT	10	10	10
Less: Interest:			
STD, 8%	2.4⎫	1.6⎫	0.8⎫
LTD, 10%	1.2⎭ 3.6	2.2⎭ 3.8	3.2⎭ 4.0
Taxable income	$ 6.4	$ 6.2	$ 6.0
Less: Taxes (50%)	3.2	3.1	3.0
Net income after taxes	$3.2	$3.1	$3.0
Expected rate of return on common equity	11.43%	11.07%	10.71%
Net working capital position (C/A − C/L)	$ 10	$ 20	$ 30
Current ratio (C/A ÷ C/L)	1.33	2.0	4.0

part of lenders. The higher the risk rating, the higher the cost of borrowing. Borrowing the needed financial resources enables the firm to use external sources of funds, whose interest is tax deductible, to increase returns to shareholders.

Depending on the tax bracket, the cost of borrowed capital is much less than using retained earnings for financing. There is increased risk, however, because the interest due is a fixed expense. There is also a loss of control, because bonds have claim on assets before owners and loans may have restrictions attached to them. The use of leverage and the composition of the capital structure of the firm are important areas of financial strategy.

Financial leverage consists of current debt and long-term debt. The degree of risk due to financial leverage is measured by the following ratios:

$$\text{Debt Ratio} = \frac{\text{Total Debt}}{\text{Total Assets}}$$

$$\text{Debt-to-Equity} = \frac{\text{Total Debt}}{\text{Total Equity}}$$

$$\text{Time Interest Earned} = \frac{\text{Earnings Before Interest and Taxes}}{\text{Interest Charges}}$$

$$\text{Times Fixed Charges Earned} = \frac{\text{EBIT + Lease Payments}}{\text{Interest + Lease Payments +}}$$
Before-Tax Sinking Fund +
Preferred Stock Dividends

The *debt ratio* measures the proportion of the firm's total assets that are financed by creditor's funds. Bond holders and long-term creditors prefer a low debt ratio, because it provides them with more protection.

The *debt-to-equity ratio* relates the proportion of debt financing to owner financing. Some analysts prefer to use long-term debt-to-equity, because the larger proportion of interest costs are incurred on long-term borrowed funds. Using the same logic, preferred stock may also be included as debt, because preferred stock dividends are usually fixed.

The *times-interest-earned ratio* employs income statement data to measure a firm's use of financial leverage. This "interest coverage" tells us the extent to which the firm's current earnings are able to meet current interest payments. The fixed charge coverage ratio measures the number of times a firm is able to cover total fixed charges, which include preferred dividends and payments required under long-term lease contracts.

As demand matures, the firm must switch from financing with debt to financing with equity. In the early stages of growth, demand is high and expanding. At this point, the firm can incur financial leverage to finance the build-up in capital assets or extensive R&D and advertising programs. As long as demand is expanding, leverage is feasible. The key is timing. The debt should be reduced before demand begins its downturn. Figure 4-5 illustrates the application of financial leverage at the various stages of the life cycle. Many firms miss the turning point altogether. In the enthusiasm of previous rounds of high demand, they continue to build both current and fixed assets in an incremental fashion and they over-build, soon finding themselves with excess capacity, large fixed costs, high financial leverage, and, ultimately, losses. If the firm has successfully leveraged profits during the growth stage, it will be favorably viewed by the market and can issue equity shares at favorable prices. When demand starts to fall or become volatile, the firm can weather the risk now that the breakeven point has been lowered.

For some companies, the degree of leverage is regulated; public utilities are an example. The degree of risk-taking allowed these firms is constrained and, of course, management must operate within those constraints.

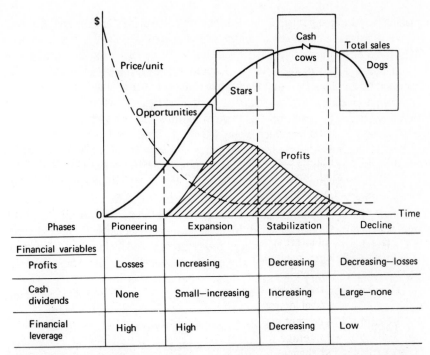

Phases	Pioneering	Expansion	Stabilization	Decline
Financial variables				
Profits	Losses	Increasing	Decreasing	Decreasing—losses
Cash dividends	None	Small—increasing	Increasing	Large—none
Financial leverage	High	High	Decreasing	Low

Fig. 4-5. The lifecycle, portfolio categories, and financial variables.
Source: Benton E. Gup, Guide To Strategic Planning, *McGraw-Hill*
Book Company, 1980, p. 184.

4.4 LEVERAGING RETURNS

Leveraging is the process of using either fixed costs or borrowed money to increase returns to the owners of the firm. The use of fixed costs to leverage returns is called *operating leverage* and the use of borrowed money is referred to as *financial leverage*.

Operating leverage occurs when the fixed costs of operations such as advertising, utilities, and salaries are a high percentage of the costs of operation. Once the volume has been obtained to meet these costs, then profits are "leveraged" due to the low level of variable versus fixed costs. Of course, this assumes that the revenue necessary to meet the fixed costs can be obtained. The breakeven point is the level of revenue which covers all the fixed costs and variable costs. Beyond the breakeven point, each additional sales dollar goes to covering variable costs, and the residual is profit.

Substituting fixed costs for variable costs then gives the firm the opportunity to increase profitability if required volumes can be sold. Replacing labor with machines, purchasing buildings versus leasing office space, and owning your own phone system are examples of shifting variables costs to fixed. Companies with high fixed costs facing high and expanding demand can maximize profits.

Table 4-4 shows the effects of operating leverage on profitability. The assumption is, of course, that the breakeven level of revenues can be obtained. This requires careful forecasting of demand and pricing. The firm may be forced by competitors to lower prices, thus, while unit levels of breakeven may be obtainable, the sales revenues would fall short. If demand falls short or starts to decline, high fixed costs have a negative leverage effect. Falling short of the breakeven point can mean large losses. Thus, operating leverage has a built-in risk. In the long-run, all costs are variable, but in the short-run, the degree of operating leverage becomes a constraint. Figure 4-6 shows us that sales revenues are the responsibility of the marketing function in terms of the volume sold and the prices obtained. Manufacturing is responsible for cost of goods sold. The degree to which the cost of goods are incurred by fixed versus variable costs will depend a great deal on the nature of operations. The airline industry, for example, has very high fixed costs. Some of the airlines have tried to shift some of the fixed burden to variable by leasing planes and subcontracting

Table 4-4. The Effects of Operating Leverage of Profitability

	Baldwin Products		Wallace Products	
	Initially	With a 50% Increase in Sales	Initially	With a 50% Increase in Sales
Sales	$100,000	$150,000	$100,000	$150,000
Sales: Fixed Operating Costs	40,000	40,000	5,000	5,000
	$ 60,000	$110,000	$ 95,000	$145,000
Less: Variable Operating Costs	40,000	60,000	75,000	112,500
Operating Profit	$ 20,000	$ 50,000	$ 20,000	$ 32,500
Percent Increase in Profits	-0-	150%	-0-	62%

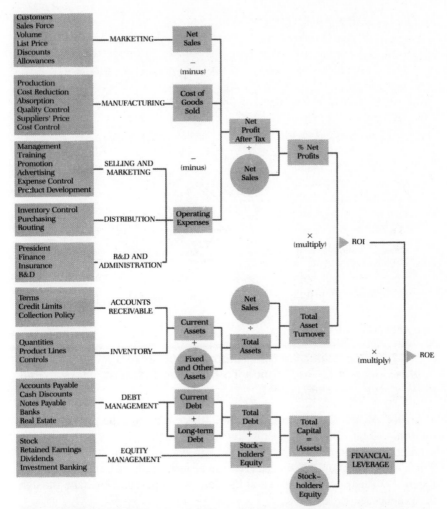

Fig. 4-6. The dimensions of ROI and ROE: the DuPont system as an analytical framework.
Source: *Lawrence J. Gitman, Michael D. Joehnk, George E. Pinches,* Managerial Finance, *Harper & Row Publishers, 1985, p. 95.*

maintenance. The reduced risk in terms of operating leverage is partially offset by the loss of accessibility and control of assets.

The degree of operating leverage constrains the firm's flexibility in using financial leverage. Operating leverage is a result of the cost structure used in producing the firm's goods or services. The use of high fixed costs increases the firm's sensitivity to returns. Once the fixed costs are covered, profits are

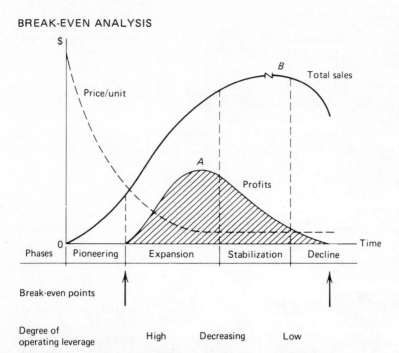

Fig. 4-7. The product lifecycle and operating leverage.
Source: Benton E. Gup, Guide To Strategic Planning, McGraw-Hill Book Company, 1980, p. 98.

leveraged. Risk is also incurred; however, there is always the probability that the firm will be unable to generate the sales volume necessary to cover the fixed costs. Thus, the risk incurred through operating leverage becomes an ultimate constraint upon how much risk can be incurred from financial leverage. Figure 4-7 illustrates the change in the degree of operating leverage through the product life cycle.

The degree of combined leverage, operating plus financial, determines the level of risk to which the firm subjects itself. Unfortunately, the two factors are not independent. It is often the case that firms requiring high fixed costs in the nature of their operations must turn to debt to finance the acquisition of the fixed assets.

4.5 ALLOCATING FINANCIAL RESOURCES

Allocation is often referred to as an investment decision, because it deals with the way the company's debt and equity are invested in assets. The finance manager must continually ask, "What is the best project or asset for us to invest our money in?" This requires taking into account the *time value* of money. A dollar invested in a treasury bill will return a low but risk-free rate. There must be a premium return for taking the risk of tying up the firm's money versus investing its money in risk-free alternatives. Thus, financial managers must continually consider the opportunity costs of capital investment.

The financial manager must calculate the present value of the future cash flows the investment will generate. The present value of these cash flows must be greater than the cost of the investment for the firm to experience a return on assets. It is quite possible for a firm to allocate resources unknowingly to projects which will not, in fact, generate the expected future returns. This happens when funds are acquired based on expected returns that did not take into account the net present value of the returns.

A case in point was Lockheed's Tri-Star project. Lockheed asked the government to guarantee a bank loan of $250 million to invest in the L-1011 wide-bodied commercial jet. At the time, Lockheed was experiencing a serious liquidity crisis due to cost overruns on military projects, so they turned to the government to guarantee their bank loan. Lockheed was prepared to invest $2.5 billion in the project, and they were confident the project would be successful. They calculated their breakeven point at 195 aircraft, with orders already in for 178. Unfortunately, the costs used in the calculation did not take into account the opportunity cost of the investment. They did not calculate the rate of return that alternative investing of the $2.5 billion would yield. By calculating net present value of the project, which takes into account the time value of cash flows, the project would have been negative at 195 planes. The project was undertaken, and it was unprofitable.[4] The difficulty with breakeven analysis is that it doesn't consider the time value of money.

We measure the effectiveness of the allocation of resources by *activity ratios* and *profitability ratios*. Activity ratios measure the effectiveness of our allocation in current assets. How soon will our current assets be cash? Profitability measures give overall indications of how well our investments in total assets are doing. Gross profit measures indicate how well our allocation of funds to operations are doing. Net profits measure our return on operations, as well as the return on our accounting strategies.

Activity Ratios

$$\text{AVERAGE COLLECTION PERIOD} = \frac{\text{ACCOUNTS RECEIVABLE}}{\text{CREDIT SALES}/360}$$

$$\text{INVENTORY TURNOVER} = \frac{\text{COST OF GOODS SOLD}}{\text{AVERAGE INVENTORY}}$$

$$\text{TOTAL ASSET TURNOVER} = \frac{\text{SALES}}{\text{TOTAL ASSETS}}$$

The activity ratios give us a measure of the payoff from each dollar invested in the various types of assets. The accounts receivable turnover is an indication of the quality of receivables and how successful the firm is in collecting them. Inventory turnover provides an indication of the amount of resources required to support a given level of operation. This ratio measures how well the investment in this current asset is being managed. The fixed asset turnover reveals how well the capacity is being utilized. A high turnover reveals a greater payoff from capital investments. Total asset turnover is sometimes called the *capital intensity ratio*. It provides an indication of the efficiency with which the firm is able to use its assets to support sales. It reveals the control management has been able to exert over its investments in assets.

Profitability ratios give a relative measure of the returns on sales, assets, or equity. These measures evaluate the firm's earnings with respect to the amount of sales necessary to generate profits, the level of assets required to support operations, and the owner's contribution. Profitability measures are closely watched by the marketplace. But, management of profitability can lead to short-term returns at the expense of long-term survival of the firm. The most commonly used profitability ratios are:

$$\text{GROSS PROFIT MARGIN} = \frac{\text{SALES - COST OF GOODS SOLD}}{\text{SALES}}$$

$$\text{NET PROFIT MARGIN} = \frac{\text{EARNINGS AFTER TAXES}}{\text{SALES}}$$

$$\text{RETURN ON INVESTMENT (ROI)} = \frac{\text{EARNINGS AFTER TAXES}}{\text{TOTAL ASSESTS}}$$

$$\text{RETURN ON STOCKHOLDERS' EQUITY (ROE)} = \frac{\text{EARNINGS AFTER TAX}}{\text{STOCKHOLDERS' EQUITY}}$$

Profitability measures will ultimately reflect early warning indications from activity ratios. When activity slows down and goes uncorrected, profits will be affected. Low activity ratios and low profit margins will show up in a low return on investment as measured by total assets. ROE will also be affected. Net profit, ROI, and ROE all use earnings after taxes. Thus, these measures indicate the performance of both the finance function and the accounting function. The accounting function is responsible for pursuing tax strategies that provide the best short-term advantage to the firm. Thus, ROE and ROI can be distorted by the current year's accounting tax strategies. Within the firm, returns are measured on cash flows provided before taxes. In other words, a firm may have positive cash flows from capital investments, yet show losses due to tax write-offs or depreciation expenses in any one year.

Both activity ratios and profitability measures are affected by the accounting strategies the firm pursues. Each of these types of measures are a combination of those strategies. Thus, profitability measures cannot be used as pure indications of how well the assets are working for the firm.

4.6 DIVIDEND PAYOUT

Another financial allocation decision concerns whether to pay out dividends or retain all the net income in the firm. The trade-off in this decision is reinvested earnings and a higher rate of corporate growth versus providing cash flow for shareholders. Each firm must determine a policy that resolves this conflict in order to balance shareholder needs with the demands of expected future growth.

Dividends are paid out in cash or stock. A *return of capital dividend* is a special type of cash dividend charged to the capital stock account on the balance sheet and represents a return of original paid-in capital. If the firm decides to pay cash dividends, the payout tends to be regular, regular plus extra dividends, or a fixed payout ratio. If the firm adopts a regular payout policy, then dividends are paid even if earnings drop. If this occurs, the firm has to borrow money to sustain its payout. This policy is more appropriate for a firm in a stable growth industry, where funds are not needed for reinvestment and earnings are not volatile.

A regular plus extra dividend policy would match the needs of a firm in a volatile earnings situation or where internal funds are used to finance growth. With this policy, the regular dividend is set at a low level and an extra is paid at the end of the year, if earnings are up and funds are not needed for internal growth.

A fixed payout ratio, a fixed percentage of earnings, is best suited for a firm with above-average growth and high needs for funds that can be profitably reinvested in the firm. The dividends obviously fluctuate with this policy and may have an erratic effect on the stock price.

It is unclear as to the relevance of dividend payout to stock valuation. The residual theory of dividends holds that dividends are passive and that only surplus funds should be distributed to stockholders. Miller and Modigliani have presented the most convincing argument for the irrelevance of dividends. They argue that the value of the stock is determined by the earning power of the firm's assets.[5] On the other side of the argument are Black and Schales, who used the capital asset pricing model to empirically relate stock prices to dividend payout. They found stocks with high payout had returns which were significantly different from those with low returns.[6]

Despite the uncertainty of the relevance of dividends, firms continue to pay them. The total amount of cash dividends has risen each year since 1962.[7]

4.7 MONITORING THE ALLOCATION OF RESOURCES

As indicated earlier in this chapter, the finance function is responsible for the monitoring of the firm's performance. Planned objectives, as often as possible, are quantified in financial and accounting measures. For this reason, the finance specialty monitors and reports how well the firm is actually performing relative to its past history and in comparison with other firms in the industry. This task of the finance function is performed using financial ratio analysis.

Through the use of comparative analysis and trend analysis, the financial manager can provide top management with information on the following questions related to survival:

- How are we doing? What is the current well-being of the firm?
- How have we been doing? What direction are we headed in?
- How are we doing compared to the industry?

Without this type of evaluation, we don't know if the firm is achieving its goals, and we don't know how effective its goal-setting process is relative to other firms. Performance is measured in financial indicators, and change or deviance in these indicators is a sign that the firm is experiencing problems. A financial ratio analysis assists in identifying weaknesses within the firm.

Financial analysis is also used by persons other than the financial managers of the firm. Credit managers, security analysts, and bankers rely heavily on this type of analysis when making decisions to loan money or invest in the equity of the firm.

Successful ratio analysis requires keeping in mind the following points:[8]

- Usually only a representative sample of ratios is presented. Additional ratios can give more insight and some industries, such as banking and insurance, health care, etc., have special ratios unique to their activities.
- Financial ratios are only "flags" of potential areas of problems. A thorough analysis requires examining other data as well.
- Financial ratios must be considered in light of their composition. A low ratio can be caused by a low numerator or high denominator.
- Standards are required for meaningful comparison. With so many conglomerates, direct comparisons and industry standards have become very difficult.
- Accounting strategies for reporting purposes make direct comparisons between firms difficult, if not impossible.

Different groups external of the firm have differing needs for knowing how well the firm is doing. Suppliers and short-term creditors are concerned with the firm's liquidity; bond holders and preferred stock owners are concerned with the firm's ability to generate funds over the long-term. Owners are concerned with profitability and return on investment.

Because of these differing needs, four groups of ratios are used. The financial manager's responsibility in each of these areas has been covered in earlier sections of this chapter.

- Liquidity ratios measure the firm's ability to meet short-term financial obligations.
- Activity ratios measure how efficiently assets generate sales.
- Leverage ratios measure the firm's capacity to meet short- and long-term debt obligations.
- Profitability ratios measure how effective the firm is at generating profits on sales, assets, and owner's investment.

4.8 ACCOUNTING STRATEGIES

The goal of accounting strategy is to choose cost reporting techniques that maximize the firm's short-term position. These choices affect financial strategies in that cash flows are increased or decreased depending on the rates of depreciation and book value of assets salvaged. Inventory costing methods affect the level of current assets and working capital management.

Depending on the reporting techniques the firm chooses, it may overstate or understate profits; it may also understate or overstate losses. The reason for pursuing these different positions is, of course, to maximize the company's current position.

By understating profits and overstating losses, the firm pays out less tax and conserves cash for use by the firm. By overstating profits in any one time period, the firm may give the impression to the market that it is performing better than it actually is. It may do this if it wishes to be bought out. Accounting strategies, then, deal with the way expenses are reported. The firm may choose to classify expenses which are to return benefits for longer than one year as capital expenditures and amortize the expense over the life of the project. If the expenses are written off as they occur, it would have the effect of understating profits. R&D expenditures may be written off currently or amortized. Thus, a firm that writes off current expenditure investments in R&D equipment will show a low level of profitability in the early stages of the project, but very high levels of profitability in later stages when returns from the investment begin to pay off.

When to expense contingent liabilities is another accounting strategy. The firm may choose to delay charging contingent expenses until they are actually paid. This strategy will result in an overstatement of profits. On the other hand, they may expense the item when the commitment is made, which can result in profits being understated. When contingent income is recognized, it also has the potential for overstating or understating profits. Waiting until it is actually realized can understate profits.

The methods used for valuation of assets can affect expenses, which in turn overstate or understate profits. The bases used for depreciation on fixed assets can be original cost, which will overstate profits, or replacement cost, which will understate profits. Current assets can be valued at FIFO, which will overstate profits during periods of inflation, or LIFO, which will understate profits during inflation.

The accounting strategies, then, affect the dollar value assigned to expenses. Any ratio that uses these dollar values has the potential of being manipulated by the methods employed. It is often difficult to get a true picture of how well a firm is doing by analyzing figures used for reporting purposes. If the firm substitutes accounting strategies for true financial strategy, it will operate in the short-term, paying close attention to changes in profitability from reporting period to reporting period. Any strategy that focuses on the short-term manipulation of costs is detrimental to long-term survival. Thus, accounting strategies must be coordinated with the financial strategies of the firm. Accounting strategies maximize short-term profitability, but financial strategies maximize the long-term wealth of the firm.

4.9 SUMMARY

Figure 4-8 summarizes the decision responsibilities of the finance and accounting function. the underlying concept in the financial planning area is the risk/return trade-off. Maintaining high levels of liquidity in the firm enables the firm to react to unforeseen circumstances in the environment and meet its financial obligations. However, funds are tied up that could be employed to generate more profits. If the firm only maintains enough liquidity to match current liabilities, it will be unable to deal with threats or opportunities that occur in the environment. Profitability will be enhanced but at the risk of rigidity. The financial manager is also responsible for the sources of funds. Will retained earnings be used to finance new projects, or will the firm assume debt? If it chooses leverage, the return to the owners will be enhanced but at the risk of multiplying losses if they should occur. Operating leverage acts as a constraint on the amount of financial leverage. The financial manager is ultimately responsible for managing the level of combined operating and financial leverage in the firm. How will funds be allocated? Will profits be reinvested or paid out in dividends? These decisions will depend on the environment of the firm's industry, the strength of its resource base, and management's risk orientation.

Cash Flow or Accounting Earnings?

When journalists report on a firm's performance, they almost always cite the firm's earnings. Similarly, when groups protest the unfairness of corporate America, they often point out the profits of these firms that they consider unjustifiably high. By contrast, the financial manager pays, or should pay, little attention to accounting earnings. Instead, the financial manager should focus on the firm's cash flow. Journalists and protesters may not even know what cash flow is all about, but in finance it is a crucial distinction.

The firm's accounting earnings are the earnings recorded on the firm's income statement and are calculated by following a complex set of accounting rules. Cash flow, by contrast, is the flow of cash into and out of the firm. In some cases, it is possible for a firm to have large reported earnings and very serious cash flow difficulties. Similarly, a firm may have very poor reported earnings and a huge cash surplus.

These large discrepancies between a firm's cash flow and its reported earnings can arise from a variety of sources. One example stems from the way in which sales are recognized and figured into earnings. Recently, this has been particularly problematic in the high tech area. Assume that a firm has a calendar year fiscal year and that today is December 15. If a product is shipped today, the sale can be recorded as of that date, according to the accounting practices of some firms. In such a situation, the sale will contribute to the reported earnings for that year. However, the payment for that shipment may not be received until a considerable time later. The sale contributes immediately to earnings, but does not contribute to cash flow until payment is finally made.

With a recent slump in high tech sales, there has been a movement to record sales as early as possible. For example, most salespeople are compensated based on their level of sales. *Business Week* reports that "aggressive salesmen have been known to ship goods without a purchase order at the end of a quarter to make their quota. Investment bankers, money managers, and accountants worry that more companies than ever may be booking sales before they have occurred."[5]

Because of abuses such as these, there is a movement to require better reporting of cash flow by firms. The Financial Accounting Standards Board (FASB), the rule-making group for the accounting profession, is studying how cash flow statements could be prepared and who should be required to present them. Banks have long been known to focus on earnings, rather than cash flow, but *Forbes* reports, "Savvy investors have long known to keep an eye on how much cash a company takes in, pays out and has in the till rather than net income it reports to shareholders. Now the bankers, sadder but wiser, are using cash flow analysis, too."[6]

5. Stuart Weiss, "High-Tech Sales: Now You See Them, Now You Don't", *Business Week*, November 18, 1985.

6. Jinny St. Goar, "Where's the Cash?," *Forbes*, April 8, 1985.

**Fig. 4-8. Responsibilities of the finance and account function.
Source: Robert W. Kolb, Financial Management Scott Foresman, 1987, p. 18.**

The finance function is also responsible for evaluating the firm's performance by monitoring the trend in its financial ratios, as well as comparing the ratios with those of other firm's in the industry.

While financial strategies are concerned with making decisions that maximize the firm's wealth, accounting strategies are concerned with short-term profitability. Activity ratios tell us how soon the investment in assets will turn into cash, while profitability measures tell us how effective our choices of assets are. Activity and profits focus on near-term returns. Many accounting decisions, such as inventory valuation and depreciation bases, are chosen to improve the firm's near-term position. It is important to make a distinction between accounting and finance strategies, because substituting short-term profitability for long-term building can cause the firm to erode its asset base and lose its ability to survive.

The finance function becomes a primary function by virtue of the fact that we use financial measures as the benchmarks by which we measure the firm's attainment of its goals. The firm must determine its sources and uses of funds before the marketing, production, and R&D functions can set their objectives. Thus, the other functional specialties are constrained by the effectiveness of the finance function.

In the next three chapters, we develop how the marketing, R&D, and manufacturing strategies contribute to the survival of the firm. And then, in Chapter 8 we show how these functions must be integrated to make the organization an efficient system of strategies.

END NOTES—Chapter 4

1. Lawrence J. Gitman, Michael D. Joehnk, George E. Pinches, *Managerial Finance* (Harper & Row, 1985), p. 5.

2. Robert W. Kolb, *Financial Management* (Scott, Foresman & Co., 1987), p. 18.

3. Federal Trade Commission, *Quarterly Financial Report: Manufacturing, Mining and Trade Corporations* (Washington, D.C.: U.S. Government Printing Office, 3rd quarter, 1983).

4. R. Charles Moyer, James R. McGuigan, William J. Kretlow, *Contemporary Financial Management, 2nd edition* (West Publishing Co.), p. 250.

5. Merton H. Miller and Franco Modigliani, "Dividend Policy, Growth, and Valuation of Shares," *Journal of Business*, 34, Oct. 1961, pp. 411-433.

6. Fischer Black and Myron Schales, "The Effects of Dividend Yield and Dividend Policy on Common Stock Prices and Returns," *Journal of Financial Economics*, 2 (May, 1974), pp. 1-22.

7. Lawrence J. Gitman, Michael D. Joehnk, George E. Pinches, *Managerial Finance* (Harper & Row, 1985), p. 818.

8. Moyer, p. 153.

Chapter 5

The Role of Marketing

5.0 THE MARKETING FUNCTION

The marketing function identifies and segments markets to be served, and selects, promotes, distributes, and prices the products and services to be offered. Figure 5-1 highlights the role of marketing for General Cinema's movie theater business. The strategy for the movie theater business is to maintain and selectively expand its leading nationwide position. The marketing function must translate this business level strategy into specific market, product, promotion, and pricing strategies. Figure 5-1 illustrates specific marketing strategies for achieving General Cinema's business level strategy. The market is family audiences; the product is first-run films, which will be premium priced. At multiscreen locations, the product will be varied to attract different audiences. The distribution strategy is to locate in regional shopping centers. The primary emphasis is to achieve a position in the high-end of the market with a premium product. Marketing and finance are integrated in that the cash from profits will be used to selectively underwrite the production of quality films to ensure the supply of first-run movies.

5.1 IDENTIFYING THE MARKET

Defining the market requires a careful analysis of demand and supply of products and services. This process is referred to as *competitive analysis*. Much of what a firm can do will depend on its competitive position within the industry. When demand is new and expanding, suppliers are attracted by profits. If demand

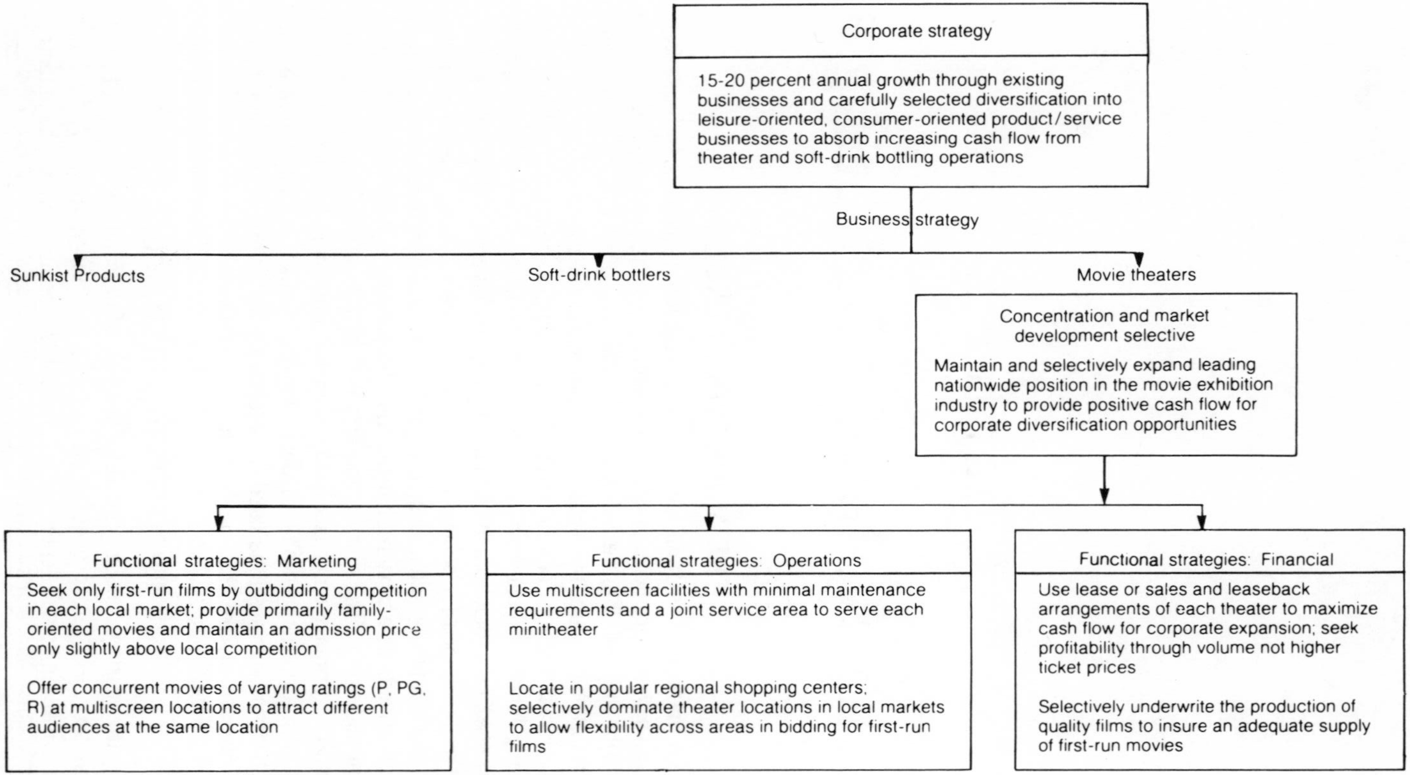
Corporate strategy
15-20 percent annual growth through existing businesses and carefully selected diversification into leisure-oriented, consumer-oriented product/service businesses to absorb increasing cash flow from theater and soft-drink bottling operations
Business strategy
Sunkist Products
Soft-drink bottlers
Movie theaters
Concentration and market development selective
Maintain and selectively expand leading nationwide position in the movie exhibition industry to provide positive cash flow for corporate diversification opportunities
Functional strategies: Marketing
Seek only first-run films by outbidding competition in each local market; provide primarily family-oriented movies and maintain an admission price only slightly above local competition
Offer concurrent movies of varying ratings (P, PG, R) at multiscreen locations to attract different audiences at the same location
Functional strategies: Operations
Use multiscreen facilities with minimal maintenance requirements and a joint service area to serve each minitheater
Locate in popular regional shopping centers; selectively dominate theater locations in local markets to allow flexibility across areas in bidding for first-run films
Functional strategies: Financial
Use lease or sales and leaseback arrangements of each theater to maximize cash flow for corporate expansion; seek profitability through volume not higher ticket prices
Selectively underwrite the production of quality films to insure an adequate supply of first-run movies

Fig. 5-1. Role of functional strategies at General Cinema Corporation.
Source: John A. Pearce, II., Richard B. Robinson, Jr.,* Strategic Management—Strategy Formulation and Implementation, *Second Edition, Richard D. Irwin, Inc., 1985, p. 300.

increases faster than supply, the structure of the industry will remain undefined. When demand slows down or the amount of supply outstrips the demand, the suppliers or competitors begin to jockey for competitive position. As long as demand is unlimited, the constraints of competition never become a threat. As profits attract new competitors in a situation of limited or declining demand, competition becomes a driving force.

An industry is defined by all the firms who seek to fill the demand for a good or service. We can describe the evolution of change in industries in terms of lifecycle stages: early development, rapid growth and takeoff, competitive shake-out and consolidation, early maturity, saturation, and decline and decay. Industries do not always follow this exact sequence and may skip phases, but it is generally recognized that all industries follow some variation of the lifecycle theory.[1] It is not always easy to predict how long a particular phase will last, but it is important to be able to recognize the current phase the industry is in and be aware of the competitive forces of that stage. Figure 5-2 depicts the stages of market evolution and the accompanying changes in market variables at each stage. It is interesting to note the relative change in importance of each of the functional areas as the market evolves, and Figure 5-3 shows the role of each function in building competitive advantage. The current stage of evolution of the industry with its opportunities and threats will determine how attractive the market is for potential entrants, as well as those already involved.

The variables that define the structure of the industry are:

• The number of sellers and their relative size.
• Market leadership.
• The number of buyers and their relative size.
• The number of value-added points in the chain from maker to user.
• The degree of vertical integration.
• Ease of entry and exit.
• The relative size of demand.
• The geographic boundaries.

Once the factors that affect the industry's structure are described, their relative importance is analyzed in terms of opportunities and threats. Table 5-1 presents a list of some of the factors and their significance.

Strategic group mapping[2], developed by Porter, is a useful technique for identifying markets. The process consists of first identifying the strategic group of rival firms with competitively similar market approaches. Similar market approaches means these firms are using identical marketing strategies; for example, offering buyers the same set of services. An industry could be one strategic group if all the firms used the same strategy. On the other hand, if each firm used a different strategy, each firm would comprise a strategic group.

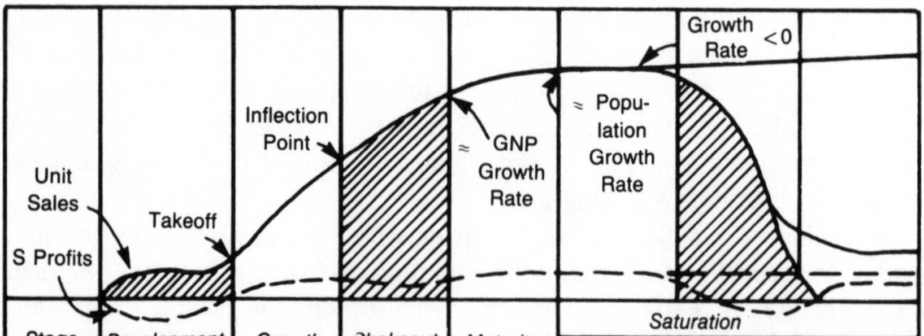

Growth Rate < 0

Inflection Point

$\approx$ GNP Growth Rate

$\approx$ Population Growth Rate

Unit Sales

Takeoff

S Profits

Saturation

Stage	Development	Growth	Shakeout	Maturity	Saturation	Decline	Petrification
Market Growth Rate	Slight	Very Large	Large	GNP Growth	Population Growth	Negative	Slight to None
Change in Growth Rate	Little	Increases Rapidly	Decreases Rapidly	Decreases Slowly	Little	Decreases Rapidly. Then Slow. May Increase then Slow.[1]	Little
No. of Segments	Very Few	Some	Some	Some-to-Many		Few	Few
Technological Change in Product Design	Very Great	Great	Moderate	Slight	Slight[2]	Slight	Slight
Technological Change In Process Design	Slight	Slight/ Moderate	Very Great	Great Moderate	Slight	Slight	Slight
Major Functional Concern	R and D	Engineering	Production	Marketing-Distribution-Finance		Finance	Marketing and Finance

[1] The rate of change of the market growth rate usually only increases during the decline stage for these products that do not die, i.e., that enter the petrification stage of evolution.

[2] Although the rate of technological change in the basic design of the product is usually low during this stage of market evolution, the probability of a major breakthrough to a different kind of product that performs the same function increases substantially during this period.

Fig. 5-2. The fundamental stages of product/market evolution.
Source: Charles W. Hofer, Edwin A. Murray, Jr., Ram Charan, Robert A. Pitts, Strategic Management, West Publishing, 1980, p. 231.

A map of strategic groups is constructed by picking several important market dimensions and plotting the relative position of the firms on these significant dimensions.

An example of strategic group mapping from Porter is presented in Fig.

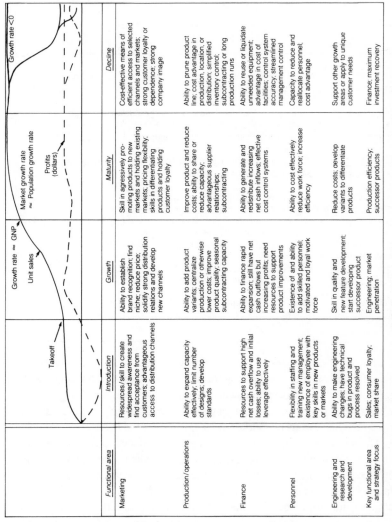

Functional area	Introduction	Growth	Maturity	Decline
Marketing	Resources/skill to create widespread awareness and find acceptance from customers; advantageous access to distribution channels	Ability to establish brand recognition; find niche; reduce price; solidify strong distribution relations and develop new channels	Skill in aggressively promoting products to new markets and holding existing markets; pricing flexibility; skills in differentiating products and holding customer loyalty	Cost-effective means of efficient access to selected channels and markets; strong customer loyalty or dependence; strong company image
Production/operations	Ability to expand capacity effectively; limit number of designs; develop standards	Ability to add product variants; centralize production or otherwise lower costs; improve product quality; seasonal subcontracting capacity	Improve product and reduce costs; ability to share or reduce capacity; advantageous supplier relationships; subcontracting	Ability to prune product line; cost advantage in production, location, or distribution; simplified inventory control; subcontracting or long production runs
Finance	Resources to support high net cash overflow and initial losses; ability to use leverage effectively	Ability to finance rapid expansion, still have net cash outflows but increasing profits; need resources to support product improvements	Ability to generate and redistribute increasing net cash inflows; effective cost control systems	Ability to reuse or liquidate unneeded equipment; advantage in cost of facilities; control system accuracy; streamlined management control
Personnel	Flexibility in staffing and training new management; existence of employee with key skills in new products or markets	Existence of and ability to add skilled personnel; motivated and loyal work force	Ability to cost effectively reduce work force; increase efficiency	Capacity to reduce and reallocate personnel; cost advantage
Engineering and research and development	Ability to make engineering changes; have technical bugs in product and process resolved	Skill in quality and new feature development; start developing successor product	Reduce costs; develop variants to differentiate products	Support other growth areas or apply to unique customer needs
Key functional area and strategy focus	Sales; consumer loyalty; market share	Engineering; market penetration	Production efficiency; successor products	Finance; maximum investment recovery

Fig. 5-3. Sources of distinctive competence at different stages of product/market evolution. Source: John A. Pearce, II., Richard B. Robinson, Jr., Strategic Management, Second Edition, Richard D. Irwin, Inc., 1985, p. 194.

Table 5-1. Factors for Determining Industry Structure
Source: Arthur A. Thompson, Jr., A. J. Strickland, III, **Strategy Formulation and Implementation,** *Fourth Edition,* **Business Publications, Inc., 1987, p. 63.**

Factor	Reason for Importance
Market size	Small markets don't tend to attract big/new competitors.
Market growth rate	Fast growth breeds new entry; growth slowdowns breed increased rivalry and a shakeout of weaker competitors.
Capacity surpluses or shortages	Surpluses push prices and profit margins down; shortages pull them up.
Relative profitability	High-profit industries attract new entrants; depressed conditions encourage exit.
Entry/exit barriers	High barriers protect positions and profits of existing firms.
Product is a big-ticket item for buyers	More buyers will shop for lowest price.
Rapid technological change	Raises risk factor; investments in technology, facilities, or equipment may become obsolete before they wear out.
Capital requirements	Big requirements make investment decisions critical; timing becomes important; creates a barrier to entry and exit.
The products of sellers are standardized	Buyers have more power because it is easier to switch from seller to seller.
Vertical integration	Raises capital requirements; often creates competitive differences and cost differences among fully versus partially versus nonintegrated firms.
Economies of scale	Affects volume and market share needed to be cost competitive.
Rapid product innovation	Shortens product life cycle; more risk because of opportunities for leapfrogging.

5-4. The two significant market dimensions are specialization and vertical integration. Strategic Group A is characterized by a full line of products with a high degree of vertical integration, while Group B, a much smaller group of firms, is characterized by a narrow line of products with limited manufacturing. A mapping of the U.S. chainsaw market in 1978 is illustrated in another example (Fig. 5-5). The significance of this map is in the choice of analytical dimensions. Brand image and the industry of dealers, mass merchandisers, and private label provide an understanding of the intermediate stage between the supply and demand factors which shape the structure of this industry.

Although strategic mapping is one way of profiling an industry, it is also important to analyze whether the industry is evolving or moving toward a different stage. Thus, we need to identify the lifecycle stage and the driving forces for change from one stage to another. The presence of these forces and the strength of the force will determine if the industry is evolving. This type of analysis requires a dynamic analysis of trends and changes overtime. The driving forces

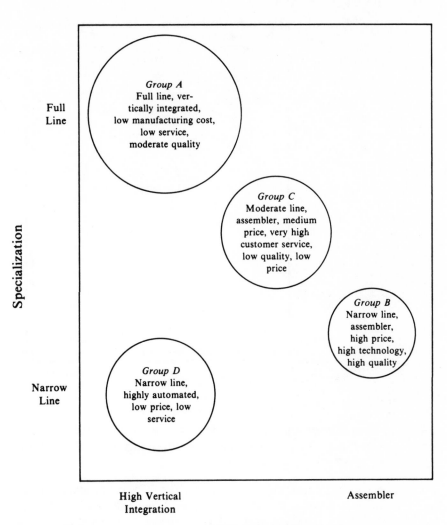

Fig. 5-4. A map of strategic groups in a hypothetical industry. Source: Michael E. Porter, *Competitive Strategy*, The Free Press, 1980, p. 131.

for change as identified by Porter[3] are:

- Changes in volume of long-term market demand. Upshifts attract new entrants, downshifts cause firms to exit. Changes in demand cause offsetting changes in supply.

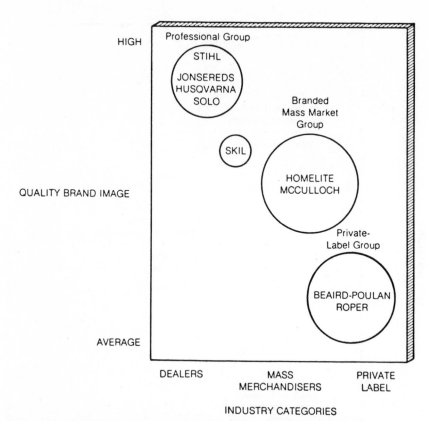

Fig. 5-5. Strategic group mapping of U.S. chainsaw market.
Source: George S. Day, Strategic Market Planning, West Publishing
Co., 1984, p. 97.

- Changes in characteristics of end-users. The ATM (automatic teller machine) is a response to end-users who need convenience banking. User friendly PC's are a response to the "non-techie" buyer segment of the personal computer market.
- Degree of product innovation. Product innovation can shift the industry demand curve out and promote product differentiation. High degrees of product innovation can cause an industry to evolve very rapidly. Electronic videogames are a case in point.
- Degree of process innovation. Process innovation can alter the supply side of the industry. It can alter the relative cost positions of the firms in the industry and change the number of cost-efficient firms the market can support.

- Degree of marketing innovation. Marketing innovation can cause shifts in demand or increase product differentiation.
- Degree of entry or exit of major firms. Again, these driving forces can change the supply side.
- Diffusion of proprietory knowledge. Rapid diffusion of proprietary knowledge increases the number of potential rivals in an industry.
- Changes in cost and efficiency. Where economies of scale and learning curve affects cause costs to decline, large firm size and experience become dominant characteristics of competitive advantage.
- Shifts from differentiated to standardized products or vice versa. Industries evolve differently depending on whether product differentiation is on the increase or decrease.
- Changes in regulatory influences and government policies. These forces can change both the supply side and demand side of the industry.

Thus, the first step in the process of defining the market is to identify the stage of evolution, map the strategic group of patterns which have emerged, and track the trends of the driving forces for change.

5.2 SEGMENTING THE MARKET

The factors to be considered in defining and segmenting markets are illustrated in Fig. 5-6.

- Customer function. What needs of customers are to be satisfied?
- Level of technology. What techniques will be employed to serve customer function?
- Customer segment. Whose needs are to be served and where are they located?
- Value-added position. Where will you position yourself in the value-added chain from maker to user?

The combination of these dimensions form a *market cell*. You may decide to meet the needs of the market as regards the ability to open cans. The technology you choose is an electric-powered cutting devise (versus a hand-operated lever and crank). Your customer segment is suburban middle income households that purchase small electrical appliances in stores located in suburban shopping centers. You will purchase the parts of the product and perform the value-added functions of assembly and distribution.

The analysis is further enhanced by identifying all possible ways of satisfying customer needs within a generic product category. Thus, we can think in terms

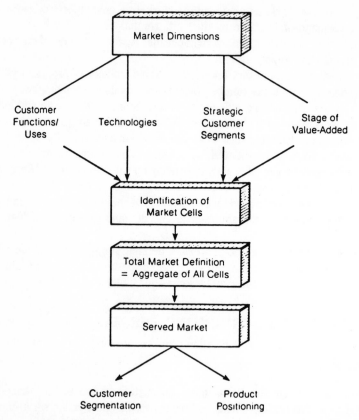

Fig. 5-6. Defining and segmenting markets.
Source: George S. Day, Strategic Market Planning, West Publishing
Co., 1984, p. 74.

of levels in a hierarchy or products within a generic product class. For example, the following distinctions are useful:

- Different product types satisfying needs beyond fundamental or generic level.
- Product variations within same overall type.
- Scented vs. unscented product variations.
- Different brands within product variations.

Market segmentation is based on distinctions among prospects who constitute the market.[4] In product differentiation, the distinctions are among products or on the supply side, whereas in market segmentations, the distinctions are among customers or on the demand side. These two seemingly different approaches to defining the market are characterized as top-down and bottom-up.[5]

The *top-down* approach is supply-side analysis. The market structure is defined in terms of competitive advantage or the resource advantages the firms have built over time. Thus, supply factors such as raw materials, production processes and technologies, the experience curve, economies of scale, barriers to entry, and change in driving forces, are all analyzed. The firm looks for groups or subgroups where these resource advantages can be used to the best advantage.

In the *bottom-up* perspective, the emphasis is on the customer. Those closest to the customer are responsible for anticipating and reacting to shifts in market demand. Changes in customers' requirements, needs, and capabilities, or competitors' ability to satisfy these requirements, are the factors to be analyzed in the bottom-up approach. The differences in the two approaches are summarized in Table 5-2.

Table 5-2. The View from the Top-Down Versus the Bottom-Up Source: George S. Day, Strategic Market Planning, West Publishing Co., 1984, p. 84.

ISSUE	TOP–DOWN VIEW	BOTTOM–UP VIEW
1. Definition of market	Markets are arenas of competition where corporate resources can profitably be employed	Markets are shifting patterns of customer requirements and needs that can be served in many ways
2. Orientation to market environment	Strengths and weaknesses relative to competition ■ cost position ■ ability to transfer experience ■ market coverage	Customer perceptions of competitive alternatives ■ match of product features and customer needs ■ positioning
3. Identification of market segments	Looks for cost discontinuities	Emphasizes similarity of buyer responses to market efforts
4. Identification of market niches to serve	Exploits new technologies, cost advantages, and competitors' weaknesses	Finds unsatisfied needs, unresolved problems, or changes in customer requirements and capabilities.
5. Time frame	2 to 5 years	1 to 3 years

Segmentation groups customers into classes whose members behave in the same way or have similar needs.[6] Besides product feature differences, these needs could include needs for information, service, technical support, and other nonproduct features. By the process of aggregation, marketing analysts determine the number of segments or groups. Each buying unit could conceivably be considered a segment; however, clustering buying units together provides economies of scale. Buying units should be clustered in such a way that there is similarity in demand within segments and differences in demand among segments. The segments must be large enough so that segmentation leads to increased profits.[7] Continuing to aggregate clusters results in a single market. Thus, the firm must determine the level of aggregation which will return the optimal profit. There are some situations in which market segmentation would be inappropriate. Examples are: the market is too small, heavy users constitute such a large share of the sales volume that they are the only relevant target, or a brand is dominant in the market.[8] Figure 5-7 illustrates the strategic relevance of effective customer segmentation by a manufacturer of electric motors. The company was able to group its customers into four segments based on common buying characteristics. The characteristics were price sensitivity, standardization, lot size, and size of customers. After segmenting their customers, the firm found it was doing poorly in Segment A, where price was the most significant key to success. They were doing much better in Segments C and D where marketing and engineering, sales coverage, and quality features were the determinants of success. This discovery led to the strategy of raising prices to eliminate themselves from Segments A and B and focus on Segments C and D, where the customers are not price sensitive.

Effective segmentation[9] yields customer groups that are:

- Measurable in terms of present and potential volume and rate of growth.
- Accessible to promotion, direct selling and advertising.
- Different so that a meaningful variation of strategy is needed to serve the segment.
- Large enough in profit potential to justify incremental costs of tailoring a marketing program.
- Durable to sustain itself past the "early adaptors" stage.

Segmentation begins with a basis for segmentation—a product specific factor that reflects differences in customer requirements and responsiveness to marketing variables.[10] The major bases for segmentation are geographic, demographic, psychographic, and behavioralistic.

Research reveals that there are product usage variations on the basis of geography and population density. For example, the usage of electric heating blankets is much higher in the northeast than in the southeast. Multinational

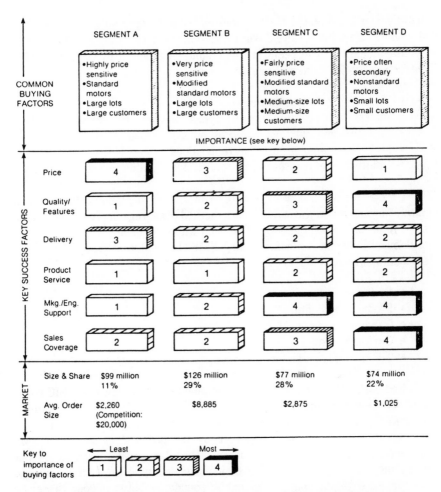

COMMON BUYING FACTORS

	SEGMENT A	SEGMENT B	SEGMENT C	SEGMENT D
	•Highly price sensitive	•Very price sensitive	•Fairly price sensitive	•Price often secondary
	•Standard motors	•Modified standard motors	•Modified standard motors	•Nonstandard motors
	•Large lots	•Large lots	•Medium-size lots	•Small lots
	•Large customers	•Large customers	•Medium-size customers	•Small customers

IMPORTANCE (see key below)

KEY SUCCESS FACTORS

	SEGMENT A	SEGMENT B	SEGMENT C	SEGMENT D
Price	4	3	2	1
Quality/ Features	1	2	3	4
Delivery	3	2	2	2
Product Service	1	1	2	2
Mkg./Eng. Support	1	2	4	4
Sales Coverage	2	2	3	4

MARKET

	SEGMENT A	SEGMENT B	SEGMENT C	SEGMENT D
Size & Share	$99 million 11%	$126 million 29%	$77 million 28%	$74 million 22%
Avg. Order Size	$2,260 (Competition: $20,000)	$8,885	$2,875	$1,025

Key to importance of buying factors: ← Least 1 2 3 4 Most →

Fig. 5-7. Segmentation based on common buying requirements.
Source: Robert A. Garda, **Strategic Segmentation: How to Carve Niches for Growth in Industrial Markets,** ***1981, AMACOM.***

firms may segment markets based on national boundaries. Another basis for segmenting markets is by demographics: age, sex, stage in family lifecycle, family income, education, occupation, and social class. Purchasing of rock albums is much larger in the 12- to 17-year-old age segment than in the 35- to 49-year-old age segment. Industrial markets can also be segmented by total sales, total assets, or total number of employees.

Behavioral characteristics related to the use of the product, such as usage rate, end use, degree of brand loyalty response to change in marketing mix, and readiness, can be used to segment markets. Usage rate is a common way to segment a market. Figure 5-8 illustrates an example of market segmentation by usage. Industrial markets are commonly segmented by end use. Other characteristics for industrial markets[11] are:

- Buyers' purchasing strategies.
- Buyers' risk preferences, rate types, and cognitive styles.
- Problems and risks perceived by different buyers.
- Differences among purchase requisitions.
- Differences in environmental forces affecting different buyers.

Garda[12] reports a new method of industrial segmentation called *strategic market segmentation (SMS)*. SMS is a method of aggregating customer groups so as to maximize homogeneity of demand within segments and differentiation of demand between segments. Using SMS, five different types of strategic segments have been defined:

- End use.
- Product segments.
- Geographic.
- Customer size.
- Common buying factor.

End-use markets are traditionally identified by *SIC codes*. Using SIC codes generally results in too many segments to be useful. SMS looks at industry groups and how customers use a product. Traditional methods of product segmentation lump products together by technological family. With SMS production, economies are also considered. Thus, large standardized orders may prove more profitable because of their ability to utilize production capacity. Geographic segments may be defined by boundaries between countries or by regional differences within them. Customer-size segments may be logically considered a subset of common buying factors. This is a special case, where buying ciriteria differs with predictable consistency by customer size. Although sales managers have grouped customers by size for planning purposes, it has only been recently that top managers have thought to develop niche strategies on this basis. There are many ways of segmenting a market. Table 5-3 presents some of the more common ones. Strategic market segmentation flows from the strategy formulation process of identifying opportunities and trends in the environment. It affords a view of competitive advantage or disadvantage, thus highlighting marketing strengths to exploit and weaknesses to correct.

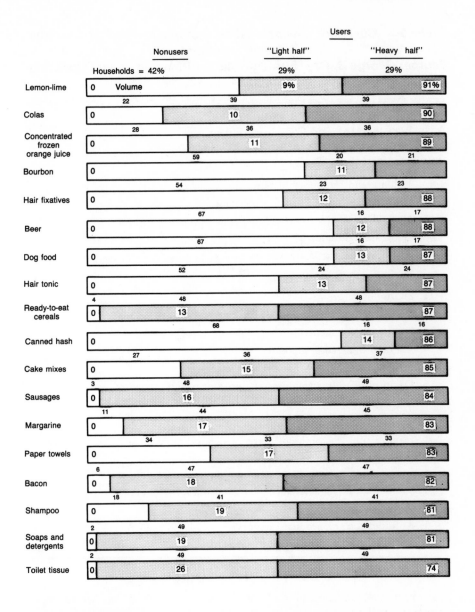

Fig. 5-8. Percentage of purchase volume accounted for by different usage groups.
Source: Douglas J. Dalrymple, Leonard J. Parson, **Marketing Management,** *Second Edition, John Wiley and Sons, Inc., 1980, p. 200.*

Table 5-3. *Customer Characteristics Commonly Used to Describe Customer Segments*
Source: *George S. Day,* **Strategic Market Planning,** *West Publishing Co., 1984, p. 92.*

A. In Both Industrial and Consumer Markets
  1. Usage situation
  2. Benefits sought or derived from product
  3. Volume and frequency of purchase
  4. Past purchasing or switching behavior
  5. Method of purchase—where and how purchases are made
  6. Geographic location
  7. Responsiveness to marketing variables (price sensitivity, etc.)

B. Primarily in Industrial Markets
  1. SIC industry group
  2. Size of organization (number of employees, sales volume)
  3. Service requirements
  4. Average transaction amount
  5. Profit margin
  6. Decision processes (number of decision makers, speed of decision making)

C. Primarily in Consumer Markets
  1. Demographic factors (age, stage of family life cycle, sex, race, religion, family size)
  2. Socioeconomic factors (income, occupation, education, social class)
  3. Psychological characteristics (activities, interests, opinions, and life-styles)
  4. Media habits
  5. Attitudes toward product category

5.3 PRODUCT POLICY

Once the market is defined, product policy is set. Product policy has two features: a program for the continuous flow of new products, and a positive plan for present product improvement.

A continuous flow of new products requires careful integration with R&D strategies. As we saw in the General Cinema strategies, profits were invested in underwriting new film opportunities. Besides research expenditures in the lab to develop new products, the firm needs to invest in market research to determine consumer needs and wants. Figure 5-9 shows the typical product lifecycle—introduction, promotion, growth, acceptance, maturity, and then decline. When a competitor introduces an imitation, sales are affected. At this point, a feature innovation may be introduced (buttery flavor for microwave popcorn), or a new promotion (the package appearance is brightened up), or price is lowered. The product moves from star to cash cow to dog and is ultimately abandoned.

Not all products follow the classical pattern. Rink and Swan have identified 12 types of product lifecycle patterns.[13] These patterns are illustrated in Fig.

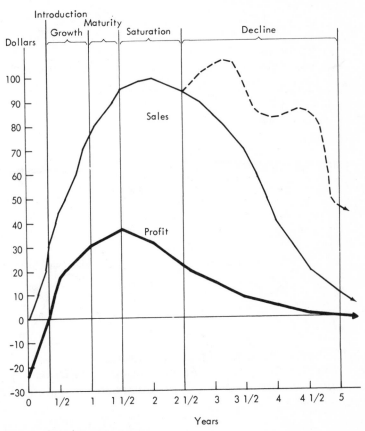

Fig. 5-9. Lifecycle of a product.
Source: James A. Constantin, Rodney E. Evans, Malcolm L. Morris, Marketing Strategy and Management, Business Publications, Inc., 1976, p. 211.

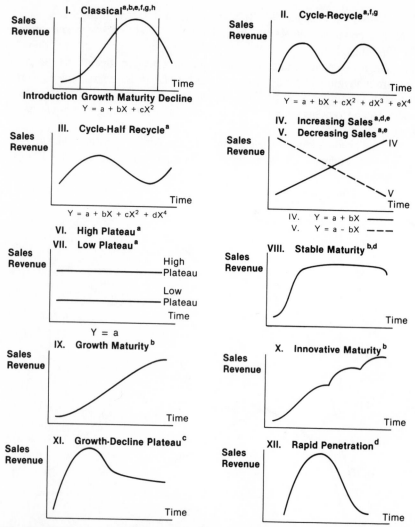

Fig. 5-10. Types of product lifecycle patterns.
Source: David R. Rink, John E. Swan, "Product Life Cycle Research:
A Literature Review," Journal of Business Research, Vol. 7,
September 1979, p. 53.

5-10. The existence of the classical pattern—introduction, growth, maturity, and decline, has been substantiated by research from 19 different studies. There seems to be evidence that the cycle-recycle pattern also exists, particularly in food products, household products, and industrial fluid measuring devices.

The usefulness of lifecycle theory in strategic planning is to help top managers determine the length of the profit stream, the magnitude of profit and cash flow in the several stages, and the length of the cash flow stream. This information is most useful in determining product mix. Thus, the lifecycle concept is a significant element in the development of strategy for growth. The following strategic questions can be answered by analyzing a product's life cycle.

- Length of time the profit stream will last.
- Amount of profit generated by each product in product mix.
- Contribution or loss from products in each stage.
- Risk involved in each stage of cycle for each product.
- Weight assigned for the quality of profit based upon risk involved.

Marketing strategies should be varied, depending upon the stages of product lifecycle. In the introductory phase, advertising and quality are very important. Price is not as important in this stage, and this presents the opportunity to skim the market with higher prices. In the growth stage, advertising becomes even more significant. In maturity, the impact of price becomes most significant. In saturation, quality again is important, as well as advertising, and the importance of service begins to increase. In decline, advertising has the greatest impact. Figures 5-11 and 5-12 summarize the impact of marketing strategies at various stages of the lifecycle.

5.3-1 PRODUCT-LINE STRATEGY

One way to increase customer interest during growth and maturity is to expand product lines. Groups of products that use the same elements of marketing strategy are called *product lines*. Thus, products sold to the same customer, or using the same channels of distribution, are grouped together. By selecting a mix of products which use similar channels of distribution, the marketing manager can promote efficiency and thus improve overall corporate profitability.

Product lines are defined in terms of their width and depth. Width is the number of different product lines offered by a single company. Depth is the number of products offered within each product line. General Motors may have three product lines, auto, truck, and buses, but within the auto line the products offered are Chevrolet, Pontiac, Oldsmobile, Buick, and Cadillac.

A major product policy decision is whether to offer many lines of goods or concentrate on a single line. Concentrating on a single line, although cost efficient, often leaves the firm vulnerable to shifts in consumer demands. The second major decision relates to the amount of variation within a product line. Needs of consumers, actions of competitors, resources of the firm and its goals should all be considered before determining the degree of product depth to pursue.

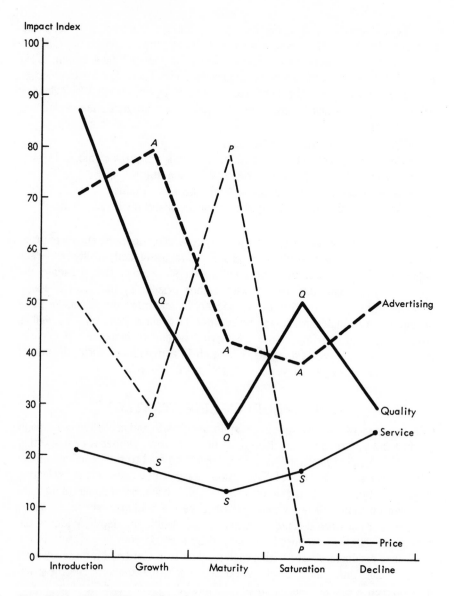

Fig. 5-11. The sigificance of the marketing mix in the stages of the lifecycle.
Source: James A. Constantin, Rodney E. Evans, Malcolm L. Morris,
Marketing Strategy and Management, *Business Publications, Inc.,*
1976, p. 218.

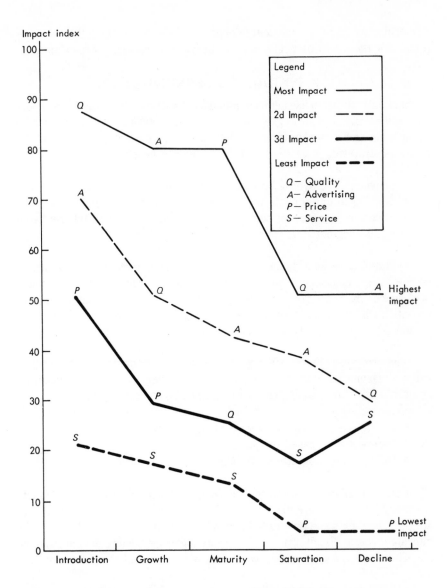

Fig. 5-12. *Relative degree of impact of elements of the marketing mix in various stages of the lifecycle.*
Source: James Constantin, Rodney E. Evans, Malcolm L. Morris, Marketing Strategy and Management, *Business Publications, Inc., 1976, p. 221.*

The firm must search for the degree of product line specialization that optimizes profits for their own particular manufacturing and marketing capabilities.

5.3-2 PRODUCT DIFFERENTIATION

Product differentiation has been identified by Porter as one of the three generic competitive business strategies that firms pursue. Business strategies involve formulating an action plan for competing in a given market. Porter found that business strategies generally follow three approaches:[14]

- Striving to be overall low-cost producer in the industry.
- Seeking to differentiate one's product offering from competitor's.
- Focusing on a market segment by pursuing low-cost or differentiation in that segment.

Differentiation as a defensive strategy provides some protection against competition, because customers establish preferences or loyalties. These preferences make the consumer willing to pay more, thus providing the profit potential. Differentiation provides a defense against the five competitive forces identified by Porter: rival competitors, customers, suppliers, potential entrants, and substitutes.

The preferred differentiation strategies are those that are most difficult to imitate. Having a distinctive competence is very crucial to successful differentiation. Long lasting competitive advantages come from:[15]

- Differentiation based on technical superiority.
- Differentiation based on quality.
- Differentiation based on customer support services.

For differentiation to work, the following conditions are necessary: (1) there are many ways to differentiate the product or service, and these differences are perceived by some buyers to have value; (2) buyer needs and uses of the item are diverse; (3) not many rival firms are following a differentiation strategy.

There are risks associated with following a differentiation strategy:[16]

- Extra costs can cause selling price to be too high for customers to switch from rival firm products.
- Market can shift away from desiring extra features to purchasing the basic or standard model.
- Rival firms may imitate to such an extent that buyers no longer perceive a difference.

When differentiation fails, the competitive strategy defaults to one of cost-leadership or price advantage. Thus, it is critical that a distinctive competence is built around the differentiated attribute. Thompson suggests selecting a basis for differentiation that makes it easy for first-time buyers to try the product, and makes it hard for regular users to abandon the product.[17]

5.4 PRICING STRATEGY

Another area of decision-making for the marketing function is price strategies and policies. The price decision is directly affected by the factors that make up the competitive structure of the industry. Thus, both the external environment of the firm, as well as the strengths and weaknesses of its resources, must be taken into consideration when determining pricing strategies.

Pricing strategies are so fundamental to the firm that they often look like the financial objectives of the firm. Setting price correctly is significant for achieving the following objectives:

- Survival.
- Short-run profitability.
- Long-run profitability.
- Minimizing the risk of loss.
- Acquiring honorable public image.
- Limiting indebtedness to a safe amount.
- Making latest discoveries and improvements.
- Return on invested capital.
- Return on sales volume.
- Attainment of market share.

This list is hard to differentiate from a list of overall corporate objectives for a firm. Because of its relationship to overall objectives and financial objectives, the pricing decision often has more decision makers involved in the process than just the marketing specialists.

The basic pricing factors of demand, competition, costs, and profit are the same for all firms; however, the optimum mix of these factors varies according to the nature of the products, markets, and corporate objectives. Figure 5-13 illustrates the dynamic relationship of these factors in the pricing decision process.

The outcome of the pricing decision is to select and implement a pricing strategy that meets the needs of the firm at a particular stage in its industry evolution. When a company is seeking to break into a new industry, prices are set low to build sales revenue rather than generate net profits. Established firms in mature industries may emphasize high-margin specialty items. Large companies may set prices to generate a minimum return on invested capital.

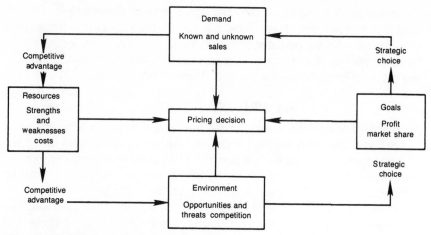

Fig. 5-13. Pricing decision process.

Another strategy is to set low prices to keep competition at a minimum. Producers of some products, such as crude oil, can restrict output and price to maximize profits.

5.4-1 EXTERNAL ENVIRONMENTAL FACTORS WHICH AFFECT PRICING

The following external factors impact on the pricing decision:

- The consumer.
- Industry structure and competition.
- Economic conditions.
- Distribution channels.
- Public policy.
- Values and ethics.

Income elasticity is a basic measure of consumer's influence on price. Elasticity is also influenced by the consumer's concept of product value. The consumer must receive value at least equivalent to the value placed on labor or else some other product will be chosen. The consumer's perceptions of the product, its manufacturer, its brand, and its relationship to other available products are all important influences on the pricing decision.

The overall condition of the economy is important to the pricing decision. An optimistic outlook has a different impact on pricing than an outlook that predicts recession. A strong dollar in the international markets means better relative prices than a weak dollar. Economic indicators have predictive value for setting both consumer and manufacturer prices.

Channels of distribution are important external determinants of price. Alternative channels of distribution perform different kinds or amounts of service for manufacturers. Services provided by different channel members must be paid for and affect the pricing of the product. The set price must be adequate to provide returns to channel members. In some cases, the channel member, a retailer, for example, may be powerful enough to dictate pricing terms.

Public policy has a significant impact on pricing decisions. Antitrust, fair trade, and unfair sales acts all restrict certain pricing practices. Ethics also cannot be ignored as an influence. Since the advent of "Nader's Raiders" and such TV programs as *60 Minutes*, unethical pricing practices have been under public review. In cases of drugs which treat rare but lethal diseases, a firm may find itself having to price the product below cost because of the moral issued involved.

5.4-2 METHODS OF PRICE DETERMINATION

Cost-oriented approaches are simple and can be used when demand is unknown or difficult to predict. Obviously, these approaches ignore external factors, especially the consumer. Another major drawback is that costs are not always easy to define. Several of the more popular cost-oriented approaches are:

- Mark-up pricing.
- Break-even pricing.
- Rate-of-return pricing.
- Variable cost pricing.
- Peak-load pricing.

The popularity of mark-up pricing is based on its simplicity. Break-even pricing can help a firm determine which price will enable it to cover its total costs, but like mark-up pricing, break-even pricing ignores the effects of demand. Rate-of-return pricing can be used to achieve a planned or target rate of return. This is a popular technique among large firms. The most serious problem with this technique is that sales estimates are used to derive a price, even though the number of units sold is obviously a function of price. With variable-cost pricing, variable costs rather than total costs are used as the lowest minimum price. This technique is based on the assumption that the recovery of fixed costs is not always realistic or necessary for the profitable operation of the business. This method is most useful when fixed costs make up a large portion of total unit costs. The airline industry is a good example of the use of variable-cost pricing. Peak-load pricing is useful when there are definite limits to the amount of goods and services a firm can provide, and consumer demand tends to vary over time. The telephone company is an example of peak-load pricing. In off-peak times, the service is discounted.

All of the above approaches to pricing assume that demand is unknown or difficult to predict. At best, the assumption is made that cost is easier to determine than demand.

Pricing with known demand, unlike cost-oriented approaches, assumes that the general shape of the demand function is known. If demand is known, then pricing can be set to maximize profit, revenue, and unit volume.

Profit maximization should be pursued if it is known that the product will have a short lifecycle. An alternative strategy would be sales or revenue maximization. This strategy is most effective in oligopolist market structures. With revenue maximization, lower prices are used to boost sales volume. The lower prices also serve as effective barriers to entry for competitors. Unit volume maximization sacrifices current profits and sales to gain dominance in number of units produced. The objective is to maximize unit volume subject to a minimum profit constraint. This type of strategy would be used in situations where unit sales data and market share figures are made available to the public.[18] In these circumstances, the firm may be under pressure to maintain its share of the total business, regardless of the effect on sales and profits.

5.4-4 USING PRICE AS COMPETITIVE ADVANTAGE

Porter's generic strategies for competing successfully include the strategy of striving to be the overall low-cost producer in the industry. This strategy evolves as a means of dealing with the five competitive forces identified by Porter. The more a strategy creates a defendable competitive position and enables a firm to earn superior profits, the better it is.

If the firm's manufacturing strategy has afforded the opportunity to pursue the generic strategy of low-cost producer, then price becomes a factor of competitive advantage. Firms with the low-cost advantage have the ability to appeal to price sensitive buyers. The low-cost producer has the advantage of setting the industry price floor.[19] Using price as strategy is most effective when[20]:

- Demand is price elastic.
- Product is standardized.
- Product differentiation is difficult.
- Buyers have common requirements.
- Switching costs are low.

Price as a competitive advantage enables a firm to protect itself against all five of the competitive forces identified by Porter.[21] Rival competitors can be

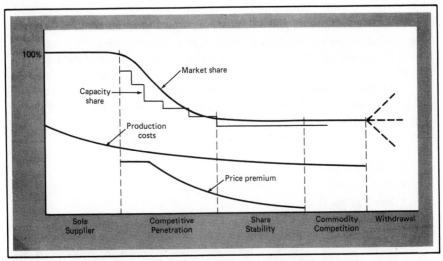

Fig. 5-14. Pricing strategies over the competitive cycle.
Source: Philip Kotler, **Marketing Management: Analysis, Planning, and Control,** *Fifth Edition, Prentice-Hall, Inc., 1984, p. 365.*

eliminated based on inefficiency. Powerful customers will be unable to bargain the price below the survival level of the next efficient firm. Cost advantage allows more pricing room to cope with increases in costs of raw materials when dealing with suppliers. Potential entrants are discouraged by the cost advantage and substitutes can be defended against by cutting prices. There are limitations to pursuing this strategy, however. A narrow focus on cost can cause the firm to overlook shifts in consumer preferences for added features of quality and service. The firm may miss declining buyer sensitivity to price and be left behind as competitors shift to differentiation strategies. Figure 5-14 demonstrates pricing strategies over the competitive cycle.

5.5 PROMOTION STRATEGIES

Promotion is the process of communicating to the market the company's products, services, prices, distributors, and ultimately the company itself. It serves as the information flow from firm to customer. The communication is persuasive in nature, because the firm's promotion objective is to influence the purchasing behavior of consumers. The role of promotion in the marketing strategy mix depends on the type of product, the nature of its markets, competition, and competitive forces. The methods used will vary with the audience to be reached, situations, and resources available. The general objective remains the same— to persuade others to respond favorably.

Promotion strategies flow from corporate goals and marketing objectives. The marketing objective will specify which promotion vehicles will be used and the optimum mix of strategies. Figure 5-15 illustrates the promotion decision model.

When the marketing objective is known, the marketing manager seeks to choose the best mix of promotion strategies to communicate his product or service to the market.

The components of promotion strategy consist of:

- Personal selling.
- Advertising.
- Sales promotion.
- Publicity.

Personal selling is the most common method of selling. Retail sales clerks, brokers, insurance salesmen, and manufacturers' representatives are all examples of the personal selling approach. The unique advantage of personal selling is the salesperson's ability to receive a direct feedback response from the customer concerning product desirability. This advantage allows the salesman to custom tailor his/her presentation to the specific audience. While personal selling is the most common method, it is also the most expensive. Personal selling accounts for 55 percent of marketing expenses.[22]

Advertising is "any paid form of non-personal presentation in promotion of ideas, goods, or services by an identified sponsor."[23] The decision to use advertising is based on an appraisal of the opportunity for stimulating primary and selective demand. Stimulating primary demand involves increasing demand for the product by increasing the amount of the product consumed by each buyer or by adding new buyers. Stimulating selective demand involves increasing the demand for a particular brand within the product category. Thus, the decision to advertise is based on the opportunity to increase total volume demanded or, in economic terms, shift the demand curve up to the right. Opportunities for increasing demand will depend on:

- A favorable trend in primary demand.
- Product differentiation exists.
- Hidden qualities important to consumer.
- Funds for advertising are available.

When demand is expanding, the opportunity for advertising is high. As the product lifecycle matures, the elasticity of advertising declines.[24] Moreover, while advertising can retard a decline, a reversal by advertising alone is highly unlikely. Thus, this stage of product lifecycle is important for determining the

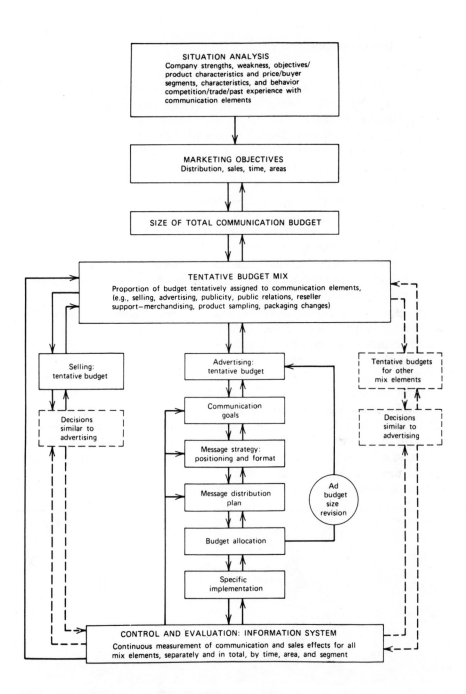

Fig. 5-15. The promotion decision model.
Source: Douglas J. Dalrymple, Leonard J. Parsons, Marketing
Management, Second Edition, John Wiley and Sons, Inc., 1980, p. 485.

effectiveness of advertising. New products are dependent on advertising to promote customer awareness. Mature products are dependent on advertising to maintain market share.

Advertising is closely connected with product differentiation, because selective appeals are more effective if the product has unique attributes. Advertising is crucial if the unique attributes are hidden. Durability as an attribute is dependent on advertising claims for consumer awareness.

The product category also has implications for the usefulness of advertising. Expensive products require a long decision horizon on the part of the buyer. Low interest items, such as soap and toilet tissues, require the constant push of advertising to create top-of-mind awareness among buyers.

Advertising objectives are sometimes categorized as *demand pull* or *demand push*. Pull advertising is designed to "pull" the product through the channels. Thus, the consumer will go directly to the distributor and ask for the product. Brand name advertising serves this purpose. Push advertising is focused on the distributors and presells the dealer on the merit of the product. Push advertising is more common with industrial products. Figure 5-16 illustrates the difference between the two approaches.

Sales promotion includes the activities that supplement and reinforce personal selling and advertising. The use of promotion by means other than advertising has been on the increase. Sales promotions are motivating activities, aimed at salesmen, middlemen, and consumers. They are generally short-term in length and noncontinuous. Dealer promotions are designed to improve dealer cooperation and include training sessions for salespeople, special gifts, and bonuses. The most popular dealer promotion is the "deal," short-run discounts designed to build dealer stocks and stimulate sales. The discount may be given

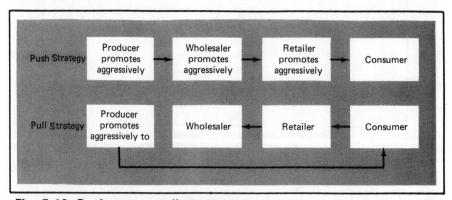

Fig. 5-16. Push-versus-pull strategy.
*Source: Philip Kotler, **Marketing Management: Analysis, Planning, and Control**, Fifth Edition, Prentice-Hall, Inc., 1984, p. 630.*

in the form of free merchandise. Another common activity is a sales contest for distributors with prizes of vacations, cash bonuses, or pink Cadillacs, as in the case of Mary Kay Cosmetics.

Consumer promotions are designed to induce customers to try products. Advertising attempts to develop favorable consumer attitudes toward the brand, while sales promotion is designed to cause some type of immediate action. These activities fall into two categories: those geared to get the nonusers to try the product, such as samples, price-off coupons, and refund offers; and those activities geared to increase the use of the product, such as price-off promotions, premiums, contests, and sweepstakes.

Other forms of promotion sometimes used include public relations, publicity, and educational seminars. Public relations frequently communicates its concern for replenishing natural resources. Oil companies, such as Mobil, sponsor public broadcasting programs to promote a more favorable image of the firm. Publicity is media communication about a company that the company does not pay for directly. A firm may be written up for its special emphasis on employees' health. Oftentimes, when a company is highlighted in a magazine article, it will also pay for an ad to be run at the same time. Because of the nature of some products, educational seminars are used as the means of promotion. This activity is very popular among financial planning firms and health care providers.

The role of promotion in the marketing mix varies by industries, companies, products, and markets. Promotion is more important in selling consumer goods than industrial goods, where the buying procedure is more formalized.

The importance of promotion varies throughout the product's lifecycle. Competitive conditions change, making it necessary to emphasize different aspects. Pricing and promotion become highly interdependent. In the maturity and saturation phases of the lifecycle, the promotion of price becomes critical.

Perhaps the single most important decision in promotion is the selection of a target market. This is the market segmentation strategy that we discussed earlier in this chapter. Markets should be selected in which the firm can achieve maximum advantage from its competitive advantages by applying its promotion resource strengths.

5.6 DISTRIBUTION STRATEGIES

Distribution is the process of organizing systems of transportation, storage, and communication so that goods and services will be readily available.[25] It is the means by which the product is placed in the hands of the user. The objective of the distribution strategy is to minimize the cost of storing and shipping, while making it as easy as possible for the buyer to acquire the product.

The first question to be answered regarding the distribution system is whether or not to use middlemen. A number of specialized middlemen exist whose function it is to move the product from factory to customer. The use of middlemen improves the efficiency of distribution and provides the services of a ready-made channel of distribution that is experienced in handling particular product lines. They also can provide warehouse facilities and even repair equipment, if needed. On the negative side, too many middlemen can raise the costs of moving goods.

A firm generally chooses from several alternatives to establish its distribution strategy. No one strategy can satisfy the requirements of moving products to reach different segments of the market, thus, the distribution strategies are highly interdependent with market segmentation strategies. The choice of alternatives will also shift as the firm grows or customer needs change.

On one end of the distribution continuum is direct distribution, which is the simplest channel. Middlemen are eliminated with direct distribution, because the producer deals directly with the consumer. Examples of direct distribution are mail-order, factory outlets, and door-to-door salespeople. Mail-order distribution works well for standardized products, such as hard-cover books and flower seeds. The disadvantage of this method is that it involves high postage and advertising costs. Factory outlets can be effective, but location is generally a problem, because only a few customers live close enough. Distribution of industrial goods is generally direct, because the number of buyers is few, and they are concentrated in geographic areas.

The first middleman to be added to the chain is the retailer. The advantage of using retailers is that they perform many useful activities, such as carrying inventory, advertising, promotion, credit, delivery, and showroom space.

It is more efficient to sell carloads of products to a few retailers than thousands of products to many buyers. Automobiles, food, and clothing are generally distributed through retailers. There has been some attempt to move forward in the channel and eliminate the retailers in the food business, clothing outlets, and catalog showrooms. To date, these attempts have not met with a high degree of success.

The second middleman added to the chain is the wholesaler. Wholesalers are critical when the firm's products are sold in different types of retail stores scattered all over the country. The wholesaler provides useful services for retailers, such as an assortment of merchandise, back-up stocks, credit, delivery, and promotional assistance. The use of wholesalers enables intensive distribution of the product. It is best utilized when contact with the retailer is not economical or needed. Brewers use wholesalers because they are better able to serve the local market of retailers.

Brokers and manufacturers' reps are another alternative source of distribution. These agents are specialized middlemen who neither own nor take possession of products. They sell, for a commission, to wholesalers and retailers in specified territories or under conditions the producer cannot handle. In the beginning of the product lifecycle, brokers may be used because the volume does not justify the establishment of a sales force. Another reason for using brokers is when the product to be distributed does not fit the specialized functions of the already established channels. Brokers are also used to distribute internationally. Usually a manufacturer will use several different channels simultaneously in an effort to minimize the cost of reaching the customer.

Services, unlike products, have no need for warehousing facilities and are usually sold through branch offices. These may be owned or franchised. Wendy's, for example, is franchised locally. Banks own their branch operations.

5.6-1 VERTICAL INTEGRATION

Companies have a strategic choice to use middlemen or own their channels of distribution. Forward vertical integration occurs when firms move forward in the value added chain. Sohio is an example of a fully integrated firm, from oil wells to service stations. The advantage of forward integration is that the firm has control over the selection of products sold, their prices, and the choice of promotional activities. Although the firm is eliminating the middlemen and the profit they collect for their value added, the primary advantage is in gaining control over marketing the product directly rather than any profits which are gained solely from the elimination of middlemen. Sherwin-Williams, which manufacturers and sells paints, has developed a strategic competitive strength in its 2,000 paint stores.

The decision to forward integrate must be carefully coordinated with the financial strategies, because forward integration requires a substantial financial investment. It also requires a shift from manufacturing driven strategies to a combination of both manufacturing and marketing strategies. There is often a reluctance on the part of the production function to relinquish power to the retail stores division. It is always more powerful to be associated with the revenue producing unit.

Forward integration should be considered a marketing strategy for purposes of increasing sales and market share. Forward integration allows the firm more flexibility in differentiation, because the firm can control more successfully the way the product is sold. The salesperson's presentation, physical facilities, and image of the store can help with product differentiation strategies. Thus, value added is increased by providing a basis for differentiation that was unavailable in the unintegrated state. Forward integration removes the problem of channel access and the bargaining power channels may have. Forward integration may be the only way to reach the market if existing channels are already locked up be competition. The closer to the consumer the firm positions itself, the better access it has to market information. The firm is better able to predict changes in demand and will be able to adjust production processes sooner than if it were not positioned in the forward chain. In industries where final demand is highly cyclical and rapidly changing, there are competitive advantages to timely market information. Another advantage may be the ability to realize higher overall prices by making it possible to set different prices for different customers for essentially the same product.

If integration is chosen, then the strategic decision involves the degree of integration and the desired degree of ownership. If middlemen are to be used, then decisions evolve around the length and width of the channel. The length is the number of institutions through which the product is sold on its way to the consumer. Figure 5-17 illustrates the basic choices. The longer the channel, the more loss of control and the more difficult it is to meet targeted sales goals. Determining the width means deciding how many different classes of middlemen there will be at a particular level in the channel. If retailers are to be used, distribution could be through drug, food, or other kinds of stores. Again, the wider the channel the greater the control problems.

The selection of channels depends largely on the buying patterns of the end consumer, the nature and availability of middlemen, and the environmental opportunities and resource strengths of the firm. The distribution strategy should provide strategic opportunities for the firm by making it easier for the end user to acquire the product.

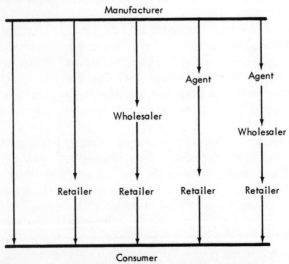

Fig. 5-17. Consumer goods distribution alternatives.
Source: James A. Constantin, Rodney E. Evans, Malcolm L. Morris,
Marketing Strategy and Management, *Business Publications, Inc.,*
1976, p. 271.

Table 5-4. Marketing Strategy

PRODUCT			
Product Line Width			
	Specialize in single product		Multiple
Depth			
	Single variation		Multiple variation
PRICING			
	High/Premium	Intermediate	Low/Aggressive
	Market oriented		Cost oriented
DISTRIBUTION			
	Exclusive	Selective	Intensive
Channel Directness			
	Owner franchise	Wholesalers	Retailers	Independents
Geographic			
	Local	Regional	National	International
PROMOTION			
Focus			
	Price/Product		Institution/Image
Timing			
	Point of purchase		Pre-purchase
Incentives for Retailers			
	Shared cost		None
Continuity			
	Discontinuous		Continuous
Warranties			
	None		Extensive
Returns			
	Restrict		Liberal

5.7 SUMMARY

In this chapter, we have developed the role of marketing in the strategic choice process. The objective of the marketing function is to identify and segment the markets to be served; to select, develop, and differentiate the products to be offered; and to price, promote, and distribute the offered products. Table 5-4 summarizes the decision processes for the marketing function.

ENDNOTES—Chapter 5

1. Michael E. Porter, *Competitive Strategy* (The Free Press, A Division of Macmillan Publishing Co., Inc.), 1980, pp. 157-162.

2. *Ibid*, Chapter 7.

3. *Ibid*, pp. 164-183.

4. Wendell R. Smith, "Product Differentiation and Market Segmentation as Alternative Marketing Strategies," *Journal of Marketing*, Vol. 21 (July, 1956), pp. 3-8.

5. George S. Day, *Strategic Market Planning* (West Publishing Co., 1984), p. 83.

6. *Ibid*, p. 89.

7. Leland L. Beik and Stephan L. Bushy, "Profitability Analysis by Market Segments," *Journal of Marketing*, Vol. 37 (July 1973), pp. 48-53.

8. Shirley Young, Leland Ott, and Barbara Feigin, "Some Practical Considerations in Market Segmentation," *Journal of Marketing Research*, Vol. 15, (August, 1978), pp. 405-412.

9. Philip Kotler, *Markerting Management, 5th Edition* (Prentice-Hall, 1984), pp. 264-265.

10. Day, p. 91.

11. *Ibid*, p. 93.

12. Robert A. Garda, "Strategic Segmentation: How to Carve Niches for Growth in Industrial Markets," 1981, AMACOM.

13. David R. Rink and John E. Swan, "Product Life Cycle Research: A Literature Review," *Journal of Business Research*, Vol. 7 (Sept. 1979), pp. 219-242.

14. Porter, pp. 35-39.

15. Arthur A. Thompson, Jr., and A. J. Strickland, III, *Strategy Formulation and Implementation, 3rd Edition* (Business Publications, Inc., 1984), pp. 162.

16. *Ibid*, p. 161.

17. *Ibid*, p. 162.

18. Robert A. Lynn, "Unit Volume as a Goal for Pricing," *Journal of Marketing*, Vol. 32 (October, 1968), p. 36.

19. Arthur A. Thompson, Jr., and A. J. Stickland, III, *Strategy Formulation and Implementation, 3rd Edition* (Business Publications, Inc., 1984), p. 159.

20. *Ibid*, p. 159.

21. Porter, pp. 35-39.

22. Patrick J. Robinson and Bert Stidsen, *Personal Selling in a Modern Perspective* (Allyn and Bason, 1967), p. 4.

23. *Marketing Definitions: A Glossary of Marketing Terms* (American Marketing Association, 1960).

24. Leonard J. Parsons, "The Product Life Cycle and Time—Varying Advertising Elasticities," *Journal of Marketing Research*, Vol. 12, (November, 1975), pp. 476-480.

25. Douglas J. Dalrymple and Leonard J. Parsons, *Marketing Management, 2nd Edition* (John Wiley & Sons, Inc., 1980), p. 414.

Chapter 6

The Role of R&D

6.0 ROLE OF R&D IN STRATEGIC PLANNING

Strategic planning and R&D are similar in that both deal with the future profits and growth of the organization. Without a continuous stream of new products, the company's strategic planning options may be limited. Today, advances in technology and growing competitive pressure are forcing companies to develop new and innovative products while the lifecycle of existing products appears to be decreasing at an alarming rate. Yet, at the same time, executives may keep research groups in a vacuum and fail to take advantages of the profit potential contribution of R&D strategic planning.

There are three primary reasons why corporations conduct research and development:

- To produce new products or services for profitable growth.
- To produce profitable improvements to existing products and services.
- To produce scientific knowledge which can assist in identifying new opportunities or in "fighting fires."

Successful R&D programs are targeted, but targeting requires a good information system and this, unfortunately, is the weakest link in most companies. Information systems are needed for optimum R&D targeting efforts and this includes assessing customer and market needs, and economic evaluation and project selection.

Assessing customer and market needs involves opportunity-seeking and commercial intelligence functions. Most companies delegate these responsibilities to the marketing group, and this may result in a detrimental effort because marketing groups appear to be overwhelmed with today's products and near-term profitability. They simply do not have the time or resources to adequately analyze other R&D activities which have long-term implications. Also, marketing groups do not have technically trained personnel who can communicate effectively with the R&D groups of the customers and suppliers.

The implications of a corporate strategic plan may be dependent solely upon that point in time where marketing tests the new products in the marketplace. Quite often, senior management will attempt to shorten the R&D time in order to increase earnings at a faster rate. The problem here is that the legality of product liability may be overlooked in the executive's haste to produce results due to stockholder pressure. In time of trouble, executives cut R&D funding in the mistaken belief that cost reductions will occur. In either event, the long-term impact on the organization may prove unhealthy.

Another major problem in industry today is budgeting amounts for new product development. Research is a costly process and is so uncertain that it is difficult to use normal investment criteria for budgeting. This problem is further compounded by the fact that the success ratio from the idea screening stage to a successful new product is 1:64, according to one author.[1]

High-tech industries such as aerospace, defense, computers, electronics, and transportation have strategic plans that include billions of dollars for R&D. These industries spend between 5 and 10 percent of their sales dollars for R&D. At the lower end of the scale are found such industries as wood products, paper, and textiles.

Budgeting for R&D, and for that matter, budgeting for any aspect of a modern business, must begin with a solid foundation of effective corporate planning. Only when there are adequate strategic plans that establish well-defined goals and objectives for the enterprise can R&D managers formulate, prioritize, and implement the needed R&D projects. These projects, once approved, generate the need for an effective method of budgeting, feedback, and control to verify that the work is progressing according to the strategic direction. Every R&D project can be viewed as part of the executive's strategic plan.

The R&D function, regardless of its position within the organizational structure of the firm, can be viewed as a strategic planning system where an input of money results in an output of products. Furthermore, as with most systems, there must exist a feedback mechanism such that the flow of money can be diverted from less promising projects to those with greater potential. This implies that the R&D systems must be continuously monitored, perhaps moreso than other systems. This leads to considering the following topics (at a minimum) in discussing the R&D budgeting process:

- New product innovation. An understanding of this process helps identify the cost/benefits of R&D and the chances of success.
- Corporate objectives and strategic plans. This provides the framework of setting technical objectives and decisions regarding the funding of a new product, program, or project.
- Project evaluation and selection. Provides method for screening and relating the potential of projects to others under consideration for funding.
- Budgeting approaches. Provides methods for linking the short-range budget plan and the long-range corporate objective and acts as a means for controlling funding flow to project activities.

6.1 INNOVATION BACKGROUND

A host of environmental forces, including changes in industrial customer needs, competitor behavior, technology, and government policy combine to make R&D and new product innovation a vital element in corporate planning. The futures of many industrial companies are closely tied to their ability to develop and successfully market new products. In addition, companies with highly sophisticated industrial products are the most prone to technological obsolescence. As a result, most successful industrial firms must pursue product innovation in addition to maintaining current product lines or risk obsolescence. One of the best ways for an industrial company to stay competitive is through active participation in the development of the latest technologies. These technologies can then be used to develop new products to satisfy changing customer needs.

An appreciation of the innovation process requires an understanding of the various types and stages of innovation. Three distinct types have been distinguished by Marquis, as follows:[2]

First, there is the complex system, such as communication networks, moon missions, and energy systems, that takes many years and many millions of dollars to accomplish. This type of innovation is characterized by thorough long-range planning that assures the required technologies will be available and fit together at the proper time in the final development stage. This type of innovation also requires large amounts of resources and effective budgeting techniques.

Second, there is the kind of innovation represented by major radical breakthroughs in technology that change the whole character of an industry. The jet engine and xerography are typical examples. Such innovations are quite rare and unpredictable, and are predominantly developed by independent inventors outside the affected industry.

Last, there is the modest type of innovation characterized by product improvement, cost cutting, quality control improvements, etc. This is the ordinary, everyday, within-the-firm kind of technological change. Without this type of innovation, industrial firms can, and do, perish.

6.2 NEW PRODUCT EVOLUTION

In a study of the new product activities of several hundred companies in all industries, Booz, Allen, and Hamilton[3] defined the new product evolution process as the time it takes to bring a product to commercial existence. This process begins with company objectives, which include fields of product interest, goals, and growth plans, and ends with, hopefully, a successful product. The more specifically these objectives are defined, the greater guidance will be given to the new product program. This process can be broken down into six manageable, fairly clear sequential stages:

- Exploration. The search for product ideas to meet company objectives.
- Screening. A quick analysis to determine which ideas are pertinent and merit more detailed study.
- Business analysis. The expansion of the idea, through creative analysis, into a concrete business recommendation including product features, financial analysis, risk analysis, market assessment, and a program for the product.
- Development. Turning the idea-on-paper into a product-in-hand, demonstrable and producible. This stage focuses on R&D and the inventive capacity of the firm. Unanticipated problems usually arise, and new solutions and tradeoffs are sought. In many instances, the obstacles are so great that a solution cannot be found, and work is terminated or deferred.
- Testing. The technical and commercial experiments necessary to verify earlier technical and business judgments.
- Commercialization. Launching the product in full-scale production and sale; committing the company's reputation and resources.

The new product process can be characterized by a decay curve for ideas as shown in Fig. 6-1. This shows a progressive rejection of ideas or projects by stages in the product evolution process. Although the rate of rejection varies between industries and companies, the general shape of the decay curve is typical. It generally takes close to 60 ideas to yield just one successful new product.

The process of new product evolution involves a series of management decisions. Each stage is progressively more expensive, as measured in expenditures of both time and money. Figure 6-2 shows the rate at which expense dollars are spent as time accumulates for the average project within a sample of leading companies. This information was based on an all-industry

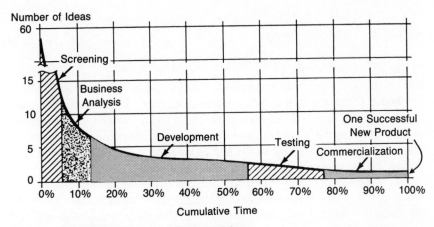

Fig. 6-1. Mortality of new product ideas.
Source: "Management of New Products," Booz, Allen & Hamilton, Inc., 1984, p. 180.

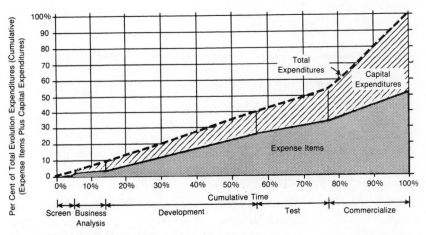

Fig. 6-2. Cumulative expenditures and time.
Source: "Management of New Products", Booz, Allen & Hamilton, Inc., 1984, p. 181.

average and should, therefore, be useful in understanding the typical industrial new product process. It is significant to note that the majority of capital expenditures is concentrated in the last three stages of evolution. It is, therefore, very important to do a better job of screening for business and financial analysis.

This will help eliminate ideas of limited potential before they reach the more expensive stages of evolution.

6.3 NEW PRODUCT SUCCESS

Mansfield and Wagner [4] investigated the success probabilities of new industrial products in different stages of their development cycles and reported a 57 percent success rate of technical completion based on the development of a working product prototype; a 65 percent success rate of commercialization (bringing the product to market) following successful technical completion; and a 74 percent probability of economic success after commercialization.

This leads to a 27 percent commercial success rate for industrial product development projects by compounding these success rates through the cycle. Although this number should be interpreted carefully because of sample size considerations and lack of agreement on the definition of commercial success, it provides a gross estimate of the risks associated with new product development activities.

The high cost of product innovation together with the high mortality rate of products makes it imperative that R&D be properly targeted through the strategic plan. This targeting includes:

- Establishing the overall company objectives in light of expected future economic and technological forecasts and development.
- Clearly communicating these objectives to the R&D organization.
- Defining the R&D mission.
- Periodic reassessment of R&D progress in light of current economic and technological developments. (i.e., balancing R&D projects against environmental [internal and external] threats and opportunities.)

6.4 PORTFOLIO MANAGEMENT

When a corporation develops its strategic plan for R&D, the plan must be aligned with the corporation's strategic business unit and product portfolio. A corporation should have a balanced mix of products. This mix consists of stars, cash cows, dogs, and question marks. Some products generate cash, while others use cash. Obviously, in order to run the company in the short-term, cash cows are required. On the other hand, in both the short- and long-term, we need stars coming into the marketplace and in development for future growth. It is doubtful that a company would want to invest very heavily in R&D for the development of new products in a declining mature market. In this example, a company may choose to have R&D work on a cost reduction program for existing products.

A company must develop product line strategies that are linked to its R&D strategies. Is marketing interested in investment and growth, thus establishing an offensive posture and building market share? Do they want to maintain position by having a defensive posture and maintaining market share? Another strategy is to harvest a product by maximizing profits and reinvesting the profits in better opportunities. The last strategy is to divest or abandon a product. By understanding this delicate balance, one can then plan future product development implications on product lifecycles.

A balanced product portfolio means new products must be under development or in their growth phase to replace those in maturity or already in decline. A continued product improvement program is necessary to remain ahead of the competition. The development of new markets for existing products prolongs the growth phase of that product. "Me-too" products require another set of capabilities, depending on the lead product's position in its product lifecycle.

6.5 PATENTS

A company must decide what type of strategy they wish to pursue regarding the protection of their technology. One course of action is to patent the technology. There are advantages and disadvantages to obtaining a patent. Some of these are as follows:

Advantages	Disadvantages
Easier to license technology	Additional demands on R&D Staff
Permits 17 years of use	Increase costs
Allows for the development of and access to a technological base	Provides competition with information

In closing, it is important to note that the evolving doctrine of "absolute novelty" states that any public disclosure prior to filing for a patent may foreclose on your company's opportunity to obtain patent coverage.

6.6 NONDISCLOSURE AGREEMENTS, SECRECY AGREEMENTS, AND CONFIDENTIALITY AGREEMENTS

In the course of doing business, few companies can develop and market a new product without some help from outside their company. When it is necessary to secure outside help, it is essential to protect the proprietary nature of the information being transmitted to the outside party. In order to do this, an agreement is drawn up between the two parties and signed by a corporate officer from each firm.

Top management must develop a policy on how to handle the transfer of confidential information regarding technological developments to outside sources.

Generally speaking, there are two types of agreements; one-way and mutual. The one-way agreement is exactly what the name implies, in that the company with the confidential information is transferring that information to the second party with nothing coming back. The mutual agreement calls for the transfer of confidential information between both parties.

6.7 GOVERNMENT

Foreign and domestic governments play a significant role in the strategic planning process for R&D. The laws and policies set forth by government can encourage or discourage research and development. This effect can be direct or indirect. The government may have tax incentives that will foster a climate for R&D to flourish. Government can also impose regulations or standards that will encourage the development of new products to meet those standards. The behavior and posture of foreign governments can influence licensing agreements, the competitive edge on new products, the ability to market new products, etc.

The Japanese robotics industry developed quickly because there was a labor shortage in some rapidly growing industries such as automobiles. A receptive atmosphere for new technology and important assistance from the government in the form of accelerated depreciation allowances and subsidized research and development were instrumental in allowing for quick success. The role of government is a subject much too broad to be covered in this book. The following list is but a sampling of how government can control and influence industrial research and development.

- Fiscal and monetary policies.
- International operations and control.
- Technology transfer restrictions.
- Patents.
- Policy impact on technological corporations.
- Taxes; monetary flow restrictions.
- Labor/management relations.
- Risk.
- Regulation.
- Sponsor of technological advance, with corporate involvement.

6.8 RESEARCH AND DEVELOPMENT RATIO

A company must determine the balance or ratio of basic research, applied research, and product development. Basic research may or may not respond directly to a specific problem or need, but it is selected and directed into those fields where advances will have a major impact on the company's future core businesses.

Applied research is the next step in using technology to accomplish business objectives, which may include processes, cost reduction, etc. Product development uses all technologies available to it to develop a product that is consistent with the direction of the company.

An industrial company needs to determine the ratio of the above mentioned areas when determining their strategy for short- and long-term decisions. Basic research is generally a long-term commitment that must be made and driven by top management. Marketing, sales, and manufacturing do not have the incentive to sponsor applied research and more product development research for short-term programs. Therefore, it is the responsibility of top management to provide direction to the research and development effort within the corporation.

6.9 MANUFACTURING AND SALES

These two groups must be included in the strategic planning process for research and development. This is particularly true in the development of new products and technologies. It is essential to know if manufacturing has the capability to make the product using existing manufacturing facilities and equipment. Will the existing manufacturing plants have sufficient capacity to meet demand? Will they be able to manufacture the product and be cost effective? If new equipment and plants are needed, this information needs to be factored into the overall plan so they will be ready when the new product is ready to be launched. Just as important is the sales force. Is the present sales force adequate? Adequacy must be evaluated in terms of numbers, training, location, etc. Will the new product require different selling skills than the company's present product line? Another factor that must be evaluated is the possible reduction in sales force due to a new product. What adverse effect might that have on the morale of the sales group? What are the behavioral ramifications of such a move?

6.10 HUMAN BEHAVIOR

One of the key factors in strategic planning is the ability to communicate effectively, with a great deal of emphasis placed on teamwork, interaction between groups, and knowing your customer. Obviously, the more top management understands human behavior, the more they can control productivity and the management of limited human resources.

One of the many problems associated with R&D is ownership. Top management may feel that they have the need and the right to constantly control a project. Management must relinquish control in order to allow R&D to inject the degree of creativity needed to make the project successful. On the other hand, the individual or team within R&D who is working on the project also needs to relinquish control once the project is ready to be released to manufacturing and marketing.

Recently, there is a greater emphasis within R&D organizations to hire behavioral psychologists to work with their staff. The driving force for this is to improve communication and increase productivity. There is also a growing trend to use behavioral psychologists to analyze the consumer and determine how to develop and position industrial products both present and future.

6.11 RESEARCH VERSUS DEVELOPMENT

Although most people consider R&D as a total entity, there are critical differences between research and development.

- Specifications. Researchers generally function with weak specifications because of the freedom to invent, whereas development personnel are paid not to create new alternatives but to reduce available alternatives to one hopefully simple solution available for implementation.
- Resources. Generally, more resources are needed for development work rather than pure research. This generates a greater need for structured supervision, whereas research is often conducted in a campus-like work environment.
- Scheduling. Researchers prefer very loose schedules with the freedom to go off on tangents, whereas developmental schedules are more rigid. Research schedules identify parallel activities whereas, in development, scheduled activities are sequential.
- Engineering changes. In the research stages of a project, engineering changes, specification changes and engineering redirection (even if simply caused by the personal whims of management) may have a minor cost impact compared to these same changes occurring in the development stage.

For simplicity sake, however, we will assume that R&D is a single entity.

6.12 R&D BENEFITS

For the past eight years, the percent of Gross National Product (GNP) spent on R&D has decreased substantially in the United States, England, and France, but increased in the U.S.S.R., Japan, and West Germany. This concern over the decline in R&D expenditures has caused observers to believe that this indicates the demise of U.S. innovation and, ultimately, economic decline. Some go beyond the economists' effort to link faltering R&D with faltering productivity.

In the near-term, a company's ability to produce innovative results may be directly related, but in the long-term, the results may not be directly measurable.

- How do we measure the R&D spillover effects across industries? (Medical benefits derived from the space program).
- How do we measure progress, if the productivity gains are not anticipated until 10 or more years from now? (SOHIO's massive investment to improve production efficiency for the mining/processing of copper is not expected to yield profitable results until 1992.)
- How do we evaluate R&D expenditures on socially valuable activities such as health and environment? (How many companies have benefited from the work of OSHA and EPA?)

If the benefits of R&D are to be measured solely by financial achievements such as ROI, then the innovation process will undergo severe restraints because executives will consider R&D planning as too costly a process, will not be able to establish projected revenue benefits from basic research, and will be unable to see future economic dividends as a result of a project that failed, even though the negative results indicate that the company should direct their efforts in a different direction.

Among the ills that plague modern management, Hayes and Abernathy identify several that bias decision making against innovation and technological aggressiveness.[5] All are reasonably construed as undermining R&D. They are interwoven to represent what is wrong about R&D planning now. Consider:

- Financial control. The prevailing profit center concept necessitates greater dependence on short-term financial measurements for evaluating managerial performance. Do tight, short-term controls stifle R&D creativity and innovation?
- Corporate portfolio management. The analytical formulas of portfolio theory push managers even further toward extreme caution in allocating resources. Is this cautious management mode directing behavior away from assuming responsibility for reasonable risk and closing the door on resource allocations for R&D?
- Market-driven behavior. Exclusive reliance on customer-driven resource allocation for product development is untenable. Customers define their needs in terms of existing products, processes, markets, and prices. So the market-driven strategy opts for customer satisfaction and lower risk at the expense of superior products in the future. Is market-driven behavior a question for lagging commitment to new technology and new capital equipment through R&D?

- Backward integration. In deciding to integrate backward because of apparent short-term rewards, managers often restrict their ability to strike out in innovative directions in the future. Are American managers subjugating R&D-based innovative products and market development to "results now" ROI-based integration? Are they paralyzing the company's long-term ability to stay abreast of technological change? Or are their near-term based decisions locking the company into long-term outdated technology?
- Limited process development. Many American managers—especially in mature industries—are reluctant to invest heavily in the development of new manufacturing processes. They tend to restrict investments in process development to only those items likely to return short-run costs. Has management lost sight of the reality that users, not producers, are the usual source of individual process innovations and that R&D-based proprietary processes can be as much a competitive edge as proprietary products?
- "Professional" managers. Modern senior managers are less informed about their industry, because there is an increasing propensity for executives to have interests in financial or legal areas, not production. The business community has developed an acceptance of the notion that an individual having no expertise in any particular industry or technology can nevertheless step into an unfamiliar company and run it successfully through strict application of financial controls, portfolio concepts, and a market-driven strategy. In the meantime, what becomes of the unglamorous, arduous process of maintaining R&D strength so that at the strategic level the business remains vigorous and competitive?

6.13 MODELING THE R&D STRATEGIC PLANNING FUNCTION

Schematic modeling of the R&D function requires an understanding of how R&D fits into the total strategic plan and the R&D functional strategy. Figure 6-3 illustrates the integration of R&D into the total strategic planning function. Once the business is defined, together with an environmental analysis of strengths, weaknesses, opportunities, and threats, the corporate goals and objectives are defined. Unfortunately, the definition of the strategic goals and objectives is usually made in financial terms or through the product/market element. This type of definition implies a critical assumption: R&D can and will develop the new products or product improvements within the required specifications in order to meet target goals and objectives.

Unfortunately, many companies have not realized the importance of soliciting R&D input into the objective-setting stage and, therefore, treat R&D simply as a service organization.

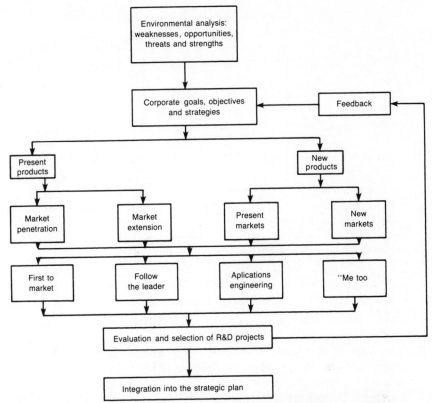

Fig. 6-3. The strategic planning process—define the business.
Source: Robert Linn, "A Setoral Approach to Strategic Planning for R&D," Research Management, Jan-Feb 1983, p. 38.

Once the objectives are set, marketing will identify the products and approach (tactics) to achieve the strategies. Here again, R&D may be treated as a service organization.

The corporate culture will dictate the selection process for R&D projects. It is not uncommon for either the entire R&D selection process to be controlled by marketing or for the entire R&D budget to be part of the marketing budget. The reason for this is because marketing wants to be sure that it can sell successfully what R&D produces.

In mature organizations, however, R&D personnel are allowed to express their concerns over the feasibility of the goals and objectives, and of the probability of successfully achieving the R&D objectives. In such a case, there exists a feedback loop from project selection to objective-setting, as shown in Fig. 6-3.

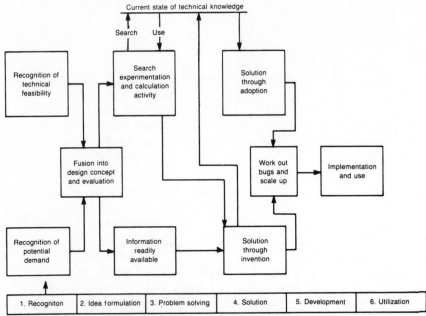

Fig. 6-4. Current state of technical knowledge.
Source: Donald Marquie, "The Anatomy of Successful Innovations,"
Innovation *Magazine, November 1969, p. 21.*

The box in Fig. 6-3 entitled "New Products" requires that the R&D strategy account for the management of innovation and entrepreneurship, and can be modeled as shown in Fig. 6-4. Not all companies have entrepreneurship strategies like 3M or Texas Instruments because of a slow and tedious permeation process into the corporate culture. The successful companies consider entrepreneurship as a "business" in itself and marry it to the mainstream of the company.

Figure 6-3 also shows that successful integration of R&D into the strategic plan requires that R&D understand the firm's production process, distribution process, market research, and market distribution channels. This requires that R&D understand marketing's decision to introduce a new product by being either first to market, second to market, application engineering, or "me too."

When a company has perceived a strategic need to enter a new market, increase growth, or improve an existing product, the company is faced with the problem of how to acquire the technical skills necessary for integration into the strategic plan. The alternatives are:

• R&D with existing resources which have the technical capability.

- R&D with existing resources through internal technical training.
- R&D through newly hired employees.
- R&D through consultants.
- Acquisition of a company with the required technology.
- Joint ventures.
- Buying technology through licensing.

As described previously, functional strategies may be performed independently up to the point of integration into the total plan. The functional R&D strategy is shown in Fig. 6-5. Each of the steps in Fig. 6-5 will be discussed in the following sections. The environmental analysis box in Fig. 6-5 is somewhat different from the environmental analysis box in Fig. 6-3. The box in Fig. 6-5 is accomplished entirely by R&D to stay abreast of the state-of-the-art and what the competition is doing. It is also important to note that the termination of each project should result in an updating of the strategic plan.

It is extremely difficult to uncouple R&D from other functions. Figure 6-6 illustrates the role of key functional units within the R&D functional strategy process. There exists several interesting points in Fig. 6-6. They include:

- Marketing and R&D are strongly coupled.
- Executives generally express more of an interest in offensive rather than defensive R&D because of the impact on the strategic plan.
- Manufacturing involvement should exist in the implementation of the R&D project because what R&D can develop on a bench may require a different approach during full-scale production runs.
- Financial involvement is limited to selection and risk assessment of R&D projects.

The models shown in Figs. 6-3, 6-5, and 6-6 are very sensitive to the length of the product lifecycle and the size of the company. Table 6-1 shows the basic differences in strategic planning as a result of short and long product lifecycles. For short product lifecycles, management must be willing to respond rapidly, especially if the environment is everchanging. Adaptability to short product lifecycles are characteristic of short organizational structures with a wide span of control. Because decision-making must be quick in short product lifecycles, organizational coupling must be high between marketing, R&D, and manufacturing. Weak coupling can result in the late introduction of new products into the marketplace.

The shorter the product lifecycle, the greater the involvement of senior management. Strategic planning at the SBU level may be cumbersome with short product lifecycles. The shorter the product lifecycle, the greater the amount of new products needed to sustain a reasonable growth. As a result, shorter product lifecycles have a greater need for superior R&D talent.

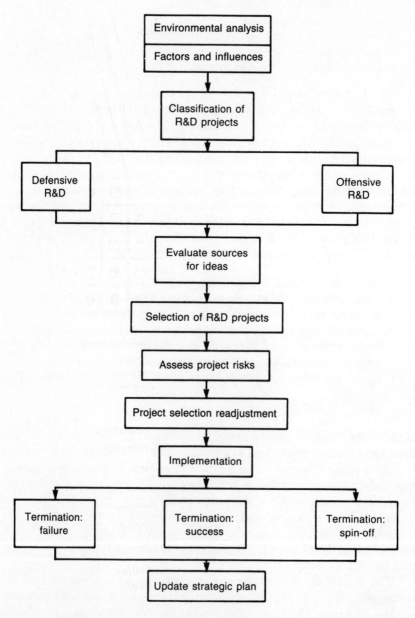

Fig. 6-5. Offensive versus defensive R&D.

Functional Decisions

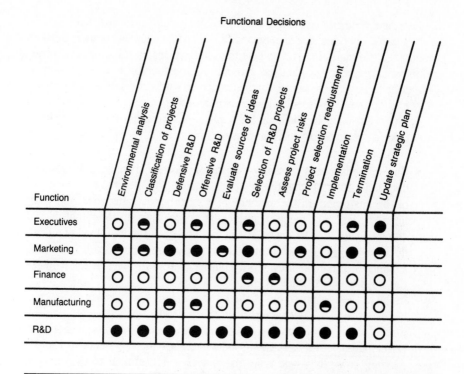

O = Little or no involvement   ◑ = Some involvement   ● = Large amount of involvement

Fig. 6-6. The involvement mix.

Table 6-1. R&D Impact Due to Length of Product Lifecycle

Variable	Short Product Lifecycle	Long Product Lifecycle
• Management Reaction	• Quick Response	• Slow Response
• Environmental Adaptability	• Quick	• Slow
• Organizational Coupling	• High	• Moderate
• Organizational Planning	• Parallel Activities	• Serial Activities
• Strategic Decision-Making level	• Executive-level	• SBU level
• Technical Talent	• Strong	• Moderate

As a final note, the strategic marketing approach to the product lifecycle can vary based upon the size of company. Small companies that compete in short product lifecycle markets must be first to market to reap profits. In short product lifecycles, large companies can commit vast resources to take advantage of experience curves, thus creating a barrier to entry for smaller companies that try to employ a follow-the-leader approach.

The process of model building for R&D is essential in order to develop a systematic framework for decision-making:

- Business managers regularly face many more technological issues and decisions, such as what the key performance parameters are in the eyes of the customer. In the absence of a systematic framework, the business context for these decisions is more difficult to establish and communicate in a company. When technology is the life-blood of a firm, decision makers cannot permit technological resources to be allocated suboptimally, nor can they afford a business strategy that fails to recognize the implications of their technological assets.[6]
- In the market-oriented era of the future, this technological push process of research that has characterized the past will further be replaced by market pull innovations. Research functions will emphasize the development of entirely new products rather than products to replace existing ones. To avoid tying the research department to the goals of specific departments, a planning process must be developed that is tuned to overall corporate objectives. Fluent communication will be necessary between the research director and other top management members. Career development patterns will have to be changed in order that research departments can take advantage of the skills to be obtained from other sectors of the corporation.[7]

6.14 FACTORS INFLUENCING R&D STRATEGIES

The development of a technical strategy is a complex process requiring the identification of numerous factors, most of which are beyond the immediate access of R&D personnel. The identification of these factors requires strong executive leadership focused on joint participation of marketing, engineering, R&D, and manufacturing. A typical list of seed questions to identify the key factors might include:[8]

Technology Objectives. Is it our objective to apply technology for product innovation, for process innovation, for product performance improvement, or for cost reduction? Do we need to replenish our technology (i.e., advance and/or catch-up) with the state-of-art?

Technology Selection. What technology(ies) to invest in for current products? What future technology(ies) to invest in to provide opportunities for future growth? How to exploit existing technological capability for maximum return and/or new products for new markets?

Technology Investment Level. How much to invest in each technology? How stable to maintain R&D investment?

External Intelligence. How much effort to expend obtaining knowledge of competitive and external direction? How to organize the technological surveillance effort?

Technological Posture. How close to state-of-the-art should the firm's technology be? Should we be the leader or just maintain an awareness? What should the balance be between basic approach, applied approach, development, and applications engineering?

Technology Acquisition. To what extent should internal vs. external sources of technology be relied on? (Licensing, joint venture, acquisition, other divisions, central research organization, contract research [government and outside companies], and internal development are possible options.)

Technology Organization and Policies. How to organize technology in the business (e.g., centralized vs decentralized)? Should a project, functional, or matrix organization be used? Is a "dual ladder" necessary? Should R&D facilities be established in other countries? Are the hiring and reward practices consistent with the strategy?

Additional questions which executives can ask include:

- What is the company's attitude toward risk-taking stability and growth?
- Can we identify the company's strengths, weaknesses, opportunities, and threats?
- How confident are we with the capabilities of our R&D personnel?
- Do we fully understand the product lifecycle and the competition?
- How well do we make decisions, especially for tradeoffs?
- Is the R&D function successfully coupled to other operational units, and how receptive are these other units towards R&D?
- Have we properly identified the costs attributed to research and development?
- Have we identified the market and financial return benefits (sales volume, sales dollars, profits, market share, ROI)?
- Have we identified the market and financial contributions (cost reduction impacts, sales facilitation of other products, reduced raw material costs to other products)?
- Have we identified the technical contributions (contribution to other products, contribution to science, contribution to know-how)?

- Have we identified our regret avoidance contributions (maintenance of our current position, reduction of losses, avoidance of lost opportunity)?

6.15 MARKETING INVOLVEMENT

Marketing often provides the largest input in identifying the critical variables. Marketing involvement includes identification of:

- Market attractiveness for each product/product line.
- Relative market share (and trend).
- Sales growth rate (and trend).
- Current business strength.
- Forecasted market share trend.
- Recommended investment strategy.

Additional factors include marketing's policy toward first-to-market, follow-the-leader, applications engineering, and "me too." Ansoff and Stewart[9] have identified the R&D impact of each of these policies:

First-to-Market. This risky but potentially rewarding strategy has a number of important ramifications throughout the business: (a) a research-intensive effort, supported by major development resources; (b) close downstream coupling in product planning, and moderately close coupling therafter; (c) high proximity to the state of the art; (d) high R&D investment ratio; and (e) a high risk of failure for individual products.

The implications of these have been discussed earlier. Taken together, they outline a clear philosophy of business. The company must recruit and retain outstanding technical personnel who can win leadership in the industry. It must see that these technical people are in close and useful communication with marketing planners to identify potentially profitable markets. It must often risk large investments of time and money in technical and market development without any immediate return. It must be able to absorb mistakes, withdraw, and recoup without losing its position in other product lines. As the nature of the market clarifies, initial plans must quickly be modified and approximation refined into precision.

Perhaps most important, top management must be able to make important judgments of timing, balancing the improved product development stemming from a delayed introduction against the risk of being second into the market. Such a company must have more than its share of long-range thinkers who can confidently assess market and competitive trends in their earliest stages and plan with both confidence and flexibility.

Follow the Leader. This marketing strategy implies: (a) development-intensive technical effort, (b) moderate competence across the spectrum of relevant technologies, (c) exceptionally rapid response time in product development and marketing on the basis of finished research, (d) high downstream coupling of R&D with marketing and manufacturing, and (e) superior competitive intelligence.

The company that follows this strategy is—or should be—an organization that gets things done. It uses many interfunctional techniques, responds rapidly to change, and often seems to be in a perpetual fire drill. It has few scientists on its payroll, but some of the best development engineers available. Its senior executives are constantly concerned with maintaining the right balance of strengths among the technical, marketing, and manufacturing functions so that the company can respond effectively to the leader's moves in any of these three areas.

Application Engineering. This strategy requires: (a) substantial product design and engineering resources, but no research and little real development; (b) ready access to product users within customer companies; (c) technically perceptive salesmen and sales engineers who work closely with product designers; (d) good product-line control to prevent costly proliferation; (e) considerable cost consciousness in deciding what applications to develop; (f) an efficiency-oriented manufacturing organization; and (g) a flair for minimizing development and manufacturing cost by using the same parts or elements in many different applications.

The applications-engineering strategy tends to avoid innovative efforts in the interest of economy. Planning is precise, assignments are clear, and new technology is introduced cautiously, well behind the economic state of the art. Return-on-investment and cash-flow calculations are standard practice, and the entire management is profit-oriented.

"Me-too". This strategy, which has flourished in the past decade as never before, is distinguished by: (a) no research or development; (b) strong manufacturing function, dominating product design; (c) strong price and delivery performance; and (d) ability to copy new designs quickly, modifying them only to reduce production costs.

Competing on price, taking a low margin, but avoiding all development expense, a company that has adopted this strategy can wreak havoc with competitors following the first-to-market or follow-the leader strategies. This is because the "me too" strategy, effectively pursued, shortens the profitable period after market introduction, when the leaders' margins are most substantial. The me-too strategy requires a "low-overhead" approach to manufacturing and administration, and a direct hard sell on price and delivery to the customer. It does not require any technical enthusiasm, nor does it aim to generate any.

6.16 R&D INVOLVEMENT

In addition to the questions identified previously, R&D must address two key questions: How costly is the process of innovation? and How easy will it be for the competition to successfully imitate our product?

High innovations cost are generally well worth the risk if the company is first-to-market and can reap the large profits associated with the leadership position. If the innovation process can be duplicated quickly by a large number of competitors, however, even if there exists a large market share, the company may not want to take the risk.

6.17 FRAGMENTED MARKETS

Fragmented markets have a tendency to discourage innovation because of high cost. In such cases, government agencies provide funding in order to stimulate innovation. Even in partially fragmented industries, such as aerospace/electronics, the government cannot expect companies to finance all innovations out of retained earnings.

6.18 PRODUCT LIFECYCLE

The length of the product lifecycle has a bearing on how much risk the company should take. Long product lifecycles may generate sufficient cash flow and lead time for new product introduction. Unfortunately, many companies put the emphasis in the wrong place. As the product lifecycle grows, emphasis shifts from a competitive position, based on product performance, to product variations and ultimately lower costs due to learning curve effects.

Many companies prefer taking the low risk (cost-wise) of developing "line extension" or "flanker" products, which are simply the same product in a different form. Needless to say, bringing out something new is a risky business, and some companies simply prefer to develop cheap imitations. Proctor and Gamble has recently introduced several new (?) products which look quite similar to existing products.[10]

Many small companies thrive on short product lifecycles even in fragmented markets. As an example, consider that if the top executive of a small engineering company is also the founding genius and top scientist, new products are developed quickly and move rapidly from R&D to the marketplace. This company has learned to cope well with short product lifecycles.

6.19 THE CORPORATE IMAGE

Regardless of how well we define the variables for technical strategy formulation, the executive's perception of the desired corporate image will overrule all else.

Some companies have a stabilized image of progressiveness and emphasize their ability to:

- Attract talented technical personnel.
- Allow technical personnel the opportunity to be creative.
- Increase public confidence in the quality of the product.

Well-managed companies can generally make the following statements:

"We can predict with some confidence that next year we will have one major new capital-absorbing development as a result of our past fundamental research. We don't know what the development will be, but we do know we can expect it."

"We figure on one major money-making discovery for roughly every 'x Ph.D. years' we invest. It is very difficult to draw a definite line between 'major' or 'minor'; we do have a fair idea of the expected impact of research in a given area."[11]

The above examples stress the long-term corporate image. Quinn and Mueller have provided another excellent example of the long-term view:

> The chairman of the operating board of a multiproduct company said: "Any damn fool can make a profit for a month—or even a year—by gutting the organization's future. Top management's job is to keep the company 'future oriented.' We try to do this by using a complex of long-term management controls. We play down the use of current profit and return standards in any rigid sense. Instead we purposely use intuitive judgments concerning how well each operating unit is building its organization and technology to meet future demands. So far, we have resisted taking on board members from banks and financial houses because we feel they overemphasize current profits, often at the expense of future strength."[12]

Quinn and Mueller have also given an example of the short-term view and the disastrous effects which can follow:

> A consumer products company, every time it spotted a poor fiscal period ahead, would defer or cut R&D expenditures in order to make periodic financial statements "look good" to stockholders and investment groups. Each such cut eventually lowered the company's competitive margin and seriously affected the research division's capacity to attract topflight people.[13]

6.20 R&D POSITION

The placement of the R&D group within the organization may have an impact on the expected role of the R&D. Foster[14] poses three stages through which organizations might pass as they mature:

- The "lab-in-the-woods stage" where R&D is an isolated organizational unit that is expected to product significant technological advances, but otherwise has little need to be connected to the main stream.
- The "marketing is the answer" stage, in which the R&D function is viewed as a potentially valuable contributor to ongoing business activity and is expected to market its product to various users in the corporation.
- The "strategic management of technology" stage, in which the R&D function is an integral part of corporate strategy and is positioned both to assist in formulating strategy and to help with its implementation in both the domestic and international context.

6.21 PLANNING ACCORDING TO MARKET SHARE

Whenever market share analysis is combined with market growth analysis, the executive is provided with an excellent tool to determine whether there exists an investment opportunity, a source of cash, or an item which should be removed from service. The general terminology for these elements of the market share/market growth matrix are cash cows, stars, dogs and either question marks or problem children. In portfolio planning, each of these has a bearing upon the direction of the R&D thrust to either maintain market share, build market share, harvest or simply withdraw.

Maintain Market Share. This strategy represents a stable market and is ideal for stars or cash cows. In this case, the accompanying R&D strategy should stress defensive R&D and applications engineering rather than diversification.

Build Market Share. This strategy is ideal for selected stars and problem children. The R&D strategy to support this would include methods for lowering production costs, improving quality, and applications engineering. This build market share strategy can also be used for dogs, provided that the company sees a technological breakthrough which will drastically increase market share and perhaps some degree of patent protection which will guarantee a profitable lifecycle.

Harvest Market Share. This strategy is used for a cash cow, where the funds are needed for other activities as R&D. A reasonable R&D strategy here would be to improve the quality or lower the cost.

Withdraw Market Share. This strategy is used with dogs, where the troublesome product has a very low market share and is marginally profitable or operating at a loss. The R&D strategy, if employed at all, should be to look for spinoffs, specialized applications if profitable, or minimal defensive R&D to support future activities which may need this technology as a bases.

6.22 THE EXTERNAL ENVIRONMENT

Every executive is paid to make decisions and take risk. In technological companies, executives are required to make rational decisions about the extent of its R&D activities, and these decisions must be made within the framework of the internal and external environments.

Many of the factors influencing the internal environment were presented in the previous section. Internally, executives may have some degree of environment control, but externally, the environment is everchanging and turbulent.

For R&D executives, increased regulation of technological change has proved to be a burden. The general public has become extremely critical of the safety of new products. Consequently, government agencies such as the Food and Drug Administration have expanded their powers to investigate and ban those products which may be unsafe. The result of this increased regulation has been higher R&D costs, a lengthening of the product lifecycle from R&D to market introduction, the funding of fewer R&D projects, and much more overseas research in countries with few health and safety regulations.

The industries impacted most by regulations appear to be pharmaceutical, food, construction, transportation, and electrical appliances. These industries must conduct a "technological assessment" of all new products/concepts before commercialization because of potentially strong opposition groups toward the construction of waste treatment plants, nuclear products, skyscrapers, projects affecting wildlife and conservation, and birth control.

6.23 LIFECYCLE MANAGEMENT

Analysis of the external environment must include lifecycle management of existing products. Lifecycle management is often the guiding light for directing new products and product mixes. Clifford has given several examples of how keen external environmental analysis can lead toward success.[15]

- Spurred by rapid technological change and by the trend toward packaging everything—a consequence of our self-service way of life—packaging has been a growth industry for well over a decade. One of the industry leaders has been E.I. DuPont de Nemours & Co. Du Pont has been strongest in cellophane, a product so well known it has become almost a synonym for transparent packaging.

With the end of World War II, flexible packaging, and cellophane in particular, entered a period of accelerated growth, but in the 1950s new products—notably polyethylene—began to meet certain packaging needs more effectively. Polyethylene film, for example, was less easily ruptured in cold weather—and in time, it also became lower in price. Consequently, cellophane began losing its share of the flexible packaging market. It became clear that sales volume would soon begin falling unless strong corrective action was taken.

Faced with the immediate threat of obsolescence in a highly profitable product, Du Pont—followed by the two other cellophane manufacturers—introduced a series of modifications designed to maintain cellophane's growth and prolong its maturity. These included special coatings, new types, and lighter grades at prices more competitive with the newer packaging materials. In all, the customers' choice of cellophane types grew from a handful to well over 100.

The cumulative effect of these improvements had an impressive impact on cellophane sales. Contrary to widespread predictions of dramatic decline, cellophane maintained the bulk of its sales volume—of which the traditional grades now represent a relatively small fraction. With more than half of a $300 million market, Du Pont has been the primary beneficiary of this reversal of fortunes.

Further testimony to Du Pont's effectiveness in lifecycle management can be found in its control over the lifecycle mix of its flexible packaging products. Recognizing the maturity of cellophane, Du Pont developed a strong position in polyethylene and in other new packaging materials. While maintaining its leadership in flexible packaging by reshaping the lifecycle of cellophane, the company also provided for growth by adding new products to strengthen its product mix.

- During the mid-1950's, Proctor & Gamble's Gleem had attained a strong position in the toothpaste market. But the total market was growing at a slow rate, and P&G wanted to grow faster. Having introduced Crest as the first decay-preventive dentifrice, P&G found the way to explosive growth by obtaining endorsement of the new toothpaste by the American Dental Association—an achievement that had evaded other manufacturers for years. P&G thus reshaped the lifecycle of the new dentifrice. Crest's share of the toothpaste market quadrupled between 1958 and 1963, while the sales curves of other brands of toothpaste showed strong signs of obsolescence, declining on the average more than 15 percent.

- Decades after the introduction of Jell-O, General Foods succeeded in converting it from a mature to a growth product by a revamping of marketing strategy. GF changed the Jell-O formula, repackaged the product, and repriced it, found a host of new uses for Jell-O, and publicized them to the housewife through stepped-up advertising. Today, Jell-O remains one of GF's biggest selling and most profitable products.

- Aggressive lifecycle management was also demonstrated when International Business Machines introduced its "Series 360" computers early in 1964. By the early 1960s, competition in this field had rapidly become severe. IBM controlled three-quarters of the computer business, but intensified competition was shortening the lifecycles of its computer line. Management foresaw that the rapid growth it had enjoyed in the 1950s would soon slow down unless the company undertook a major shift in product and marketing strategy.

  The solution adopted by IBM was to rapidly obsolete its own equipment—much of which had been on the market for less than four years. At the same time, the company moved to secure its entrenched position in computers by providing an expandable system that would make it uneconomic or inefficient for customers to switch to competing systems as their computer needs grew.

These examples clearly indicate that executives must be willing to search for "opportunities." This is a much more common strategy for small companies which must continuously examine changing consumer behavior in order to maintain a competitive advantage. Small companies generally look for a short-term product plan based upon opportunism, and within the constraints of available dedicated resources.

Another objective of a small company is to develop a "customer-efficiency" strategy by offering products or services that can improve the efficiency of the customer's operations. As described by Curtis:[16]

The greatest success is achieved when the product or service brings about a structural improvement in the customer's businesses, not just an increase in manufacturing efficiency. Structural improvements can be achieved by offering a product or service that reduces the amount of inventory a company must carry, or that reduces or eliminates complex scheduling of the sort that occurs on a production line, which makes products with different sets of custom features. This strategy is similar to opportunism since it requires a detailed understanding of the customers' needs. However, it does not require the rapid response that the opportunism strategy does.

6.24 EXTERNAL INFLUENCES

Robert A. Linn, in his article on "A Sectoral Approach to Strategic Planning for R&D[17]," has identified four major external influences on R&D:

Stability and the Need for Change. Including the stability of the external environment, the ability to reach a goal by more than one competitive means, and the perceived need for stability or change. Consider first a market which is stable or static because of some prior action taken by the firm. Such stable situations, in which the firm has gained appreciable control over the market, can be highly profitable, and a rational strategy may be to preserve or enhance the situation.

An R&D program effectuating this strategy may comprise the following:

- A search to uncover possible substitutes for the technology that confers the leadership position. The goal is to discover and patent such substitutes before the competition.
- A program to lower costs and thereby increase margins.
- Evaluation of competitors' innovations as they become known to determine whether they threaten the firm's leadership position.
- A technical service program to further develop the firm's relationships with its customers.
- A search for new ways to capitalize on the firm's proprietary position.

The program should be designed to reflect the product lifecycle, product-process lifecycle, and experience curve. For example, during the lifecycle growth phase, product quality improvement may be stressed. Later on, cost cutting and technical service may be employed.

To implement the first case, R&D should use structures and procedures designed for thoroughness. The technical service program would be designed for speed, a quick, satisfactory response to customer needs being the goal. The intensity of the program will reflect the firm's interest in the particular market. Furthermore, the program can be modified if the firm perceives a need for change. For example, if a price change will require substitution of a new raw material, additional process and product research may be required.

For a second case, consider a static market caused by a patent owned by a competitor that refuses to license. If the firm wishes to compete, it must either develop technology which circumvents the patent coverage or wait until it expires.

Usually, learning curve experience will grant the patent owner lower costs over time, and this poses a threat of price competition should the firm enter the market. Hence the firm may not adopt either strategy without one or two signals: knowledge that the market perceives a change to be desirable (e.g., customer companies would welcome a second supplier to guarantee supply), and/or an acceptable probability that the firm can develop technology that will allow it to remain competitive even if the patent owner lowers its price.

In the first case, the firm may have already qualified raw materials from several suppliers or guaranteed delivery by a long-term contract with one of them. Alternatively, research may be undertaken to develop an internal source of critical raw materials. Further, the firm in the second case may consider such research in an attempt to have a cheaper source of such materials so it can better meet any price competition by the patent owner. In stable, mature product lines, vertical integration helps profitability, but in changing (growing or declining) markets, the opposite is true.

Today, most business climates are changing rather than static. The more unstable the external environment, the more innovative the firm must be. Hence, each company must position itself to meet the level of change posed by external technical or market requirements. This has deep-seated ramifications, because such positioning requires suitable strategies and internal structures.

If there is a market shift from a stable to an unstable environment, then the firm must radically change its internal environment to meet the challenge. For example, Table 6-2 illustrates the contrasting requirements for the commodity and specialty chemical businesses. As shown, a specialty chemical company cannot enter the commodity chemical business without undergoing many important changes. The same holds true for commodity chemical companies that want to enter the specialty chemical business. This point is currently important, because commodity chemical companies are being lured by higher profits in specialty chemical businesses.

The Prior Art. Before imitating a research project, technical and patent literature must be reviewed to prevent "re-inventing the wheel" or working within claims of a blocking patent for which a license is unavailable. Frequently, the patent situation uncovered falls within one of the following categories, or a combination thereof:

- Much prior art is uncovered, most of which falls short of present commercial requirements. In many instances, commercial exploitation stemming from this art will depend on finding a heretofore unobvious solution to what made the art commercially unacceptable in the first place. This means the firm will be unable to remedy the deficiencies of the prior art without making an invention or discovery, perhaps through application of its own proprietary technology. If the firm views the probability of invention or discovery as slim, the uncovered prior art should not be replowed, but another approach should be taken.

- A fair amount of prior art is uncovered, much of which pertains to commercialized technology. This situation can arise when a firm wishes to apply its superior development or engineering skills to enter a market presently being served by others with patented technology. There are two possibilities:

Table 6-2. Contrasting Requirements for the Commodity and Specialty Chemical Businesses

	Commodity Chemicals	Specialty Chemicals
Definition	Sold on the basis of chemcial composition or physical properties e.g., monomers and solvents.	Sold on the basis of performance,e.g. detergents, antioxidants, stabilizers.
Composition	Usually a pure or near pure chemical compound. Competitors may make identical products.	Often the combination of several materials. Composition can vary among suppliers.
Growth	Generally markets are growing slower than specialties markets.	Generally faster growing than commodity chemicals.
Life Span	Can be long, 10 or more years.	Generally shorter lifecycles, perhaps five or fewer years.
Markets	Relatively stable, many markets are mature. Customers consider different brands interchangeable.	Opportunities for market segmentation and targeted market mix. Customers develop loyalty toward reliable supplier.
Price Competition	Much competition on price.	Market changes seldom on price alone.
Capital Requirements	High, e,g, one dollar of capital for each dollar of annual sales.	Should be kept low, e.g., 50¢ of capital per each dollar of annual sales.
Processes	Automated, continuous. Little flexibility.	Batch, specialty operations. Much flexibility.
Operating Margins	Low	High
Sales Expenses	Low; service component is low.	Very high, cut deeply into margins. A high service committment is required.
Strategies for Success	A product and technology orientation. Thorough, careful research. Emphasis on low cost product volume ad product standardization.	Entrepreneurial spirit. Ability to act quickly. A market focused orientation. Emphasis on good service and high quality products.
Research	Diminished synthesis effort Much engineering development. Look for a cheaper process to make a product of reliably, uniform quality.	Considerable chemical synthesis effort required. Look for a unique product.
Protection of Know-how	Frequently no protection on products is obtainable. For processes, trade secrets or patents can be relied upon depending on the state of the art and patent enforceability.	Product composition and process frequently protected by trade secrets.

(1) The patents belong to one party. When more than one patent is directed to commercially used technology and variations thereof, this coverage may be difficult to design around. When researchers spend too much time conducting experiments within the scope of patent coverage presently in force, this could indicate that the researchers lack meaningful ideas on how to circumvent the coverage, or else that management has not defined the project broadly enough to allow probes at alternative technology. In either case, a collegial review of the program, including its goals, key problems, and progress to date should be conducted to see if alternative approaches can be identified. If not, the program should be terminated.

(2) The patents belong to several firms. In this situation, the patents may be easier to design around, especially if the program has the benefit of advice from skilled patent counsel. Each firm owning patents was trying to protect its own technology, and in a crowded art, gaps will be left between patents when distinguishing what is claimed from what is old in the art.

When the firm tries to thread its way between the patents, the developed technology may have different engineering requirements than the art being designed around. Hence, the development process must have close coupling with engineering to keep the project focused toward a commercially viable innovation.

If the firm is entering into a market late, but before expiration of important adverse patents, the "best" technology may already be covered by patents issued to unwilling licensors. In such a situation, a project objective to improve over the prior art may be unrealistic, and a realistic goal may be to discover infringement-free technology that is "just as good" as the competition. For such a project, the profit potential may be low. This is especially true if the technology being developed will require more expensive engineering to put it into commercial practice, or if the involved engineering is outside the scope of the firm's prior experience. Therefore, the firm should not undertake too many "me-too" or applications engineering development projects unless content to settle for relatively low profit levels.

- Little prior art is found. If the uncovered art is old enough to be in the public domain, it can be used free of any infringement question. Sometimes, however, very recent prior art is uncovered, and this prompts research utilizing the technology reported. Researchers will feel they can confidently use the reported technology if it is not directly covered by claims within the disclosing document. However, caution is advised. The document itself shows that someone with a head-start is working in the area and troublesome patents may be forthcoming, or the other party will beat the firm to commercialization.

- No prior art is uncovered. In this event, the firm should consider a redundant search using a different data bank to make sure nothing of consequence was missed. Also, if there is no prior art to guide researchers, the research project may be lengthy (and the introductory phase of the product lifecycle may also be lengthy if the research is successful).

The Effect of Market Share. A firm must understand its position in the market. Being first has many advantages, it confers the greatest relative benefits of the experience curve and thereby allows pricing to be used as a competitive weapon. Usually companies with leading market shares have the highest profits and return on investment. Moreover, market share is fundamental to superior accomplishments during a substantial future period.

If the company is first in market share, then its strategy should be to maintain that position. If it is second or third, then the strategy is to get out of that position, or if that is impossible, to minimize the disadvantages. Usually, the latter is accomplished by segmenting the market to find a niche in which the firm can assume a leadership position. Winning market share from the leader is a lengthy, expensive proposition unless the leader is asleep. On the other hand, share can be lost quite rapidly to a firm that knowingly applies share-building strategies. Market share is so important that the portfolio of R&D projects and the motivation of employees from the highest level down must focus on performance relative to it.

Current Business and Political Factors. Current external factors such as high cost-push inflation, slow economic growth, greater worldwide competition, low predictability, and high turbulence will continue to increase the obsolescence rate of present products, and operating and investment costs, and decrease productivity and real profitability. In light of these factors, management has lessened margin for error and an enhanced need to plan.

Increasingly, formulation of corporate strategy is of major importance to shareholders. Institutional investors play a major ownership role in leading technological companies; hence, the degree of company appeal to the institutional investor has a significant impact on the market price of a share of stock. Also, the goal of management is to maximize shareholder wealth. This goal is quantified in two ways. First, management must seek to maximize the return and the cost of capital to be as large as possible. Second, management needs to maximize the value of a share of common stock. The immediate market value of a share is of importance to management because it bears on the ability to arrange beneficial mergers, or to raise new equity through issuing new shares.

6.25 EXECUTIVE INVOLVEMENT IN R&D

In order for product innovation to be successful, the implementation of R&D policy and funding should be based on the overall long-range corporate strategy and objectives. Without a clear company position and direction, a company defeats itself. Warner and Strong[18] estimated that about 80 percent of all industrial products fail to meet company objectives and thus are considered failures by their firms. This rate appears to be rather high and may be due to the particular definition of a product failure as one that does not achieve its objectives. Before technical objectives can be established, corporate objectives must be set and communicated downward. Unspecified objectives can result in technological failure.

The following list identifies the basic criteria for choosing an objective:

- Specific, not general.
- Not overly complex.
- Measurable, tangible and verifiable.
- Realistic and attainable.
- Established within resource bounds.
- Consistent with resources available or anticipated.
- Consistent with organization plans, policies, procedures.

For projects which are definable and well-structured, almost all of these criteria can be met. For R&D projects, however, only a small portion may be appropriate, and prioritization of the criteria may be necessary. Because the prioritization may be different at each level of management, senior management must take an active role so that corporate position is known to all.

Understanding the corporate position, its finances, its technological level, and current condition leads to setting realistic long-term objectives. With these objectives and long-term growth goals, the level of technological spending can be set. This level considers all or some of the following:

- The long-range company position in the industry.
- Overtaking specific competitors.
- Maintaining market share.
- A lead or lag position technologically.
- Growth in specific market segments.
- Quality or value relative to competition.
- Technological diversification plans.
- New markets for existing technology.

Hanson and Nason[19] reported the following three recommendations for budgeting and control of R&D expenditures related to firm objectives and planning:

- Budgeting and control of expenditure can only be effective if based on sound planning. Even if prepared on an annual basis, plans should look forward over the period for which resources are already largely committed; a rolling five-year plan is recommended.
- Long-term and exploratory research programs should not be exclusively originated by the research staff. If such work is funded on a corporate basis, its origin and review must be at corporate level, research direction taking its due part in these processes. Funds for such corporate research should be protected from short-term fluctuations.
- R&D funded by operating divisions of the company, and directed to their objectives, must be reported and reviewed against these targets, but the divisions should be encouraged not to take too short-term a view.

Unfortunately, many executives have found that there are other strategic objectives that compete for the same resources. According to Hanson and Nason,[20]

It should be noted that most companies have had to direct more and more of their already scarce resources to problems resulting from legislation and regulation with respect to such items as:

- Product liability
- Environmental matters
- Health
- Safety
- Energy supplies

The end result is a very small residual for investment in innovation, growth and productivity.

There are two critical questions that companies must ask: In what direction should we grow? Should we change our image and, if so, what should it be?

If a company decides to grow vertically, then growth can be directed towards either markets or raw material sources. Horizontal growth is normally directed to new markets or new applications for existing markets. The methods for growth in either direction will be based upon acquisition, merger, licensing, or internal R&D.

In each method for growth, the company's image must be considered. If a company wishes to be considered as progressive, then the company's image may be to attract top technical talent or to increase public acceptance of its products. Today, many companies advertise an image of compliance with government policies on pollution, health, safety, EEO, and minority group hirings. Then years ago, companies were less concerned about their social values and more concerned with maximizing stockholder wealth. Today, there appears to be a changing trend.

Obviously, there are other objectives that must be considered, such as:

- Geographic markets.
- Market size.
- Market share.
- Company size.
- Dependence on suppliers.
- Dependence on limited customer base.
- Profitability.
- Return on investment.
- Bond market rating.

6.26 ALIGNING GOALS AND OBJECTIVES

The chief executive officer must make sure that the R&D goals and objectives are in line with the corporate goals and objectives. The first step in aligning the goals and objectives is to define the types of businesses. There are essentially four types of businesses:

- Selling technical products.
- Selling technical services.
- Selling materials.
- A combination of the above.

When a company sells technical products, the customer owns, rents, or operates the products. Corporations which sell technical products must maintain a strong R&D group capable of introducing a continuous stream of new products. Such companies usually stress advanced state-of-the-art achievements rather than applications engineering or customer service. Technical products companies measure success by how many new customers abandoned their current but still serviceable products to buy ours, and by how many of our existing customers wanted to be upgraded to better equipment. Such companies would include IBM, Control Data, Digital Equipment, Burroughs, Polaroid, and the automotive industry.

Companies which sell technical services include ATT, Bechtel, and hospital administration companies. These companies own and operate the systems themselves. In such organizations, the target for the R&D groups may be to improve the value of the service sold by upgrading rather than to seek out new products. In these organizations, executives should continuously ask, "How can our technical services be improved?"

Companies that sell materials are in the most volatile position, because they must rely heavily upon extensive market analysis to see if a continuous need exists. Chemical companies are an example. Such companies emphasize patent protection or patent dodging and may stress all-purpose material to take advantage of learning curves rather than specialty products. These types of companies stress long lifecycles and encourage new product development. The number of patents which an individual or group has is a strong motivational force.

6.27 PRIORITY SETTING

Priorities create colossal management headaches for the R&D project manager because R&D projects are usually prioritized on a different list than all of the other projects. Functional managers must now supply resources according to two priority lists. Unfortunately, the R&D priority list is usually not given proper attention.

As an example of this, the Director of R&D of a Fortune 25 corporation made the following remarks:

"Each of our operating divisions have their own R&D projects and priorities. Last year, corporate R&D had a very high R&D project geared toward cost improvement in the manufacturing areas. Our priorities were based upon the short-run requirements. Unfortunately, the operating divisions that had to supply resources to our project felt that the benefits would not be received until the long-run and therefore placed support for our project low on their priority list."

Communication of priorities is often a problem in the R&D arena. Setting of priorities on the divisional level may not be passed down to the departmental level, and vice versa. We must have early feedback of priorities so that functional managers can make their own plans.

6.28 WORKING WITH MARKETING

In most organizations, either R&D drives marketing or marketing drives R&D. The latter is more common. Well-managed organizations maintain a proper balance between marketing and R&D. Marketing-driven organizations can create havoc, especially if marketing continuously requests information faster than R&D can deliver it and if bootleg R&D is eliminated. In this case, all R&D activities must be approved by marketing. In some organizations, R&D funding comes out of the marketing budget.

In order to stimulate creativity, R&D should have control over at least a portion of its own budget. This is a necessity, because not all R&D activities are designed to benefit marketing. Some activities are simply to improve technology or create a new way of doing business.

Marketing support, if needed, should be available to all R&D projects regardless of whether they originate in marketing or R&D. An R&D project manager at a major food manufacturer made the following remarks:

"A few years ago, one of our R&D people came up with an idea and I was assigned as the project manager. When the project was completed, we had developed a new product, ready for market introduction and testing. Unfortunately, R&D does not maintain funds for the market testing of a new product. The funds come out of marketing. Our marketing people did not understand the product and placed it low on their priority list. We, in R&D, tried to talk to them. They were reluctant to test the new product because the project was our idea. Marketing lives in their own little world. To make a long story short, last year one of our competitors introduced the same product into the marketplace. Now, instead of being the leader, we are playing catch-up. I know R&D project managers are not trained in market testing, but what if marketing refuses to support R&D-conceived projects? What can we do?"

Several organizations today have R&D project managers reporting directly to a new business group, business development group, or marketing. Engineering-oriented R&D project managers continuously voice displeasure with being evaluated for promotion by someone in marketing who really may not understand the technical difficulties in managing an R&D project. Yet, executives have valid arguments for this arrangement, asserting that these high technology R&D project managers are so in love with their projects that they don't know how and when to cancel a project. Marketing executives contend that projects should be cancelled when:

- Costs become excessive, causing product cost to be non-competitive.
- Return on investment will occur too late.
- Competition is too stiff and not worth the risk.

Of course, the question arises, "Should marketing have a vote in the cancellation of each R&D project or only those that are marketing-driven?" Some organizations cancel projects upon consensus of the project team.

The role of an executive may change because of his working relationship with other executives. Items such as decision-making, authority, and power can be changed. Kotler[21] has elaborated on the working relationship between marketing and R&D:

The company's desire for successful new products is often thwarted by poor working relations between R&D and marketing. In many ways, these groups represent two different cultures in the organization. The R&D department is staffed with scientists and technicians who pride themselves on scientific curiosity and detachment, like to work on challenging technical problems without much concern for immediate sales payoffs, and like to work without much supervision or accountability for research costs. The marketing/sales department is staffed with business-oriented persons, who pride themselves on a practical understanding of the world, like to see many new products with sales features that can be promoted to customers, and feel compelled to pay attention to costs. Each group often carries negative stereotypes of the other group. Marketers see the R&D people as impractical, long-haired, mad-scientist types who don't understand business, while R&D people see marketers as gimmick-oriented hucksters who are more interested in sales than in the technical features of the product. These stereotypes get in the way of productive teamwork.

Companies turn out to be either R&D dominated, marketing dominated, or balanced. In R&D-dominated companies, the R&D staff researches fundamental problems, looks for major breakthroughs, and strives for technical perfection in product development. R&D expenditures are high, and the new-product success rate tends to be low, although R&D occasionally comes up with major new products.

In marketing-dominated companies, the R&D staff designs products for specific market needs, much of it involving product modification and the application of existing technologies. A higher ratio of new products succeed, but they represent mainly product modifications with relatively short product lives.

A balanced R&D/marketing company is one in which effective organizational relationships have been worked out between R&D and marketing to share responsibility for successful market-oriented innovations. The R&D staff takes responsibility not for invention alone but for successful innovation. The marketing staff takes responsibility not for new sales features alone but also for helping identify new ways to satisfy needs. R&D/marketing cooperation is facilitated in several ways: (1) Joint seminars are sponsored to build understanding and respect for each other's goals, working styles, and problems; (2) each new project is assigned to an R&D person and a marketing person, who work together through the life of the project; (3) R&D and marketing personnel are interchanged so that they have a chance to experience each other's work situations (some R&D people may travel with the sales force, while some marketing people might hang around the lab for a short time); and (4) conflicts are worked out by higher management, following a clear procedure.

6.29 PLANNING FOR R&D

Planning for R&D in today's economy presents many problems. When resources become more scarce, vision tends to become shorter. Senior management must communicate with R&D managers in order to develop the proper balance between the many tradeoffs. The tendency to give up on strategic planning and resort to operational-type planning must be resisted. Good planners still practice good strategic planning while recognizing today's economy. The tool that will permit this is effective scheduling coupled with short-range milestones, carefully designed to permit aborting, if that alternative is in the best interest for the company.

One approach to the formulation and construction of a corporate R&D activity is to use a procedure which requires participative involvement of both corporate executives and the R&D staff. Corporate executives from Marketing/Sales, Manufacturing/Production, and Corporate Planning are invited to a series of informal meetings carefully designed to obtain their input into the R&D budget. At the same time, the R&D staff is given an opportunity to participate in the formulation of R&D programs. This is accomplished through a series of meetings involving successively lower levels of supervision, including the first level, which would involve the individual bench chemist or engineer. Subordinates are requested to cost out a suggested budget in a three-level format:

- Level 1—Assume that the total resources available for R&D will be at the "current level."
- Level 2—Very desirable projects which could require the displacement of certain Level 1 projects.
- Level 3—Projects which identify the backlog of quality R&D investment opportunity projects.

This overall approach has several important strengths, such as:

- Providing for participative involvement of corporate departments.
- Developing a better understanding within R&D of other departments.
- Establishing a sound foundation for effective management by objectives.

There are, however, some weaknesses such as:

- Creating personal conflict and misunderstandings.
- Awakening some "sleeping dogs."
- Creating conflicts in the event that the management style is highly authoritarian.[22]

The chemical group of a large corporation uses two principal documents in their R&D project planning format. The first of these is the R&D project plan and authorization which summarizes the proposed project activities and its costs, increments, and incentives and provides informational linkages to other planning and budgeting documents. The second document is an Incremental impact summary which provides more detail on the specific tasks and other resources required for each increment.

Prioritizing of R&D projects is essential to the process. One method used by the chemical group is as follows:

- Support required for existing business.
- Expansion programs of the existing budget base.
- Deferrable programs.

After prioritization, R&D management should meet with operating division/unit management until agreement is reached on details. Next, group and corporate management review and evaluate the proposed budgets leading to final approval.[23]

Several attempts have been made to identify effective planning practices for R&D. Perhaps the best document known to the authors was prepared by Hughes Aircraft Company[24] and includes:

- Ensure that all affected organizations and individuals are involved in the planning.
- Quantize plans whenever possible.
- Examine all pertinent tradeoffs.
- Eliminate all unnecessary items and avoid excessive detail.
- Ensure realistic cost and schedule parameters.
- Optimally time-phase all important elements of a plan—delays at any part of an effort may adversely impact the remaining.
- Examine ("debug") plans critically before implementing them.
- Develop contingency plans well in advance of potential events that may have a negative effect on the effort.
- Recognize that plans can succeed only if they are communicated effectively, are understood, and are properly carried out.
- Orient budgets to the future, not the past—base them on future needs, not on past actuals.
- Assure that planned budgets adequately represent the realities of effective operation. (Unfortunately, in practice, budgets are often increased for organizations which traditionally overrun and decreased for organizations which consistently underrun).

- Assign specific responsibilities for adhering to budgets—stress accountability.
- Make potential return-on-investment a major consideration in selecting and planning R&D projects.
- Optimize cash flow in financial planning.
- Plan major capital investments well in advance of actual need.
- Have managers annually prepare plans for the overall improvement of their organizations in the coming year and review progress against their plans at the end of the year.
- Maintain an ongoing program/plan for replacement or updating of obsolete plant and facilities.
- Plan for proper maintenance of plant and facilities.
- Make optimum use of computers as an aid to planning.
- Avoid overplanning.

6.30 LOCATION OF THE R&D FUNCTION

R&D project management in small organizations is generally easier than similar functions in large organizations. In small companies, there usually exists a single R&D group responsible for all R&D activities. In large companies, each division may have its own R&D function. The giant corporations try to encourage decentralized R&D under the supervision of a central research (or corporate research) group. The following problems were identified by a central research group project manager.

- Parallel projects going on at the same time.
- Duplication of effort because each division has their own R&D and quality control functions. Poor passing of information between divisions.
- "Central research originally developed to perform research functions which could not be effectively handled by the divisions. Although we are supposed to be a service group, we still bill each division for the work we do for them. Some pay us and some don't. Last year, several divisions stopped using us because they felt that it was cheaper to do the work themselves. Now, we are funded entirely by corporate and have more work than we can handle. Everyone can think of work for us to do when it is free."
- "I know that there is planning going on now for activities which I will be doing three months from now. How should I plan for this? I don't have any formal or informal data on planning as yet. What should I tell my boss?"

Executives should not try to understaff the R&D function. Forcing R&D personnel and project managers to work on too many projects at once can drastically reduce creativity. This does not imply that personnel should be used on only one project at a time. Most companies do not have this luxury, but this situation of multiproject management should be carefully monitored.

As a final note, executives must be very careful about how they wish to maintain control over the R&D project managers. Too much control can drastically reduce bootleg research and, in the long run, the company may suffer.

6.31 SCHEDULING

Overall scheduling of R&D projects becomes a must at this point in the budgeting for R&D projects. Prior to this point, the R&D manager will have assembled a package of continuing and new projects. Each will have been evaluated and prioritized, but only by assembling a master schedule of all proposed projects will it be possible to have the necessary information on hand for the reviews with senior management that will lead to the ultimate funding.

Master scheduling, together with the next step, funding, becomes an iterative process. One of senior management's roles is to examine the tradeoffs between available resources, current economic conditions, and corporate goals and objectives. Conceivably, the package of R&D projects could exceed the availability of internal R&D manpower. In this event, senior management would be faced with considering contract R&D as opposed to dropping the lowest priority projects.

There are basically two types of R&D projects that have to be placed in the master schedule: non-well-defined projects and well-defined projects.

The non-well-defined projects are the most difficult to schedule because they are simply ideas that require "seed money" to explore. If the results are positive, then the project may become a well-defined effort and combined with other projects as part of the R&D selection portfolio. "Seed money" projects can occur at any time and can easily cause major shifts in the master schedule.

Scheduling activities for R&D projects is extremely difficult because of the previously mentioned problems. Many R&D people believe that if you know how long it will take to complete the objective, you do not need R&D. Most R&D schedules are not detailed, but are composed of major milestones where executives can decide whether or not additional money or resources should be committed. Some executives and R&D managers believe in the philosophy that, "I'll give you 'so much time' to get an answer." In R&D project management, failure is often construed as an acceptable answer.

There are two schools of thought on R&D scheduling, depending of course upon the type of project, the time duration, and resources required. The first school of thought involves the tight R&D schedule. This may occur if the project is a one-person activity. R&D personnel are generally highly optimistic and believe that they can do anything. They, therefore, have the tendency to lay out rather tight, optimistic schedules. This type of optimism is actually a good trait. Where would we be without it? How many projects would be prematurely cancelled without optimistic R&D personnel?

Tight schedules occur mostly on limited resource projects. Project managers tend to avoid tight schedules if they feel that there exists a poor window in the functional organization for a timely commitment of resources. Another reason is that R&D personnel know that in time of crisis or fire-fighting on manufacturing lines (which are yielding immediate profits), they may lose their key functional project employees, perhaps for an extended period of time.

The second school of thought believes that R&D project management is not as mechanical as other forms of project management and, therefore, all schedules must be loose. Scientists do not like or want tight structuring, because they feel that they cannot be creative without having sufficient freedom to do their job. Many good results have been obtained from spinoffs and other activities where R&D project managers have deviated from predetermined schedules. Of course, too much freedom can prove to be disastrous, because the individual might try to be overly creative and "reinvent the wheel."

The second school says that R&D project managers should not focus on limited objectives. Rather, the project manager should be able to realize that other possible objectives can be achieved with further exploration of some of the activities.

An interesting problem facing executives is how much of an input the bench researcher should have in selecting R&D projects. This does not imply that researchers should have complete freedom in selecting projects. Well-planned R&D strategic planning programs hire researchers because of their abilities in specific technical disciplines. Some organizations boast of one new money-making effort or one new product each year.

Researchers may already be predisposed with the technical problems of new product development, and to burden the researchers further with project selection committees may distract from their usefulness. Thus, the interrelationship between executives (specifically R&D executive) takes on paramount importance. According to Quinn and Cavanaugh,[25] the researchers input to project selection should be between the researcher and the research executive:

"We expect the individual researcher to come up with proposals within his specialty. He discusses any major new approach with his director. Normally, the director encourages the researcher to perform some exploratory investigations and come back in about a month to discuss the areas again. If the approach then looks scientifically promising to the researcher and his director, he goes ahead for another three months. His progress and the promise of the field are then checked again by a small group of research directors. If things are still encouraging, he is given a commitment for another six months. If the project continues after this checkpoint, it is looked at annually by the research committee in the regular review cycle. This system only works because we are a research-oriented company, and there is strong mutual respect between the researchers, our research executives, and our top management.''

The authors have also commented on the individual relationship with the scientist himself:[26]

''One of our biggest problems is that our scientists become 'organization men' too rapidly. We hire them for their brilliance, objectivity, and willingness to try things no one has done before. Within two to three years, they begin second-guessing 'what we want' from them in the way of science and start worrying about organizational status, and the like. Sure, we want a man to know the company's needs, so he doesn't feel frustrated by not seeing his work applied. But we don't want him to lose the very creativity we hired him for, just because he is trying to 'make a mark' for himself in the organization and please everybody in sight.''

Because each R&D project is part of an executives' strategic plan, executives are expected to be actively involved in R&D activities. As an example:[27]

As one vice president of research said, ''A new product is like a baby. You don't just bring it into the world and expect it to grow up and be a success. It needs a mother (enthusiasm) to love it and keep it going when things are tough. It needs a pediatrician (expert information and technical skills) to solve the problems the mother can't cope with alone. And it needs a father (authority with resources) to feed it and house it. Without any one of these, the baby may still turn out all right, but its chances of survival are a lot lower.''

The following situations indicate the difficult role of an executive in managing and interfacing with R&D personnel:

Isolating R&D. The vice-president for R&D did not understand the necessity for developing a good liaison with marketing personnel and decided to shield his group from ''commercial pressures.'' The result of this sheltering was that the operations group did not hear about technical achievements until the very last moment and, consequently, technology transfer from R&D to manufacturing required years.

Integrating Research with Development. A chemical company maintains a pure research group. Unfortunately, although a large expense was incurred in supporting the group, only "lip service" was given to achievements, and many promising results were simply shelved because of weak development activities. As a result of this frustration, there was a large turnover in personnel, many of whom opened their own companies.

The R&D Vacuum-Suppliers. A medium-sized electrical equipment manufacturer prided themselves on their ability to develop new products for their customers. Unfortunately, what was proven valid with bench testing could not be mass-produced in manufacturing because suppliers could not keep up with the company's rapidly changing needs. As a result, the company found it necessary to develop a better liaison with its suppliers during R&D activities.

Organizational Aging. An industrial products company appointed a 62-year-old executive in charge of new product development. He immediately set up a project selection committee composed of senior company managers. During his four-year tenure, only short-term R&D projects were selected. It appeared that the selection committee was reluctant to accept new technology projects that would yield profits only after they retired.

Organizational Approval Process. An electrical equipment manufacturer was forced to cut back on R&D expenditures during the 1979-1982 downturn in the economy. As a result, numerous approval committees were established to approve each R&D project depending, of course, upon the size of the requested budgets. In many cases, by the time that the projects were approved, many of the key individuals had been reassigned to other activities and interest in the project dissipated.

The Integration Vacuum. A small appliance company maintained an aggressive approach toward R&D, quite often as the industry leader. Unfortunately, the manufacturing personnel preferred the status quo, and worker resistance to new technologies was very strong. Management alleviated the problem by allowing manufacturing to participate in the R&D strategic planning process. As a result, strategic R&D planning helped smooth the way for anticipated technological changes in manufacturing.

The Central Research Vacuum. A Fortune 500 food company established a central research group to keep all non-technical managers abreast of all corporate R&D. However, the objectives of corporate R&D appeared to be quite different from divisional objectives. As a result, the liaison between the divisions and R&D dissipated to such a degree that central research is now reduced to the status of a separate division.

6.32 CLASSIFICATION OF R&D PROJECTS

R&D projects can be classified into seven major categories. The first category is the *grass roots* project. This type of project may be simply an idea with as few as one or two good data points. Grass roots projects are funded with "seed money," which is a small sum of money, usually under the control of the R&D manager. The purpose of the seed money is to see if the grass roots project is feasible enough to be developed into a full-blown, well-funded R&D project to be further incorporated into the strategic plan.

The second category is the *bootlegged* project. This type of project is one in which funding does not exist either because the selection team did not consider this project worthy of funding or because funding had been terminated (or ran out) and funding renewal was not considered appropriate. In either event, a bootlegged project is done on the sly, using another project's budgeted charge numbers. Bootlegged projects run the complete spectrum for conceptual ideas to terminated, well-defined activities.

The third category is the *basic research* project and may include the grass roots and bootlegged project. Basic research activities are designed to expand knowledge in a specific scientific area, or to improve the state-of-the-art. These types of projects do not generally result in products that can be directly sold by marketing and, as a result, require special handling.

The fourth category is the *applied research* project. The applied research project is an extension or follow-on to the basic research project and explores direct application of a given body of knowledge. These types of projects hopefully result in marketable products, product improvements, or new applications for existing products.

The fifth category is the *advanced development* project. These types of activities follow the applied research or exploratory development projects with the intent of producing full-scale prototypes supported by experimental testing.

The sixth category is the *full-scale engineering development* project. This activity includes complete working drawing design of the product together with a detailed bill of materials, exact vendor quotes, and specification development. This type of R&D activity requires strong manufacturing involvement.

The seventh and final category is the *production support* R&D project. This category can include either applications engineering to find better uses of this product for a customer, or internal operations support to investigate limitations and feasibility of a given system with hopes of modification or redesign. Projects designed to find ways of lowering production costs or improving product quality are examples of internal production support projects.

Contract R&D is another form of strategic planning and can be used with any of these seven classifications for projects. There are different reasons for conducting contract R&D, depending whether you are the customer or the contractor. Customers subcontract out R&D because they may not have the necessary in-house technical skills; have in-house skills, but the resources are committed to higher priority activities; and/or may have the available talent, but external sources have superior talent and may be able to produce the desired results in less time and for less money.

From a subcontractor's point of view, contract R&D is a way to develop new technologies at someone else's expense. Subcontractors view contract R&D as a way to:

- Minimize the internal cost of supporting R&D personnel.
- Develop new technologies to penetrate new markets/products.
- Develop new technologies to support existing market/products.
- Maintain technical leadership.
- Improve resource utilization by balancing workloads.
- Maintain customer goodwill.
- Look for spinoffs on existing products.

There also exists disadvantages to contract R&D from the customer's point of view:

- How dependent should I become on a subcontractor to produce the desired results within time and cost?
- What criteria is used to evaluate subcontractors?
- What type of communication network should be established?
- How do I know if the subcontractor is being honest with me?
- If tradeoffs are needed, how will decisions be made?
- Who controls patent rights resulting from the research under contract?
- Will project failures impact strategic planning process?

From the subcontractor's point of view:

- What influence will the customer try to exercise over my personnel?
- Will project success generate follow-on work?
- Will project success enhance goodwill/image?
- Will project failure damage goodwill/image?
- Based upon the type of contract, are there risks that we will have to finance part of the project with our own money?
- Can this contract generate legal headaches?

Contract research, licensing, joint ventures, acquisitions, and the luxury of hiring additional personnel are taken for granted in the United States. Foreign countries may not have these luxuries, and additional classifications are needed, usually by the level of technology. According to one foreign country, the following levels are used:

- Level I: Technology exists within the company.
- Level II: Technology can be purchased from companies within the country.
- Level III: Technology can be purchased from outside country.
- Level IV: Technology must be researched in other countries and brought back into parent country.

Because a great many foreign countries fall into Levels III and IV, several foreign corporations have established employee sabbatical funds. Each month, the company withholds 3 percent of the employee's salary and matches this with 7 percent of company funds. Every five or six years, each participating employee is allowed to study abroad to bring technical expertise back into the country. The employee draws his full salary while on sabbatical in addition to the sabbatical fund.

For strategic R&D planning, this type of sabbatical leave creates a gap in the organization. Management can delay a sabbatical leave for an employee for one year only. What happens if the employee is in a strategic position? What if the employee is working on a critical project? What if the employee is the only person with the needed skills in a specific discipline? Who replaces the employee? Where do we put the employee upon his return to the organization? What happens if the employee's previous management slot is no longer vacant? Obviously, these questions have serious impact on the strategic planning process.

6.33 OFFENSIVE VERSUS DEFENSIVE R&D

Should a company direct its resources toward offensive or defensive R&D? Offensive R&D is product R&D, whereas defensive R&D is process R&D. In offensive R&D, the intent is to penetrate a new market as quickly as possible, replace an existing product, or simply satisfy a particular customer's need. Offensive R&D stresses a first-to-market approach.

Defensive R&D, on the other hand, is used to either lengthen the product lifecycle or to protect existing product lines from serious competitive pressures. Defensive R&D is also employed in situations where the company has a successful product lein and fears that the introduction of a new technology at this time may jeopardize existing profits. Defensive R&D concentrates on minor improvements rather than major discoveries and, as a result, requires less funding. Today, with the high cost of money, companies are concentrating on minor product improvements, such as style, and introduce the product into the marketplace as a new, improved version when, in fact, it is simply the original product slightly changed. This approach has been used successfully by the Japanese in copying someone else's successful product, improving the quality, changing the style, and introducing it into the marketplace. A big advantage to the Japanese approach is the product can be sold at a lower cost, because the selling price does not have to include recovery of expensive R&D costs.

Defensive R&D is a necessity for those organizations which must support existing products and hopefully extend the product's age life. According to Goldring,[28] properly managed defensive research can provide six operational improvements:

- Improved coordination between R&D personnel and operational groups.
- Improved contact with the marketplace.
- Better judgment in corporate and R&D planning.
- Better acceptance by operating personnel, especially decision-making personnel in operating divisions.
- Better access to varied sources of technological innovation.
- Greater emotional satisfaction for R&D personnel through improved perception of the value of their contributions.

Goldring concludes his argument by stating that:

> "Payoffs from defensive research performed by the corporate R&D group will occur through the application of lower cost materials, design and manufacturing improvements, higher speed machinery, reduced defect rate in manufactured goods, and so forth. These payoffs should be clearly visible and directly demonstrable. When this defensive research is consistently sustained over long periods of time, the cumulative effect can produce technological innovation with relatively little scientific discovery. These innovations develop almost without planning and with little extra expense.
>
> Although defensive research lacks the glamor of technological breakthrough, it is a pragmatic approach for maintaining technological innovation in the firm. Properly directed, it can maintain the firm's competitive position, broaden markets, and give timely warning when technological developments threaten a product or process with obsolescence. It is a powerful tool for stimulating technological innovation by bringing needs and technical ability together."[29]

A firm's strategic posture in the marketplace is therefore not restricted solely to new product introduction. Companies must find the proper technological balance between offensive and defensive R&D.

6.34 SOURCES OF IDEAS

Unlike other types of planning, strategic R&D planning must be willing to solicit ideas from the depths of the organization. Successful companies with a reputation for continuous new product introduction have new product development teams which operate in a relatively unstructured environment to obtain the best possible ideas. Some companies go so far as to develop idea inventories, idea banks, and idea clearing houses.

These idea sessions are brainstorming sessions and not intended for problem-solving. If properly structured, the meeting will have an atmosphere of free expression and creative thinking, an ideal technique for stimulating ideas. Arguments against brainstorming sessions include no rewards for creators, attack of only superficial problems, possibility of potentially good ideas coming out prematurely and being disregarded, and lack of consideration for those individuals that are more creative by themselves.

Principles which can be used in brainstorming sessions include:

- Select personnel from a variety of levels; avoid those responsible for implementation.
- Allow people to decline assignments.
- Avoid evaluation and criticism of ideas.
- Provide credit recognition and/or rewards for contributors.
- Limit session to 60 minutes.

Ideas are not merely limited to internal sources. There are several external sources of new product ideas[30] such as:

- Customers.
- Competitors.
- Suppliers.
- Purchase of technologies.
- Licensing of technologies.
- Unsolicited ideas from customers or others.
- Private inventors.
- Acquisitions.
- Trade Fairs.
- Technology fairs.
- Private data banks.
- Technical journals.
- Trade journals.
- Government-funded research programs.
- Government innovation/technology transfer programs.
- Government agencies.

Perhaps the best method for idea generation is to monitor the competition for information on new products.[31] This includes:

- Current Product Information.
  - —Product quality and performance
  - —Breadth of line
  - —Product costs
  - —New product developments
- Technological Information.
  - —R&D activities
  - —Patent & licensing activities
  - —Technical capabilities
- Financial Information.
  - —Sales
  - —Profits and losses
  - —Operating expenditures
- Production Information.
  - —Production capacity
  - —Facility location
  - —Capital investment
  - —Volume
- Market Information.
  - —Pricing, discounts, volume
  - —Market share
  - —Distribution methods
  - —Advertising
  - —Customer relations
  - —New market potentials and plans

6.35 STRATEGIC SELECTION OF R&D PROJECTS

The selection of R&D projects must, in the final analysis, be the responsibility of top management. Unfortunately, too many executives wait for the following symptoms[32] to occur before considering some type of systematic process for project selection:

- The executives who want new products, but do not know or cannot agree on what kinds of projects in which to be interested.
- The laboratory crowded with development products, but with few new products coming out, and too many of these not paying off.
- The "orphan" project that goes on and on because nobody has given it much thought or had the heart to kill it.
- The "bottomless hole" product that took three times as long and cost five times as much as expected, and finally got to market behind all other competitors.

- The product with "bugs" that were hidden until 10,000 units came back from consumers.
- The "me too" product that has no competitive reason for existence.
- The scientific triumph that turned out to have no market value when someone thought to investigate it.

It is no wonder that companies waste large sums of money on projects that are not justified for commercial usefulness (excluding basic research). If the R&D project selection process is not aligned to the corporate posture, there will undoubtedly be a dissipation of critical resources.

The ideal situation is for a company to select a low risk project with a high payout. Unfortunately, this seldom happens, because most projects do not fall within these limits. Therefore, it is imperative for companies to develop some type of selection criteria.

Roussel[33] suggests that what is needed is a common language between management and R&D technical staff. He acknowledges that managers in American industry often lack a research background. He suggests that R&D and management learn to communicate comprehensibly and credibly by employing a series of simple tasks in project evaluation:

- Define the research objective in commercial and technical terms. The definition must specify all the successful technical steps required for commercialization.
- By a series of approximations, estimate the potential of real commercial reward.
- Redefine all the major technical steps in terms of assumptions, postulates, or theories that must be found valid for each to succeed.
- Determine whether the validity of these assumptions, postulates, or theories can be tested within the state of the art. Redefine any that are found untestable.
- Estimate the probability of conducting a conclusive test of each assumption, postulate, or theory with the desired level of research resources.
- Put the various tests in a logical and chronological sequence.
- Forecast the cost and time required for completion of crucial tests.
- Decide whether the risk-reward-time strategic relationships justify the project.

Roussel suggest that employing the eight-step process will make it possible to convert R&D uncertainties to risks, thus providing managers a rational basis for decision making.

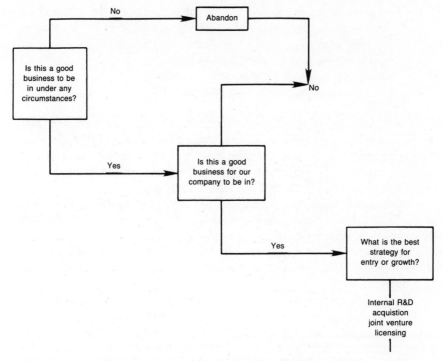

Fig. 6-7. Logical approach to project selection.

There are numerous approaches that companies can use for project selection. Figure 6-7 illustrates one such approach by asking a logical sequence of questions:[34]

- Is this a good business for anyone to be in?
  - —What is the probability of commercial success?
  - —What is the sales/profit potential?
  - —What is the yearly growth potential?
  - —How strong is the competition?
  - —Is the market easy or difficult for competitors to enter?
  - —How might competition react?
  - —What socio-political factors must be considered?
  - —Is there a value added by manufacturing?
- Is this a good business for us to be in?
  - —What are the risks to the company?
  - —What capital needs must be considered?
  - —Is our cash flow compatible with capital needs?

—Do we have the marketing/sales force to support the product?
—Is in-house manufacturing capability strong enough to support production?
—How strong is our technical capability?
—How strong is our management capability?
—Is raw material availability a problem?

These last eight questions require further comment. Some companies may not be willing to accept the risks of developing a new product (even if considered to be profitable) because it may be *too good* of a fit with the other products (all your eggs in one basket). In other words, if capital is limited, it may be best to undertake those projects that can lead to diversification.

Although a product that requires a small amount of capital may be a low financial risk to the company, the overall risk to the company may be quite high if it invites competition. On the other hand, a capital intensive project may serve as a barrier to entry for the competition but requires a better understanding of the potential risks. High capital intensive projects require reasonably good cash flows.

All too often, companies forecast a market need or an untapped market niche and proceed "full speed ahead" without giving serious thought to the availability of an adequate marketing/sales force. Training a new sales force or developing a new marketing approach may take years. By the time that the training is completed, the lifecycle of the product could be expired, the product could be obsolete, the market niche could disappear, or a new technology could have been developed. In any case, if training is necessary, it should be done concurrently with product development if at all possible.

Manufacturing capability is a decisive factor in project selection. Simply because the R&D personnel have the capability to develop the product and the associated pilot plant and prototype, does not imply that full commercial production capability exists. Developing manufacturing capability concurrently with development may not be possible until the design and performance specifications are frozen. One alternative to this would be to delay commercial production until the prototype is complete; this may result in late market entry and a large loss in profits. A second alternative may be to subcontract the manufacturing, but this places the company at the mercy of the subcontractors. An untimely increase in the subcontractor's costs could eliminate all profits, if the margins are already tight.

Technical capability strength is measured in four areas: R&D, production, customer service, and patent protection. Simply maintaining a strong R&D group does not mean that the company can respond quickly to changes in the state-of-the-art, customer application engineering, or customer service. To compete effectively, a company's technical base should be at least at the same strength as that of the competition.

The most frequently documented cause of failure of potentially good products is due to the fact that the company does not know how to manage a newly acquired product line. As an example, Company A buys out Company B in order to diversify. Company B has several new products, many of which have solid potential. However, the executives in Company A believe that both companies should be managed the same. The moral is to diversify into areas in which you possess the managerial skills.

Full scale commercialization of a new product requires accessibility to raw materials. It is not uncommon for a company to select those projects for development that fit their suppliers, even though other higher profit potential projects are available. Obviously, the best situation and least risk would be to select high profit potential projects which fit a backwards integration strategy.

For the R&D selection process to be meaningful, there must exist a systematic approach based upon a well-defined criteria. For military application, the following approach may be useful:

- Cost-benefit ratio. This criterion involved comparing the cost required to complete the research project with the advantages to be received by the Air Force because of its successful completion. Formal procedures existed for performing such comparisons.
- Technical merit. This criterion involved arriving at a judgment regarding the extent to which the research project provided a new or better technical capability to the Air Force. This process was administratively formalized but subjective in nature, as estimates of the future were involved.
- Resource availability. This criterion involved a decision about the availability of the appropriate personnel, equipment, facilities, and other resources needed to complete the research project. In general, this factor was concerned with the capability to perform the required research involved in the proposed project.
- Likelihood of success. This criterion was concerned with the likelihood that the proposed research project would achieve technical success, given its planned time and resource constraints. The likelihood involved resulted from subjective probability estimates.
- Time period. This criterion involved the length of time that was required to complete the proposed research project. In general, with all other things equal, relatively short research projects were favored over relatively long research projects. It was generally agreed that extremely long research projects have almost no chance of being selected, given the resource constraints that existed at the time of the study.

- Air Force need. This criterion involved examining the extent to which it had been established that an actual need existed within the Air Force for the technical capability to be provided by a particular research project.

For industrial applications, the criteria list must be subdivided into two parts: a business criteria list[35] and an R&D criteria list.[36]

- Business enterprise R&D criteria.
    —Ratio of research costs to profits
    —Percentage of total earnings due to new products
    —Share of market due to new products
    —Research costs related to increases in sales
    —Research costs to ratio of new and old sales
    —Research costs per employee
    —Research costs as a ratio of administrative and selling costs
    —Cash flows
    —Research audits
    —Weighted averages of costs and objectives
    —Project profiles
- Some suitability criteria.
    —Similar in technology
    —Similar marketing methods are used
    —Similar distribution channels are used
    —Can be sold by current sales force
    —Will be purchased by same customers as current products
    —Fits the company philosophy or image
    —Uses existing know-how or expertise
    —Fits current production facilities
    —Both research and marketing personnel are enthusiastic
    —Fits the company long range plan
    —Fits current profit goals

The need for two lists should be obvious. Regardless how well a new product idea fits the business criteria list, the organization must have adequate resources for support.

The criteria list can be transformed into rating models as shown in Figs. 6-8, 6-9, and 6-10. Unfortunately, these criteria must be further elaborated, such as in Table 6-3, so that a clear understanding of the criteria is available to all evaluators.[37]

6.36 STRATEGY READJUSTMENT

Many R&D projects are managed by overly optimistic prima donnas who truly believe that they can develop any type of product if left alone and provided with

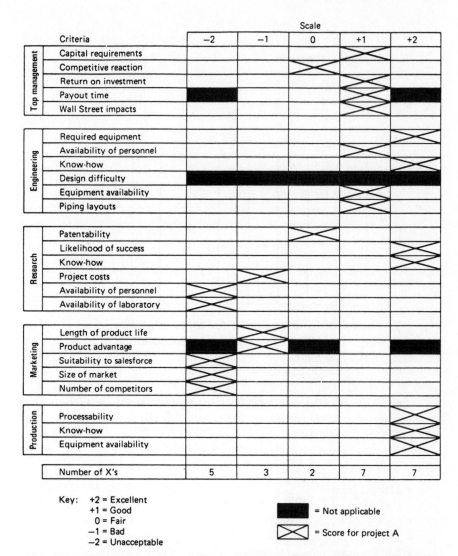

Fig. 6-8. Illustration of a scaling model for one project, Project A.
Source: William E. Souder, Project Selection and Economic Appraisal,
Van Nostrand, 1984, p. 66.

sufficient funding. Unfortunately, such projects never end, because the R&D managers either do not know when the project is over (poor understanding of the objectives) or do not want the project to end (exceeding objectives). In either event, periodic project review and readjustment action must be considered.

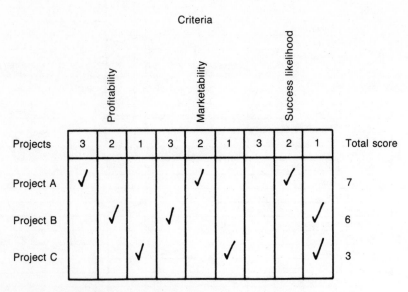

Fig. 6-9. Illustration of a checklist for three projects.
Source: William Souder, **Project Selection & Economic Appraisal,** *Van Nostrand, 1984, p. 68.*

The primary reason for periodic review is to reassess the risks based upon current strategic thinking and project performance. Souder has identified several types of project risks:[38]

- Technical failure.
- Market failure.
- Failure to perform.
- Failure to finish on time.
- Research failure.
- Development failure.
- Engineering failure.
- Production failure.
- User acceptance failure.
- Unforeseen events.
- Insurmountable technical obstacles.
- Unexpected outcomes.
- Inadequate know-how.
- Legal/Regulatory uncertainties.

Criteria	Profitability	Patentability	Marketability	Produceability
Criterion Weights	4	3	2	1

Projects	Criterion scores*				Total Weighted Score
Project D	10	6	4	3	69
Project E	5	10	10	5	75
Project F	3	7	10	10	63

Total weighted Score = $\sum$, Criterion score, X Criterion Weight

*Scale: 10 = excellent; 1 = Unacceptable

Fig. 6-10. *Illustration of a scoring model.*
Source: *William Souder*, Project Selection and Economic Appraisal, Van Nostrand, 1984, p. 69.

Project risks generally result in project selection readjustment. Souder has also provided a list of readjustment actions:[39]

- Replanning project.
- Readjusting portfolio of projects.
- Reallocating funds.
- Rescheduling project.
- Backlogging project.
- Reprioritizing projects.
- Terminating project.
- Replacement with backlogged project.
- Replacement with new project.

Table 6-3. Factor and Subfactor Ratings for a New Product
Source: Robert R. Rothberg, Corporate Strategy and Product Innovation, Second Edition, The Free Press, Addison and MacMillan Publishing Co., Inc., 1981, p. 316, 317, 318.

	Very Good	Good	Average	Poor	Very Poor
I. Marketability					
A. Relation to present distribution channels	Can reach major markets by distributing through present channels.	Can reach major markets by distributing mostly through present channels, partly through new channels.	Will have to distribute equally between new and present channels, in order to reach major markets.	Will have to distribute mostly through new channels in order to reach major markets.	Will have to distribute entirely through new channels in order to reach major markets.
B. Relation to present product lines	Complements a present line which needs more products to fill it.	Complements a present line that does not need, but can handle, another product.	Can be fitted into a present line.	Can be fitted into a present line but does not fit entirely.	Does not fit in with any present product line.
C. Quality/price relationship	Priced below all competing products of similar quality.	Priced below most competing products of similar quality.	Approximately the same price as competing products of similar quality.	Priced above many competing products of similar quality.	Priced above all competing products of similar quality.
D. Number of sizes and grades	Few staple sizes and grades.	Several sizes and grades, but customers will be satisfied with few staples.	Several sizes and grades, but can satisfy customer wants with small inventory of nonstaples.	Several sizes and grades, each of which will have to be stocked in equal amounts.	Many sizes and grades which will necessitate heavy inventories.
E. Merchandisability	Has product characteristics over and above those of competing products that lend themselves to the kind of promotion, advertising, and display that the given company does best.	Has promotable characteristics that will compare favorably with the characteristics of competing products.	Has promotable characteristics that are equal to those of other products.	Has a few characteristics that are promotable, but generally does not measure up to characteristics of competing products.	Has no characteristics at all that are equal to competitors' or that lend themselves to imaginative promotion.
F. Effects on sales of present products	Should aid in sales of present products.	May help sales of present products; definitely will not be harmful to present sales.	Should have no effect on present sales.	May hinder present sales some; definitely will not aid present sales.	Will reduce sales of presently profitable

II. Durability

A. Stability	Basic product which can always expect to have uses.	Product which will have uses long enough to earn back initial investment, plus at least 10 years of additional profits.	Product which will have uses long enough to earn back initial investment, plus several (from 5 to 10) years of additional profits.	Product which will have uses long enough to earn back initial investment, plus 1 to 5 years of additional profits.	Product which will probably be obsolete in near future.
B. Breadth of market	A national market, a wide variety of consumers, and a potential foreign market.	A national market and a wide variety of consumers.	Either a national market or a wide variety of consumers.	A regional market and a restricted variety of consumers.	A specialized market in a small marketing area.
C. Resistance to cyclical fluctuations	Will sell readily inflation or depression.	Effects of cyclical changes will be *moderate*, and will be felt *after* changes in economic outlook.	Sales will rise and fall with the economy.	Effects of cyclical changes will be *heavy*, and will be felt *before* changes in economic outlook.	Cyclical changes will cause extreme fluctuations in demand.
D. Resistance to seasonal fluctuations	Steady sales throughout the year.	Steady sales—except under unusual circumstances.	Seasonal fluctuations, but inventory and personnel problems can be absorbed.	Heavy seasonal fluctuations that will cause considerable inventory and personnel problems.	Severe seasonal fluctuations that will necessitate layoffs and heavy inventories.
E. Exclusiveness of design	Can be protected by a patent with no loopholes.	Can be patented, but the patent might be circumvented.	Cannot be patented, but has certain salient characteristics that cannot be copied very well.	Cannot be patented, and can be copied by larger, more knowledgeable companies.	Cannot be patented, and can be copied by anyone.

III. Productive Ability

A. Equipment necessary	Can be produced with equipment that is presently idle.	Can be produced with present equipment, but production will have to be scheduled with other products.	Can be produced largely with present equipment, but the company will have to purchase some additional equipment.	Company will have to buy a good deal of new equipment, but some present equipment can be used.	Company will have to buy all new equipment.

Table 6-3. (continued)

	Very Good	Good	Average	Poor	Very Poor
B. Production knowledge and personnel necessary	Present knowledge and personnel will be able to produce new product.	With very few minor exceptions, present knowledge and personnel will be able to produce new product.	With some exceptions, present knowledge and personnel will be able to produce new product.	A ratio of approximately 50-50 will prevail between the needs for new knowledge and personnel and for present knowledge and personnel.	Mostly new knowledge and personnel are needed to produce the new product.
C. Raw materials' availability	Company can purchase raw materials from its best supplier(s) exclusively.	Company can purchase major portion of raw materials from its best supplier(s), and remainder from any one of a number of companies.	Company can purchase approximately half of raw materials from its best supplier(s), and other half from any one of a number of companies.	Company must purchase most of raw materials from any one of a number of companies other than its best supplier(s).	Company must purchase most or all of raw materials from a certain few companies other than its best supplier(s).
IV. Growth Potential					
A. Place in market	New type of product that will fill a need presently not being filled.	Product that will substantially improve on products presently on the market.	Product that will have certain new characteristics that will appeal to a substantial segment of the market.	Product that will have minor improvements over products presently on the market.	Product similar to those presently on the market and which adds nothing new.
B. Expected competitive situation— value added	Very high value added so as to substantially restrict number of competitors.	High enough value added so that, unless product is extremely well suited to other firms, they will not want to invest in additional facilities.	High enough value added so that, unless other companies are as strong in market as this firm, it will not be profitable for them to compete.	Lower value added so as to allow large, medium, and some smaller companies to compete.	Very low value added so that all companies can profitably enter
C. Expected availability of end users	Number of end users will increase substantially.	Number of end users will increase moderately.	Number of end users will increase slightly, if at all.	Number of end users will decrease moderately.	Number of end users will decrease substantially.

6.37 PROJECT TERMINATION

Previously, we stated that R&D projects should be periodically reviewed so that readjustment actions can be taken. One technique for readjustment is to terminate the project. The following are the most common reasons and indications that termination is necessary:

- Final achievement of the objectives. This is obviously the best of all possible reasons.
- Poor initial planning and market prognosis. This could be caused by a loss of interest in the project by the marketing personnel or an overly optimistic initial strategy.
- A better alternative has been found. This could be caused by finding a new approach that has a higher likelihood of success.
- A change in the company interest and strategy. This could be caused by a loss of the market, major changes in the market, development of a new strategy or simply a lack of commitment and enthusiasm of project personnel.
- Allocated time has been exceeded.
- Budgeted costs have been exceeded.
- Key people have left the organization. This could be caused by a major change in the technical difficulty of the project with the departure of key scientists who had the specialized knowledge.
- Personal whims of management. This could be caused by the loss of interest by senior management.
- Problem too complex for the resources available. This could be caused by an optimistic initial view when, in fact, the project has insurmountable technological hurdles which did not appear until well into the project.

Executives normally employ one or more of the following methods to terminate the R&D projects:

- Orderly planned termination.
- The hatchet (withdrawal of funds and cutting of personnel).
- Reassignment of people to higher priority projects.
- Redirection of efforts toward different objectives or strategies.
- Bury it or let it die on the vine.

R&D personnel are highly motivated and hate to see projects terminate in mid-stream. Executives must carefully assess the risks and morale effects of project termination.

6.38 STRATEGIC BUDGETING FOR R&D

Formulation of the R&D budget is a complex mechanism involving feedback loops and decision methodologies. As was the case with project screening and planning, several questions must be considered in analyzing the environment:

- Company strategy.
  - —First in with new product.
  - —Close follower to industry leader.
  - —Produce a "me-too" product.
- Technological effort.
  - —Present size of R&D effort.
  - —Level of morale of R&D staff which, in part, is due to freedom to choose interesting and challenging projects.
  - —State of the art of the technology utilized now and required in the future.
- Financial considerations.
  - —Availability of money from internal or external sources to fund both the technical segment as well as the commercial segment of the innovation.
  - —Return on investment in R&D projects versus investment in other projects such as purchasing new product machinery or building a new warehouse.
  - —Requirements for stable financial support for R&D.
- Production capability.
  - —Availability or ability of the production facilities to produce the new innovation at a competitive cost.
- Market conditions.
  - —Highly competitive versus stable market environment.
  - —Length of the product lifecycle.
  - —Profit opportunities or market niches.

Unfortunately, many of the environmental questions identified above do not carry equal weight. The authors have found that, most often, financial considerations may dominate. The following list further expands the financial considerations:

- What are the risks?
  - —Technical risk is often quite modest.
  - —Commercial risk is often substantial.
- What makes for success?
  - —Economic success is the product of three separate factors: the

probability of technical success, the probability of commercialization, and/or the probability of economic success.

—A close link between marketing and R&D is a must.

• What is the right portfolio?

—The right proportion of low-risk R&D activity and technically more ambitious projects whose probability of economic success is higher is needed.

—A good mix of both long-term and short-term projects is important.

—Economic evaluation of both project proposals and continuing projects using rate of return or discounted cash flow methods is necessary.

• What is the rate of return?

—The rate is different for products than for processes.

—There is both a private rate and a social rate.

—A generous time horizon is needed by senior management, because short-term fluctuations in returns do occur.[40]

Budgeting methodologies range from "what the chief executive wants" to some very analytical models that are organized in highly logical and consistent steps. These steps, which may use the above questions as a basis, are necessary to determine the level of the R&D budget so that requirements can be specified for:

• Manpower/management-planning activities.
• Facilities/services.
• Capital equipment expenditures.
• Documentation.

Also, the budgeting environmental activities attempt to identify the following major elements of the financial plan:

• Source of Funds (Where?).
• Allocation of Costs (To Whom?).
• Funding Decision-Makers (By Whom?).
• Schedules and Milestones (When and How?).

A major consideration in any budgeting process is the ability to identify those features that distinguish an effective budget from an ineffective one. According to Bunge,[41] there are seven major considerations involving high-risk ventures:

• The budget is built around people. R&D budgets must be built around and controlled through the human and nonhuman resources, not by the reports, account classifications, or computer printouts.

- The budget must have the support of top management. Continuous support by top management should create enthusiasm for lower level managers. Likewise, if top management simply provides lip service, lack of enthusiasm will appear down the entire line and budgeting controls may be disregarded.
- The budget must be realistic. Unrealistic budgets cause people to lose respect for the project. Unfortunately, many managers and executives set unrealistic budgets on the assumption that the budget will eventually be overrun. Enthusiastic executives normally set a budget slightly more than what is needed in hopes that R&D managers will be motivated enough to exceed performance requirements.
- The budget is flexible. Because the R&D environment is extremely turbulent and uncertain, flexible budgets are a must in R&D. Inflexible budgets are merely a series of appropriations and are appropriate to static rather than dynamic operations.
- The budget is comprehensive and complete. A good budget includes all types of income and all types of expenditures. Good budgets include every area and every level of responsibility from the president's office on down.
- The budget is based upon information, communication, and participation. A good budget is a synthesis, not an analysis. It is developed through participation of all who have a hand in spending the company's money and upon whom management has placed the responsibility of some measure of authority.
- There is an effective program of follow-up. Good planning alone does not assure success. There must exist a method for follow-up such that tradeoffs on time, cost and performance can be made. Follow-up is usually accomplished with reports which identify the slippages or variations from the target, as well as an explanation of the corrective action to be taken and the impact on the constraints of time, cost and performance.

6.39 CONTROLLING COSTS

Top management must retain a fair amount of cost control for these types of projects. As stated earlier, resources are becoming more scarce and R&D, by its very nature, is a high-risk operation. Simply monitoring a project is not adequate. There must be a cost and control system in place.

Controlling is a three-step process of measuring progress toward an objective, evaluating what needs to be done, and taking the necessary corrective action to achieve or exceed the objectives.

The project manager is basically responsible for ensuring the accomplishment of group and organizational goals and objectives.

Effective management of a program during the operating cycle requires that a well-organized cost and control system be designed, developed, and implemented so that immediate feedback can be obtained in order that the up-to-date usage of resources can be compared to those which were established as target objectives during the planning cycle. The requirements for an effective control system (for both cost and schedule/performance) should include:

- Thorough planning of work to be performed to complete project.
- Good estimating of time, labor, and costs.
- Clear communication of scope and required tasks.
- Disciplined budget and authorization of expenditures.
- Timely accounting of physical progress and cost expenditures.
- Periodic re-estimation of time and cost to completion.
- Frequent, periodic comparison of actual progress and expenditures to schedules and budgets both at the time of comparison and at project completion.

This periodic appraisal allows for tracking and reporting as well as reapportionment of committed funds. After initiation of most R&D programs, they quickly fall into the following categories:

- Project right on stream.
- Project ahead of progress plans.
- Project has encountered unforeseen problems.
- Project is in real trouble.
- Project requires major enlargement and/or acceleration.

Projects falling into the first two categories are not major problems and fortunately, comprise the majority of R&D programs. The latter three categories can cause major revisions to both the budget and funding exercises. The "unforeseen problem" project may result in being a fund contributor to other projects if the problem is identified as not being able to effectively utilize appropriated funds. The "real trouble" project must be watched closely, and continuance of the project may result in disaster, because the project manager is not prone to killing his own project.

The fifth project may result when technological break-throughs or new vistas are gained during the original project. Additional funds required may necessitate reductions or elimination of other projects. This may require a totally new process of budgeting and funding and may also hold the greatest future rewards for the company.

6.40 LIFECYCLE COSTING (LCC)

For years, many R&D organizations have operated in a vacuum, where technical decisions made during R&D were based entirely upon the R&D portion of the plan with little regard for what happens after production begins. Today, industrial firms are adopting the *lifecycle costing* approach that has been developed and used by military organizations. Simply stated, LCC requires that decisions made during the R&D process be evaluated against the total lifecycle cost of the system. As an example, the R&D group has two possible design configurations for a new product. Both design configurations will require the same budget for R&D and the same costs for manufacturing. However, the maintenance and support costs may be substantially greater for one of the products. If these downstream costs are not considered in the R&D phase, large unanticipated expenses may result.

Lifecycle costs are the total cost to the organization for the ownership and acquisition of the product over its full life. This includes the cost of R&D, production, operation, support, and, where applicable, disposal. A typical breakdown description might include:

R&D Costs. The cost of feasibility studies; cost/benefit analyses; system analyses; detail design and development; fabrication, assembly, and test of engineering models; initial product evaluation; and associated documentation.

Production Cost. The cost of fabrication, assembly and testing of production models; operation and maintenance of the production capability; and associated internal logistic support requirements including test and support equipment development, spare/repair parts provisioning, technical data development, training, and entry of items into inventory.

Construction Cost. The cost of manufacturing facilities or upgrading existing structures to accommodate production and operation of support requirements.

Operation and Maintenance Cost. The cost of sustaining operational personnel and maintenance support, spare/repair parts and related inventories, test and support equipment maintenance, transportation and handling, facilities, modifications and technical data changes, and so on.

Product Retirement and Phaseout Cost. The cost of phasing the product out of inventory due to obsolescence or wearout, and subsequent equipment item recycling and reclamation as appropriate.

Lifecycle cost analysis is the systematic analytical process of evaluating various alternative courses of action early on in a project with the objective of choosing the best way to employ scarce resources. Lifecycle cost is employed in the evaluation of alternative design configurations, alternative manufacturing methods, alternative support schemes, and so on. This process includes:

• Define the problem (what information is needed).

- Define the requirements of cost model being used.
- Collect historical data/cost relationships.
- Develop estimate and test results.

Successful application of LCC will:

- Provide downstream resource impact visibility.
- Provide lifecycle cost management.
- Influence R&D decision-making.
- Support downstream strategic budgeting.

There are also several limitations to lifecycle cost analyses. They include the assumption that the product has a known, finite lifecycle, that it has a high cost to produce and may not be appropriate for low cost/low volume production, and that it has a high sensitivity to changing requirements.

Lifecycle costing requires estimates to be made. The estimating method selected is based upon the problem context (decisions to be made, required accuracy, complexity of the product, and the development status of the product), and the operational considerations (market introduction date, time available for analysis, and available resources).

The estimating methods available can be classified as follows:

- Informal estimating methods.
  —Judgment based on experience
  —Analogy
  —SWAG method
  —ROM method
  —Rule of Thumb method
- Formal estimating methods.
  —Detailed (from Industrial Engineering Standards)
  —Parametric

Table 6-4 shows the advantages/disadvantages of each method.

Figure 6-11 shows the various lifecycle phases for Department of Defense projects. At the end of the demonstration and validation phase (which is at the completion of R&D), 85 percent of the decisions affecting the total lifecycle cost will have been made, and the cost reduction opportunity is limited to a maximum of 22 percent (excluding the effects of learning curve experiences). Figure 6-12 shows that, at the end of the R&D phase, 95 percent of the cumulative lifecycle cost is committed by the government. Figure 6-13 shows that for every $12 that DOD puts into R&D, $28 are needed downstream for production and $60 for operation and support.

**Table 6-4. Advantages and Disadvantages
of Informal and Formal Estimating Methods**

Estimating Technique	Application	Advantages	Disadvantages
Engineering Estimates	Reprocurement	*Most detailed technique	*Requires detailed program and product definition
	Production Development	*Best inherent accuracy *Provides best estimating base for future program change estimates	*Time consuming and may be expensive *Subject to engineering bias *May overlook system integration costs
Empirical			
Parametric Estimates and Scaling	Production and low cost Development	*Application is simple	*Requires parametric cost relationships to be established
		*Statistical data base can provide expected values and prediction intervals	*Limited frequently to specific subsystems or functional hardware of systems
Statistical		*Can be used for equipment or systems prior to detail design or program planning	*Depends on quantity and quality of the data base *Limited by data and number of independent variables
Equipment/Subsystem Analogy Estimates	Reprocurement	*Relatively simple	*Require analogous product and program data
	Production Development	*Low cost *Emphasizes incremental program and product changes	*Limited to stable technology *Narrow range of electronic applications
Comparative	Program Planning	*Good accuracy for similar systems	*May be limited to systems and equipment built by the same firm
Expert Opinion	All Program Phases	*Available when there are insufficient data, parametric cost relationships, or program/product definition	*Subject to bias *Increased product or program complexity can degrade estimates *Estimate substantiation is not quantifiable

Lifecycle cost analysis is an integral part of strategic planning, because today's decisions will affect tomorrow's actions. Yet there are common errors made during lifecycle cost analyses:

- Loss or omission of data.
- Lack of systematic structure.
- Misinterpretation of data.
- Wrong or misused technique.
- Concentration on insignificant facts.
- Failure to assess uncertainty.
- Failure to check work.
- Estimating wrong items.

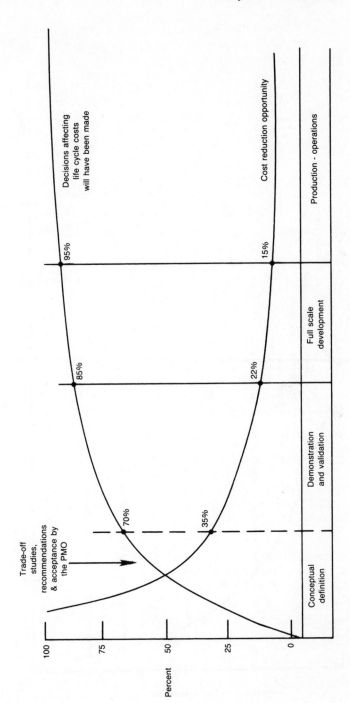

Fig. 6-11. Lifecycle phases for Department of Defense projects.

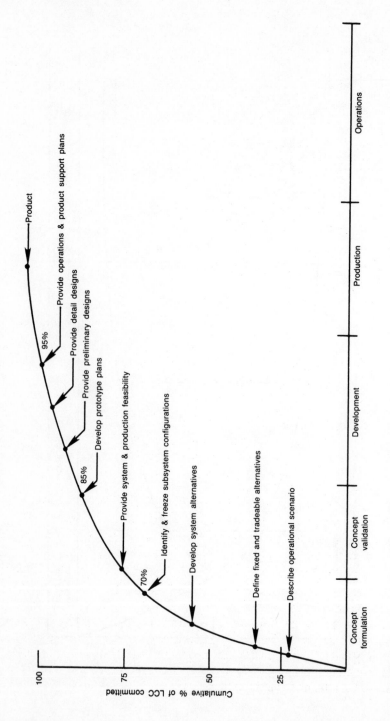

Fig. 6-12. Actions affecting lifecycle cost (LCC).

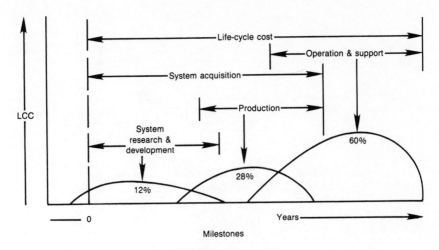

Typical Communication System Acquisition LCC Profile

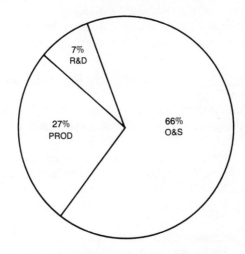

Fig. 6-13. Downstream production and operations costs.

6.41 INTEGRATING R&D INTO THE STRATEGIC PLAN

In the previous sections, we indicated that proper coupling of R&D to marketing and manufacturing is a necessity to integrate R&D into the strategic plan. Figure 6-14 illustrates the degrees of downstream coupling. There are several reasons why companies prefer strong downstream coupling. First, as described previously under lifecycle costing, downstream costs such as service engineering must be considered during R&D tradeoffs. Second, R&D planning and decision-making must attempt to minimize the disruptive effects on manufacturing. Third,

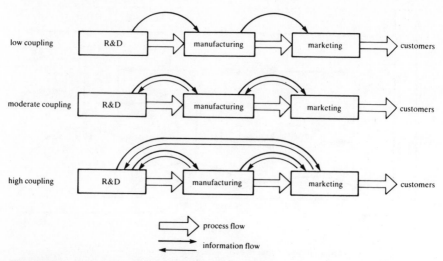

low coupling

moderate coupling

high coupling

R&D — manufacturing — marketing — customers

process flow
information flow

Fig. 6-14. Degrees of downstream coupling.
Source: H. Igor Ansoff, Implanting Strategic Management, *Prentice-Hall International, Englewood Cliffs, New Jersey, 1984, p. 122.*

R&D must be planned for with consideration for the quality control efforts needed in manufacturing.

Highly coupled systems are generally dynamic rather than static and respond better to changes in the strategic planning system. Figure 6-15 shows the matrix that couples R&D plans to the business objectives. For a highly dynamic, highly coupled system, there exists a continuous reassessment of the technical efforts necessary to support the business-technical portfolio.

Quinn and Mueller[42] have developed a four-step program to improve the flow of technical innovation from research into operations:

Step 1. Examine technological transfer points.
- Analyze the critical points across which technology must flow if it is to be successfully exploited.
- Recognize the potential resistances to the flow at each of these interfaces.

Step II. Provide information to target research.
- Generate adequate information so that research can be targeted toward company goals and needs.
- Develop a comprehensive long-range planning program to determine what technology is relevant to the company's future and to serve as a focal point for information flows.
- Establish special organizations, where needed, to seek specific new technological opportunities for the company, to provide commercial

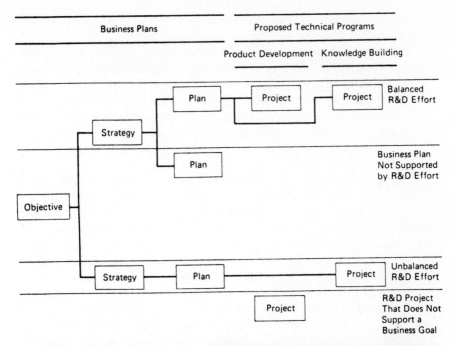

***Fig. 6-15. Matrix that couples R&D plans and business objectives.
Source: James F. Lyons, "Strategic Management and Strategic
Planning in the 1980's,"* The Strategic Management Handbook,
*Kenneth J. Albert, Editor-in-Chief, McGraw-Hill, 1983, p. 3.***

intelligence information about competitive activities, and to make careful economic evaluations of technologically based new ventures.

Step III. Foster a positive motivational environment.
- Establish a motivational environment which actively stimulates technological progress and its associated organizational change.
- Develop tough-minded top-management attitudes, policies, and long-range term controls which foster—rather than hinder—the production and use of new technologies.

Step IV. Plan and control exploitation of R&D results.
- Design special exploitation organizations and procedures to ensure (a) that competent groups have both the authority and the obligation to develop new technologies at each of their critical stages; (b) that each major technological transfer is planned and monitored to control effort expenditures, cash flows, and timing; and (c) that the entire transfer system implements the critical strategy—which determines success or failure—at each major technological transfer point.

Quinn and Mueller also provide an example of a company that has knitted all of the pieces together into one well-developed plan:[43]

- A large chemical company regularly follows this planning procedure. It prepares its long-range plan semiannually, in conjunction with its operating and capital budgets—each of which extends five years into the future. The executive committee—acting on information from a central long-range planning staff—establishes overall company objectives for the next five years. These objectives—specifying "what" should be done and "when" it should be done—are fed down to operating and service groups, who then draw up specific programs to meet them.

Each program tells "how" the organization will effect its part of the company's objectives and estimates the financial implications (both capital and expense) of the program. The central staff group and a long-range planning committee work with each group to see that each program is coordinated with other phases of the total corporate plan. Special subcommittees then review each of the final budgets before they go to the long-range planning committee and executive committee for final recommendations and approval.

Here is how research needs and aspirations are fitted into the long-range plan. Working from technological forecasts and past program information, research draws up a tentative program. It checks this with each major operating division and with the key corporate executives individually. It then draws up a modified program (and budgets) and submits this to a formal review by the research subcommittee which looks for issues of balance, project priorities, and program scope. The long-range planning committee makes a few final recommendations, sees that operating division plans adequately anticipate research technology, and then sends the final plans to the executive committee for approval. Of course, throughout the entire process there is a constant modification of objectives and plans as mutual interaction dictates.

The coupling of R&D to marketing is extremely critical, especially in organizations with short product lifecycle. Figure 6-16 shows the two-dimensional characteristics of products classified by product objectives. Figure 6-16 can be transformed into Fig. 6-17 to show the relationship of new product responsibilities by department. Regions where there exists joint responsibilities indicates the need for highly coupled downstream integration of people and activities.

Frohman and Bitondo have indicated several ways that technical strategy can be coupled to business strategy:[44]

- Positioning the R&D strategy from defensive to offensive, depending on the market attractiveness and business position (Fig. 6-18).
- Posturing of the R&D effort with the spectrum from state-of-the-art research (technology invention) to prototype development (minor application

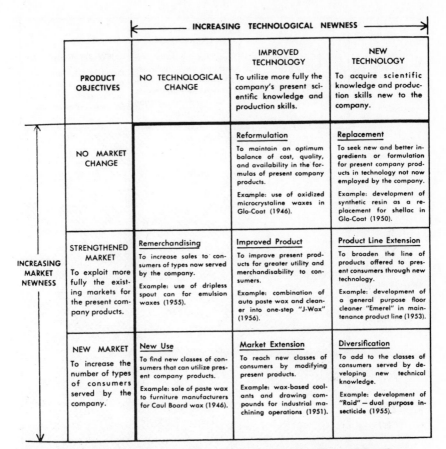

← INCREASING TECHNOLOGICAL NEWNESS →

INCREASING MARKET NEWNESS ↓

PRODUCT OBJECTIVES	NO TECHNOLOGICAL CHANGE	IMPROVED TECHNOLOGY To utilize more fully the company's present scientific knowledge and production skills.	NEW TECHNOLOGY To acquire scientific knowledge and production skills new to the company.
NO MARKET CHANGE		Reformulation To maintain an optimum balance of cost, quality, and availability in the formulas of present company products. Example: use of oxidized microcrystaline waxes in Glo-Coat (1946).	Replacement To seek new and better ingredients or formulation for present company products in technology not now employed by the company. Example: development of synthetic resin as a replacement for shellac in Glo-Coat (1950).
STRENGTHENED MARKET To exploit more fully the existing markets for the present company products.	Remerchandising To increase sales to consumers of types now served by the company. Example: use of dripless spout can for emulsion waxes (1955).	Improved Product To improve present products for greater utility and merchandisability to consumers. Example: combination of auto paste wax and cleaner into one-step "J-Wax" (1956).	Product Line Extension To broaden the line of products offered to present consumers through new technology. Example: development of a general purpose floor cleaner "Emerel" in maintenance product line (1953).
NEW MARKET To increase the number of types of consumers served by the company.	New Use To find new classes of consumers that can utilize present company products. Example: sale of paste wax to furniture manufacturers for Caul Board wax (1946).	Market Extension To reach new classes of consumers by modifying present products. Example: wax-based coolants and drawing compounds for industrial machining operations (1951).	Diversification To add to the classes of consumers served by developing new technical knowledge. Example: development of "Raid" — dual purpose insecticide (1955).

Fig. 6-16. Classification of new products by product objective. Source: Robert R. Rothberg,* Corporate Strategy and Product Innovation, *Second Edition, The Free Press, 1981, p. 191.

of existing technology), depending on product line need and Market Share Strategy (Fig. 6-19).

- R&D meeting objectives ranging from eliminating products to developing new products to new specifications (Fig. 6-20).
- Matching the needs of the product, depending where it is in the lifecycle requiring R&D from product innovation to cost reduction (Fig. 6-21).

After the investment and product line needs have been defined, the functional responsibility for reaching the goals and the role of R&D must be determined.[45] Note that from Fig. 6-20, for a product strategy relying on existing products,

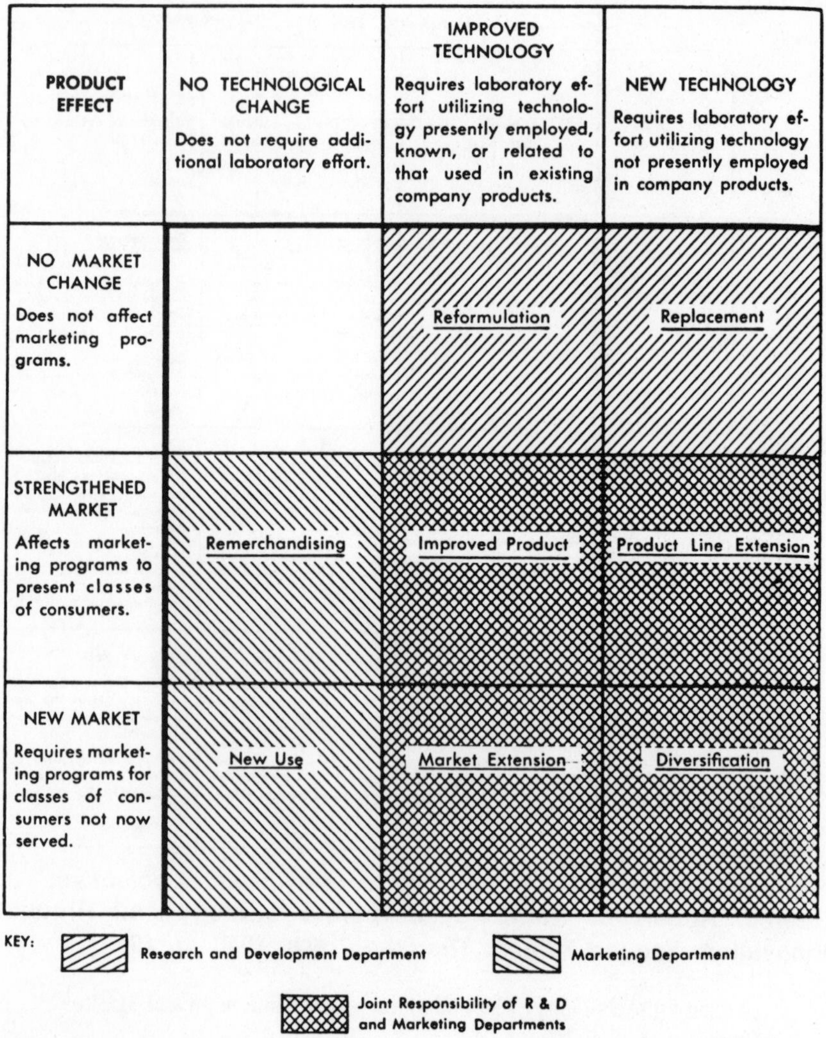

PRODUCT EFFECT	NO TECHNOLOGICAL CHANGE	IMPROVED TECHNOLOGY	NEW TECHNOLOGY
	Does not require additional laboratory effort.	Requires laboratory effort utilizing technology presently employed, known, or related to that used in existing company products.	Requires laboratory effort utilizing technology not presently employed in company products.
NO MARKET CHANGE Does not affect marketing programs.		Reformulation	Replacement
STRENGTHENED MARKET Affects marketing programs to present classes of consumers.	Remerchandising	Improved Product	Product Line Extension
NEW MARKET Requires marketing programs for classes of consumers not now served.	New Use	Market Extension	Diversification

KEY:

⬚ Research and Development Department	⬚ Marketing Department

⬚ Joint Responsibility of R & D and Marketing Departments

Fig. 6-17. Relationship of new product responsibilities by department. Source: Robert R. Rothberg, Corporate Strategy and Product Innovation, Second Edition, The Free Press, 1981, p. 192.

a market strategy is mainly required. For improved or new products, the emphasis is placed on the technology strategy for each product. The function responsible for leading and developing the specific strategy for each product will depend on the emphasis of the strategy. The implications of the investment strategy for the R&D strategy is shown on Fig. 6-22. This chart is intended

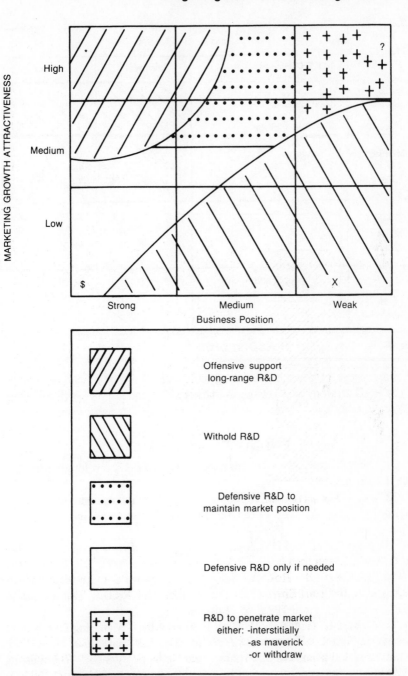

Fig. 6-18. Positioning the R&D strategy.

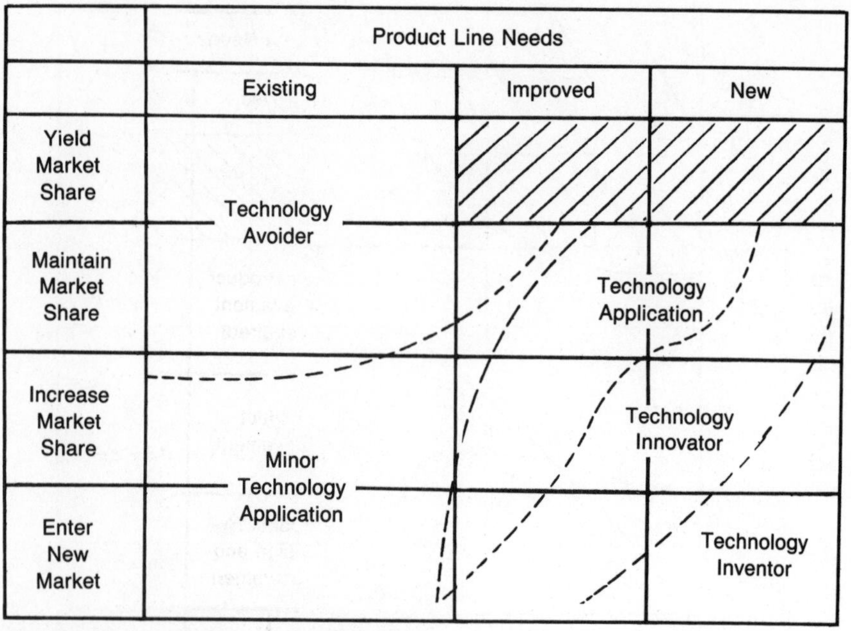

Fig. 6-19. Posturing of R&D effort.

for the purpose of general positioning and getting correlation and agreement on the R&D strategy as it relates to market share and sales growth rate (Fig. 6-22).

ENDNOTES—Chapter 6

1. Philip Kotler, *Marketing Management, 4th Ed.* (New Jersey: Prentice Hall, 1980), p. 314.

2. D. G. Marquis, "The Anatomy of Successful Innovations," *Managing Advancing Technology*, American Management Associations, Inc., 1972, Vol. 1, pp. 35-48.

3. Allen, Booz, and Hamilton, "Management of New Products," 1968, pp. 7-12.

4. E. Mansfield and S. Wagner, "Organizational and Strategic Factors Associated with Probabilities of Success in Industrial R&D," *The Journal of Business*, No. 48, April 1978, pp. 179-196.

5. Robert H. Hayes and William J. Abernathy, "Managing Our Way to Economic Decline," *Harvard Business Review*, July-Aug. 1980, pp. 67-77.

6. Adapted from Alan L. Frohman and Domenic Bitondo, "Coordinating Business Strategy and Technical Planning," *Long Range Planning*, Vol. 14, No. 6, Dec. 1981, pp. 58-67.

		Product Line Needs		
		Existing	Improved	New
Market Share Strategy	Yield Market Share	Reduce Products	///////	///////
	Maintain Market Share	Consolidate Products	Minor Product Improvement (if required)	New Product Existing Specifications
	Increase Market Share	Reduce Cost of Products	Product Improvement	New Product Improved Specifications
	Enter New Market	Apply Products to New Uses	Product Re-Design and Improvement	Diversification
	Functional Responsibility	↑ Marketing: Market Strategy	↑ Engineering: Product Development	↑ Research: Basic and Applied R&D

Fig. 6-20. R&D meeting objectives.

7. J. G. Wisseman, "Industrial R&D Prepares for the Eighties," *Research Management*, Vol. 22, No. 5, Sept. 1979, pp. 22-26.

8. Alan L. Frohman and Domenic Bitondo, "Coordinating Business Strategy and Technical Planning," *Long Range Planning*, Vol. 14, No. 6, Dec. 1981, p. 64.

9. H. Igor Ansoff and John M. Stewart, "Strategies for a Technology-Based Business," *Harvard Business Review*, Nov-Dec 1967; also *R&D Management: Part II*, No: 8.032, Reprints from *Harvard Business Review*, p. 12. Copyright © 1967 by the President and Fellows of Harvard University; all rights reserved. Reprinted by permission.

10. *The New York Times*, Thursday, December 13, 1984, p. D1.

11. James Brian Quinn and Robert M. Cavanaugh, "Fundamental Research Can be Planned," *Harvard Business Review*, Jan-Feb 1964. Also, *R&D Management, Part I*, No. 8.031, p. 106, Reprints of *Harvard Business Review*. Copyright 1964 by the President and Fellows of Harvard University; all rights reserved. Reproduced by permission.

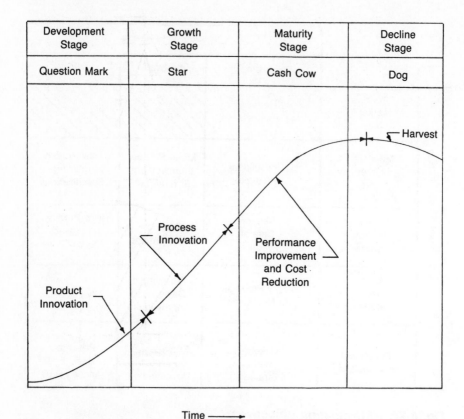

Development Stage	Growth Stage	Maturity Stage	Decline Stage
Question Mark	Star	Cash Cow	Dog

Harvest

Process Innovation

Performance Improvement and Cost Reduction

Product Innovation

Time ⟶

Fig. 6-21. Matching the needs of the product.

12. James Brian Quinn and James A. Mueller, "Transferring Research Results to Operations," *Harvard Business Review*, Jan-Feb. 1963. Also, *R&D Management Series: Part I*, Reprints from *Harvard Business Review*, No: 8.031, p. 32. Copyright 1963 by the President and Fellows of Harvard University; all rights reserved. Reproduced by permission.

13. *Ibid.*

14. R. N. Foster, "Organizing for Successful Research and Development," unpublished paper, McKinsey and Co., Inc., New York, 1983.

15. Donald K. Clifford, Jr., "Managing the Product Life Cycle," *The Arts of Top Management: A McKinsey Anthology*, Roland Mann, editor, pp. 216-226. Copyright 1971 by McGraw Hill Book Co., used by permission of McGraw Hill Book Company.

16. David A. Curtis, *Strategic Planning for Smaller Businesses* (Lexington Books, 1983), p. 75.

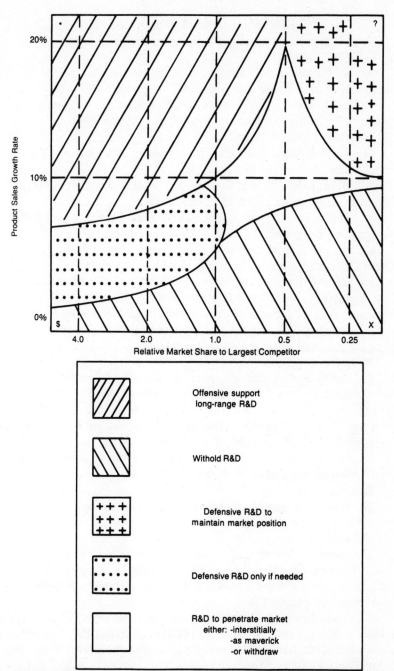

Fig. 6-22. Implications of the investment strategy for the R&D strategy.

17. The remainder of this section has been taken from Robert A. Lunn, "A Sectoral Approach to Strategic Planning for R&D," *Research Management*, Jan-Feb 1983, pp. 33-36.

18. R. Warner and S. Strong, "Out of the Lab and into the Market," *Industrial Marketing*, 56 (December 1971), p. 20.

19. W. T. Hanson and H. K. Nason, "Funding and Budgeting Corporate Research Programs," *Research Management* (March 1980), p. 38.

20. *Ibid*, p. 39.

21. Philip Kotler, *Marketing Management, 5th Edition* (New Jersey: Prentice Hall, 1984), pp. 729-731.

22. E. M. Kipp, "How to Contract an Effective Corporate R&D Budget," *Research Management*, May 1978, pp. 14-17.

23. Matthew J. Liberatore, "An Incremental Approach for R&D Project Planning and Budgeting," *Research Management*, pp. 17, 18, 20.

24. Hughes Aircraft Company, *R&D Productivity* (Culver City, California: Hughes Aircraft Company, 1978), pp. 14-15.

25. James Brian Quinn and Robert M. Cavanaugh, "Fundamental Research Can be Planned," *Harvard Business Review*, Jan-Feb. 1964. Also *R&D Management: Part I*, No: 8.031; reprints of *Harvard Business Review* articles, p. 108. Copyright, 1964 by the President and Fellows of Harvard University, all rights reserved. Reproduced by permission.

26. *Ibid.*

27. James Brian Quinn and James A. Mueller, "Transferring Research Results to Operations," *Harvard Business Review*, Jan-Feb 1963. Also *R&D Management: Part I*, No. 8.031; reprints of selected *Harvard Business Review* articles, p. 23. Copyright 1964 by the President and Fellows of Harvard University; all rights reserved. Reproduced by permission.

28. Lionel S. Goldring, "Defensive R&D as a Management Strategy," *Research Management*, May 1974, pp. 25-28.

29. *Ibid.*

30. William E. Souder, *Project Selection and Economic Appraisal* (New York: Van Nostrand Publishers, 1984), p. 6.

31. *Ibid.*

32. Samuel C. Johnson and Conrad Jones, "How to Organize for New Products," *Harvard Business Review*, 35, May-June 1957, pp. 49-63. Copyright 1957 by the President and Fellows of Harvard University; all rights reserved. Reproduced by permission.

33. Philip A. Roussel, "Cutting Down the Guesswork in R&D," *Harvard Business Review*, Sept-Oct. 1983, pp. 154-160. Copyright 1983 by the President and Fellows of Harvard University; all rights reserved. Reproduced by permission.

34. Adapted from D. Bruce Merrifield, "Selecting Projects for Commercial Success," *Research Management*, November 1981, p. 15.

35. Source unknown.

36. William E. Souder, *Project Selection and Economic Appraisal* (New York: Van Nostrand Publishers, 1984), p. 44.

37. David B. Montgomery and Glen L. Urban, *Management Science in Marketing* (New Jersey: Prentice Hall, 1969), pp. 303-312.

38. William E. Souder, *Project Selection and Economic Appraisal*, p. 43.

39. *Ibid.*

40. Edwin Mansfield, "How Economists See R&D," *Research Management*, July 1982, pp. 23-27.

41. Adapted from Walter A. Bunge, *Managerial Budgeting for Profit Improvement*, (New York: McGraw Hill Book Company, 1968).

42. James Brian Quinn and James A. Mueller, "Transferring Research Results to Operations," *Harvard Business Review* Jan-Feb. 1963; also *R&D Management, Part I, Harvard Business Review,* No: 8.031, p. 31. Copyright 1963 by the President and Fellows of Harvard University, all rights reserved. Reproduced by permission.

43. *Ibid*, p. 26.

44. Alan L. Frohman and Domenic Bitondo, "Coordinating Business Strategy and Technical Planning," *Long Range Planning*, Vol. 14, No. 6, 1981, pp. 58-67.

45. *Ibid*, pp. 60-61.

Chapter 7

The Role of Manufacturing in Strategic Planning

7.0 INTRODUCTION

Both American and foreign corporations are surprised and concerned over the way that once powerful American businesses are now struggling for survival. Foreign corporations, especially in Europe and the Far East, have continually increased their American and international market shares by enjoying low cost labor and manufacturing advantages. Hayes and Wheelwright have identified several causes for why the United States appears to be losing its vitality and capacity for organic growth:[1]

> The usual explanations included (1) the growth of governmental regulation, taxes, and other forms of intrusion into business affairs; (2) a deterioration in the American work ethic which, combined with an adversary relationship between labor and business, had produced crippling strikes, inflexible work rules, and wage increases not justified by productivity increase; (3) interruptions in the supply, and rapid increases in the prices, of various forms of energy since the first OPEC oil shock in 1973; (4) a massive influx of new people into the work force—teenagers, women, and minority groups—who had to be conditioned to work in an industrial environment and trained in new skills; and (5) the advent of unusually high capital costs brought on in part by high rates of inflation.

Perhaps the main cause for America's ills is the continuous pressure placed upon executives for quick decisions and near-term financial successes. As a result, more emphasis is placed upon marketing and R&D strategies than upon manufacturing strategies. The reason for this is self-evident; manufacturing strategies may require substantially much more capital (for facilities, equipment, personnel, training, etc.) and may very well be irreversible. The results of the manufacturing strategy may not be measurable for three years or more and, in the meanwhile, executives are being pressured for short-term profits.

Even under situations where R&D and marketing strategies are long-term, manufacturing strategies may be short-term and often expressed in terms of obtaining more efficient utilization of existing resources. Short-term manufacturing strategies incur little risk, whereas long-term strategies for manufacturing incur high risks in the development of new products and processes to generate lower cost products with increased productivity.

These short-term strategies have existed for so many years that even many of our prime manufacturing industries are plagued by severely aging equipment. According to Roger Smith, Chairman and Chief Executive Officer of General Motors,[2]

"Most of the industrial base in this country is 30 to 60 years old. And too many of our business systems are really not systematic at all—they are a maze of disconnected, uncoordinated, and even competing systems. This is because most of our companies developed through rapid growth. And as they grew bigger, the small basic systems that originally brought them success were simply enlarged.

"And unless we want to play a perpetual game of catch-up, we in American business have to do more than just meet our competition on a day-to-day basis. We have to beat them in long-term strategy. We have to anticipate their future competitive moves. We have to understand their ultimate strategies and outstrategize and outsmart them."

Long-term manufacturing strategies require a serious commitment to long-term capital investment. Although the United States appears to be spending more and more each year on capital investment, the actual expenditure, when adjusted for inflation, appears to be at a much lower rate than French, German, and Japanese corporations. As a result, while the foreign competition becomes capital intensive, American corporation remains labor intensive. And because capital intensive companies maintain a long-term cost advantage over labor intensive companies, the final result will be that Americans will ultimately be able to meet the competition on quality not on cost.

These trends are significant and have been criticized by economists and executives alike:

The rate of net investment is not only very low by international standards, but has fallen sharply in recent years. In the second half of the 1960s, the U.S. devoted 4.2 percent of GNP to increasing the stock of plant and equipment. By the second half of the 1970s, the investment share had fallen by 40 percent to only 2.6 percent of GNP.[3]

In the U.S., the average employee works with $50,000 worth of plant and equipment. This means each new entrant into the labor force must be equipped with $50,000 worth of capital if he is to reach the average productivity level. If Americans decide to have a baby boom, as they did in the 1950s and early 1960s, they are making an implicit promise that they will, approximately 20 years later, cut their consumption and provide each of those babies with the $50,000 in plant and equipment he or she needs to enter the work force as a productive worker. It is this implicit promise that Americans are failing to keep.[4]

Somehow or other, American business is losing confidence in itself, and especially confidence in its future. Instead of meeting the challenge of the changing world, American business today is making small, short-term adjustments by cutting costs and by turning to the government for temporary relief... Success in trade is the result of patient and meticulous preparations, with a long period of market preparation before the rewards are available... To undertake such commitments is hardly in the interest of a manager who is concerned with his or her next quarterly earnings report.[5]

Management of many U.S. companies today are unwilling to commit wholeheartedly to available manufacturing concepts and technologies. According to Thomas Gunn, the reasons for this foot-dragging are eight-fold:[6]

First, articles and discussions of high technology factory automation often focus on technical features instead of the proven strategic benefits that such factory automation can deliver.

Second, because most U.S. Chief Executive Officers and board members come from financial, legal, or marketing backgrounds, they often lack knowledge and a true understanding of design and manufacturing as it was 10 years ago, as it is today, and, more important, as it will be in the next five to 10 years. In addition, few of them have the backgrounds or interest that allows them to understand the powerful role of today's computer systems in integrating business functions.

Third, with their traditional capital budgeting techniques, they (or their lower level managers) haven't been able to justify investing in risky long-term factory automation program. They have no base of experience to deal with factoring benefits other than direct labor reduction or increased capacity into their justification calculations. Then, too, most top executives seldom adopt a truly corporatewide outlook to planning their design and manufacturing strategy and capital improvements to increase their strategic effectiveness, as well as efficiency/productivity.

Fourth, many top managers simply don't know who to believe anymore. They seldom have complete trust in their own managers, since they are well aware of vested departmental or functional interests and the political maneuvering that often accompanies requests for capital expenditures. Vendors often have even less credibility due to the inherent conflict of interest their recommendations represent, and especially due to the fact that each vendor seems to have a different solution to the problem.

Fifth, many executives simply don't have (and perhaps have never had) an objective picture of where their company currently stands with respect to competing by its ability to execute its design and manufacturing mission effectively. They also lack knowledge of their competitor's design and manufacturing capability. Thus, they have difficulty planning or implementing change because they lack any frame of reference about their current position vis-a-vis their competitors or the state-of-the-art in their industry, in addition to what they will have to accomplish to be competitive as a manufacturer for world markets in the future.

Sixth, many companies lack an explicit manufacturing strategy that firmly supports that company's business strategy. Often, we find companies whose so-called "manufacturing strategy" is a vague motherhood statement espousing that they will be the high-quality, low-cost producer that will strive to increase its inventory turns. While these goals are all desirable, they are the strategies of every manufacturing company.

What will separate winners from losers is a process that will transfer these vague manufacturing strategies into an implementable action plan that achieves concrete measurable results against standards established by the competitive business world.

Seventh, top managers often lack an understanding of how factory automation and the increased permeation of the business environment by computing technology will affect their company's organizational structure and policies or their human resource, education, and training requirements.

Finally, top managers do not understand the consequences of not investing in factory automation or reviewing their design and manufacturing competitiveness. History teaches us that change and technological innovation are inevitable and inexorable, yet for many companies, even if they reversed field and made the financial and management commitment to implement "the Factory of the Future" in their company today with unlimited funds, it is too late for them.

If management is to attack these problems head-on, then the starting point must be a shift in corporate thinking. A reasonable set of criteria might include:

- Focusing on and measuring results in the long-term, rather than the short-term.
- Developing a strategic plan which integrates marketing, R&D, and financial goals with manufacturing goals, rather than at the expense of manufacturing goals.
- Developing a new breed of manager with encouragement for hands-on experience.

There are two critical issues that influence the planning for today's and tomorrow's manufacturing function. In the past, it was possible to develop strategic planning groups which would meet periodically. These groups might not have been headed up by an executive. Today, with a constantly changing environment, manufacturing technology breakthroughs can occur at any time and, therefore, without continuous monitoring and involvement by top management, strategic windows, and opportunities may be issued.

Second, manufacturing today is highly innovative and manufacturing executives must foster a climate conducive to creativity and new idea development. To take advantage of this creativity, management must consider the *total* manufacturing function, rather than the automation of small islands. This step requires a genuine and total commitment by senior management to depart from the static environmental thinking of the past three decades and to encourage an atmosphere of creativity.

Strategic planning in the United States appears to be dominated by financial considerations, especially in the calculation for ROI. If the strategic goals are to improve ROI, then it can be obtained by either increasing the numerator (profits) or decreasing the denominator (investment). Obviously, the latter is easier to accomplish. Reducing investment can be achieved by either delaying the replacement of aging equipment, reducing preventive maintenance to as-needed maintenance, or replacing worn-out equipment with equipment encompassing the same technology, rather than looking for newer technology. In any event, the facilities continue to age to the point where the construction of a completely new and more costly facility may be the only solution.

If manufacturing strategies are not properly integrated with other strategies, the result is like a two-legged stool. Marketing, R&D, and financial strategies are designed for compression, whereas manufacturing strategies stress expansion. To illustrate this, marketing has assessed a market need for a new product. The financial people, being optimistic, prophesize a substantial profit and market share. The project is then turned over to the R&D group, who are asked to create the impossible in an unbelievable short time frame. Marketing executives pressure R&D to work faster to achieve a first-to-market position. Financial executives pressure R&D to cut corners and use low cost, readily available materials. By the time the product gets to manufacturing, the manufacturing personnel are asked to mass-produce a product which they have never seen or have seen but which has undergone numerous design changes so as to shorten their schedule. And, as is often the case, manufacturing is now told to "fast-track" the job by going into production without complete manufacturing plans, without proper quality control, without proper time to evaluate sources for raw material and subcontracts, without proper facilities and equipment, without properly trained personnel, and without any consideration that what is developed on an R&D bench may not be able to be mass-produced with the same quality. Finally, if the product does not meet up to specifications, let's simply blame manufacturing.

If integration is to be successful, then it must be based upon a total systems approach. Roger Smith states that:[7]

> To develop a total systems approach, each business must create an integrated, coordinated, decision making way of functioning which comprehends business plans, budgets, product programs, and everything else that helps run the business. It must build an integrated worldwide database that brings all parts of the business together. Such a database finally marries those two great singles, the manufacturing systems and the business systems, with no chance of divorce.
>
> The bottom-line benefit of such a wedding is that it allows business people to understand their total business in a comprehensive way that was not possible before. They can actually see those cases where two can live more cheaply than one. They can simultaneously review all parts of the business—as well as the linkages which hold them together. And this new-found ability enables them to make more informed, more timely, and shrewder business decisions—decisions that can give a company a long-term competitive edge.

The third criteria involves the development of a new breed of executive. The job description of an executive is to develop strategic and long-term plans so as to assure the growth and survivability of the corporation over the next five to ten years. But every Christmas, the executive receives a bonus based upon 12-month profitability, rather than the results of the strategic planning process. Executive compensation must be married to the strategic planning process, rather than short-term profitability.

Employees climbing the corporate ladder must be given sufficient time in any given assignment to obtain hands-on experience. All too often, managers move from job to job and company to company without a chance to gain in-depth experience. The result is that they never stay in one job long enough to see the long-term impact of their decisions.

Many companies develop corporate cultures for allowing talented employees to climb the corporate ladder to success. All too often, the ladder to success avoids positions which require hands-on experience. As discussed by Hayes and Wheelwright:[8]

American companies increasingly turned to people with financial, accounting, and legal backgrounds to fill their top positions. By the late 1970s, the percentage of newly appointed CEOs with such backgrounds in the 100 largest U.S. corporations was up 50 percent from its level 30 years earlier. As a result, correspondingly fewer hands-on experience in the more competitively oriented functions such as marketing, production, and engineering. The absolute change in numbers has not been as important as the change in attitude precipitated by this trend. Young managers searching for ways to get ahead tended to choose jobs and career paths that they perceived to be on the road to the top. If this road appeared to emphasize staff assignments, the best were attracted to staff positions.

Properly developed executives with an insight toward long-term strategic planning may very well be the starting point to meet the competition head-on.

7.1 UNDERSTANDING MANUFACTURING OPERATIONS[9]

Manufacturing (production) is the conversion of raw materials into products and/or components thereof, through a series of manufacturing procedures and processes. It includes such major functions as manufacturing, planning, and scheduling; manufacturing engineering; fabrication and assembly; installation and checkout; demonstration and testing; product assurance; and determination of resource requirements.

Manufacturing management is the technique of planning, organizing, directing, and controlling the use of people, money, materials, equipment, and facilities to accomplish the manufacturing task economically. A manufacturing management system is composed essentially of three phases: planning, analysis, and control.

During the planning phase, consideration must be given to such factors as material acquisition, an adequate work force, engineering design, and provisions for subcontractor support. Production feasibility and producibility of the engineering design are critical factors that must be considered early in a program. This consideration must include planning, new processes, facilities, tools and test equipment, and cost control during design.

During the analysis phase, answers must be provided to such questions as: Is the manufacturing process working? Is it efficient? Is manufacturing being accomplished by the most economical method? Is the manufacturing plan being followed and are the established goals being met? During system design and development, these questions need to be projected into the future manufacturing effort to identify required preparatory actions and to assess risks.

During the control phase, the manufacturing effort must be monitored to ensure that the manufacturing management function is performing within the constraints and limits that have been established.

These three phases of a manufacturing management system can also be redefined as the three phases for strategic manufacturing planning. The objectives or strategic manufacturing planning are:

- To ensure that proper manufacturing planning has been accomplished early in a program so that the manufacturing effort will be performed smoothly.
- To ensure that the system design will lead to efficient and economical quantity manufacture.
- To assess the status of the program at any point during the production phase to determine if schedule, costs, and quality standards are being met, and whether or not changes must be made to the strategic and operational plans.
- To conduct assessment and reviews of the manufacturing effort required to meet decision points at each phase in the lifecycle of a program.

To achieve these objectives, strategic manufacturing planning must begin in the product design phase, well before the product ever reaches manufacturing. There are significant costs associated with the manufacturing effort. The current view is that those costs, to a great degree, are inherent in the design phase. As a design evolves and comes off the drawing board, certain costs are essentially fixed. Given the objective of minimizing cost and the existence of forward projections that indicate that limited dollars may be available for future manufacturing effort, it is necessary to identify costs at the point in time when they are being fixed.

These types of problems have especially plagued government organizations in the past to such a degree that the operational readiness of government/military equipment may be questionable. The government can no longer support private industry by providing government furnished manufacturing facilities. In a speech

in October, 1975, the then Vice-Commander of the Air Force Systems Command, Lt. Gen. Robert Marsh, stated that the Air Force is searching,
". . . for new opportunities to save money without hurting efficiency or performance. We think we found one of these opportunities in the manufacturing area. In the past, our government engineers have concentrated on performance design requirements and relied almost entirely on the contractors in manufacturing matters. That was a mistake. We must devote the same management attention to our design-to-cost goals as we do to our performance goals. That can only be done by active and continuous involvement in manufacturing and planning operations from the very outset of conceptual design until the last item rolls down the production line."

It requires very early manufacturing involvement together with a strong coupling of manufacturing with R&D, marketing, and especially engineering design. This statement indicates a perception that the ability to influence the manufacturing cost requires a change in manufacturing management practices and strategy.

7.2 INDUSTRIAL BASE

Success in developing and producing products relies heavily on the technological and industrial capability of industry as a whole. In managing development and production programs, managers need to specifically assess and understand the capabilities of the industrial base and its capability to support the strategic plan.

Weaknesses in the industrial base often appear first on defense industry activities. A report by the House Armed Services Committee (HASC) on December 31, 1980, titled, "The Ailing Defense Industrial Base: Unready for Crisis," sums up the perception that prevailed in government and industry. The chairman of the HASC Defense Industrial Base Panel, Representative Richard H. Ichord, stated in the letter of transmittal:

"The panel finds that there has been a serious decline in the nation's defense industrial capability that places our national security in jeopardy. An alarming erosion of crucial industrial elements, coupled with a mushrooming dependence on foreign sources for critical materials, is endangering our defense posture as its very foundation."

The panel reported the following:

- A continuing deterioration and contraction of the defense industrial base.
- The lack of plan for defense industrial base preparedness.
- Turbulence in defense system (weapons) programs.

- A shortage of critical materials and a growing dependence on uncertain foreign sources for these materials.
- Restrictive procurement policies and procedures.
- Tax and profit policies that discourage capital investment.
- Diffused responsibility for the condition of the industrial base.

A number of problems, including those cited by the HASC, have degraded the ability of the industrial base to respond to near-term readiness, surge, and mobilization requirements in a timely manner. The same problems have resulted in a deterioration of the subcontractor and vendor base, which has diminished the likelihood of competition and contributed to the emergence of production bottlenecks. These problems apply equally well to all industrial bases, not merely the defense industry industrial base.

The impact of crucial industrial base elements on program success is apparent when one examines lead times, the contractor/subcontractor/customer/supplier base, productivity, and industrial strategic planning.

Lead Times

Lead times for material and components tend to be volatile. There are various reasons for this situation, including imbalances between capacity and demand, competition from commercial suppliers, and raw materials availability. The changing nature of lead times from 1978 for selected material is illustrated in Fig. 7-1.

Lead times are also severely impacted by capacity limitations. As orders increase beyond existing capacity, the facility has the option of increasing capacity or adding the new orders to backlog. For a facility with a reasonably steady demand and no capacity expansion, this increase in time is communicated to

	Dec 78	May 80	Apr 82
Aluminum small forgings	48	83	44
Aluminum extensions	54	81	26
Titanium large forgings	74	121	60
Titanium extensions - heavy	47	80	35
Fasteners - non-titanium	40	52	23
Integrated circuits	34	44	40
Diodes	26	33	28

Fig. 7-1. Material lead times (in weeks).
Source: U.S. Government Document.

the facility's customers, and their response to the lead time is to issue orders immediately to ensure material availability. With constant capacity, these new orders must also be added to backlog, which must then be reflected in increased lead time. As this self-fueling process, often called the *lead time capacity syndrome,* continues, a relatively small increase in demand can result in extremely large increases in lead times. The area of component and material lead time is extremely critical to meeting production schedules and defining long lead requirements.

Customers/Contractors/Suppliers

Numerous reasons have caused the reduction in the size of the supplier base. The primary reasons include economic conditions, material shortages, foreign competition, and government regulations. The impact is fewer companies in the market place, some loss of competition (with all that entails), and a possible increase in lead times. The implications are obvious as numerous demands are placed upon a few suppliers.

These problems can be illustrated by the following finds:

- The steel industry is hampered by aging plants, foreign competition, and environmental restrictions. Alloying elements such as chromium, cobalt, etc., are in short supply.
- During the period 1977 to 1979, the number of titanium fabricators dropped from 16 to 4, primarily as a result of titanium sponge shortage.
- In the past decade, more than 400 foundries have gone out of business, many due to the cost of meeting environmental requirements.

To further complicate these problems, some companies prefer to limit their growth and customer base so as not to invest in additional facilities and equipment. As an example, the machine tool industry is characterized by a large number of small companies, most of which are selective of their customers base.

Capacity and Investment Decisions

Capacity can be defined as the maximum rate of productive or conversion capability of an organization's operations. Capacity is normally constrained by physical facilities, available productive equipment, tooling and/or test equipment. The portion of this capacity actually utilized is determined by the demand on the plant for current and known future workload. Firms must be particularly aware of a need for excess capacity, because customer demand tends to be somewhat unstable over time.

Operational and investment decisions, which could increase capacity, are influenced by return on investment or profit in relation to the risk perceived and the potential return from other opportunities. Since the early '70s, there are indications that a majority of industrial facilities have been growing older and new investment has not been keeping pace with equipment obsolescence or the advances in manufacturing technology which could lead to higher productivity and lower costs. During this period of time, thousands of suppliers have closed their plants and many others have been reluctant to increase capital investment. This has led to an industrial bottleneck, where certain limited suppliers are taxed to capacity. Lead times for the items produced at these facilities tend to be extremely volatile and subject to the demand lead time syndrome described previously.

7.3 STRATEGIC DECISIONS

Manufacturing decisions cannot be made on an instantaneous basis, but must be made over time. Therefore, it is useful to try to classify the strategic variables into categories. Hayes and Wheelwright identify the following eight categories:[10]

- Capacity. Amount, timing, type.
- Facilities. Size, location, specialization.
- Technology. Equipment, automation, linkages.
- Vertical integration. Direction, extent, balance.
- Work force. Skill level, wage policies, employment security.
- Quality. Defect prevention, monitoring, intervention.
- Production planning/materials control. Sourcing policies, centralization, decision rules.
- Organization. Structure, control/reward systems, role of staff groups.

Hayes and Wheelwright categorized the first four decision categories as long-term, structural decisions, whereas the last four are tactical decisions to support the ongoing business. There are, of course, other factors that are important to the business in general, and have an impact upon the manufacturing strategies. According to Schmenner, they can be summarized as:[11]

- Access to markets/distribution centers.
- Access to suppliers and resources.
- Community and government aspects.
- Competitive considerations.
- Environmental considerations.
- Interaction with the rest of the corporation.
- Labor.
- Site attractiveness.

- Taxes and financing.
- Transportation.
- Utilities and services.

The exact location of a facility may be of far less importance than how the facility is managed once it is in place.

It is highly unlikely that strategic manufacturing decisions will be black or white. In almost every situation, tradeoffs are required. Skinner has identified several of the important tradeoff decisions in Table 7-1.[12]

On the international scene, the list of typical decisions can be much more complicated. According to Skinner, typical decisions might include:[13]

- How to deal with vendors who are habitually late in delivery and marginal in performance but are nevertheless the best vendors available.
- How to minimize investment in inventory and yet prevent stockouts—when replacement of a missing item may require four to six months and the cost of local working capital is 12 to 20 percent per year, and when it is difficult to hire stock clerks who can keep accurate records.
- How to maintain a fair, motivating wage and salary rate in the midst of inflation, secrecy regarding practices of other companies, and traditional patterns of compensation such as automatic annual increments and "dearness allowances."
- How to select and train employees in the face of (a) language differences and often a low general-education level; (b) difficulties in testing applicants potential; (c) the necessity of relying on new or weak lower-level supervision for the bulk of recommendations and training; and (d) high penalties for mistakes made (such as heavy compulsory severance pay to employees discharged).
- How to choose between (a) equipment or processes characterized by high initial cost, automated features, high maintenance, and low labor cost; and (b) alternatives with lower initial cost which may require more direct labor and tighter control in terms of quality and supervision. Such decisions are often complicated by unpredictable future costs and markets.

7.4 CRITICAL ISSUES

The long-term objective of any business entity is the generation of profits for the shareholders. In achieving profitability, a manufacturing enterprise must assure the effective application of the production resources to the task of building and delivering the product. Other pressures also exist which dictate the need for carefully defined plans. The pressure to control manufacturing costs and the

Table 7-1. Some Important Trade-Off Decisions in Manufacturing—or "You Can't Have It Both Ways"

Decision area	Decision	Alternatives
PLANT AND EQUIPMENT	Span of process	Make or buy
	Plant size	One big plant or several smaller ones
	Plant location	Locate near markets or locate near materials
	Investment decisions	Invest mainly in buildings or equipment or inventories or research
	Choice of equipment	General-purpose or special-purpose equipment
	Kind of tooling	Temporary, minimum tooling or "production tooling"
PRODUCTION PLANNING AND CONTROL	Frequency of inventory taking	Few or many breaks in production for buffer stocks
	Inventory size	High inventory or a lower inventory
	Degree of inventory control	Control in great detail or in lesser detail
	What to control	Controls designed to minimize machine downtime or labor cost or time in process, or to maximize output of particular products or material usage
	Quality control	High reliability and quality or low costs
	Use of standards	Formal or informal or none at all
LABOR AND STAFFING	Job specialization	Highly specialized or not highly specialized
	Supervision	Technically trained first-line supervisors or nontechnically trained supervisors
	Wage system	Many job grades or few job grades; incentive wages or hourly wages
	Supervision	Close supervision or loose supervision
	Industrial engineers	Many or few such men
PRODUCT DESIGN/ ENGINEERING	Size of product line	Many customer specials or few specials or none at all
	Design stability	Frozen design or many engineering change orders
	Technological risk	Use of new processes unproved by competitors or follow-the-leader policy
	Engineering	Complete packaged design or design-as-you-go approach
	Use of manufacturing engineering	Few or many manufacturing engineers
ORGANIZATION AND MANAGEMENT	Kind of organization	Functional or product focus or geographical or other
	Executive use of time	High involvement in investment or production planning or cost control or quality control or other activities
	Degree of risk assumed	Decisions based on much or little information
	Use of staff	Large or small staff group
	Executive style	Much or little involvement in detail; authoritarian or nondirective style; much or little contact with organization

need to meet schedules demand a carefully planned application of manufacturing resources and proper strategy planning.

Strategic planning for manufacturing falls into three categories.

- More efficient utilization of existing resources (process development).
- Increasing/decreasing demand for existing products (product development).
- Resource planning for new products (product development).
- A combination of the above.

Based upon the product manufacturing demands, a manufacturing framework can be developed, such as shown in Fig. 7-2, for a new product development process. This framework should define the specific elements of the organization that will be involved in the program and the amount and types of subcontractors and vendors that may be required. The decision regarding subcontractors and vendors should be made from the standpoint of contractor and vendor capability as well as capacity. Within the context of the defined business structure, there should be an identification of the specific resources required. Personnel should be identified in terms of both quantity and specific skill types required, time-phased over the planning horizon.

Feasibility and Capability

The issues of manufacturing feasibility and capability must be addressed in the initial phases of the strategic manufacturing planning. The evaluation of manufacturing feasibility and capability are directed toward analysis of the compatibility of the demands of the manufacturing task and the manufacturing facility and equipment required to accomplish it. The capability of a firm to successfully execute the manufacturing effort depends upon that firm having:

- Complete understanding of the manufacturing task.
- Adequate qualitative production skills.
- Sufficient personnel (on hand or available).
- Sufficient facility floor space.
- Equipment in satisfactory condition.
- Adequate, operable test equipment.
- Assured, capable suppliers.
- Management capability.
- Plan to coordinate all resources.

Manufacturing Resources

Manufacturing management can be defined as ''the effective use of resources to produce on schedule the required number of end items that meet specified

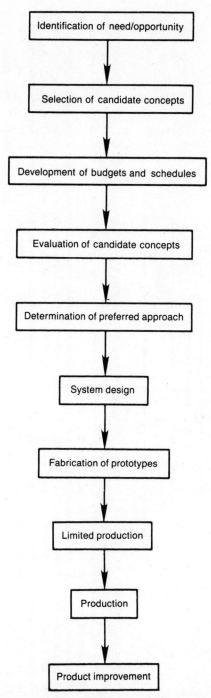

Fig. 7-2. The generic product development process.

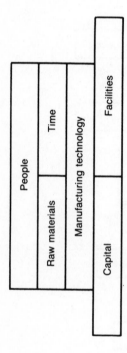

People	
Raw materials	Time
Manufacturing technology	
Capital	Facilities

1. *People*. People include those in program management, design engineering, manufacturing engineering, and (probably the most important) factory operations — the direct labor personnel and the indirect person personnel who support them.

2. *Facilities*. Facilities are the real property in the factory; the environment in which the products are built. The term includes the industrial equipment, the machine tools, and the shop aids to manufacturing.

3. *Manufacturing Technology*. Manufacturing technology is that set of efforts undertaken to improve the manufacturing process, techniques, or equipment required to support current and projected requirements. This area involves advancements in the way things are done in the factory, including the processes that are available to take raw material, enter it into a productive process, and transform it into something useful that meets DOD needs.

4. *Raw Materials*. Raw materials are the basic materials used in the manufacturing process. The focus of the government and contract effort should be on the most efficient utilization of the required raw materials.

5. *Capital*. Capital represents the monetary assets which are available to the contractor. Capital can be used to finance on-going work, as an investment to improve capacity or capability, to broaden the market base or any of a large number of competing uses within the contractor's organization.

6. *Time*. Time is a resource available to all contractors. It provides a constraint on the contractor, since performance and delivery commitments are related to specific dates.

Fig. 7-3. Manufacturing resources.

quality, performance, and cost." A few comments can be made about this definition to serve as a basis for consideration of the manufacturing planning issue. The first significant word is "effective." The question is: "Measured against what baseline?" How does something that has to be defined on a specific program in terms like relative or absolute cost, compare to other similar programs or performance within resource constraints?

The classic manufacturing resources required are: people, facilities, manufacturing technology, raw materials, capital and time (Fig. 7-3).

Manufacturing Risk Assessment

Manufacturing risk assessment is a supporting tool for the decision-making process. It seeks to estimate the probabilities of success or failure associated with the manufacturing alternatives available. These risk assessments may reflect alternative manufacturing approaches to a given design or may be part of the evaluation of design alternatives, each of which has an associated manufacturing approach.

Manufacturing processes and materials may be divided into three broad groups: state-of-the-practice, state-of-the-art, and experimental.

State-of-the-practice implies that the material or process is in general use in industry, is well understood, and has a long usage record. These processes and materials generally represent low-riskapproaches.

State-of-the-art implies that a material or process has had some factory usage, but was recently developed and is available from only one or a limited number of sources. These types of processes often provide the potential for cost or time savings but may introduce risk if they have not been used in the particular application or by the producer.

Experimental processes or materials have been demonstrated in the laboratory, but not in the factory environment. These processes and materials often hold great promise in terms of reduced cost, improved material properties, and better performance. Their use should be demonstrated in the factory environment prior to use in a manufacturing program.

As the design of a new product or process evolves, the manufacturing implications of various design options should be evaluated as part of the on-going review process, as shown in Fig. 7-4. The appropriate manufacturing concepts should be identified by the manufacturing engineers so that the risk levels associated with those approaches can be evaluated. This is a critical procedure if the selected system design alternative requires the use of an experimental material or process. If it does, or if a state-of-the-art material or process is to be used, two actions should be taken:

- Establish a plan to prove out the material or process prior to initiation of manufacturing.

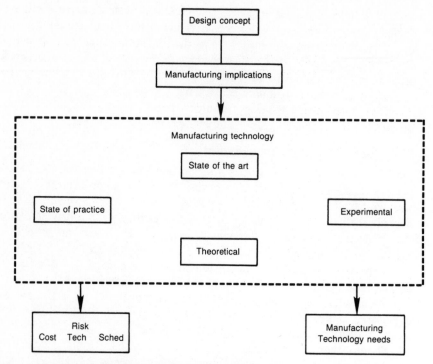

Fig. 7-4. Manufacturing risk assessment.

- Identify a fall-back approach if the material or process cannot be used successfully in manufacturing.

Personnel Planning

In developing a personnel plan, the company needs to consider the number of personnel, the specific skill types, the time phasing of the requirements, and the ability of the organization to absorb the additional personnel. The ability to meet the personnel demands will be a function of the labor pool currently available within the organization as well as the ability of the local area to provide the quantity and types of people required.

There needs to be a clearly defined profile of the required work force and a plan for the acquisition and training of new hires. Although on-the-job training (OJT) may be an effective mechanism for providing required knowledge, its effectiveness is limited. Where the skills involved are relatively complex, there should be some form of formal training provided and planned for as part of the strategic planning process.

Management should review the adequacy of the planned personnel manloadings to ensure that adequate numbers of the required skill types can be made available. When a large personnel increase is planned, the sources of those personnel should be determined and evidence of their potential availability should be clearly indicated in the plan.

Facility Planning

The facility includes the plant and productive equipment that is to be made available to accomplish the production task. In developing the facility plan, both the quantitative and qualitative demands of the product must be considered. The qualitative analysis determines the types of processes required. The firm then has the option of utilizing currently existing facilities, acquiring new facilities, requesting customer-furnished facilities, or subcontracting a portion of the effort. The quantitative analysis determines the size of the various processing departments within the facility. This requires consideration of the number of units to be delivered and the rate of delivery. The information collected in these analyses will provide a measure of the number of work stations and the floor space required.

After determination of the facility requirements, the next concern is layout and flow planning. In most cases, the layout is constrained by the existing facility; however, it may be possible to revise the layout for a new strategic program where future products can use some of the existing flow plan.

7.5 CAPACITY DECISIONS

A major element in any manufacturing strategy is the decision of whether or not to increase manufacturing capacity. Increasing manufacturing capacity may allow firms to take advantage of economies of scale, thus lowering unit cost. But excess capacity, which is underutilized, could have a detrimental effect. Capacity strategies are based upon an understanding of the following:

- Predicted demand for product.
- Lifecycle of product.
- Behavior of competitors (domestic and international).
- Rate of change of technology.
- Cost of construction and operation for additional capacity.

Capacity can be added in increments, as shown in Fig. 7-5. In each of the three situations, the demand is assumed to be linear and known. In Situation 1, capacity leads demand. This would be representative of a firm that is afraid of running short and desires to maintain a capacity cushion or buffer zone. Although unused capacity is expensive, the firm may benefit through faster re-

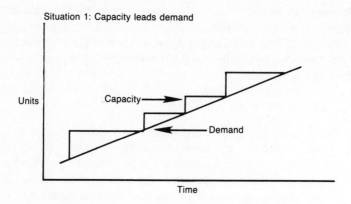

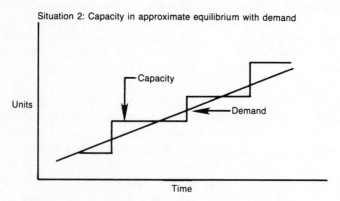

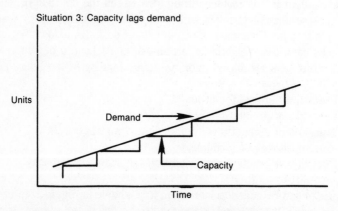

Fig. 7-5. Alternative capacity expansion strategies.
Source: Robert H. Hayes, Steven C. Wheelwright, Restoring Our
Competitive Edge, *John Wiley Publishers, 1984, p. 49.*

sponse to an increased demand (without overtime expenses), and a "good will" environment with customers by avoiding shortages.

In Situation 2, capacity and demand are in equilibrium. This case is dangerous because not only does it permit shortages to exist, but it assumes that capacity can be added as needed. In Situation 3, shortages can be large, because the firm may fear that demand will be reduced in the future. The firm will consider capacity expansion only when backlogged orders approach a certain critical point.

Unused capacity has both positive and negative considerations. On the positive side, it acts as a barrier to entry. On the negative side, the company may have to change the manufacturing processes to handle increased capacity, and must plan for an adequate work force, properly trained, to handle the increased work load. In addition, the changeover cost from one product line to another may create additional complexities.

Long-term excessive capacity can push a company well below the breakeven levels. Porter has prepared a list identifying the causes for overbuilding manufacturing capacity.[14]

- Technological factors.
    - —Adding capacity in large increments
    - —Economies of scale
    - —Long lead times in adding capacity
    - —Minimum efficient scale increasing over time
    - —Changes in production technology
- Structural factors.
    - —Significant exit barriers
    - —Motivation from suppliers
    - —Building credibility with customers
    - —Integrated competitors
    - —Effect of capacity share on market share
    - —Effect of age and type of capacity on demand
- Competitive factors.
    - —Large number of firms
    - —Lack of credible market leaders
    - —Entry of new competitors
    - —Advantages of being an early mover
- Information flow factors.
    - —Inflation of future expectations
    - —Divergent assumptions or perceptions
    - —Breakdown of market signaling
    - —Structural change
    - —Financial community pressures

- Managerial factors.
  - —Management background and industry experience
  - —Attitude toward different types of risk
- Governmental factors.
  - —Perverse tax incentives
  - —Desire for indigenous industry
  - —Pressures to increase or maintain employment

The geographical area plays an important part of any capacity decision. Consider the following:

- Will the required work force become too big in relation to the population in the immediate area?
- Is the population skilled, or will the employees require training?
- How will the training be provided?
- Will the economies of scale offset the possible increased freight charges to other locations?
- How vulnerable are we if a natural disaster occurs (i.e., flood, earthquake, etc.)?

When the industry begins to mature, firms tend to prefer smaller facilities in order to minimize confusion, maintain better control, and to avoid becoming too dominant a force in the local community.

7.6 PERSONNEL AVAILABILITY

In deciding where to locate a new facility, there are two critical issues associated with personnel availability: the size of the population and community expectations. If a plant becomes a major community employer, then the community becomes heavily dependent upon the plant. In such cases, the community may become actively involved in the activities of the plant (as well as the parent corporation), and a hostile environment can develop. Some companies limit plant size (employment ceilings) to 5 percent of the population within a fifty mile radius. (There are other reasons for wanting low employment ceilings such as to keep the plant too small to be a union organizing target.)

The second critical issue involves the social concerns of the corporation in regards to employee training and development. If the employment community is unskilled, then the community may have high expectations that the company will develop training programs to convert personnel from unskilled to skilled or semi-skilled workers. From a social perspective, the idea has merit, but from a financial point of view, large-scale training may not be cost-effective.

If a company converts a large portion of its work force from unskilled to skilled, then the increased salary demands could cut into profits. In small communities, the turnover of personnel may be so small that each year, the average age of the work force increases, thus driving up the fringe benefit costs and the adjoining overhead rates. If the community is large, then a high employee turnover rate could force the company to reassess whether it is getting a return on investment for its training dollars. Finally, if a company does, in fact, provide training programs for employee upgrading together with salary increases, then the most logical benefit to the company would be to take advantage of learning curve effects on production quantities.

7.7 PRODUCTIVITY

Productivity enhancement is an important part of strategic planning, because productivity growth leads to lower costs and provides an opportunity for lower priced products and/or higher profits. It also makes possible increased compensatory benefits for employees. Productivity growth helps to ensure that production will meet cost and schedule targets, thus providing more resources for other manufacturing activities.

The productivity of any firm is a measure of how well the resources in that firm are brought together and used to accomplish a set of results. Productivity isn't just an increase in the volume of shipments, although this is one element. Traditionally, productivity has been defined as the acceptable output per labor hour. Using this definition, we would quickly discover that in a firm with many employees and little automation, productivity depends principally upon human achievement. On the other hand, in a firm where automation predominates, the human contributions to productivity play a lesser role.

Productivity is more than output over input. It is the relationship of the quantity and quality of products, goods, and services produced to the quantity of resources (personnel, capital facilities, machine tools and equipment, materials, and information) required to produce them. In order to improve productivity, both the output (performance achieved) and the input (resources consumed) must be capable of measurement. The ratio set forth below provides a measure of how well the expended resourced are able to accomplish the established performance objectives, i.e., the ratio provides a measure of the value added.

Although several productivity ratio formulas exist, the preferred productivity ratio for any endeavor is the one that best fits the purpose and resources of the organization involved. Practice, comparative use, and historic validation are some of the methods for giving productivity ratios meaning and/or validity.

7.8 TRENDS IN PRODUCTIVITY GROWTH

In recent years, both the United States and Europe have been losing their dominance in many different industries to the Japanese. The results of recent studies

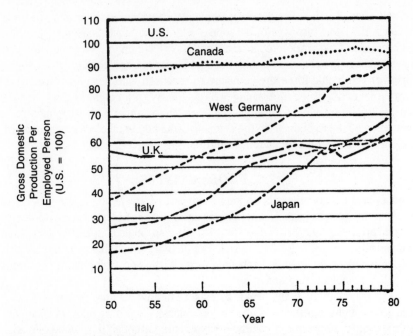

Fig. 7-6. International productivity rating relative to manufacturing: 1960-1980.
Source: Bureau of Labor Statistics, 1980.

of Japanese improvements in productivity, product quality, and management have become the basis for changes in industrial practices worldwide.

During the 1950s and 1960s, the United States maintained a relatively high productivity growth rate. During the 1970s, the growth rate declined, but the United States is still ahead of the rest of the world. The Bureau of Labor Statistics in the Department of Labor indicates that when comparing the real gross domestic production per employed person—the national measure of productivity—the United Kingdom is 39.5 percent behind the United States, Italy trails by 39.4 percent, Japan by 31.6 percent, West Germany by 11.3 percent, France by 10.6 percent, and Canada and the Netherlands by 8 percent. The challenge to the United States from other countries is a real one. It will take commitment—commitment to more innovation and commitment to strong leadership; see Fig. 7-6.

Factors that Influence Productivity

The factors that influence productivity growth are the work force, management, capital investment, and technology.

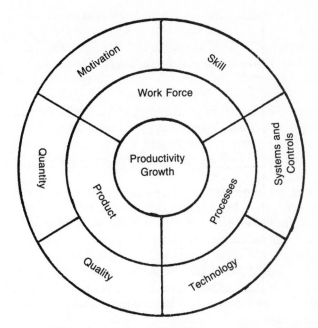

Fig. 7-7. Productivity results from effective interaction of the work force, the processes, and the product.

Work Force. The members of the work force represent an integral part of the productivity picture. This is portrayed in Fig. 7-7. Referring to this figure, you can see that each of the three categories—work force, process, and product—is composed of subordinate elements, any one of which can impact productivity growth. Productivity growth occurs when the cumulative effect of the interdependent elements is imposed.

The quality of the work force effects productivity. As the quality increases or decreases, the productivity increases or decreases. There has been a decline in the quality of the work force in the United States during the past few years. This decline can be attributed to a rise in the proportion of young and inexperienced workers in the work force and the decrease in the average work effort. Also, the lack of motivation of many young workers has had an adverse affect on productivity.

Management. One of the keys to productivity enhancement within any organization is management. The attitudes, actions, and personal examples of management pervade the organization and directly affect the attitudes, actions, and motivation of the work force. It is from management that the workers generally take their cues. Accordingly, astute managers must convey clearly the importance they place on productivity and their desire to enhance productivity throughout the organization. Unfortunately, actions that management takes to improve productivity in one organization may not work out well when applied to another. Therefore, it is important for managers to assess the situation within their organization before taking specific actions to enhance productivity.

Capital Investment. Capital investment is absolutely necessary if productivity is to be enhanced. At the start of the 1980s, the picture is grim. The cumulative U.S. capital investment requirement for the 1980s is about $5 trillion. This figure exceeds the sum total of all capital investments made between 1900 and 1980. It will average $350 billion more per year than was spent in the last 20 years.

According to some surveys, capital investment—after adjustment for inflation—may not show much growth in the early 1980s. What causes a decline in capital investment? Inflation. In the early 1980s, when we needed more capital than ever before in our history, industry earnings were low, interest rates were high, equity financing was low, profits had eroded, and bond ratings were down. The portion of U.S. capital stock (technology, equipment, and facilities) that was 5 years old or less had been declining steadily since 1869, and the share of our total investment identified for building technological capital was declining at an alarming rate.

Inflation has an uncontrollable effect on productivity. Inflation tends to shed a negative light on productivity and capital investment. The volatile rates of inflation over the past 20 years, with its attendant negative impact on economic activity, has discouraged investment because of the perceived risks. It is very difficult for any business, including defense, to plan adequately when accurate forecasts of inflation rates are difficult to obtain.

Productivity is influenced by the dollars industrial firms are able to set aside for investment in new technology, equipment, and facilities. If the United States is looking for a way to improve productivity, it needs to stimulate capital spending.

New Technology. A well-managed industrial firm is one in which there is an effective integration of the work force and advanced technology. The genesis of such an organization is an implementation plan that includes education of the work force for factory automation, early identification of new manufacturing processes that will lend themselves to automation, manpower/workload forecasting that takes into account factory automation, and a mechanism for worker feedback.

United States industry and the government must foster more widespread use of industrial robots. The application of robots was one of the keys to the remarkably high levels of productivity achieved by the Japanese in the 1970s. The Robot Institute of America (RIA) suggests that U.S. industry assign high priority to the installation of robots, especially in dangerous, dirty, and dull jobs, "recognizing that robots are one of the quickest and cheapest ways to increase productivity." Also, industry must accept the responsibility for retraining workers who are displaced by robots. Industry managers will have to communicate with the work force and help the workers to understand the advantages of using robots. Further, industrial managers will have to develop plans so workers will share in the benefits of increased productivity.

Someone has said that "if robots are becoming the tireless arms and eyes of production, then computers are their minds." The versatility of the computer has made it one of the principal elements leading to the automation of the factory. According to the Center for Productivity of the National Science Foundation, computer-aided design (CAD), computer-aided manufacturing (CAM), and computer-aided test (CAT) have more potential to radically increase productivity than any development since electricity.

New flexible manufacturing systems, in which several numerically controlled production machines are grouped along with a transport system, under a control of a main computer, are impacting productivity substantially. Using this type of manufacturing system, machine tool utilization has increased as much as 45 percent in some companies.

7.9 CRITICAL MATERIALS AND COMPONENTS

There is a growing dependence in the private industry, as well as the defense industry, on materials and products from foreign countries. The dependence ranges from relying entirely on imported minerals to using electronic components in our weapons systems that are manufactured abroad.

The critical materials stockpile is not at established goals. Of the 62 family groups and individual materials that are to be stockpiled, about 60 percent do not meet the goals. U.S. industries have become dependent on foreign sources for materials and components. Japan has taken almost half of the U.S. market for the computer memory chip, and Japan is posing a serious threat to the U.S. semiconductor industry. Also, approximately 90 percent of all assembly work on U.S. manufactured semiconductor devices is being done offshore.

7.10 FACILITY LIFECYCLES

For years, marketing students were taught that products go through various lifecycle stages from R&D to ultimate death. These same concepts can be used to show that every factory has a lifecycle. The lifecycle approach to facility decisions, just as in marketing/product decisions, allows companies to plan for the use of the facility during each evolutionary stage. The more thoroughly a company plans for the long-term use of its plants, the more efficient the resources will be utilized, productivity can be planned for, and contingency planning becomes easier.

A facility's lifecycle can be defined in three stages; initial planning and start-up, growth and maturity, and deterioration. Companies expect the new facility to be up and running as quickly as possible so that revenue and profitability can be planned for. Schmenner has identified several critical issues that should be considered in the initial planning and startup phase:[15]

- The definition of the products to be manufactured and their desired output levels.
- The plant's capacity and technological capabilities.
- The specific process technology to be used, and the workflow pattern to be followed within the plant.
- The number of workers and the mix of their skills.
- The recruiting, training, and other human resource policies to be adopted in pursuit of the work force goals.
- The production scheduling and control systems to be employed.
- The interrelationship between this facility and other facilities, as well as with suppliers, the distribution system, and ultimate customers.
- The overhead functions and support staff to be provided—both those contained within the facility and those "borrowed" from outside sources.
- A provision for the subsequent expansion and development of the facility and its human resources.
- The capabilities and tasks that will not be required of the plant (at least during early stages).
- The events that would cause a change in the basic plan for the facility.

During the growth and maturity stage, emphasis should be placed upon maintaining or improving productivity and preparing for possibly a new role. Included in this phase are:

- Searching for ways to maintain or improve productivity of the plant.
- Investigating state-of-the-art technology, such as computer integrated manufacturing techniques.
- Investigating better ways for production planning and materials control.
- Reassessing employee skill levels and accompanying salary levels.
- Searching for better ways to improve quality.
- Investigating the possibility for plant expansion to new product lines.
- Evaluating the potential advantages/disadvantages of vertical integration.
- Looking for ways for the plant to "stay alive" even as it ages.

Every lifecycle has a termination point, and termination must be planned for with the same accuracy as initiation planning. Planning for termination, the closing of a plant, is one of the most difficult decisions facing any manager. Schmenner has identified several signs of a failing plant which indicate that the distasteful contingency of plant-closing must be planned for:[16]

- Obsolescence reflected in technology deterring plant layout, poor materials handling, or problems with other physical aspects of the plant.
- Severe and unremitting sales declines.
- Substantial cost increases in labor, transportation, or raw materials.
- Militant union or other personnel problems.
- Needless duplication of operations of other plants.

In preparing for the closing of a plant the company must consider:

- Disposition of human and nonhuman resources.
- Financial and tax considerations.
- Reaction by suppliers and customers.
- Reaction by community.
- Reacton by other organizational units.
- Impact on other plants, product lines, services.

7.11 ENVIRONMENTAL PROTECTION

Restrictions imposed on manufacturing plants by regulations enforced by the Environmental Protection Agency have had a severe effect on many industries in the United States. Pollution control regulations have diverted capital and R&D funds into meeting these requirements. Many companies have ceased operations entirely, because the costs of compliance would make their profit margin so low that the resulting return on investment would not be acceptable. Funds have been diverted from R&D, plant modernization programs, and start-up of new operations by many companies in order to stay in business and be competitive. The net effect has been the loss of innovation and a stagnant or even negative productivity rate.

EPA regulations have limited exploration and development of critical minerals in the U.S. and caused our dependence on foreign supplies for strategic materials to be intensified. Mining of certain strategic materials is limited.

Easing of certain regulations as they now exist would do much to alleviate the curtailments that have been outlined. Legislative reform may be needed to repeal or amend some of the existing laws pertaining to environmental restrictions.

needed to repeal or amend some of the existing laws pertaining to environmental restrictions.

7.12 PRODUCIBILITY

In the previous sections, we have emphasized the fact that manufacturing strategic planning must be coupled with R&D and engineering design. The purpose of this coupling is to develop and manufacture an item that is "producible." Specifically, producibility is a measure of the relative ease of producing a product. Producibility is the coordinated effort by design engineering and manufacturing engineering to create a functional design that can be easily and economically manufactured. The product must be designed in such a manner that manufacturing methods and processes have flexibility in producing the product at the lowest cost without sacrificing function, performance, or quality.

Producibility limitations must be recognized and addressed in each of the lifecycle phases of manufacturing strategic planning. Broad producibility considerations might include the selection of materials and manufacturing processes. The iterative design process mapped in Fig. 7-8 is filled with decision points, each of which permits a potential tradeoff against some other requirement. However, all demands upon the system such as reliability, availability, maintainability, safety, or producibility heavily interact with each other throughout the foreign process creating the need for tradeoffs.

Producibility Objectives and Design

Considerations should include but not be limited to these areas:

- To maximize:
  - —Simplicity of design.
  - —Use of economical materials.
  - —Use of material choices and process alternatives.
  - —Use of economical manufacturing technology.
  - —Standardization of materials and components.
  - —Confirmation of design adequacy prior to the production phase.
  - —Process repeatability.
  - —Product inspectability.
- To minimize:
  - —Procurement lead time.
  - —Generation of scrap, chips, or waste.
  - —Use of critical (strategic) materials.
  - —Energy consumption.

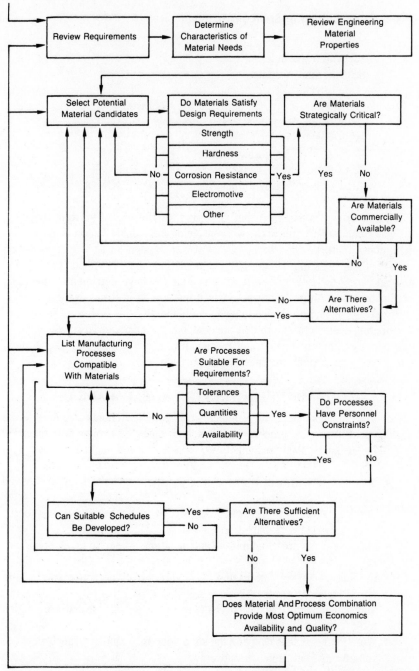

Fig. 7-8. Producibility considerations during the iterative design process.

—Special manufacturing tests.
—Special test systems.
—Use of critical processes.
—Pollution.
—Skill levels of manufacturing personnel.
—Unit costs.
—Design changes during manufacture.
—Use of limited availability items and processes.
—Use of proprietary items without "production right" release.

Too often, it is assumed that designing for the use of existing tooling is the most economical approach, without giving due consideration to new more economical materials and processes. Further, designers also tend to design around their existing processes, without due consideration to ongoing manufacturing technology developments. This can have detrimental effects on producibility and future purchases, which may result in excessive engineering change orders. The producibility plan should identify the system of reviews of engineering designs to assure that the composite of characteristics which, when applied to equipment design and manufacturing planning, leads to the most effective and economic manufacturing approach.

7.13 MANUFACTURING PROBLEM AREAS

When strategic manufacturing planning is performed, it should also include the development of policies, procedures, rules, and guidelines to overcome recurring problems. A list of major manufacturing problem areas might include:

- Inventory investment is excessive, yet there are shortages of needed material.
- Crash programs to reduce inventory to some arbitrary level occur frequently and care based on edicts.
- Delivery dates are often missed and overtime is used to meet new must-have dates.
- Production control, purchasing, plant supervisory personnel, and others are in constant mode of expediting.
- Many manufacturing and purchase orders are past due but are needed to fill current shortages.
- Work in progress is clogging the shop floor and manufacturing orders are sometimes lost, albeit temporarily.
- Rejected material accumulates, and its disposal is usually made when a part is short on the assembly floor.
- There is a lack of rapport and communication among production control,

inventory control, purchasing, sales, engineering, data processing, accounting, and shop floor personnel.

- Bills of material and routing and inventory records are inaccurate or incomplete.
- Overhead cost levels are excessive because current planning and control systems are not timely.
- Productivity is low because of excessive shortages, causing idle time and frequent equipment changeovers.
- Dates on which engineering changes become effective are not highly visible to everyone and configuration control is lost.
- The majority of shipments are made during the last week of the month.
- Lower output is achieved from a given amount of resources.
- Higher unit costs are incurred at all levels of manufacturing.
- Amount of waste is increasing in performing operations.
- Extra operations and equipment are increasingly needed to perform these operations.
- No improvements in the budgeting process are made, thus providing a poor basis for price estimating.
- No improvement in manufacturing control activities and delivery time estimation are made.
- Not enough attention is focused on cost reduction and cost control.

Needless-to-say, these areas must be accounted for in the strategic planning process.

7.14 ROBOTICS

It is important to recognize today's manufacturing environment. Figure 7-9 presents a breakdown of typical manufacturing costs, by percentage. This breakdown is representative of the situation in defense, aerospace, electronics, and heavy industries in the United States. Materials account for the biggest "slice of the pie."

The opportunity for reducing manufacturing costs by introducing robots has generally been in the area of direct and indirect labor tasks. With costs distributed, as shown in Fig. 7-9, the first inclination is to consider replacing direct and indirect labor with a robot due to the similarity of robot motions to human arm movements. However, the potential for cost savings is greater if ways are also found to use robots to save materials.

For many years, robots were marketed as the answer to many of the problems faced by industry in the United States. U.S. industry was beset by rising direct labor costs; pressures to improve productivity; challenges posed by environmental and occupational health and safety authorities, based upon

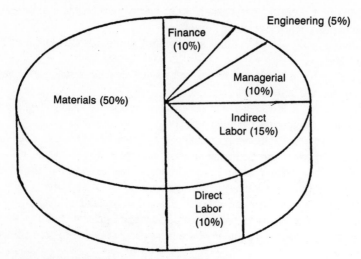

Fig. 7-9. Manufacturing cost distribution.

unpleasant and hazardous working conditions; and the need for better product quality. A modest, but increasing number of products have not only been able to solve these problems, but have been able to save materials and provide a manufacturing flexibility not available previously.

Robots are justified within the production volume ranges shown in Fig. 7-10. When less than 200 parts are to be manufactured per year, manual labor is usually less costly. Above 20,000 parts per year, hard automation is generally more cost effective.

Today, about 80 percent of the U.S. industrial robots are being applied to welding, material handling, and machine loading/unloading. The remainder of the robots are being used in such activities as spray painting, machining, assembling, and palletizing. About 40 percent is divided almost equally between foundries and the light manufacturing industry that is producing nonmetal products. The remainder of the applications are in the heavy equipment, electrical/electronics, and aerospace industries.

Over the years, the capabilities of robots have continued to increase. Much of the current robot technology was unknown just a decade ago—particularly control technology and programming. Now, robot manufacturers have discovered electronic logic and computer software. These technologies are making robots adaptable to an increasing variety of complex tasks. Therefore, it is very important that each proposed application be carefully considered and the robot selected be properly engineered to ensure success. Such a robot will inherently increase manufacturing flexibility and improve product quality and productivity.

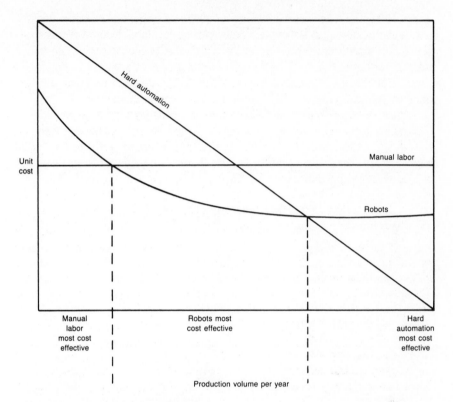

Fig. 7-10. Robotics justification.

Labor and other production costs continue to rise, but robot manufacturers have generally held the line on the price of robot installations in recent years. Thus, we can expect many more manufacturing companies to give serious consideration to purchasing robots. When they do so, they may find themselves on their own. Although the number of applications will increase, each application will be unique in some respects. Robot technology is still relatively new, and there is, therefore, little in-depth experience to call upon. As a consequence, the experience of most robot users is being guarded jealously, because they believe this experience gives them a competitive edge. It is quite possible that the "wheel" is being reinvented many times over by industry in developing robots for new applications.

Although robots are used to save workers from health hazards and fatigue, reduction in labor cost is still the most popular reason for employing robots in manufacturing operations. Let's examine this finding in more detail.

In 1981, the true cost of an hourly employee in the metal working industry (except automobiles) was about $15/hour. In the automobile industry it was about $20/hour. At the same time, the "all included" cost of applying a medium-priced robot was about $6/hour. The hourly operating cost of a robot has only risen $2 since 1967. GMC Chairman Roger B. Smith once said, "Everytime the cost of labor goes up $1/hour, 1000 more robots become economical."

In the design or redesign of every manufacturing system, management has the opportunity to explore options concerning the relationships between people, technology, and cost. Managers, normally concerned with technological improvements and reduction in cost, can ill afford to neglect the changes that will be wrought on the social system in the workplace by robots.

7.15 LEARNING CURVES

The profitability of a corporation is often measured as a function of the relative market share. As market share increases, profitability will increase more because of lower production costs than due to increased margins. Large market shares allow companies to build large manufacturing plants so that the fixed capital costs are spread out over more units, thus lowering the unit cost. This increase in efficiency is referred to as *economies of scale* and may be the main reason why larger manufacturing organizations may be more efficient than smaller ones. Capital equipment costs follow the rule of six-tenths power of capacity. As an example, consider a plant which has the capacity of producing 35,000 units each year. The plant's construction cost was $10 million. If the company wishes to build a new plant with a capacity of 70,000 units, what will the construction cost be?

$$\left(\frac{\$ \cdot \text{new}}{\$ \text{ old}} = \frac{70,000}{35,000} \right)^{0.6}$$

Solving for $ new, we find that the new plant will cost approximately $15 million, or one and one-half times the cost of the old plant. (For a more accurate determination, the costs must be adjusted for inflation.)

Large manufacturing also generates lower costs through "experience" or "learning" curves whereby the manufacturing costs (specifically direct labor) will decline each time a company doubles their output. Typically, experience curves produce a cost savings of 10 to 30 percent each time a company's experience at producing a product doubles. As an example, consider a company which is operating on an 85 percent experience curve and is currently producing its 1000th unit. If the experience curve holds true, then when production reaches 2000 units, the cost of the 2000th unit should be only 85 percent of the cost of the 1000th unit. And if the production level doubles again to 4000 units, then the cost of the 4000th unit should be 85 percent of the cost of the 2000th unit. Simply stated, each time production doubles, the costs should decrease by the same fixed amount. In this example, the fixed cost decrease was 15 percent. Theoretically, this decrease could occur indefinitely.

These types of costs are often referred to as *value-added costs*, and can also appear in the form of lower freight and procurement costs through bulk quantities. The value-added costs are actually cost savings for both the customer and contractor.

The usefulness of the experience curves requires a close working relationship between marketing and manufacturing, especially during the development of the manufacturing strategic plan. Scale effects provide large cost savings and can increase competitiveness. However, manufacturing must have the capacity to produce the required number of units. Therefore, marketing must provide manufacturing with an estimate of market share and demand.

Concept

The learning curve was adapted from the historical observation that individuals performing repetitive tasks exhibit an improvement in performance as the task is repeated a number of times. Empirical studies of this phenomenon yielded three conclusions on which the current theory and practice is based. For a constant rate:

- The time required to perform a task reduces as the task is repeated.
- The amount of improvement decreases as more units are produced.
- The rate of improvement has sufficient consistency to allow its use as a prediction tool.

This consistency in improvement has been found to exist in the form of a constant percentage reduction in time required over successive doubled quantities of units produced. This can be seen graphically in Fig. 7-11.

Comments of Improvement

By its title, the learning curve focuses attention on worker learning, or job familiarization. This is just one of the components which contribute to the reduction of time requirements. Table 7-2 lists a number of elements which have been shown to contribute to the manufacturing improvement. From Table 7-2 it can be seen that the total improvement is a combination of personnel learning and management action. Although some study has been done, there is no general rule concerning the relative contribution of the specific elements. The critical

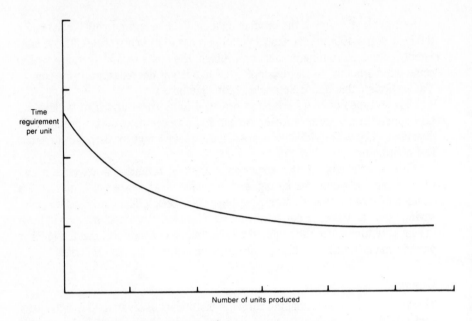

Fig. 7-11. Manufacturing improvement curve.

Table 7-2. Factors Affecting Learning

- *Worker learning*
- *Supervisory learning*
- *Reductions in crowded workstations*
- *Tooling improvements*
- *Design producibility improvements*
- *Reduced engineering liaison*
- *Improved work methods*
- *Reduced parts shortages*
- *Improved planning and scheduling*
- *Increased lot sizes*
- *Reduced engineering change activity*
- *Reduction in scrap and reworks*
- *Operation sequencing and synchronization*

issue is to recognize the role of management in achieving these reductions and to ensure that appropriate management actions are taken.

Characteristics of Learning Environment

While learning is found in almost all elements of the manufacturing function, its impact is most pronounced when certain characteristics are present. The first characteristic is the building of a large, complex product requiring a large number of direct labor hours. The second characteristic is continuity of manufacturing to preclude losses of accrued improvements during production breaks. The third characteristic is an element of continuing change in the product. This third characteristic can present some problems in analysis using the manufacturing improvement curve.

Key Words Associated with Learning Curves

To utilize learning curve theory, certain key phrases listed below are of importance:

- *Slope of the Curve.* A percentage figure that represents the steepness (constant rate of improvement) of the curve. Using the unit curve theory, this percentage represents the value (e.g., hours or cost) at a doubled production quantity in relation to the previous quantity. For example, with an experience curve having an 80 percent slope, the value of unit two is 80 percent of the value of unit one, the value of unit four is 80 percent of the value at unit two, the value at unit 1,000 is 80 percent of the value at unit 500, and so on.
- *Unit one.* The first unit of product actually completed during a production run. This is not to be confused with a unit produced in any reproduction phase of the overall acquisition program.
- *Cumulative average hours.* The average hours expended per unit for all units produced through any given unit. When illustrated on a graph by a line drawn through each successive unit, the values form a cumulative average curve.
- *Unit hours.* The total direct labor hours expended to complete any specific unit. When a line is drawn on a graph through the values for each successive unit, the values form a unit curve.
- *Cumulative total hours.* The total hours expended for all units produced through any given unit. The data plotted on a graph with each point connected by a line form a cumulative total curve.

Unit Curve

There are two fundamental models of the learning curve in general use; the unit curve and the cumulative average curve. The unit curve focuses on the hours or cost involved in specific units of production. The theory can be stated as follows: As the total quantity of units produced doubles, the cost per unit decreases by some constant percentage. The constant percentage by which the costs of doubled quantities decrease is called the rate of learning.

The "slope" of the learning curve is related to the rate of learning. It is the difference between 100 and the rate of learning. For example, if the hours between doubled quantities are reduced by 20 percent (rate of learning), it would be described as a curve with an 80 percent slope.

To illustrate the unit curve concept, assume that the first unit required 100,000 labor hours to produce. If a curve with an 80 percent slope is assumed, the second unit would require 80,000 labor hours, the fourth 64,000, and so forth.

The difference or amount of labor-hour reduction is not constant. Rather, it declines by a continually diminishing amount as the quantities are doubled. But the *rate* of change or decline has been found to be a constant percentage of the prior cost, because the decline in the base figure is proportionate to the decline in the amount of change.

A labor-hour graph of this data curve drawn on ordinary graph paper (rectangular coordinates) becomes a hyperbolic line. The nonlinear appearance in Fig. 7-12 pictures the relationship between two variables, units produced in sequence (X) and labor hours per unit (Y). When labor hour figures that conform to the learning process are plotted on log-log paper against the units of production to which they apply, the points thus produced lie on a straight line called the learning curve. This is shown in Fig. 7-13.

Cumulative Average Curve

The cumulative average curve may be obtained from the following formula:

$$T_a = T_1 X^{-K}$$

when:

T_a = cumulative average direct labor hours
T_1 = the direct labor hours for the first unit, (unit one)
X = the cumulative unit produced
$-K$ = a factor derived from the slope of the experience curve (values for the cumulative average curve are available in tables)

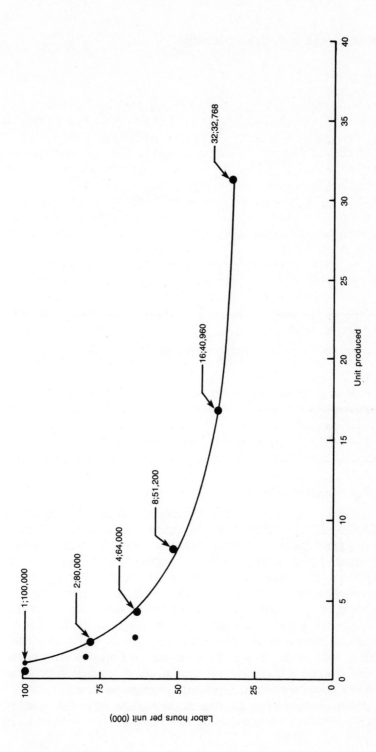

Fig. 7-12. An 80 percent learning curve on arithmetic graph paper.

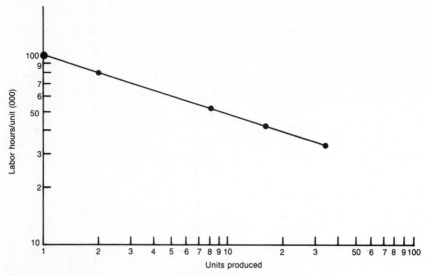

Fig. 7-13. An 80 percent learning curve on log-log paper.

The best solution for this formula is through the use of logarithmic tables and is expressed as:

$$\text{Log } T_a = -K \text{ Log } X + T_1$$

Developing Slope Measures

Research by the Stanford Research Institute revealed that many different slopes were experienced by different manufacturers, sometimes on similar manufacturing programs. In fact, manufacturing data collected from World War II aircraft manufacturing industry had slopes ranging from 69.7 percent to almost 100 percent. These slopes averaged 80 percent, giving rise to an industry average curve of 80 percent. Other research has developed measures for other industries such as 95.6 percent for a sample of 162 electronics programs. Unfortunately, this industry average curve is frequently misapplied by practitioners who use it as a standard or norm. When estimating slopes without the benefit of data on the item being manufactured from the plant of the manufacturer, it is better to use learning curve slopes from similar items at the manufacturer's plant rather than the industry average.

The analyst needs to know the slope of the learning curve for a number of reasons. One is to facilitate communication, because it is part of the language of the learning curve theory. The steeper the slope (lower the percent), the more rapidly the resource requirements (hours) will decline as production increases. Accordingly, the slope of the learning curve is usually an issue in production contract negotiation. The slope of the learning curve is also needed to project follow-on costs, using either the learning tables or computational assistance of a computer. Another need for a slope is that for many production situations, a given slope may be established as a standard based on reliable historical experience. Learning curves developed from actual experience on current production can then be compared against this standard slope to determine whether the improvement on a particular contract is or is not reasonable.

Unit Costs and Use of Midpoints

The use of the learning curve is dependent on the methods of recording costs that companies employ. An accounting or statistical record system must be devised by a company so that data is available for learning curve purposes. Otherwise, it may be impossible to construct a learning curve. Costs, such as labor hours per unit or dollars per unit, must be identified with the unit of product. It is preferable to use labor hours rather than dollars, because the latter contain an additional variable, the effect of inflation or deflation (both wage-rate and material cost changes), which the former does not contain. In any event, the record system must have definite cutoff points for such costs permitting identification of the costs with the units involved. Most companies use a lot-release system, whereby costs are accumulated on a job order in which the number of units completed are specified and costs are cut off at the completion of the number of units. In this case, however, the costs are usually equated with equivalent units rather than actual units. Because the job order system is commonly used, the unit cost is not the actual cost per unit in the lot. This means that when lots are plotted on graph paper, the unit value corresponding with the average cost value must be found.

Selection of Learning Curves

Existing experience curves, by definition, reflect past experience. *Trend lines* are developed from accumulated data plotted on logarithmic paper (preferably) and "smoothed out" to portray the curve. The type of curve may represent one of several concepts. The data may have been accumulated by product, process, department, or by other functional or organizational segregations, depending on the needs of the user. But whichever experience curve concept or method of data accumulation is selected for use, based on suitability to the experience pattern, the data should be applied consistently in order to render meaningful information to management. Consistency in curve concept and data accumulation cannot be overemphasized, because existing experience curves play a major role in determining the projected experience curve for a new item or product.

When selecting the proper curve for a new production item when only one point of data is available and the slope is unknown, the following, in decreasing order of magnitude, should be considered.

- Similarity between the new item and an item or items previously produced.
- Physical comparisons.
  - —Addition or deletion of processes and components
  - —Differences in material, if any
  - —Effect of engineering changes in items previously produced
- Duration of time since a similar item was produced.
  Condition of tooling and equipment
  - —Personnel turnover
  - —Changes in working conditions or morale
- Other comparable factors between similar items.
  - —Delivery schedules
  - —Availability of material and components
  - —Personnel turnover during production cycle of item previously produced
  - —Comparison of actual production data with previously extrapolated or theoretical curves to identify deviations

It is feasible to assign weights to these factors as well as to any other factors that are of a comparable nature in an attempt to quantify differences between items. These factors are again historical in nature and only comparison of several existing curves and their actuals would reveal the importance of these factors.

If at least two points of data are available, the slope of the curve may be determined. Naturally the distance between these two points must be considered when evaluating the reliability of the slope. The availability of additional points of data will enhance the reliability of the curve. Regardless of the number of data points and the assumed reliability of the slope, comparisons with similar items are considered the most desirable approach and should be made whenever possible.

A value for unit one may be arrived at either by accumulation of data or statistical derivation. When production is under way, available data can be readily plotted, and the curve may be extrapolated to a desired unit. However, if production has yet to be started, actual unit one data would not be available, and a theoretical unit one value would have to be developed. This may be accomplished in one of three ways:

- A statistically derived relationship between the preproduction unit hours and first unit hours can be applied to the actual hours from the preproduction phase.
- A cost estimating relationship (CER) for first unit cost based upon physical or performance parameters can be used to develop a first unit cost estimate.
- The slope and the point at which the curve and the labor standard value converge are known. In this case, a unit one value can be determined. This is accomplished by dividing the labor standard by the appropriate unit value.

Follow-On Orders

Once the initial experience curve has been developed for either the initial order or production run, the values through the last unit on the cumulative average and unit curves can be determined. Follow-on orders and continuations of production runs, which are considered extensions of the original orders or runs, are plotted as extensions on the appropriate curve. However, the cumulative average value through the final point of the extended curve is not the cumulative average for the follow-on portion of that curve. It is the cumulative average for both portions of the curve, assuming no break in production. Thus, estimating the cost for the follow-on effort only requires evaluation of the difference between cumulative average costs for the initial run and the follow-on. Likewise, the last unit value for both portions of the unit curve would represent the last unit value for the combined curve.

Manufacturing Breaks

The *manufacturing break* is the time lapse between the completion of an order or manufacturing run of certain units of equipment and the commencement of a follow-on order or restart of a manufacturing run for identical units. This time lapse disrupts the continuous flow of manufacturing and constitutes a definite cost impact. The time lapse under discussion here pertains to significant periods of time (weeks and months) as opposed to the minutes or hours for personnel allowances, machine delays, power failures, and the like.

It is logical to assume that because the experience curve has a time/cost relationship, a break will affect both time and cost. Therefore, the length of the break becomes as significant as the length of the initial order or manufacturing run. Because the break is quantifiable, the remaining factor to be determined is the cost of this lapse in manufacturing (that is, the additional cost incurred over and above that which would have been incurred had either the initial order or the run continued through the duration of the follow-on order or the restarted run).

When a manufacturer relies on experience curves as management information tools, it can be assumed that the necessary, accurate data for determining the initial curves have been accumulated, recorded, and properly validated. Therefore, if the manufacturer has experienced breaks, the experience curve data for the orders (lots) or runs involved should be available in such form that appropriate curves can be developed.

George Anderlohr, in the September 1969 issue of Industrial Engineering, suggests a method that assumes loss of learning is dependent on five factors:[17]

- Manufacturing personnel learning. In this area, the physical loss of personnel, either through regular movement or layoff, must be determined. The company's personnel records can usually furnish evidence on which to establish this learning loss. The percentage of learning lost by the personnel retained on other plant projects should also be ascertained. These people will lose their physical dexterity and familiarity with the product, and the momentum of repetition.
- Supervisory learning. Once again, a percentage of supervisory personnel will be lost as a result of the break in repetition. Management will make a greater effort to retain this higher caliber of personnel, so the physical loss, in the majority of cases, will be far less than in the area of production personnel. However, the supervisory personnel retained will lose their overall familiarity with the job, so that the guidance they can furnish will be reduced. In addition, because of the loss of production personnel, the supervisor will have no knowledge of the new hires and their individual personalities and capabilities.
- Continuity of productivity. This relates to the physical positioning of the line, the relationship of one work station to another, and the location of lighting, bins, parts, and tools within the work station. It also includes the position adjustment to optimize the individual needs. In addition, a major factor affecting this area is the balanced line or the work-in-process build-up. Of all the elements of learning, the greatest initial loss is suffered in this area.
- Methods. This area is least affected by a break. As long as the method sheets are kept on file, learning can never be completely lost. However, drastic revisions to the method sheets may be required as a result of a change from soft to hard tooling.
- Special tooling. New and better tooling is a major contributor to learning. In relating loss in tooling area to learning, the major factors are wear,

physical misplacement, and breakage. An additional consideration must be the comparison of short-run or so-called soft tooling to long run or hard tooling, and the effect of the transition from soft to hard tooling.

The S-Curve

The S-curve is a formulation of the learning curve which has been supported by actual cost experience observed in industry, particularly by their manufacturing personnel. This S-curve describes the situation where the initial units in the production cycle exceed the anticipated "normal" learning curve values by a significant percentage and at a relatively low learning rate. This is illustrated in Fig. 7-14.

As the production cycle continues to produce units of the product, these units costs begin to drop sharply, actually dropping below the normal learning curve generally anticipated at that point and then begin to proceed at a lesser slope rate.

This pattern may reflect the fact that during the introduction of a new product, intensive demands are placed upon the entire organization. These demands are the result of frequent design changes and production interruptions, causing new requirements for training production and supervisory personnel in new manufacturing techniques and possibly requiring the development of new procedures for production planning and control.

If this situation exists and is not recognized by using an analysis based upon the S-curve rather than the standard learning curve, the result could be that sufficient funds would not be available during the early part of a program.

If the strategic planners decide to use the S-curve approach, Fig. 7-15

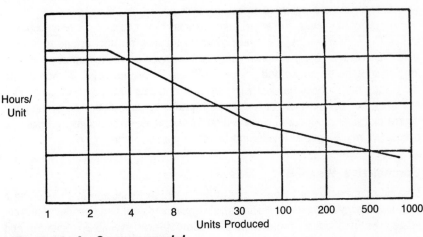

Hours/
Unit

1   2   4   8   30   100   200   500   1000
Units Produced

Fig. 7-14. An S-curve model.

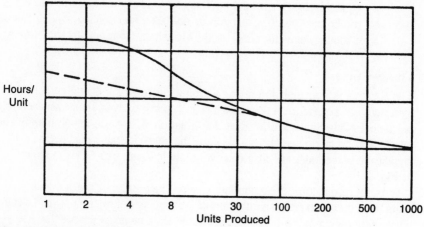

Fig. 7-15. The S-curve.

illustrates a method that could be used for modeling this procedure. The figure reflects an initial period of slow learning followed by a period of more rapid learning, and then followed by a slower learning level. To use this approach, it would be necessary to evaluate the specific company's experience to determine where the break points would occur and the appropriate slopes for the curve segments. This illustration (Fig. 7-15) indicates the first break point at unit 3; the actual break point may come much later in the program, and some research has indicated that near unit 30 is the most likely point for the first break.

In stable, competitive markets, unit price will decrease proportionally to the price decrease (due to the experience effect). This is shown in Fig. 7-16, with a constant gap between price and cost.

In reality, however, the actual relationship is closer to an S-curve as depicted in Fig. 7-17. In Phase A, it is quite common for new product prices to be less than the average costs, especially if pricing policies are based upon expected, long-term units produced and prices. In Phase B, profits begin to increase to the point where it becomes attractive for new entrants to the marketplace. This indicates the beginning of Phase C, where prices begin to decrease to the point where marginal producers are forced out of the marketplace. During Phase D, profits approach normal levels and begin to parallel industry costs.

Competitive Weapon

Learning curves are a strong competitive weapon especially in developing a pricing strategy. The actual pricing strategy depends upon the product lifecycle stage, the firm's market position, the competitors' available resources and

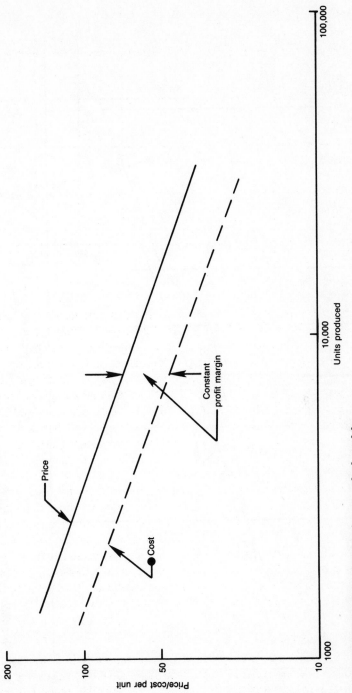

Fig. 7-16. Idealized price/cost relationship.

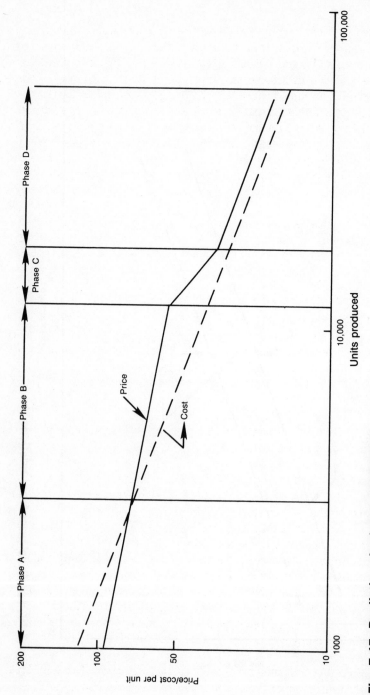

Fig. 7-17. Realistic price/cost relationship.

market position, the time horizon, and the firm's financial position. To illustrate corporate philosophy towards pricing, although companies such as Texas Instruments (TI) and Digital Equipment Corp. (DEC) have used "experience curve pricing" to achieve an early market share and a subsequent strong competitive position, companies such as Hewlett-Packard Co. (HP) have used completely different approaches to achieve a commanding portion in the market. The focal point of TI's and DEC's strategy has been to price a new product in relation to the manufacturing costs that they expect to achieve when the product is mature. In contrast, HP, instead of competing on price, concentrates on developing products so advanced that customers are willing to pay a premium for them. Mr. David Packard, chairman of HP, drives the point home by saying,

"The main determinant of our growth is the effectiveness of our new product programs . . . Anyone can build market share, and if you set your price low enough, you can get the whole damn market. But I will tell you it won't get you anywhere around here."[18]

7.16 COMPUTER-INTEGRATED MANUFACTURING (CIM)

CIM advocates that all functions in a manufacturing plant can be integrated by a computer system with strong communications channels. The manufacturing plant then becomes responsive as an organized unit. The best way to define CIM is to quote individuals from various industries:

From the management consulting business, Ray L. Discasali, Vice President of Management Science of America, says:

This host of new technology is beginning to be collectively referred to as computer-integrated manufacturing (CIM). CIM is the umbrella under which all the independent pieces—CAD, CAM, GT, robotics and others—are organized to work together. We're still in the process of defining what it is, but we're at a point, I believe, where we can see several of the major pieces that will comprise CIM.

Certainly, CIM is computer-based. It is hardware. It is also software. At the core, CIM is a view of the manufacturing plant layout from an information processing perspective. It is a way of managing information as much as machinery and manpower.

CIM is also firmware—dedicated pieces of automation be they robotic, CAD/CAM, or automated storage and retrieval systems for material handling. These three components, as well as pieces not yet envisioned, comprise a powerful new tool for manufacturing.

From the computer hardware industry, Stephen J. Gondert, Manager of Industry and Product Promotion for Computervision Corporation, says:[20]

Computer-integrated manufacturing is not a "thing." It is rather an evolutionary process that has been going on in the manufacturing community ever since the advent of the computer. CIM is a global concept that includes far more than the traditional manufacturing processes found in the factory. CIM is truly a technological imperative that can help to ensure economic survival in an increasingly competitive international marketplace. CIM integrates all data processing functions within the company, including financial accounting, purchasing, inventory, distribution, payroll, engineering, and management, as well as the traditional manufacturing operations. Calling it a computer-integrated business functional system might be more appropriate.

From the plastics industry, Agostino von Hassell, Associate Editor of "Plastics Technology," says:[21,22,23,24]

Fundamentally, CIM means transforming a manufacturing operation that today consists of an assemblage of systems and subsystems operating more or less independent of each other into a single organism with an electronic "nervous system" of sensors and controllers. Everything that happens in the plant—from receiving a customer's order to shipping the finished product—is known to a central computer and can be controlled by it. The three fundamental phases of manufacturing—product design, production planning, and manufacturing—are integrated and accomplished without direct human effort, by the utilization of intelligent distributed control and effective machine intercommunication.

The details of each industry's definition of CIM will focus on different aspects of the general concept because the specific needs of each industry differs to some extent.

As with any advanced technology, it is easy to begin to think of CIM as an end in itself; but the real reason for investing in computer-integrated manufacturing is productivity. The pressures for increased productivity are very clearly explained by James A. Baker, Executive Vice President of General Electric Company, in the following:[25]

Any manufacturing operation of any size that is not actively pursuing automation is on death row. It's a factory—and a business—with no future. Failure to automate will lead to the death of a business. Bad economic times and low capital funds are no argument against automation. The wait-until-good-times approach is custom-made for losers. The winners are begging, borrowing, betting everything on smart automation, using the leverage of technology to fight back. The losers are frozen like deer in the Japanese headlights, hoping for some outside force to save them. It won't. But automation can. We're running out of excuses, and we're running out of time. It is not only the rich companies that are spending on automation. The hardest hit industries are doing it as well. Chrysler's going in hock up to its ears to automate. Iacocca knows, as do Ford and GM, that automation is the last, best hope for American industry and must be pursued no matter what the cost. The choice is between biting the bullet or biting the dust.

Ray L. Discasali, Vice President of Management Science of America, makes the same point as Baker when he says:[25]

With all the excitement surrounding CIM and what it will mean for U.S. manufacturing, we must keep in mind that CIM is not the goal. The goal is competitive survival. We must shorten development time, reduce costs, and improve quality. We must be both responsive to the market and more profitable.

Computer-integrated manufacturing is not a quick fix. CIM is basically a way to put computer power to use in manufacturing. Although it may be relatively easy to conceptualize what CIM should be, it is much more difficult to implement CIM technology in an organization. Implementation takes careful planning and step-by-step strategy, but a company that is willing to put forth the effort can realize the benefits.

ENDNOTES—Chapter 7

1. Robert H. Hayes and Steven C. Wheelwright, *Restoring Our Competitive Edge* (John Wiley Publisher, 1984), p. 2.

2. Roger B. Smith, Chairman and Chief Executive Officer, General Motors Corporation, "The 21st Century Corporation," delivered before The Economic Club of Detroit, Cobo Hall, Detroit, MI, September 9, 1985.

3. Martin Feldstein, "Reviewing Business Investment," *Wall Street Journal*, June 19, 1981.

4. Lester Thurow, "A Productivity Disaster and a Saving Solution," *Boston Globe*, January 7, 1981, p. 52.

5. Ryohei Suzuki, "Worldwide Expansion of U.S. Exports—a Japanese View," *Sloan Management Review*, Spring 1979, p. 67-70.

6. Thomas G. Gunn, "CIM Must Start at the Top," *Production Magazine*, March 1985, pp. 43-44.

7. Roger B. Smith, speech before the Economic Club of Detroit, September 9, 1985.

8. Robert H. Hayes and Steven C. Wheelwright, *Restoring Our Competitive Edge*, p. 10.

9. Several of the remaining sections in this chapter have been adapted from *Manufacturing Management Handbook*, AD-A146-901, 2nd Edition (Fort Belvoir, VA: Defense Systems Management College), July 1984.

10. Robert H. Hayes and Steven C. Wheelwright, *Restoring Our Competitive Edge*, p. 31.

11. Roger Schmenner, *Making Business Location Decisions*, (New Jersey: Prentice Hall Publishers, 1982), p. 33-36.

12. Wickham Skinner, "Manufacturing-Missing Link in Corporate Strategy," *Harvard Business Review*, May-June, 1969; also *Harvard Business Review* reprints, Production Managements Part III, P. 33; © 1969 by the President and Fellows of Harvard College; all rights reserved.

13. Wickham Skinner, "Management of International Production," *Harvard Business Review*, September-October 1964; also, *Harvard Business Review* reprints, Production Management: Part II, p. 56; © 1964 by the President and Fellows of Harvard College; all rights reserved.

14. Adapted from Michael Porter, Competitive Strategy (New York: Free Press, A Division of MacMillan Publishers, 1980) pp. 324-339.

15. Roger Schmenner, *Making Business Location Decisions*, p. 28.

16. Roger Schmenner, "Every Factory has a Life Cycle," *Harvard Business Review*, March-April 1983, p. 128. Copyright 1983 by the President and Fellows of Harvard University; all rights reserved. Reproduced by permission.

17. George Anderlohr, *Industrial Engineering*, September 1969.

18. "Hewlett Packard: Where Slower Growth is Smarter Management," *Business Week*, June 9, 1975.

19. Ray L. Discasali, "Developing Your CIM Strategy," *Manufacturing Systems*, March 1985, pp. 42-43.

20. Stephen J. Gondert, "Understanding the Impact of Computer-Integrated Manufacturing," *Manufacturing Engineering*, 93, September 1984, pp. 67-69.

21. Agostino von Hassell, "Computer Integrated Manufacturing: Coming Sooner Than You Think," *Plastics Technology* 29, May 1983, pp. 37-42.

22. Agostino von Hassell, "Computer Integrated Manufacturing: Here's How to Plan For It," *Plastics Technology* 29, November 1983, pp. 54-69.

23. Agostino von Hassell, "CIM Guidelines on Buying Hardware, Software," *Plastics Technology* 29, December 1983, pp. 59-69.

24. Agostino von Hassell, "New Controls Technology Aids Complete Plant Automation," *Plastics Technology* 30, July 1984, pp. 20-27.

25. James A. Baker, "Winning Your Case for Automation," *Manufacturing Engineering*, 93, July 1984, pp. 72-73.

Chapter 8

Integrating
Functional Strategies

8.0 THE NEED FOR INTEGRATION

In on-going firms, each functional area has a set of activities related to the achievement of objectives set by previous rounds of strategic planning. These within-function activities are in various stages of development and change. For example, the firm may be in the process of phasing out focused product promotion and phasing in a program related to image or institutional promotion. Thus, with the complexity of activities underway, it is possible that even within a functional area, a company can find itself pursuing conflicting activities. If goals have not been integrated from the top down, it is also possible that functional areas themselves are in conflict with each other. For example, the desires of the marketing function to stay close and responsive to the market often result in activities which conflict with the desires of the manufacturing and accounting functions to reduce costs and maintain efficiency. Figure 8-1 illustrates what happens if each of the functional areas are left to set their own objectives. The activities of the separate objectives soon begin to cancel out each others' effectiveness. In order to make sure that all the activities move the organization in the same direction, mutually dependent activities must be coordinated. The interrelatedness within strategies and across strategies can be complex. Figure 8-2 depicts the complexity, as seen by one author, in the area. If the functional strategies are not coordinated, the organizational objectives probably won't be achieved. If they are achieved, it is due to the luck of chance, rather than planning.

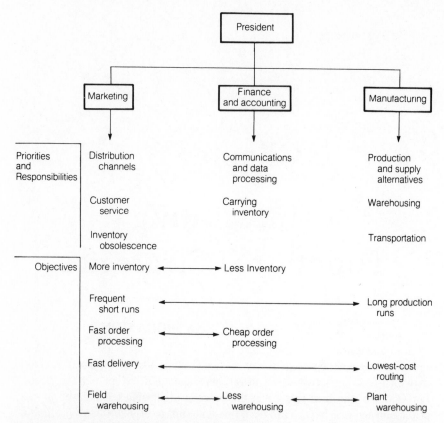

Fig. 8-1. Responsibilities and objectives of functional areas within a typical manufacturing company.
Source: John F. Stolle, "How to Manage Physical Distribution",
Harvard Business Review 45 (July-August 1967), p. 95.

Figure 8-3 shows the flow of functional strategies for General Cinema Corporation's business level strategy for movie theaters. The business level strategy specifies concentration and selective market development. Obviously, the choice of this goal was arrived at by analyzing environmental opportunities and threats and matching these with resource strengths and weaknesses. This business is in the growth, cash cow stage, and Cinema plans to take advantage of its competitive position to provide cash for diversification when the movie theater business hits the mature and declining stages.

Under functional strategy, Cinema chooses to improve profitability by increasing volume rather than sales price. It chooses to lease rather than own

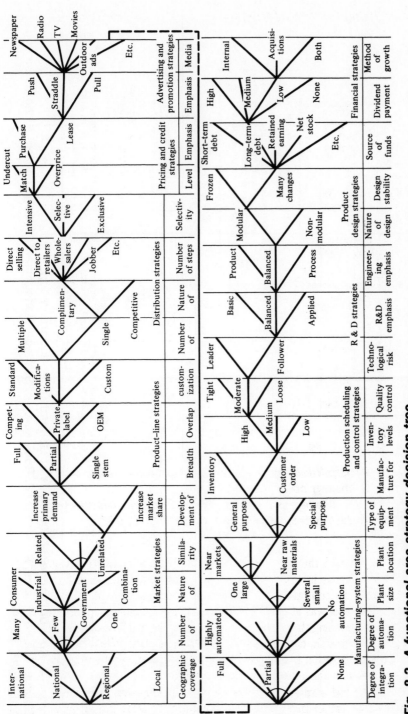

Fig. 8-2. A functional area strategy decision tree.
Source: C. W. Hofer, The Uses and Limitations of Statistical Decision Theory. (Boston: Intercollegiate Case Clearing House, 9-171-653, 1971), p. 34.

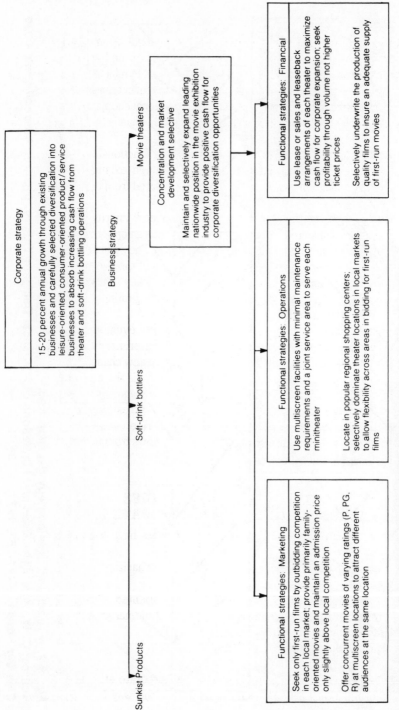

Corporate strategy

15-20 percent annual growth through existing businesses and carefully selected diversification into leisure-oriented, consumer-oriented product/service businesses to absorb increasing cash flow from theater and soft-drink bottling operations

Business strategy

Sunkist Products

Soft-drink bottlers

Movie theaters

Concentration and market development selective

Maintain and selectively expand leading nationwide position in the movie exhibition industry to provide positive cash flow for corporate diversification opportunities

Functional strategies: Marketing

Seek only first-run films by outbidding competition in each local market; provide primarily family-oriented movies and maintain an admission price only slightly above local competition

Offer concurrent movies of varying ratings (P, PG, R) at multiscreen locations to attract different audiences at the same location

Functional strategies: Operations

Use multiscreen facilities with minimal maintenance requirements and a joint service area to serve each minitheater

Locate in popular regional shopping centers; selectively dominate theater locations in local markets to allow flexibility across areas in bidding for first-run films

Functional strategies: Financial

Use lease or sales and leaseback arrangements of each theater to maximize cash flow for corporate expansion; seek profitability through volume not higher ticket prices

Selectively underwrite the production of quality films to insure an adequate supply of first-run movies

Fig. 8-3. Role of functional strategies at General Cinema Corporation.
Source: John A. Pearce, II., Richard B. Robinson, Jr., Strategic Management, Second Edition, Richard D. Irwin, Inc., 1985, p. 194.

theaters, thus avoiding tying the corporation's capital up in long-term, fixed assets. One of the uses of cash resources will be to underwrite production ventures to produce quality films. Operations will seek to minimize costs, because their objectives call for multiscreen facilities with low maintenance and a common snack bar service area. Distribution is to be in regional shopping centers. They will seek to selectively dominate in local markets to enhance their bidding power for first-run films.

General Cinema's business level strategy and functional strategy tie back to its corporate strategy, which is to grow through existing business with selective diversification using the cash being generated from bottling and movie theaters.

Figure 8-4 shows the strategic decision choices if improving performance is the overall goal selected by corporate. Cinema has an opportunity to increase performance by choosing to increase sales volume. They will seek to penetrate the market for first-run family films. Underwriting of the production of quality films is their product development strategy. They will pursue market development by offering concurrent movies of differing ratings to try and attract different market segments at multiscreen locations.

General Cinema is in the mature stage of market evolution in its film business. The marketing/distribution function takes on primary emphasis at this stage. Strong distribution, with the ability to develop new channels while holding existing markets and skills at differentiating products, is the marketing function that fits with this stage of evolution. At the mature stage, the finance function is also of primary significance. Net cash flows are increasing and these funds need to be allocated to projects which will generate subsequent rounds of profitability. We see General Cinema using its cash flows from the movie theaters for corporate diversification opportunities.

8.1 GENERIC STRATEGIES—
INTEGRATION AT THE CORPORATE LEVEL

Four basic types of generic management strategies have been identified:[1]

- Performance improvement strategies emphasizing increasing sales volume.
- Performance improvement strategies, oriented toward increasing profitability through improved productivity or margins.
- Harvesting or divestment strategies.
- Turnaround strategies.

These generic management strategies or corporate strategies are broad patterns of functional actions which characterize the way businesses tend to

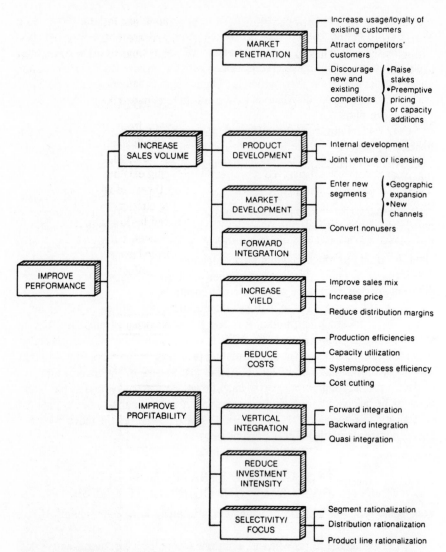

Fig. 8-4. Developing strategy options: the role of generic strategies.
Source: George S. Day, Strategic Market Planning, *West Publishing*
Co., 1984, p. 103.

compete. They have also been referred to as recipes. Each basic type has
different implications for functional objectives, and each type has a choice of
alternatives for achieving the corporate objective. From Fig. 8-4, we see that
we can increase sales volume through a variety of marketing strategies; market

penetration, product development, market development, and forward integration. Not all firms follow the generic strategy, and these are not offered as ideal "shoulds," rather these are patterns of activity that tend to emerge and that have been observed and reported.

8.1-1 INCREASING SALES VOLUME

The opportunity to increase sales volume derives from the possibility of expanding along one or more of the dimensions of the business definition. Figure 8-5 illustrates how the business definition can be expanded.

Market penetration involves strategies for keeping existing customers while trying to lure the competition's customers. If the threat of retaliation is high, then it is best to focus energy on reinforcing existing customers. Entry barriers may be pursued, such as preemptive pricing offered by low cost advantages. The probability of success for this strategy is enhanced when demand in the whole industry is high and expanding, and the established leaders are complacent or overly concerned about the "cannibalization" effects of new product development.

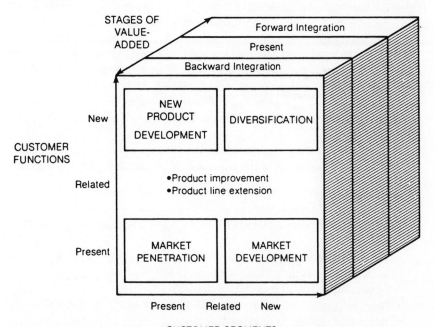

Fig. 8-5. Directions for expanding the business definition.
Source: George S. Day, Strategic Market Planning, West Publishing Co., 1984, p. 104.

Another strategy for increasing sales volume is through product development for the present served market. This can be done by extending the present product line, improving the performance of existing products, or using a technology that is new to the firm to provide a new function to the served market. Option one and two build on existing competencies.

Market development is achieved by entering new segments or using new channels to reach unserved customers. If the new market has similarities with existing markets served, then the additional volume will reduce unit costs through better utilization of capacity.

The gains from forward integration will depend on how close the firm is to the ultimate customer. There is the potential of reduced marketing and servicing costs, lower production costs, and increased sales. If competition with present customers becomes severe or costs are too high, then the potential is wiped out. As was already discussed in Chapter 5, forward integration is sometimes the only way to reach the market if existing channels are already locked up by competitors.

8.1-2 IMPROVING PROFITABILITY

Figure 8-6 shows the components of profitability. If the overall generic strategy is to improve profitability, opportunities exist in increasing sales volume, increasing sales yield, reducing costs, or reducing investment intensity.

To increase sales yield, detailed knowledge of costs is required. The firm seeks to achieve the highest average price per unit across the product line. When unit costs are known with accuracy, it is possible to shift the sales mix toward high profit items. High gross margins should be sought from products facing limited direct competition, while margins on highly competitive commodity products should be low.

We have already discussed elsewhere the strategies of unit-cost reductions. The following list summarizes the activities to be pursued with that option:

- Improving production efficiencies by standardization of design, components, and/or processes.
- Improving production efficiencies through mechanization of labor-intense activities.
- Cutting material costs by substituting new materials, finding cheaper sources, or subcontracting where cost will warrant.
- Increasing purchasing power by pooling.
- Improving systems and process efficiency by using computers.
- Increasing utilization of capacity.

Vertical integration is often pursued as a cost reduction strategy. This occurs if transaction costs can be eliminated. Thus, the advisability of vertical integration as a cost reduction strategy lies in a careful analysis of the transaction costs

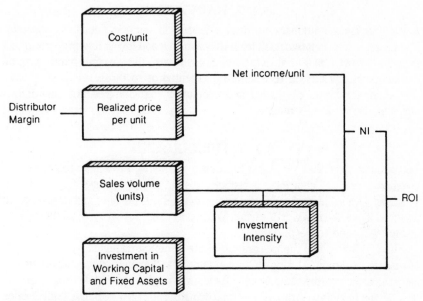

Fig. 8-6. Components of profitability.
Source: George S. Day, **Strategic Market Planning,** ***West Publishing***
Co., 1984, p. 108.

at each stage of the value-added system and, of course, the opportunity for elimination of the cost if the function is taken over.

Significant profit improvement can be achieved by the following strategies of reducing investment intensity:

- Reduce inventories, both of finished goods and work-in-process.
- Reduce accounts receivable.
- Reduce capital intensifying investments in systems and automation unless they provide a competitive advantage.
- Subcontract elements of manufacturing which require heavy capital commitment.
- Develop captive volume.

Most of the above strategies focus on reducing the denominator in the ROI ratio; this will manipulate the ratio and make the firm appear to be more efficient, thereby also manipulating the profitability ratios.

Profitability can also be enhanced by selective focus. This will result in a decline in volume and revenue as the firm focuses on its most profitable items. This is also referred to as a *retrenchment strategy*. The selectivity can be along market segment, product line, or distribution elements of the marketing mix.

8.1-3 HARVESTING

Harvesting is recommended for market leaders in mature or declining markets. The purpose is to remove cash from the cash cow and invest it in projects which promise growth potential. Operating costs are cut to the bone. Capital expenditures are limited to absolutely essential or to those required by law. Customer service is cut, sales and promotion expenditures are cut, and, if possible, prices are increased.

8.1-4 TURNAROUND

Turnaround strategies focus on improving cash flow. Payables are stretched, inventories are cut, labor force is reduced, discretionary expenses are cut. These strategies are employed when the firm is in a serious decline, and its long-term potential looks like it is worth saving. When pursuing a turnaround, all the options in Fig. 8-5 need to be pursued.

Figure 8-7 shows the integration of the generic strategies with the stages of market evolution. During the development and growth stage, strategies to increase sales volume are pursued. As growth begins at an increasing rate, the firm begins to shift to strategies of improving profitability with maintaining sales volume. The improvement in profitability enables the firm to survive the shakeout stage and lays the ground work for harvesting during the mature and saturation stages. Harvesting strategies are employed during the saturation and decline stages. At this point, financial resources are redeployed to begin the cycle over with a new business or a new product. A turnaround may be attempted if long-term potential warrants it. A product may be redesigned and recycled at this point.

8.2 INTEGRATING GENERIC STRATEGIES WITH FUNCTIONAL AREA STRATEGIES

The importance of distinctive competence within a specific functional area changes with market evolution and the generic strategy pursued. Figure 8-8 illustrates the shift in primacy of the functional areas as the market or industry matures. In the introduction and development stage, the R&D strategy and its distinctive competence are of primary importance. As the product shifts into production, the engineering and production capabilities of the manufacturing function become important, because capacity for later volumes is established and standardized efficient procedures are developed. The distinctive competence of marketing is critical in the maturity and saturation stages as competitive advantage is established and maintained. In decline, the finance function's ability to squeeze out cash flows and reallocate funds becomes critical to the firm's long-term survival.

Thus, as the market evolves, the power and primacy of the functional areas

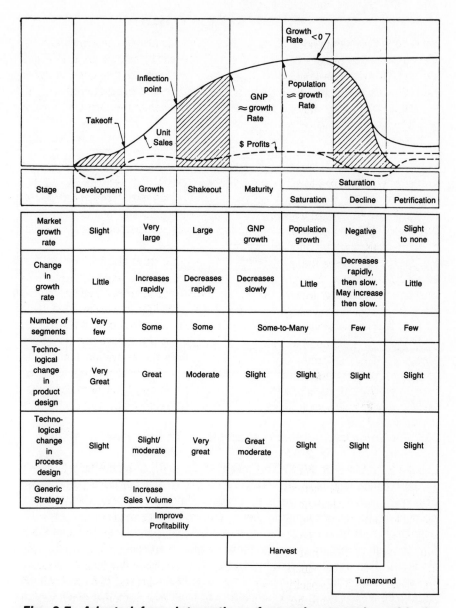

Fig. 8-7. Adapted from integration of generic strategies with the fundamental stages of product/market evolution.
Source: *C. W. Hofer,* **Conceptual Constructs for Formulating Corporate and Business Strategy** *(Boston: Intercollegiate Case Clearing House, 9-378-754, 1977), p. 7.*

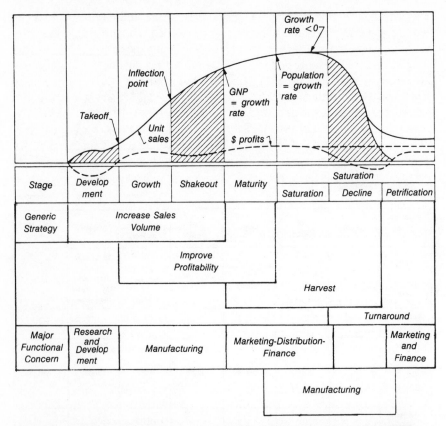

Fig. 8-8. Integrating generic strategies with functional strategies.

builds and declines or shifts. This means that the organization must be ready to deploy personnel and budgetary resources to the functional area whose distinctive competence is currently needed. Unfortunately, the ability to shift power is easier to talk about in theory than to achieve in practice. In reality, functional areas build power during their "hey-day" and then block and sabotage the shift of resources to what they perceive as competing functional areas. Goodyear Tire was dominated by the power of its R&D function and its Tire Division. This power and dominance was held long after it should have shifted to marketing. It's not the cost or quality of Goodyear tires that holds it back in the competition; the foreign competition has done a much better job of promoting the image of their products. Goodyear was never a marketing organization. After the 1986 takeover attempt by Goldsmith, it now faces a dilemma as its diversification strategy is foiled, and it must now attempt to rebuild in a mature market. Goodrich, in contrast, never developed a strong Tire

Division and was able to take their R&D competence in the chemical area and develop diversified markets. Without a strong position in original equipment tires, they were never able to develop their tire business into the cash cow they needed to generate the resources for a strong marketing function. Instead, they attempted to make PVC (Polyvinyl Chloride) their cash cow. PVC is a commodity and amongst the manufacturers of this product, Goodrich was a small fish. In an effort to purchase a marketing function, Goodrich merged with Uniroyal. The organizations were very dissimilar. Goodrich finally quit the tire business by selling off their portion of the merged company to an investment firm in late 1986. GenCorp harvested the tire business in its early growth stage and diversified their business unit portfolio. GenCorp focused more on financial strategies than R&D and manufacturing. They also sold their tire division off in 1986.

8.3 WITHIN FUNCTION INTEGRATION

As the primacy of each of the different areas increases or declines, it becomes necessary to assure that the activities within the areas are coordinated to achieve the overall functional objective, as well as the overall corporate objective. Each of the functional areas must be cross-integrated so that the activities of one area don't cancel out the effectiveness of activities in other functional areas. In the next four sections of this chapter, we will focus on integrating activities within functional strategies and integrating activities across functional areas.

8.3-1 INTEGRATING MARKETING STRATEGIES

Table 8-1 summarizes the marketing strategy activities from Chapter 5. Continuums are presented for each activity representing a range of strategy. Some of the strategies are mutually dependent. For example, the following activities form an integrated marketing strategy:

- Premium pricing.
- Exclusive distribution.
- Image promotion.
- Pre-purchase timing.
- Retailer incentives.
- Extensive warranties.
- Liberal return policy.
- Single-product.

The choice of product strategy is based on the marketing function objective, which in turn flows from the overall corporate strategy. The corporate mission directs the marketing function by answering the questions: "Who is the customer?" "What customer needs should we satisfy?" "What value should

Table 8-1. Marketing Strategy

PRODUCT
    Product Line Width

    Specialize in   **Multiple**
    single product

    Depth

    Single variation   *Multiple variation*

PRICING

    High/Premium   Intermediate   Low/Aggressive

    Market oriented   Cost oriented

DISTRIBUTION

    Exclusive   Selective   Intensive

    Channel Directness

    Owner fran-
    chise   Wholesalers   Retailers   Independents

    Geographic

    Local   Regional   National   International

PROMOTION
    Focus

    Price/Product   Institution/Image

    Timing

    Point of purchase   Pre-purchase

    Incentives for
       Retailers

    Shared cost   None

    Continuity

    Discontinuous   Continuous

    Warranties

    None   Extensive

    Returns

    Restrict   Liberal

we provide the customer?'' For example, Levi Strauss & Co. defines their basic corporate mission as: ''Provide clothing to individuals from cradle to grave, regardless of sex or interests.''

Levi Strauss, in their mission statement, has specified the product strategy to be pursued by the marketing function. The product is clothing, and the product line will be broad (all ages, sex, or interest). This mission statement was chosen after a careful assessment of the market opportunity. From the product strategy, then, the pricing, promotion, and distribution strategies will be formulated with activities to reach all individuals, regardless of age, sex, or interest.

Polaroid's corporate mission statement is to: ''Diversify to build a broader and more balanced product line.''

Thus, the product strategy is to increase the breadth of products. The diversification goal comes from the environment assessment of the opportunities and threats of a mature industry with mature products. Both Levi Strauss and Polaroid will emphasize heavy product development. The corporate strategy statement will determine which functional strategy will be primary and, within the functional strategy, which of the substrategies will be primary and secondary.

The choice of a primary strategy may preclude the choice of some alternative secondary strategies. If pricing is the primary strategy, as would be the case if the mission is to ''maintain price—leadership arrangement,'' then some of the possible choice alternatives for promotion, distribution, and product would be excluded. On the other hand, premium priced products are promoted on the basis of image at pre-purchase. Retailers are given exclusive dealerships and sales incentives for handling the product and allowing returns. Extensive warranties are offered as part of the image promotion.

A primary emphasis on product strategy, as in the examples of Levi-Strauss and Polaroid, does not exclude choices of promotion, pricing, or distribution. In each case, a multiple product mix strategy with multiple pricing, promotion, and distribution will be pursued.

Within the four main categories of marketing strategy, product, pricing, distribution, and promotion, the activities must be aligned to produce a pattern of behavior which moves in an integrated direction. If the pricing strategy is cost-oriented, then all pricing activities must be consistently cost-oriented. The choice of cost-oriented pricing is based on the stage of product lifecycle or industry maturity that the firm finds itself. Thus, the choice of pricing strategy must be consistent with the choice of product.

Of the marketing strategies, product and/or pricing can be primary strategies depending on the competitive structure of the industry. Distribution and promotion are almost always dependent strategies to be integrated with the choice of product or pricing strategies. Product strategies are primary when consumer demand is high and expanding; pricing strategies become primary when markets reach maturity. The choice of distribution strategy flows from the marketing mix objective determined by product strategy. In 1959, Mead Johnson and Co. produced a product for diet-conscious consumers, Metrical, and the product line was narrowly defined as "health products." Because Mead Johnson already had existing pharmaceutical distribution channels, synergy was employed, and the same channels were used. They were quite successful. The profits attracted Pet Milk into the market with Sego. The product was synergistic with Pet's already existing manufacturing processes, but Pet's distribution channels were food stores. The product was broadly defined for the liquid food market so that Pet was able to capitalize on manufacturing and distribution synergy. Pet was even more successful.

If the mission statement specifies products for East Coast consumers, then a regional distribution strategy is required. In the Levi Strauss example, the consumers are widely dispersed, so the use of middlemen retailers will be required. If the product is perishable, then a local channel must be selected.

Figure 8-9 shows the shift in focus of the marketing mix components during the product lifecycle. In the introductory stage, promotion is high, but during the growth stage distribution takes on primary emphasis. Once the market is established, distribution becomes important, and finally, price is the component emphasized. Product development takes on primary emphasis again in the decline stage, because new products must be developed or old products redesigned and redeveloped.

8.3-2 INTEGRATING MANUFACTURING STRATEGY

The objective of the manufacturing strategy is to maximize the output of goods with the minimum use of resources. The choice of manufacturing strategy must be integrated with the assessment of the competitive structure of the industry. Given the choice of pursuing a corporate strategy of growth, stability or retrenchment, it becomes the goal of the manufacturing strategy to maximize productivity. Productivity is measured by the ratio of output versus cost. Thus, increases in productivity can be achieved by increasing output while maintaining costs, or conversely maintaining output while decreasing costs. In Chapter 7, we talked about the dilemma of U.S. companies seeking to increase productivity measures by decreasing the numerator (cost) and thus eroding their productive strength. Although cost containment is important, it is not the key to increasing productivity. Major increases in productivity are the product of the relationship between productive volume and cost. The cost advances accrue from spreading the costs of production over the volume of more output units. Unfortunately, the tradeoff of increasing productivity is at the risk of reducing flexibility. Thus, high volume, low cost manufacturing resources are unsuitable for environments which require ability to adapt quickly to change. Some flexibility is occurring

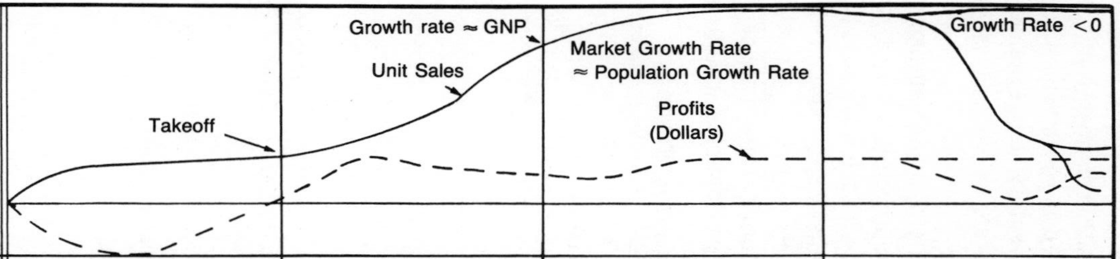

Functional Area	*Introduction*	*Growth*	*Maturity*	*Decline*
Marketing	Resources/skill to create widespread awareness and find acceptance from customers; advantageous access to distribution channels	Ability to establish brand recognition; find niche; reduce price; solidify strong distribution relations and develop new channels	Skill in aggressively promoting products to new markets and holding existing markets; pricing flexibility; skills in differentiating products and holding customer loyalty	Cost-effective means of efficient access to selected channels and markets strong customer loyalty or dependence; strong company image
Activity	Promotion	Distribution	Price	Cost Reduction

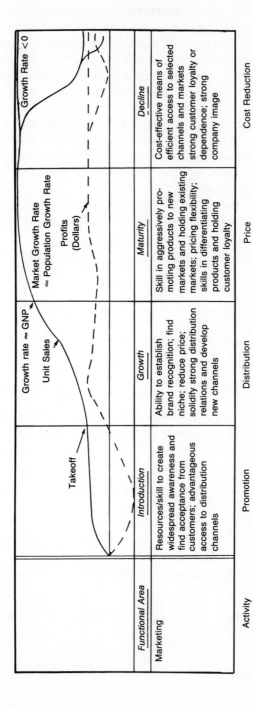

Fig. 8-9. Emphasis on marketing strategies during product/market lifecycle.
Source: John A. Pearce, II., Richard B. Robinson, Jr.,* Strategic Management, *Second Edition, Richard D. Irwin, Inc., 1985, p. 194.

with the advent of multipurpose robots and reprogrammable machines. However, at present manufacturing flexibility is still a high cost strategy.

When it is possible to forecast demand, firms may plan adjustments by buffering or leveling. Fluctuations are planned and prepared for, and buffers are used to create flexibility. Producing for inventory is an example of buffering. Car manufacturers build up buffer inventories for the anticipated spring and summer demand.

Another method of adapting is to level production demands by combining products which have opposite peak demand cycles. Thus, a sporting goods manufacturer can use the same facilities to produce water skis and snow skis. By maintaining volume through leveling production, manufacturers can maintain their cost/output ratio advantage.

The strategic activities of the manufacturing strategy are depicted in Table 8-2. A firm can choose to build capacity for economics of scale to meet industry

Table 8-2. Manufacturing Strategy

	Inflexible Low Cost	Flexible High Cost
CAPACITY		
Scale	Economies	Diseconomies
Utiliation	High	Low
FACILITIES		
Location	Centralized	Decentralized
Specialization	Special Purpose or Reprogrammable	General Purpose
PROCESS TECHNOLOGY		
	State of practice State of art	Experimental
CONTROL PROCESSES		
Inventory - Raw material -	EOQ minimize	When needed
Inventory - Finished Goods	Enlarge minimum order	No minimum order
CONTROL OF SUPPLY		
Backward Integrate Bargaining with	Make supply	No control
Suppliers	Dominate	Submit

demand. Building such a plant would give the firm the lowest production cost curve in the industry and enable it to follow a cost leadership strategy. Once this decision is made, the firm is locked in to going after the volume required to produce the cost advantage. The alternative is to incur diseconomies by adding on productive capacity in increments as demand evolves. This approach is costly, but allows the firm the flexibility to scale up and down in a reactive mode.

Utilization of capacity is another manufacturing decision variable. High utilization results in low costs and locks the firm into the product in process. Lower utilization allows flexibility for adjustment but at the cost of increasing the firm's breakeven point.

The location and type of facilities are also important decision variables. Centralized facilities minimize costs, while decentralized facilities enable the firm to react and adjust to local conditions. Special purpose facilities produce many standardized products in a maximum amount of time at minimum cost. General purpose facilities are costly but more adaptive.

Process innovation is very important in some industries. When cost leadership is the generic strategy, there is constant pressure to continually innovate lower cost processes. Demand is on the decline, the firm has market share, but the declining market share makes it necessary to capture competitor's market share with the strategic advantage of cost. Many firms stick with state of practice or even obsolete processes rather than invest the initial high cost required to experiment or roll over to state-of-the-art processes. This can occur when the firm decides to mine-out the production facilities too soon. During the growth stage, there needs to be high investment in longer term processes. To remain with the same processes is a short-term, low cost decision that results in a production process too obsolete to compete longer term.

Control processes need to be streamlined, centralized, and inflexible when low cost strategies are primary during the maturity and decline stages. Control is the mechanism that keeps cost at the level necessary to break even at lower prices. EOQ techniques are implemented to contain raw material costs, and guidelines are set for minimum orders to ensure reduced inventory carrying costs. Once control procedures are in place, the system becomes inflexible. Thus, increasing levels of flexibility incur the risk of reduced control.

If control over supplies of raw materials is crucial to cost control, the firm may choose to backward integrate. The cost advantages of backward integration do not always materialize. Matching economies of scale is not often easy. The firm may find itself with excess capacity of raw materials and then have to enter new markets to sell the excess. Or, it may find itself short of supply and have to buy the extra that is needed at extreme price disadvantages. Often, backward integration is accomplished by purchasing a firm that may be in trouble, thus increasing the financial and managerial burden to the acquiring firm. Backward integration should be pursued to relieve dependence on suppliers, rather than to achieve cost advantages. The so-called synergistic effects of backward integration have not stood up to their claims.

The decision variables of the manufacturing strategy result in the firm having to make a tradeoff between cost efficiencies and flexibility. The choice of one strategy versus another depends on environmental assessment and resource analysis. The manufacturing objective then flows from a grand strategy derived during the formulating process.

Within the set of manufacturing strategies, activities must be aligned to move the total function in a unified direction. If decisions have been made to scale up capacity to be the lowest cost producer in the industry, then production must be scheduled to assure high utilization of capacity, facilities should be centralized for cost advantage, and equipment should be special purpose for speed and efficiency. R&D on process must be such that there is continual ongoing research and information seeking on more efficient processes. The efficiency can be in terms of increased quantity or improved quality of output. Inventory control processes must be in place to minimize ordering and carrying costs. The firm must seek to control supply of raw materials for cost containment. This is accomplished through backward integration or domination of suppliers. Inconsistencies must be avoided if maximum production is to be achieved with minimum resources. If is not possible to minimize the use of resources when facilities are decentralized and general purpose in nature. Although the decentralization and general purpose provide some flexibility, they do so at the loss of the cost advantages of using minimum resources.

The choice of the inflexible cost advantage strategy has built-in consequences. Product differentiation becomes difficult. The ability to adjust rapidly to technological change is lost. The need to use existing technology to achieve scale economics precludes experimenting with new processes. The pursuit of the inflexible approach means capitalizing on the experience curve. But the relationship is a curve, and there are diminishing returns to the aggressive pursuit of cost advantages. The pursuit itself results in a single-minded focus on production advantage, which can draw attention away from market shifts and technological development that can obsolete both the firms' product and processes.

Manufacturing strategy becomes a primary driving strategy when the assessment of the environment indicates the growth of demand has begun to decline, and competitors are moving to maintain growth through aggressive pursuit of each other's market share. When these conditions begin to develop, the competitive emphasis shifts to cost advantage. If firms have miscalculated capacity relative to demand, excess capacity can occur at this point, stimulating price wars for the needed volume to make breakeven. Figure 8-10 shows the shift in the mix of manufacturing choices as the market and product lifecycle

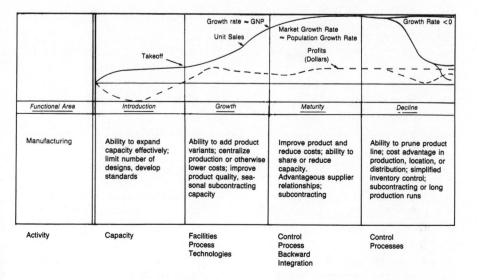

Functional Area	Introduction	Growth	Maturity	Decline
Manufacturing	Ability to expand capacity effectively; limit number of designs, develop standards	Ability to add product variants; centralize production or otherwise lower costs; improve product quality, seasonal subcontracting capacity	Improve product and reduce costs; ability to share or reduce capacity. Advantageous supplier relationships; subcontracting	Ability to prune product line; cost advantage in production, location, or distribution; simplified inventory control; subcontracting or long production runs
Activity	Capacity	Facilities Process Technologies	Control Process Backward Integration	Control Processes

Fig. 8-10. *Adapted from emphasis on manufacturing strategies during product/market lifecycle.*
Source: *C. W. Hofer,* **Conceptual Constructs for Formulating Corporate and Business Strategy** *(Boston: Intercollegiate Case Clearing House, 9-378-754, 1977), p. 7.*

matures. In the introduction stage, manufacturing seeks to build economies of scale capacity. In the growth stage, cost advantages are gained by centralizing facilities and developing new process technologies. Control of costs through sophisticated process control techniques becomes a distinctive competence when market evolution reaches the maturity stage. During this stage, firms also seek to gain control over supply through backward integration. Cost advantages may also accrue as a result of this process. In the decline stage, all strategies of efficient production must be employed, but control process strategies are primary as they provide the information and techniques for cost containment across the manufacturing mix.

Manufacturing and marketing strategies must be integrated to assure a common direction in pursuit of a grand strategy. The inflexible cost advantage strategy requires a high relative market share, a wide product line of related products, serving all major market segments, aggressive pricing, product/price promotion, and direct distribution. Figure 8-11 illustrates the decision choices in marketing and manufacturing which lead to an integrated grand strategy of improving profitability through cost leadership. The choice of cost leadership

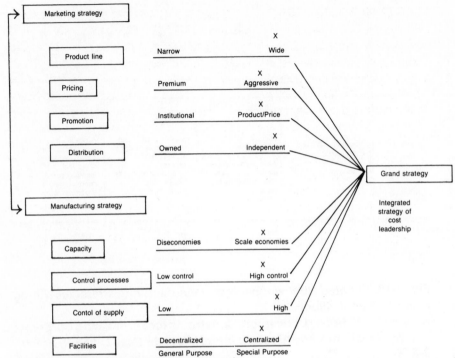

Fig. 8-11. Across function integration.

is based on the maturity of growth in the industry. Competitive advantage is now gained through manufacturing strategy and marketing decisions must support the maintenance of the production advantage.

8.3-3 INTEGRATING FINANCE STRATEGY

The objective of the finance function is to maximize the benefits to owners by choosing the sources and allocation of funds which maximize the wealth of the firm. The financial decision choices are closely tied to corporate and business level objectives. Often it is difficult to differentiate the corporate objective from the finance objective, because we use financial measures to set corporate objectives. In large diversified firms, the corporate objective literally becomes a financial strategy of diversifying the risk of its investment in a portfolio of businesses.

Much of the financial decision concerns the capital allocation question. What are the priorities for capital allocation and how will the firm finance the allocations? Will the firm finance allocations from within by using retained earnings or will financial leverage be used? If leverage is used, what is an acceptable cost of capital? What is the desired capital structure? How much liquidity is desired? Should funds be used to pay dividends? The choice of financial strategies is dependent upon the risk/return tradeoff. The degree of risk a firm may assume will depend upon the assessment of the opportunities and threats in the environment and the strengths or weaknesses of the firm's financial resources. Delta Airlines, for example, seeks to minimize its level of debt financing, preferring to use equity and internal funds. Delta operates in a highly volatile industry with high fixed operating costs. Management chooses to reduce the risk of incurring fixed capital costs.

Table 8-3 illustrates the decision variables for the finance strategies. The firm must decide on the degree of operating leverage. Operating leverage is a tradeoff of fixed versus variable costs. With a high investment in fixed costs (plant, equipment, computer systems), the firm is able to leverage profits by spreading those fixed costs over high volume. Thus, returns are magnified. Losses are also magnified so high degrees of operating leverage are risky. The use of operating leverage is consistent with an inflexible low cost manufacturing strategy. As volumes increase, the costs per unit decrease giving the firm a cost leadership advantage. On the other hand, a firm may decide not to acquire fixed costs and instead keep the costs of operating variable by leasing. This approach keeps capital expenditures low and marginal costs high. The advantage is the flexibility of being able to shift into different methods and types of operations.

Financial leverage is often combined with operating leverage to determine total risk. By using debt versus equity, the firm can leverage the return. Interest is a tax deductible charge, thus the cost of financing capital expenditures through borrowing is partially underwritten by the government. The cost of financing with retained earnings is essentially the opportunity cost of investing the earnings in alternative investments. The risk is lowest with retained earnings and highest with short-term financing. The relationship between leverage and risk is not linear. A firm may add increments of debt with no increase in risk rating up to a point where the market decides the degree of leverage is too much, and then the risk factor may increase dramatically. If the firm has a high degree of operating leverage, then financial leverage increases the risk. Thus, the degree of operating leverage is a constraint on how much financial leverage the firm can safely take on. Financial leverage will be high in the introductory stage of a market or product lifecycle, but in the mature stages, the firm should decrease its level of financial leverage.

The firm must also decide on the level of liquidity it chooses to maintain. Conservative working capital management dictates that high levels of current assets are maintained relative to current liabilities. This reduces risk but at the cost of returns, because the funds tied up in current assets could be employed to increase returns to the firm. An aggressive approach would call for lower

Table 8-3. Financial Strategy

	Low risk Low return	High risk High return
LIQUIDITY **Level of Current Assets**	High/Conservative	Low/Aggressive
LEVERAGE **Degree of Combined** **Leverage**	Low	High
Use of Financial Leverage	Low/Equity	High/Debt
Financing Current Assets	Long-term debt conservative	Short-term debt aggressive
Asset Costs	Ownership of assets	Lease of assets
Dividend Payout	Payout 100% in dividends	Reinvest payout 0% in dividends
ACCOUNTING STRATEGIES	Overstate profits low cash flow	Understate profits high cash flow
Depreciation	Straight-line	Accelerated
Inventory Valuation	Fifo during inflation	Lifo during inflation

levels of current assets and increased risk. Whether or not to extend credit or lengthen the terms of the credit arrangement will also determine the level of liquidity required. If the firm decides to "carry" its customers, then the need for working capital increases.

Ownership of assets versus leasing is another decision choice of the finance function. The decision is tied to the leverage decision. Ownership of assets results in fixed costs while leasing results in variable costs. Shifting fixed to variable costs lowers the firm's breakeven point, reducing the risk of losses due to decreased volume.

Accounting strategies support finance strategies and need to be integrated with finance strategies. When liquidity is low due to capital being tied up in current assets, accounting should seek to understate profits in order to generate as much cash flow as possible. Accounting strategies should seek to keep as much cash in the firm as possible at points when funds are heavily invested in capital projects.

Figure 8-12 illustrates the shift in emphasis of the finance function as the market or product lifecycle matures. At the introductory stage, profits are in

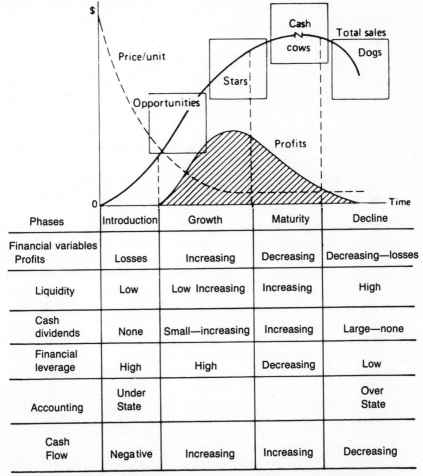

Phases	Introduction	Growth	Maturity	Decline
Financial variables Profits	Losses	Increasing	Decreasing	Decreasing—losses
Liquidity	Low	Low Increasing	Increasing	High
Cash dividends	None	Small—increasing	Increasing	Large—none
Financial leverage	High	High	Decreasing	Low
Accounting	Under State			Over State
Cash Flow	Negative	Increasing	Increasing	Decreasing

Fig. 8-12. Finance strategies during product/market lifecycle.

the loss area, liquidity is low, cash dividends are not paid out, and financial leverage is high. The firm uses resources to support high net cash cashflow. As growth starts to occur, the firm must be able to finance rapid expansion and product improvements. As positive cash flows develop in the maturity stage, decisions must be made for redistributing cash for new products and projects. Overstating of profits at this stage is employed as a strategy for establishing a sound position for the next round of financial borrowing required at the introductory stage.

Finance strategies must be cross-integrated with marketing, manufacturing, and R&D strategies. Finance strategies support the activities of all other functional areas. Figure 8-13 shows the choice of finance strategies which will provide across function integration for a corporate or business level strategy of cost leadership.

8.3-4 INTEGRATING R&D STRATEGY

The objectives of R&D strategy are to produce new products or services; to produce profitable improvements to existing products and services. R&D is closely linked to strategic planning. A continuous stream of new products provides options for the company's strategic planners. With increasing competitive pressures and rapidly changing technology, firms are under constant pressure to develop new and innovative products.

Table 8-4 illustrates the strategic decision variables for the R&D function. The first decision the firm faces is the technological involvement decision. Will the firm do research and development internally or will they acquire it from the outside through patents, licensing, or joint ventures or even purchase other firms with R&D functions already in place? Once the firm has decided to do its own research, the next decision deals with the level of research to undertake. Will they engage in basic research whose results are very long-term, difficult to measure, and risky, or will they mainly focus on applications research whose results are shorter-term, easier to measure, and safer? Depending on the phase of market evolution, the firm may focus on product innovation and product improvement. If the industry is characterized by commodity-type products, the focus for research and development will be toward process innovation and cost reduction innovations which enable the firm to maintain a cost leadership position in the industry. If the firm chooses process innovations, will they be focused at state = -of-the-industry changes whose results are quicker and the chances of investment risk are low, or will they be geared to the processes of the future? Some bankers, for example, have not invested in ATM's because they feel banking transactions in the future will all be centralized, with the replacement of money by a plastic card. What level of budget allocation is the firm willing to commit? Firms with high commitment to R&D allocate between 5 and 10

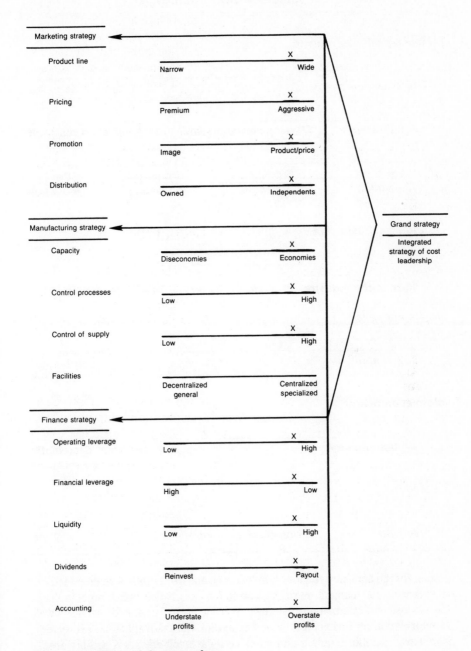

Fig. 8-13. Financial strategies.

Table 8-4. R&D Strategy

Technological Involvement

Internal sources			Externally acquired
Basic resarch	Developmental research		Application research
Production innovation	Product improvement	Process innovation	Cost reduction

Technological Selection

State of the industry	State of the art	Advanced futuristic

Investment Level

Low budget	High budget 5-10% revenue

Information Search

Ad hoc random	Systematic surveillance

Protection

Patents	Non-disclosure agreements	None

percent of the annual revenues. For research and development to be effective, an extensive commitment must be made to the information search process. This means designing information systems to provide both market information as well as information on technology. To what extent will innovations be protected? The use of patents requires an extensive legal involvement. If patents aren't employed, will nondisclosure agreements and confidentiality agreements be entered into? Polaroid tried to protect the SX-70 from duplication through patenting its unique process. Kodak was able to duplicate the process in one year, and Polaroid was unable to win a patent infringement against Kodak.

Because of its significance for the survival of the firm, R&D plays a major role in all the functional decisions of the firm. It is also necessary to integrate R&D activities with the marketing, finance and manufacturing strategies. Figure 8-14 illustrates the cross functional involvement of R&D with other areas of speciality. Marketing provides the largest input by providing information on market attractiveness for new products and product lines. Finance provides capital budgeting information. How attractive are the cash flows from the investment in the proposed project? Manufacturing provides the "can do" answers. How long from prototype to manufacturable product? Manufacturing provides cost data for the finance function's capital investment decision.

Figure 8-15 illustrates the shift in focus of the R&D function in the different stages of the product/market evolution. From the introduction stage, product innovation shifts to product development as the research prototype is prepared for mass production. As growth declines, emphasis shifts back to product development. The next new product must be researched and developed, but at the same time the current product's manufacturing process should be researched for cost reduction ideas to be implemented during the maturity and declining stages of the product lifecycle.

8.4 METHODS FOR ACHIEVING INTEGRATION

If the functional areas are integrated and activities are coordinated within functional areas, the firm's probability of success is greatly enhanced. Failure can occur, because the firm chose the wrong goals. It can also occur because the right goal was chosen but the firm's activities were not coordinated to achieve the goal.

The first step in integrating functional areas is the analytical diagnosis of which activities within a function support the corporate goal. The next step is to cross-check functions to make sure interdependencies are coordinated and conflicts are resolved. The third step is to set up the managerial systems which support the formulation of integrated goals.

Several of the methods for achieving integration are:

- MBO.
- Integrated reward systems.
- Lateral relations/project management.
- Rationalized tradeoffs.

MBO, with objectives established from top-down, provides an integrated hierarchy for communicating corporate goals. It must be a top-down approach,

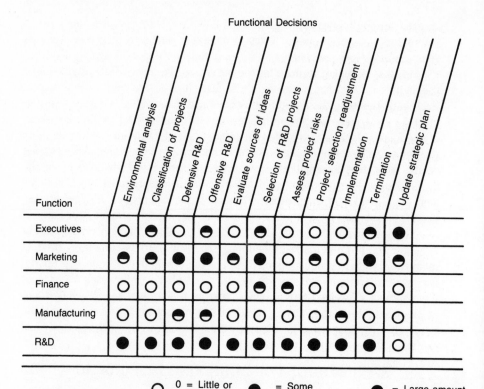

Fig. 8-14. The involvement mix.

Functional Area	Introduction	Growth	Maturity	Decline
Research and Development	Ability to make engineering changes; have technical bugs in product and process resolved	Skill in quality and new feature development; start developing successor product	Reduce costs; develop variants to differentiate products	Support other growth areas or apply to unique customer needs
Activities	Product Development	Product Innovation	Process Innovation	Cost Reduction

Fig. 8-15. *R&D strategies during product lifecycle.*
**Source: *John A. Pearce, II., Richard B. Robinson, Jr.*, Strategic
Management, *Second Edition, Richard D. Irwin, Inc., 1985, p. 194.***

because corporate strategy is the responsibility of top level management. MBO not only provides a means of communicating the goal down through the organization, it also provides assignment of responsibility in achieving the goal. This method provides the vertical linkages which are necessary for the goal attainment.

Reward systems need to be integrated with the goal of integrating functions. Rewards which favor one function over another are dysfunctional for the purposes of achieving integration. Profit centers are also sometimes dysfunctional, because a cost center may find it more effective to purchase goods and services from outside vendors rather than use internal sources. If integration is to be achieved, rewards must be tied to those activities which foster integration.

Structures which support or establish lateral relations in the organization also promote integration. Project management is one example. Any structure which supports the use of personnel across functions will enhance the transference of information which is necessary for effective integration. Linking relations through committees and counsels are also helpful. Quality circles enhance integration efforts while promoting product quality.

Finally, a rationalized system for tradeoffs in the organization will promote integration. If the tradeoffs are rationalized in terms of the larger corporate goal, individual functional areas are less likely to get involved in power wars to the detriment of integration. Anytime one area "wins" and another "losses," integration efforts are foiled. If the functional areas are seen as part of the integrated whole of the organization's survival, there is less likelihood of internal conflict destroying the organization's objective.

8.5 SUMMARY

The need for integration of functional areas is everincreasing as organizations grow in size and complexity. Depending on the nature of opportunities and threats which exist in the environment, one function may become a primary focus for the firm. Over the life of the product/market evolution, the primacy of functions change based on the specialized needs of each phase. Regardless which function is the primary emphasis of the current moment, the functions must be cross-integrated for the firm to achieve its corporate goals. Analysis of interdependent functions and management practices of MBO processes help achieve the integration of functions.

ENDNOTES—Chapter 8

1. Day, p. 102.

Chapter 9

Small Business Strategies

9.0 INTRODUCTION

Small firms that are growth intensive have to develop a marketing posture that strategically balances sales and new product development. The essential areas with which marketing is concerned are:

- Understanding goals of the business.
- Growth objectives.
- Product marketing.
- Advertising and promotion.
- Sales and distribution.

One major difference between a growth oriented company and its competitors is the amount of income spent on marketing. If, for example, the industry average marketing expenditure is 10 percent of new sales, a growth company may spend 20 to 30 percent. Of course, the trick is to be successful, which means marketing must use its budget wisely.

The goals of the business, when clearly defined, provide a beginning point from which the marketing strategy must be developed. The strategic market plan may be thought of as involving four sets of related decisions:

- Defining the business[2][1]. The CEO and top level managers must decide, "What business are we in?" The definition must state:

—Scope: The products and markets. Customers (which) to be served, needs which can be satisfied. What ways (technologies) are to be used.

—Product and market segmentation: A definition of how a firm groups customers with respect to needs and how they are satisfied.

- Determining the mission of the business. Performance expectations in terms of sales growth, market share, return to investors, net income and cash flow must be determined. Short-term expectations should be balanced with long-term alternatives.
- Formulating functional strategies. The costs and benefits of various alternatives functionally determine how marketing, manufacturing, R&D, service, and physical distribution interact.
- Budgeting. The planning cycle produces a resource allocation plan. At this stage, specific financial decisions are made and operating budgets are determined.

This should work quite well for a large company with enough staff and the time required. The smaller company has limited resources and so many pressing daily problems that it may be very difficult for them to plan. But successful growth companies have to develop goals to achieve.

The marketing strategy defines what will be offered to buyers, which buyers will be targeted, and how. The market definition evolves from what has been sold and to whom. The starting point for small business strategic planning is the identification and analysis of past and present customers. If there exists an industry posture, whether fragmented or not, research has to be conducted to determine the company's present market share, growth average for all competitors in that industry, and the size of the market the company may serve. The customer list can be checked to determine common markets, number of applications successful, and why the client decides to buy. This information may be gathered from field sales feedback.

9.1 PRODUCT MARKETING

Every company has to consider its customer's needs. The mission and definition of the business define the general market and what types of customer needs will be served. Following that, products and services are the responsibility of the marketing team.

Growth-oriented small companies spend a major portion of their resources developing new products. Ideas for new products come from many sources including:

- Sales feedback from customers.
- CEO and marketing brainstorming sessions.

- Customer surveys.
- Competitive pressures.
- Defensive R&D for product quality and productivity improvements.

Products have a lifecycle, beginning at introduction to the market and ending as the market moves on to another preference. Each stage of the product lifecycle has to be estimated and managed in conjunction with the company's goals and objectives, external environment, and competitive pressures. The sales history of most products follows a pattern of:

- Introduction. A period of slow sales growth as the product is introduced in the market. Profits are low and cash flow is high in this stage due to the initial costs.
- Growth. A period of rapid market acceptance and substantial profit improvement.
- Maturity. A period of slowdown in sales growth because the product has reached acceptance by most of the potential buyers. Profits begin to decline as costs to compete increase.
- Decline. The period when sales show a strong decline and profits erode.

Small companies very often struggle with acceptance of product lifecycle strategies because of severely limited resources and poor management. New product strategies are the most important growth element for the small business. Unfortunately, the products/services of small business may have a much shorter lifecycle than the larger companies, and therefore the cost and resources necessary for lifecycle phase analysis may not be beneficial.

9.2 MARKETING STRATEGIES

All companies, large and small, have competitors, need to grow in sales and profits, and many market opportunities. To decide how the small company will grow requires one of the following market strategies, regardless of whether the company management knows and accepts it. Firms in industry pursue different competitive strategies and enjoy different positions in the market. Arthur D. Little, a consulting organization, rates firms in one of five competitive positions:

- Dominant. This firm controls the behavior of other firms and has a wide choice of options.
- Strong. This firm can take independent action without endangering its long-term position, regardless of competitors' actions.
- Favorable. This firm has a strength that is exploitable in particular strategies and can improve its position.

- Tenable. This firm is performing at a level to warrant continuing in business.
- Weak. This firm has unsatisfactory performance and no opportunity for improvement.

Growth-oriented small companies must assess their competitive position. If the markets being served are growing, then growth companies may be satisfied to be favorable or tenable if the strategy is a developing one. In stagnant or declining markets, growth companies have to be strong or dominant to sustain growth.

Market leadership strategy is well-suited to small growth-oriented firms that must act on three fronts. First, the firm must create ways to expand total demand. Second, the firm must protect its current market share through solid defensive and offensive actions. Third, the firm can try to expand its market share further as the market rate slows.

Market-challenger strategies are used by smaller firms that are new in a market or have acquired a company or product line gaining access to a market. Challengers are generally more successful if their strategy objectives are well-defined and within their means to improve market share. An aggressor can choose to attack one of three types of firms:

- Attack the market leader. The risk is high, but the payoff is greatest if the market leader is not serving the market well.
- Attack other firms of similar size. Works best if the competitive firm's resources are limited.
- Attack smaller firms that are underfinanced. Works well to displace entrepreneurial firms in startup mode.

Market follower strategies fit smaller growth companies if the market is expanding rapidly and enough business is available to suit the growth goals of the firm. Challenging the industry leader can weaken the firm if the leader has sufficient defenses. The follower defines a growth path but one that does not invoke retaliation from the leaders. Three strategies can work for followers:[2]

- Following closely. Here, the follower lives off the market expansion of the leader and is basically a copy of the leader.
- Distant follower. The company differentiates in some ways from the leader but follows similar pricing and distribution channels.
- Selective follower. The firm picks key areas to follow, but this company is innovative and may become a challenger if the market slows in growth.

One major goal of followers is relatively high profits, perhaps in a short time. Market-niche strategies are excellent for small growth-oriented companies. These firms try to find a market niche that is safe and profitable. The difficulty is finding a niche market that will grow steadily. An ideal market niche has the following characteristics.

- Sufficient size and purchasing power to be profitable.
- Growth potential.
- Negligible interest to major competitors.
- Required skills and resources available to serve the niche effectively.
- The firm can defend itself against an attacking competitor.

Niche marketing requires the firm to specialize in a particular market with specific customers along a narrow product line. Notably, the firm will act as a specialist in one of several categories including:

- End-use.
- Application orientation.
- Specific customer type.
- Geographic area—this may be anywhere in the world.
- Product or product line.
- Product feature specialist.
- One-of-a-kind specials.
- Quality/price.
- Service.

The risks are high that the niche will evaporate. Small firms in the growth phase must consider diversification to insure growth and long term success.

9.3 SUCCESSFUL MARKETING PLANS

Once a strategy has been selected, the marketing plan must be developed. The initial planning requires that the following questions be asked:

- Where does the company stand now?
- What will the future be like for the firm?
- Where should the company be heading?
- How can the firm get there?
- Who is going to do it and when?
- How much will it cost, and what do these costs cover?
- What are the results?
- What changes need to be made?

For any business, the implementation of a growth strategy concept begins with marketing issues. For small companies, one fact is always true: "Nothing happens until a sale is made."

The first two questions above, when answered, produce what large company planners refer to as a *situation analysis*. A detailed look at the products or services that are offered by the business is necessary to understand the dynamics of customer needs, market growth, and product-line demand. The major input for the situation analysis comes from company sales records. This record is generally available by product, market, geographic location, price, channel of distribution, and even end-use application within the industry. Table 9-1 identifies what information (and the respective issues) should be analyzed using the situation analysis planning tool.

A second logical market tool that will help the small company develop growth strategies is consideration of the *STEEP factors*. The evaluation of sociological, technical, economic, environmental, and political (STEEP) factors help put the data developed from the situation analysis into perspective. Consideration of how the company fits into the world situation identifies the opportunities and threats the firm faces. An example of this analysis for a growth-oriented company is presented in Table 9-2.

Previous discussion introduced the product lifecycle concept. During the introduction phases, small quantities are produced that must absorb fixed costs and depreciation. As more units are produced and experience is gained in producing and selling the product or providing the service, unit costs drop. As costs are reduced, prices can be adjusted to reflect cost reductions. Thus, as the firm moves forward on the experience curve, market interest may improve and growth in market share results. The experience curve relationship leads directly to the idea that market share level is critical for business success, because it is achieved by economies of scale and learned expertise. This holds true for both large and small companies. Small growth-oriented companies can often develop economies of scale quicker than large firms.

9.4 THE INTEGRATED STRATEGY

Strategy is the term we use to define what the business will be and which direction the company resources will be applied to sustain growth. Strategy development begins with a situation analysis for the business. Next comes the definition of why the company is in business. From these two steps, a purpose for the company can be clarified. Following these two steps comes an analysis of possible resource deployment moves. Competitive moves in the market can be anticipated at this point, and marketing resource deployment can be assessed, together with the financial state of the company.

Table 9-1. Situation Analysis Planning Tool

Issues to Be Addressed	Purpose	Sources and Techniques to Use in the Analysis
1. Product Sales.	To track trends in business sales.	Company sales records.
2. Product sales by market.	To examine trends in product sales by market	Management Information System (MIS) segregating sales by market, industry, or SIC.**
3. Product sales by market by geographic area.	To examine strengths of products and markets by location.	MIS.
4. Sales by method of distribution.	To determine volume of sales by direct and indirect methods.	Company sales records.
5. Sales by size of customer.	To evaluate quality of sales provided by large, medium, and small accounts	Company sales records augmented by data on customer output or number of employees.
6. Key-customer sales.	To identify most important customers.	Listing of customers in descending order of sales volume.
7. Key-customer economic-power factors.	To evaluate key customers' ability to dictate marketing terms.	Survey of their impact on your business; fraction of their purchases of your product; possible backward integration (to produce your product).
8. Total market size.	To track trends in market share by product and to determine degree of market saturation.	Survey of salesforce; general survey of sample customers and extrapolation of results.
9. Growth of markets.	To determine product growth trends in existing markets.	Survey of literature; data from survey in issue 8.
10. Market development opportunity.	To determine underdeveloped sales opportunity in unexploited markets.	Survey of sample of suspected markets and extrapolation of results.
11. Product attributes.	To develop data on customer likes and dislikes.	Survey of customers in issue 8.

After these factors are known, several alternative strategies are compared. From this analysis, a strategic business plan is written to direct the company either forward on a growth program or possibly to a retrenchment position. The strategic plan identifies the most effective means of deploying corporate

Table 9-2. Forecast Problems and Opportunities Based on STEEP Factors—Acme Machine Tool Co.

STEEP Factors	Marketing	Research and Development	Manufacturing	Others (Financial, Legal, Human Resources, Materials Management, Product Reliability)
Sociological • Toolmaker shortage. • Sunbelt migration. • Extended work career.	• Point out time-saving aspects to management. • Sell on ease of use and simplicity of design.	• Design for use by less-experienced worker. • Use computer-assisted design (CAD). • Institute training sessions for customers.	• Use computer-assisted manufacture (CAM). • Recruit older, experienced craftspeople.	• Assist in picking attractive areas for expansion (human resources). • Train and retrain employees.
Technological • Direct numerical control (DNC). • Computer-assisted design (CAD). • Computer-assisted manufacture (CAM). • Robotics.	• Sell virtues of DNC, CAD, CAM, and built-in automatic features as value/price purchase incentives. • Sell advantage of low reject rate.	• Design state-of-the-art products for productivity improvement. • Improve internal production processes to reduce costs constantly. • Do not overdesign.	• Use latest cost-effective methods to stay competitive.	• Make sure new equipment purchased for production is cost effective (finance). • Assist marketing in developing ROI justifications for customers (finance).
Economic • Inflation. • Productivity. • Depreciation. • Interest rate levels. • Devaluation/revaluation. • GNP growth. • Funds availability.	• Institute purchase plans. • Sell productivity improvement aspects. • Point out faster write-off possibilities. • Sell to low-profit as well as high-growth industries. • Take advantage of high relative value of dollar overseas.	• In high-growth periods, use outside assistance to keep permanent staff low. • Design modular units that can be purchased piecemeal.	• Use outside vendors if cash flow and funds availability are tight. • Make sure capacity is not outstripped by forecast demand. • Keep work-in-process inventory low.	• Keep all inventory levels as low as possible to minimize interest expenses for working capital (materials management). • Work out advantageous lease-purchase plans (financial, legal). • Consider last-in, first-out, (LIFO) accounting controls (finance). • Evaluate new distribution methods (materials management).
Environmental • Energy costs. • OSHA requirements. • Nonproductive capital expenditures.	• Point out safety features. • Branch out into environmental protection.	• Develop designed-in safety features. • Design for lowest energy consumption possible.	• Adhere to OSHA regulations. • Reduce energy consumption.	• Examine new products for safety (product reliability). • Train employees to work safely.
Political • Imports to less-developed countries (LDCs). • Tariff negotiations. • Antitrust regulations.	• Work to eliminate restrictions.	• Design products with specific country markets in mind.	• Consider plants or joint ventures inside growing LDCs.	• Use hedging procedures to minimize exchange losses (finance). • Check potential acquisitions or mergers for antitrust implications.

* Source unknown.

resources in relation to the changing characteristics of the business environment. More directly stated, strategic planning is the process by which a business prepares to maintain or change its competitiveness in the marketplace. Strategic plans are dynamic and must change to insure business continuity. The frequency of change in small firms may be more often than in the larger firms.

9.5 DEFINING THE BUSINESS

Strategy formation begins with an analysis of what the company is doing presently. To get started, one must first define the boundaries of the business. The major boundaries of a business include:[3]

- Geography served.
- Products and services.
  - —Currently offered
  - —Planned
- Customers served.
  - —By geography
  - —Buying patterns
  - —Industry
  - —Distribution

These boundaries must be compared with the results obtained with expanded boundaries that may result from penetration of related businesses or unserved market sectors.

Next, the main company operations must be examined for resource definition. For example, the following outline can be used as a guide:

- Staff.
  - —Skills
  - —Experience
- Technology.
  - —Product
  - —Process
  - —Operation
- Cost structure.
  - —Value added
  - —Experience curve
  - —Inventories and accounts receivable
- Financial aspect.
  - —Cash flow sources and uses
  - —Profit and loss
  - —Balance sheet

- Strengths and weaknesses.
- Historical performance.
  - —Reason for changes
  - —Original strategies

As the analysis proceeds, a definition of what the firm is and does will unfold.

Timing issues are extremely important to small business. All plans involve both achievement and schedules. Industries and companies have natural rhythms which have to be planned for. For example, one major growth strategy may be as simple as changing the timing of new product introductions. To change requires knowledge of the present conditions so that the timing of the following can be identified:

- Product development.
- Manufacturing.
- Product lifecycle.
- Technology lifecycle.
- Order completion cycle.
- Capital purchasing.
- Acquisition of staff.
- Acquisition of capital.

At this time, the firm may have identified many problem areas. A typical list of the problems that are presently common to the small business includes:[4]

- Standards of costing/pricing.
- Irrational competitors.
- Product lifecycles.
- Situation dynamics.
- R&D funding.
- Lack of data.
- No apparent strategy.

The last important area necessary to defining the business is the firm's environment. For small firms intent on growth, this is the weakest analysis area. The present environment is always changing. Successful growth companies read these changes quickly and capitalize on the opportunities presented. The environment can be characterized into the following elements:

- Economic environment.
  - —Government regulation
  - —Inflation

—Interest rates
—GNP
- Technical environment.
  —Trends
  —Other technologies available
  —Lifecycle
- Ecological social/political environment.
  —New processes
  —Modernization vs. new plant and equipment
  —Changes in industries served

9.6 STRATEGY FORMULATION

There are several steps that can be taken to reduce the complexity of the planning process. The most common, which is usually available to most small businesses, is to merge strategies. Most small companies should develop a corporate strategy. Market and product strategies need not be separated and developed on their own. For a small growth-oriented company, the corporate strategy will lead to the appropriate action plans when concentration on objectives is stressed.

The next task in the strategic planning process is to identify discrepancies between the conditions revealed in the situation analysis and the desirable conditions. Three areas should be stressed at this point:

- Compare and contrast the firm's capabilities in each identified key success factor.
- Competitive strengths and weaknesses.
- Current situation compared with corporate objectives.

There may be discrepancies in each area, and adjustments must be made in order to point the strategic plan in a position toward reducing or eliminating the variances. The strategic plan will involve risks, and the strategy planner has to make the distinctions between avoidable and unavoidable risks that can be successfully dealt with.

Creativity in studying the discrepancies is important. The company may not be strong enough in a key area for success; for example, numbers of engineers in R&D. But the firm may recognize that a computer-aided design system will leverage the design team and improve the competitive position. The strategic plan should consider whether the acquisition of a computer-aided design system will improve the company's competitive position or whether other changes are necessary. If the value added from marketing, sales, and service is increasing rapidly, perhaps part of engineering can be subcontracted without sacrificing quality or margins.

Similarly, the impact of weaknesses in comparison to competitors may be minimized by strategies that hasten changes in the industry or change the importance of key success factors. Improving product reliability to reduce service calls is a strong selling point against a competitor with a strong service organization.

Formulating strategies is not a cook-book process. The following ideas are suggested as a framework from which a successful strategy can be developed. No guarantees are available in defining the one best strategy. The firm will evolve into the best strategy by practice, careful analysis of competitive moves, and periodic planning updates.

Describing the business after the situation analysis is complete will differ from the original analysis, but it should be consistent with the owners/CEO personal objectives, strategic logic, and corporate objectives. It is the description of what the business should be after the strategic plan is implemented. The business activities included in the description must be aimed at exploiting the firm's strengths. As far as possible, the description should be consistent with long-term defensible goals.

Several possible strategies should be examined. Examples of one-dimensional strategies that can be used as patterns for formulating custom growth strategies are presented below:[5]

- Technology—Strategy options.
  - —Create a new technology
  - —Exploit advanced technology
  - —Follow up on technology development
  - —Apply technology in product, processes or services
  - —Improve firm's share of available technology
  - —Protect critical technologies
  - —Ensure security of technology base
- Product—Strategy options.
  - —Product offering by type
  - —Differentiated products from competition
  - —Product breadth
  - —Product plus limited service
  - —Product plus application expertise
  - —Product plus full line service
- Product pricing—Strategy.
  - —High, sell on performance, quality, and specification
  - —Equal to competition, sell on substitution or system-cost criteria
  - —Low, sell on limited substitution criteria

This list is not exhaustive but is intended to focus on those strategies that will promote growth for the small industrial manufacturing firms.

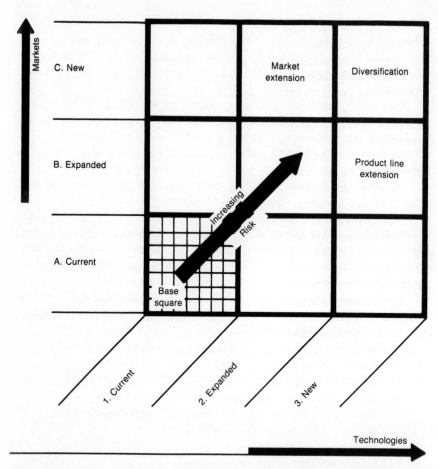

Fig. 9-1. The basis for discussing alternative two-dimensional strategies.

Two-dimensional strategies are more sophisticated than those already discussed, but a simple graphical technique shown in Fig. 9-1 adds clarification.[6] The figure depicts a way of describing alternative strategies, recognizing that markets and technologies are interrelated. The figure shows, in a two-dimensional format, a company's current position and future opportunities in both technology and markets.

The six two-dimensional strategy alternatives are to:

• Maintain the status quo.

- Create new base squares (A1).
- Insure markets.
- Maintain markets by technology changes.
- Maintain technology by market changes.
- Improve both market and technology position.

Notice that as the company moves outside the base square, increasing risk is suggested.

However, maintaining the status quo will not proceed toward growth. Competitive strategies, changes in the environment, and the market work against this strategy. It can be shown that trying to keep the company products in square A-1 will cause a decline in the company's competitiveness.

Formulated strategies have to account for experience and company resource deployment to develop and achieve implementation of a strategic plan. One illustration of a company's style of approach to developing strategies and plans is shown in Fig. 9-2.[7] Coupled with the two-dimension strategy matrix, the firm can consider many strategies and plan implementation styles.

Unfortunately, intended strategies do not usually happen by plan. Unstructured considerations not planned for always have to be dealt with. Quite often small company business leaders fail to see that experience and its value can be overestimated. Changing the strategy results from a decision made outside of or without consideration for the strategic plan. The decision may be correct, but it must be made weighing all the alternatives and elements affected that are a part of the formal strategic planning process.

In summary, the main points to consider when developing a strategy for the firm are:[8]

- Use of a list of business discrepancies identified by the situation analysis.
- Consideration for the fact that the strategic plan will call for a change in the business.
- Strategies and the business are dynamic.
- Capitalize on strengths and understand weaknesses.
- Use strategies that share costs between activities.
- Consider costs, cash flow, and growth alternatives.
- Develop contingency ideas for future planning.

Following the development of several strategies, each should be tested for clarity and consistency with the goals of the CEO and owners. Further, each strategy should be compared with unexpected changes in the market and business environment.

	Maintain Status Quo	Create New Base Squares	Insure Markets	Maintain Markets via Technology Changes	Maintain Technology via Market Changes	Improve Market/ Technology Position
Caution						
Risk Reduction	●		●			●
Risk Hedging	●		●	●	●	●
Risk Diversification		●				●
Risk Spreading	●	●				●
Evolution						
Mandatory			●	●	●	
Elective			●	●	●	●
Revolution		●				●
Aggression		●		●	●	●

Fig. 9-2. Strategic planning for smaller businesses.

9.7 EVALUATION AND SELECTION

To select a strategy from several alternatives, the firm has to evaluate the research done in the strategy formation process. Often, several strategy alternatives will not pass a cursory examination. But, for those alternative strategies that remain, a systematic process should be used. Techniques include:

- Quantifying qualitative information.
- Handling the lack of data.
- Financial evaluation.
- Growth rate check.
- Nonfinancial criteria.
- Final selection.

These techniques do not insure that the ultimate strategy will be selected. Success is a painfully slow process when evaluation of much subjective data is involved. However, the alternative is not acceptable for growth-oriented companies.

Quantifying qualitative data is a precise way to present and evaluate information of which the firm can't be totally sure. Generally, a weighting is used. Major activities performed or involved are listed for the company that are common to competitors, the market, the industry, and the environment. Justification of the weights is subjective but can be enhanced using past experience.

Handling the lack of data requires decision-making analysis and the knowledge of the associated cost to gain the information. Essentially, the task is to assess the probability that perfect information does not exist about competitors or costs of implementation in the future. For example, if the firm's competitor is entering a new market and market share information is desired, the company may have to pay a consultant to study the market. Suppose it is enough to know the competitor is entering this market. Then the cost of additional "better" information is prohibitive. A computer software package can estimate the cost of perfect information and further increase confidence by probability analysis. These techniques include Monte Carlo analysis, histogram probabilities, and various "What If" analysis techniques.

The financial evaluation has to emphasize the time value of money. Present value and discounted cash flow analysis should be applied to relate the costs involved of strategy alternatives. If capital investments are called for, the net present value, internal rate of return, and payback period have to be considered. For growth-oriented small businesses, the main concern is how much cash is required before the program starts to generate revenue.

The direct cash flow calculation method should be employed to check the discounted cash flow method. Often, a small business does not have the necessary month-to-month cash flow, even though an investment passes all other tests.

Next a breakeven analysis should be applied if the strategy calls for financial investment. Breakeven analyses can be generated graphically to help determine whether the rate of return from the activity is acceptable. The breakeven calculation shows the point at which revenues equal the total of fixed and variable costs.

Return on investment made in a new program can be deceiving in a small business. Calculating profit from the investment does not account for cash flow. The issue is that of establishing a figure for profit and a suitable investment time frame without examining the fluctuations in cash flow that occur on a daily basis over the period.

The question of growth rate for a small business is quite serious. Rapidly growing businesses are most often derailed due to under-capitalization. In other words, the growing concern can't bring in enough cash from operations, loans, and equity to cover the short-term needs. Aggressive growth strategies require a sanity check, because a firm has to balance debt and equity financing with short-term cash flows. The formula included here is useful to measure the capability of the business to grow.[9]

$G = P [R + (D/E) \times R - I]$ where
G is sustainable growth rate/year
P is the percent of earnings retained
R is the return on net assets
D/E is the debt-to-equity ratio
I is the effective interest rate on debt after allowing for income tax

Caution has to be used when applying this formula, because debt has to be repaid from earnings. It would be better to use the ratio of extra debt to be incurred for the strategic plan under consideration to the incremental equity available to calculate the program's sustainable growth rate.

The final quantitative evaluation comes from generating pro-forma operating statements. These statements do not provide the same precision as the cash flow test, but the time horizon is extended over several years. In this way, alternative strategies can be assessed over the longer term.

Nonfinancial criteria include the evaluation of contingency plans and a description of the risk involved. The action plans called for by the strategic plan have to be backed up with alternative plans to satisfy the strategy. The problem is to isolate what caused missed sales targets so a correction plan can be implemented. Early feedback is the key to using contingency plans successfully.

Classification of risks is again a judgemental process. However, if the results of the previous planning period have been recorded, then risks can be compared from experience. The final analysis rests with the CEO, and his decisions are the final strategy criterion.

To make the final decision on selecting the growth strategy for the firm requires a choice of trade-offs between sustaining cash flow and maintaining the growth objectives. If no strategy can be selected after this process, then modifications to the strategy must be considered. In some cases, a combined strategy will work. More likely, the successful firm will implement the simplest strategy that receives the highest evaluation. The surviving strategy is reduced to action plans, and the results measured for success.

ENDNOTES—Chapter 9

1. Derek F. Abell, *Strategic Market Planning* (New Jersey: Prentice-Hall, 1979).

2. Bernard A. Rousch, *Strategic Marketing Planning* (Boston: Amacom, A Division of American Management Associations, 1982).

3. David A. Curtis, *Strategic Planning for Smaller Businesses* (Lexington: D.C. Heath & Co., 1983), p. 94.

4. *Ibid*, p. 96.

5. *Ibid*, p. 121 (adaptation).

6. *Ibid*, p. 124.

7. *Ibid*, p. 134.

8. *Ibid*, p.135.

9. *Ibid*, pp. 154–155.

Chapter 10

Multinational Strategies*

10.0 INTRODUCTION

Multinational enterprises that manage global systems of trade, productions, technology, and finance demonstrate the highest degree of multinational involvement and foreign-marketpenetration. Although most of these companies tend to be large (they include almost all the Fortune 500), several medium-size companies have also become multinational in the scope of their international operations. Even though multinational enterprises are impressive in the international sophistication of their management, they did not start that way. The actual historical experience of U.S. manufacturers indicates that the process of internationalization is likely to be a gradual evolution over time.

10.1 WHY GO INTERNATIONAL?

Ultimately, the answer to this question is specific to each company. In general terms, however, it can be said that companies go international when they can no longer achieve their strategic objectives by remaining at home. They may go abroad to:

- Achieve profitable growth which is blocked at home by saturated or slow-growing markets.

---

*The authors are indebted to Kenneth Smith, Executive MBA Student at Baldwin-Wallace College, for much of the research on this chapter.

* Keep up with domestic competitors; the so-called bandwagon effect.
* Follow their domestic customers who are going international.
* Earn additional income on existing technology.
* Take advantage of faster-growing foreign economies.
* Spread fixed manufacturing and development costs over larger sales volume.
* Compete more effectively with foreign companies invading their home markets.
* Achieve other objectives.

For the most part, however, these objectives become explicit only after a company has made its first, tentative venture into foreign markets. The impulse behind that first entry—almost always as an exporter—is simply the prospect of obtaining profits on immediate sales. Only later, after some success in casual exporting, do companies begin to design strategies for a sustained build-up of international business over the long run. To do so, their management must cast off popular misconceptions about international business.

10.2 MISCONCEPTIONS ABOUT INTERNATIONAL BUSINESS

Several misconceptions about international business have prevented U.S. manufacturers from taking the first step into foreign markets. The following are some of that more prominent ones.

Misconception #1. The skills needed to manage international payments (handling foreign exchange, financing sales, insuring payment, etc. are beyond the capabilities of our managers, who have only domestic experience. Most certainly, the management of international payments appears mysterious and often threatening to the domestic executive; however, these fears are unwarranted, because the executive can easily obtain the assistance of banks that specialize in international payments arrangements. Furthermore, because most U.S. export shipments are payable in dollars, the risk of adverse fluctuations in exchange rates is usually borne by the foreign imported.[1] The executive with an open mind will find that he can learn what he needs to know about international payments in an intense, but short learning experience.

Misconception #2. Export sales are just too complicated, with all sorts of documentary requirements, like special price quotations, involved transportation arrangements, foreign customs clearance, etc. It certainly is true that the requirements of export shipments are more demanding than domestic shipments. However, once again, the manufacturer can easily obtain the assistance of specialists, such as international forwarders, who will take care of most of the details of export shipments. Because shipment is intimately linked with financing and payments, banks also offer assistance in meeting documentary requirements.

Misconception #3. We jut don't know anything about foreign markets, and it's hard to find out anything about them. As a matter of fact, a great deal of information about foreign markets may be acquired quickly and at little cost from a variety of secondary sources: the U.S. and State governments, foreign governments, international and regional organizations, banks, trade associations, and other agencies, as well as from numerous publications.

Misconception #4. Risks are far higher in international business than in domestic business. This statement is inapplicable unless both the risk and the foreign country are identified. Once this is done, it becomes evident that risks vary within the same country or between countries. More fundamentally, the international economy should not be viewed as a jungle. For example, the major trading countries are committed to observe certain rules in their treatment of foreign trade as participants in the General Agreement on Tariffs and Trade (GATT). Furthermore, the United States has scores of bilateral agreements with foreign countries covering trade, investment, industrial property rights, taxation,, and other subjects of concern to international business. Beyond these formal agreements, national governments are unlikely to introduce radical changes in their treatment of foreign trade and investment because they fear retaliation, to say nothing of other economic costs. For the most part, therefore, the international economy can be considered a regulated environment.

All this is not to deny that political risks (the risks that arise from government actions adverse to foreign business interests) may be much higher in some countries than in the United States (where they are by no means entirely absent). However, it is possible for the U.S. company to manage political risks in the same objective way it manages the usual business risks. There is no basis, therefore, for describing international business as generally riskier than domestic business. Indeed, for some risks in some foreign countries, business may be less risky than business at home!

Misconception #5. International business demands a great deal of capital and management time. This misconception derives from ignorance about the many modes of foreign market entry, ranging from indirect exporting to full-scale foreign manufacturing. At one extreme, indirect exporting requires zero or only most commitments of capital and management because the export job is undertaken by an intermediary located in the United States. At the other extreme, full-scale manufacturing abroad may involve substantial capital investment and specialized management teams at both the parent company and the subsidiary. The important point here is that international business is open to small and big companies alike, as long as they offer distinctive products and skills to the market place.

The foregoing misconceptions reduce to a general misconception that international business is totally different from domestic business. Certainly, business environments in foreign countries differ from the U.S. business environment, but the principles of good management are the same everywhere. Less common is an opposing general misconception that international business is the same as domestic business. This misconception springs from narrow attitudes that predispose U.S. managers to believe that what works best for their companies in the United States will also work best abroad. This misconception (ordinarily implicit rather than explicit) has caused many blunders and unfortunately encourages U.S. companies to undertake foreign ventures that are ill-designed for success.[2]

10.3 THREE-STAGE EVOLUTION

The transition from domestic to multinational enterprises may be described as an evolution in three stages: the export stage, the foreign production stage, and the multinational enterprise stage.

The Export Stage

The export stage ordinarily starts with an unsolicited inquiry about a company's products from a domestic-export intermediary or direct from a prospective foreign buyer. When the inquiry results in a profitable sale, the manufacturer follows up subsequent inquiries and makes sales to other foreign buyers, probably through domestic export middlemen. At some point, however, the manufacturer decides that his or her export business should be actively developed, and to that end, he or she appoints an export manager with a small staff. If the manufacturer experiences a continuing growth of export sales, the inadequacy of a small, built-in export department becomes evident. The next step, then, is to establish a full-service export department at the same level as the domestic sales department. Further growth of export sales may justify the establishment of sales branches overseas to replace foreign agents and distributors and even assembly operations to obtain lower transportation and/or tariff costs.

The manufacturer has now evolved toward a systematic export program supported by market research, advertising, and other forms of promotion. The company may be selling full-product lines in many of the foreign markets, and his other export sales may be 10 percent or more of total company sales. However, the manufacturer still depends entirely on exports (including assembly operations) to penetrate foreign markets.

For a comparatively small number of high-technology firms, licensing may be the mode of first entry into international business. Licensing does not require capital investment and poses few risks to the newcomer. The manufacturer simply licenses the use of his patents, production know-how, or trademarks to an independent foreign producer in return for royalty payments. A pure licensing agreement means that the manufacturer has substituted an export of technology for the export of his own products.

The first stage in the evolution of a multinational company ends when the manufacturer decides to enter foreign markets by means of foreign production under one or more arrangements.

The Foreign Production Stage

Most exporting manufacturers prefer to stay out of foreign production. Exports and licensing, however, are not always sufficient to achieve a manufacturer's objectives in foreign markets. The most common explanations of this situation are high tariffs or other import barriers imposed by governments, and more intense competition within a foreign market. Consequently, the motivation behind the first entry into foreign production is usually a defensive step taken to maintain an existing export market. Nevertheless, the first direct investment by a manufacturing company in foreign-production facilities marks a critical step in its evolution as an international company. (Because most U.S. manufacturers are inclined to view their first investment in Canada as domestic rather than foreign, it is their first investment outside the United States and Canada that becomes the critical step). For the first time, the manufacturer commits substantial financial, managerial, and technical resources to an international venture. He now becomes exposed to risks (such as expropriation) that go far beyond the risks associated with exporting or licensing. To a far greater extent than before, the entry into foreign production most often involves top management of a company in decisions relating to international business.

The first investment abroad traditionally paves the way for later investments. Eventually, plants may be established in several countries to produce all or part of the manufacturer's product lines. At the same time, the manufacturer will continue to export domestic products to other countries and, increasingly, to his own foreign subsidiaries. He also continues to license technology abroad, but mostly to his own affiliates rather than to independent foreign manufacturers. At the end of the foreign production stage, the U.S. manufacturer will be penetrating markets throughout the world by means of several foreign production bases, in conjunction with exports from the United States. The management of these diverse, far-flung operations places new strains on the planning, organizing, and controlling functions of the parent company. To accommodate those strains, management moves toward a global concept of a single-enterprise system that marks the beginning of the multinational-enterprise stage.

The Multinational-Enterprise Stage

A company becomes multinational when its management starts to plan, organize, and control its total operations on a worldwide scale. Such a company both poses and answers questions such as:

- Where in the world are our best markets?
- Where in the world should we manufacture products for these markets?
- Where in the world should we obtain financing for our capital investments and current operations?
- Where in the world should we recruit people to staff our global system?

During the foreign production stage, a manufacturer tends to follow a binational strategy with respect to foreign markets. He may perceive each foreign market as unique and separate from other national markets, thereby ignoring potential relations among them and among his manufacturing affiliates located in different countries. However, at the multinational stage, the manufacturer replaces binational strategy with global strategy. National markets are now viewed as segments of broader regional and world markets. As a consequence, managers must concentrate their energies on building intraenterprise flows of products, technology, capital, and personnel among their many affiliates in order to take advantage of international specialization and economies of scale.

Only a minority of international companies have reached the multinational stage.[3] Although their numbers will almost certainly grow both in the United States and in other advanced countries, the majority of U.S. manufacturers engaged in international business will probably remain in the exporting stage, and other manufacturers will probably not move beyond the foreign production stage. Of course, the great majority of U.S. manufacturers will remain wholly domestic in their orientation. Thus, there is no inevitable progression to the multinational stage. Nor should one consider multinational strategy necessarily superior to exporting strategy. Limitations of size will prevent many U.S. manufacturers from entering foreign production or will permit entry only on a modest scale. The important point is that manufacturers should choose those entry strategies that promise to be most effective in attaining company objectives. For some, a succession of entry strategies over time will bring an evolution to becoming a multinational enterprise and, for others, an evolution to more and more sophisticated export management and operations.

10.4 DESIGNING ENTRY STRATEGIES

A company may choose as its corporate strategy one or more paths to long-run profitable growth:

- Greater penetration of old markets at home with old products (increased market share).
- The development of new markets at home for old products (adding market segments).

- The introduction of new products to serve old markets (product replacement).
- The introduction of new products to serve new markets at home (product diversification).
- The entry into foreign markets with old and/or new products (international business).

It follows that foreign growth strategies should be assessed against domestic growth strategies if a company intends to allocate its resources rationally over the long-term future. For the purposes of this analysis, it is assumed that such an assessment has been made in favor of foreign market entry. The next section is directed at how a company should plan that entry.

10.5 A PLANNING MODEL

The foreign market entry strategy of a company is a comprehensive plan that determines the objectives and policies that will guide the growth of its international business over a period of time long enough to encompass economic, political, and other factors critical to success in foreign markets. For most companies, the entry-strategy period probably runs from three to five years. For some companies, it may be only a year; for other companies, a decade or more. The important point is that the planning period should be long enough to compel managers to raise and answer fundamental questions about the future direction and scope of their company's international business operations. Also, the planning period should encompass the effects of decisions that are taken in accordance with the plan. For the convenience of this analysis, it is assumed that the entry-strategy period is on the order of from three to five years.

Although one may speak of a company's foreign-entry strategy as if it were a single plan, it is actually the end result of many individual product-market plans. Basically, managers should plan the entry (or reentry) of each product in each foreign market. The individual plans should then be brought together and reconciled to form the overall foreign market-entry strategy of the company. The constituent product-market plans often involve:

- The choice of a target market.
- The choice of market objectives.
- The choice of a market-entry mode or modes.
- The monitoring of market performance that may lead to a subsequent revision of market objectives and entry modes.

Thus, each product-market plan defines a course of action over the next three to five years to achieve defined objectives in a target foreign market. When we speak of exporting, licensing, and production abroad as foreign market entry strategies, we are speaking, therefore, of the complete strategic plans.

Some managers in small and medium-size companies may believe that only big companies can afford strategic planning for foreign market entry. They often identify such planning as using elaborate analytical techniques applied by expert planners to a large body of quantitative data. This approach, however, is unlikely to succeed. Fundamentally, market-entry planning is an effort to chart the future course of a company's international operations by using reason and facts rather than depending on hunch or day-to-day decisions. What is important is the idea of planning a foreign market entry strategy. Once a company accepts this idea, it will find ways to plan foreign-market entry, irrespective of how limited its resources may be. The very activity of systematically thinking about where a company's international business should be five years from now, and what will be needed to get there, can instill a creative spirit in managers. To say that a company cannot afford a foreign market entry strategy is to say that it cannot afford to think systematically about its future.

The elements of the entry-strategy planning process for a specific product and a specific target market are shown in Fig. 10-1. Although these elements are presented as a logical sequence of activities and decisions, this sequence is not unidirectional. Quite the opposite, the planning process is iterative through time and has many feedback loops (only some of them are shown in Fig. 10-l). Evaluation of alternative market-entry modes, for instance, may cause a revision of market objectives or initiate a reassessment of the firms' resources and capabilities. Planning for foreign market entry is a continuing, open-ended process, and, from Fig. 10-1, treatment of planning as a sequence of logical steps should not be allowed to obscure this basic fact.

Planning the foreign market entry strategy usually begins with an evaluation of a firm's resources and capabilities. For example, What are the firm's resources in personnel, materials, technology, and capital? Does the firm have distinctive products that can gain a competitive niche in foreign markets? How well has the firm done with those products in domestic markets? If the firm is already in some foreign markets, what are the strengths and weaknesses of its international business performance? In brief, what are the driving and restraining forces within the firm with respect to foreign market entry? Such questions need to be raised and answered by managers if they are to establish reasonable objectives for a market-entry strategy.

10.6 CHOOSING TARGET MARKETS

Step 2 in Fig. 10-1 is the evaluation of foreign market opportunities to choose the best target market for the company. Listed below are some questions that

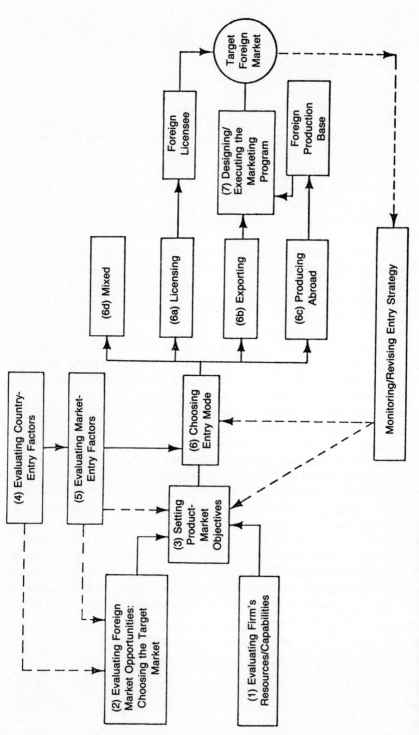

Fig. 10-1. Entry strategy planning.

must be answered in the evaluation:

- Which countries are prospective target markets for the company's product type?
- Of these prospective target markets, which countries offer high market potentials?
- Of the high-potential countries, which country offers the highest sales potential for the company's own products?
- Which market segment, or mix of segments, is optimal in this target market?

The analytical steps by which managers can get answers to these questions are shown in Fig. 10-2.

Preliminary screening identifies foreign markets that warrant further investigation. Because of the large number of national markets, preliminary screening should be done quickly and economically, using readily available information and simple techniques. At the same time, it should be sufficiently discriminating to select prospective target markets from a heterogeneous set of markets. Because the screening is preliminary, it should be comprehensive. Otherwise, managers may ignore countries that offer good prospects for their product types and leave them to more discerning competitors.

Although there is no single best set of screening criteria, they may be classified as general criteria that relate to a particular country and criteria that relate directly to the generic product. Country-specific criteria include population, gross national (or domestic) product, geography, manufacturing as a percentage of national product, per capita income, energy consumption, total imports, imports from the United states, and other significant features of the country. In contrast, product-specific criteria vary from company to company. Based on their experience at home or elsewhere, managers should decide what criteria will discriminate among countries with respect to market opportunities for their product. For example, manufacturers of industrial products may use criteria that measure the size and growth of the industries they serve; manufacturers of the consumer products may use criteria that measure significant household-consumer characteristics. When a country exceeds the minimum (or threshold) values of the criteria employed by a company, it becomes a prospective target country.

The next task is to estimate the market potential of a prospective target country. Market potential can be described as the most probable total future sales of a product by all sellers in the designated country over the company's planning period. Several techniques are available to estimate market potentials, such as trend analysis, correlation, and survey methods. However, it is always important to know current and past sales of the product in the market under

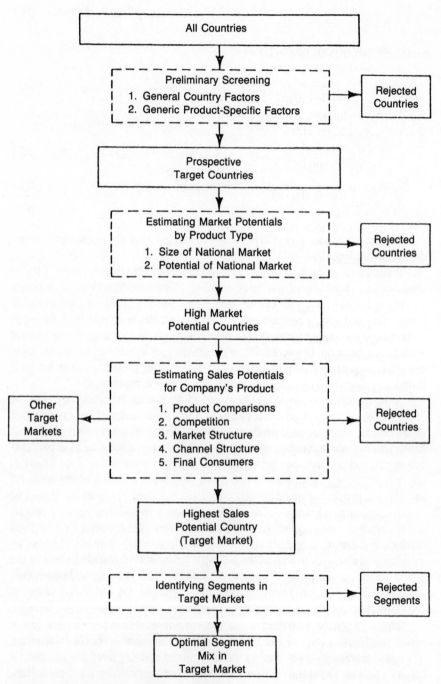

Fig. 10-2. Screening target markets.

study. When a generic product is wholly new to a foreign market, then experience in other markets, comparisons with older products serving the same market needs, surveys of consumer attitudes, etc., may prove useful. If actual sales data are not available, managers may be able to estimate apparent consumption from local production, import, and export data. The estimate of a country's market potential provides a quantitative measure of a market in which the manufacturer must find a place if entry is to be successful. It can tell him how big the market is, and how it is most likely to grow over the next three to five years.

The third step is the estimation of the sales potential of a company's own products in a high market potential country. Sales potential can be described as the maximum sales that a company can reasonably plan for in the foreign market. Alternatively, sales potential is the projection of a company's maximum share of the market potential over the next three to five years. The sales potential is not the same as a sales forecast, which determines the sales goal of current operations; rather, it is usually considered the basis of a market-entry strategy.

To estimate a company's sales potential in a foreign market, managers should evaluate and measure (when feasible) several factors. Probably the first area of investigation should be an appraisal of any entry restrictions imposed by the foreign government on inflows of products, technology, and equity investment. This is indicated in Fig. 10-1 by the dashed line connecting Box 4 and Box 2. Consideration of country-entry factors, together with market-entry factors, presents a key element: The sales potential in a given foreign market will ordinarily depend on the mode of entry chosen by the company. At this stage in planning market-entry strategy, however, country-entry factors are usually evaluated only to the degree necessary to answer the question: Is there an acceptable way the company can enter the market? Full evaluation of these factors is usually undertaken only after the selection of the target market. Thus, sales potential estimates at this stage are tentative, becoming definite for the target market only after the entry mode is decided by management. Although tentative, sales potential estimates should be firm enough, to identify with an acceptable degree of confidence, the country with the highest sales potential, which then becomes the company's target market.

Next, a series of comparisons can be made between the manufacturer's product line and those of competitors in the foreign market. The comparisons should go beyond price to encompass quality, design, and other aspects of product differentiation. Nor should the comparisons be confined to the tangible product alone; comparisons also need to be made in before—and after—sales services provided to customers. Finally, comparisons should be made among all products—whether or not in the same industry—that satisfy the same function or need. In the final analysis, the U.S. manufacturer is competing not against other products, but for the favor of potential customers. Other areas of investigation include competition, market structure, channel structure, and the behavior of the final consumers or users of the manufacturer's product line.

The target country market may be heterogeneous, consisting of several sub-markets (market segments) that differ significantly in sales potential and in their responses to marketing variables such as price, quality, promotion, and so on. It is desirable, therefore, for the manufacturer to undertake segment analysis of the target market, using criteria that influence sales potential, such as age, sex, income, lifestyle (for a consumer product) or industry, firm size, and geographical location (for an industrial product). Market-segment analysis can be an important input into the design of the marketing program, apart from its bearing on the choice of market-entry mode.

10.7 CHOOSING ENTRY MODES

Once the U.S. manufacturer has selected a foreign target market and has determined his objectives in that market over the planning period, he must decide on the most appropriate mode of entry for his product or product line. A logical entry-decision process requires awareness of the different entry modes available to the company and a comparison of the benefits and costs associated with alternative entry modes for a particular combination of product and market. There are several reasons why the entry-decision process cannot be reduced to a formula or even to a complex quantitative model that is manipulated by a computer. In this regard, it is the same as any other strategy decision.[4]

One reason is the multiplicity of entry modes. Although there are only three primary modes for foreign market entry—exporting, licensing, and producing abroad— there are many secondary modes within each primary mode. The number of entry modes is further magnified by the possibility of mixed modes of entry that combine two or all three primary modes. Consequently, as companies expand their international operations, mixed modes of entry may be preferable to primary modes. Thus, a search for alternative entry modes is an indispensable element of a rational entry-decision process.

Several other reasons make it difficult to compare alternative entry modes. The benefits and costs of each mode must be evaluated in terms of the company's multiple objectives, which are sometimes in conflict. An entry mode that scores highly on one objective (rate of growth in sales) may score low on another objective (profitability). Therefore, managers must decide on the tradeoffs between conflicting objectives. In addition, some of the benefits and costs associated with a particular entry mode may be difficult to identify and/or measure. For example, the use of licensing precludes the opportunity to enter a target market with a new mode later on or licensee's emergence as a competitor in export markets.

Another reason why entry decisions are so complex is that comparisons are made between projected benefits and costs over a future planning period. Managers are, therefore, comparing expected benefits and costs under conditions of partial ignorance. Because a company new to international business is often aware of its ignorance, it is inclined to choose an entry mode that appears to require less experience than other modes. Also, the different entry modes are subject to different sets of risks, with different amounts of company assets exposed to those risks. Therefore, it is management's responsibility to adjust benefits and costs for both market and political risks.

The complexity of the foreign market entry decision makes all the more desirable an analytical framework that facilitates systematic comparisons among alternative entry modes. The framework presented here assumes that one of the key objectives (if not the overriding one) of management is profitability over the planning period. Even though management may not choose that entry mode with the highest profitability because of other objectives, internal constraints, or risk preference, it remains important to know the sacrifice in profitability resulting from an alternative. Furthermore, profitability analysis may rule out certain entry modes because they do not satisfy a company's profitability threshold (internal rate of return).

Profitability analysis regards the entry decision as an investment decision. As used here, investment includes not only capital, but the allocation of any of a company's resources with the purpose of generating income over a lengthy future period. Thus "start-up costs" to enter a new business environment, hiring new skills, negotiating with the host government and local business people, conducting market research, planning product adaptation, etc.) are just as much a part of a company's "entry-investment base" as a cash investment in a new foreign plant.

Major steps that are applied by a company in preparing a profitability analysis are:

- Identify, measure, and project over the planning period all incremental revenues (net after foreign and U.S. taxes) that will be received by the company as a direct or indirect result of each entry mode (including mixed modes).
- Do the same for all costs.
- Using the projections from the first two steps, calculate the incremental net cash flow of each entry mode over the planning period.
- Adjust the net cash flows for the time value of money (the cost of capital to the company) by calculating the net present value of each net cash flow.
- Rank-order the alternative entry modes by their net present values.

Entry Mode	Projected Cash Inflow[1]	Projected Cash Outflow[2]	Net Cash Inflow[3]	Time-Adjusted Cash Inflow[4]	Other Criteria	Recommended Entry Mode
Indirect Export						
Direct Export						
Foreign Assembly						
Licensing						
Foreign Contract Manufacturing						
Joint Venture						
Wholly Owned Manufacturing Subsidiary						
Mixed						

[1] Based on unit sale and price projections and/or any other projected cash inflows (royalties, management fees, dividends, and so on), net after foreign and U.S. taxes, and repatriable in U.S. dollars.
[2] Based on projections of the U.S. company's foreign investment base and operating costs borne by the U.S. company.
[3] Projected cash inflow less projected cash outflow.
[4] Net present value.

Fig. 10-3. Financial analysis of entry model alternatives.

Once the profitability analysis is completed, management needs to evaluate each entry mode with other criteria it considers significant, such as other objective, risk, control, the exchange rate, and internal constraints. Therefore, the entry mode chosen by management may not be the mode with the highest net present value. Figure 10-3 summarizes this approach to the foreign-entry decision with a comparison matrix.

10.8 MONITORING AND REVISING ENTRY STRATEGY

The discussion, thus far, of foreign market entry strategy has been for a single planning period. However, the entry strategy that is optimal for a company in a given target market at one time may not be optimal at a subsequent time. To maintain optimal entry strategy over time, therefore, managers need to continually monitor and evaluate changes in factors that bear on the direction and effectiveness of the current entry strategy. These factors include changes in the target market (such as country and market entry conditions, competition, buyer preferences), changes in company objectives, changes in company resources and capabilities, and changes in the company's actual performance in the target market.

The evolution of international companies may be described as a sequence of entry strategies, adopted to sustain and strengthen their positions in foreign markets over time. It is a cumulative process: entry strategies today prepare the way for new entry strategies in the future. This interdependence among entry strategies becomes evident when we further examine the three primary market-entry vehicles: exporting, licensing, and production abroad. Interdependence is revealed by Behrman's study of the investment-export relations of 53 companies.[5] Twenty-two percent of the companies reported situations where changes in import tariffs and quotas led to a shift from exporting to foreign production in order to preserve or develop the market.[6] Twenty percent reported a similar shift after the appearance of local and third-country competitors in the foreign market.[7] Twenty-seven percent indicated situations where export products were displaced by foreign investment but where new and different export products were induced by the investment, or where foreign investment opened up export opportunities for new finished products.[8] Other situations of interdependence were also cited by the companies.

ENDNOTES—Chapter 10

1. S.L. Srinivasulu, "Strategic Response to Foreign Exchange Risks," *Columbia Journal of World Business,* Spring 1981, p. 127.

2. David Ricks, *International Business Blunders* (Columbus, OH: Grid, Inc., 1974).

3. William A. Dymsza, *Multinational Business Strategy* (New York: McGraw-Hill, 1972), p. 257.

4. Igor H. Ansoff, *Corporate Strategy* (New York: McGraw- HIll, 1965), p. 116.

5. Jack N. Behrman, *Direct Manufacturing Investment, Exports, and the Balance of Payments* (New York: National Foreign Trade Council, Inc., 1968).

6. *Ibid,* p. 41.

7. *Ibid,* p. 41.

8. *Ibid,* p. 41.

Chapter 11

Developing Strategic Planners: A Project Management Approach

11.0 INTRODUCTION

The ambition of every MBA student is, upon graduation, to go directly into a strategic planning position for a Fortune 500 Corporation. Somehow, students have become convinced that simply because they have correctly analyzed several college-designed case studies, they are now prepared to perform strategic planning, regardless of prior work experience or background. The more recognition that the graduate school has achieved, the greater the propensity that the new graduate will seek out immediate positions in strategic planning.

Corporations today are critically reassessing not only the staffing for the strategic planning function, but even the hiring of MBA students in general. The glamor of MBA degrees during the 1960s and 1970s seems to have diminished during the 1980s. With regard to the strategic planning function, this is understandable. Strategic planning cannot be effective unless the strategic plan can be implemented. Creative thinking, ingenuity, and the desire to achieve are good personal attributes for planners, provided that the output of the planning process is meaningful, realistic, and attainable.

Perhaps the best solution appears to be the training of the new MBA as a project manager, where he/she can understand the difficulties of strategy implementation and execution by physically executing projects. For the past 25 years or so, industry has been using project management for the implementation of tactical and operational plans. It is therefore only fitting that there be a scale up to strategic planning as well.

After having served as a project manager for at least three to five years, the individual is placed into a strategic planning position. The advantages of this technique are as follows:

- Most projects cut across the entire organization and the project manager learns how each functional unit operates and how they should work together.
- The project manager must work with each functional manager to plan, staff, execute and monitor status. The project manager, therefore, has the opportunity to develop strong interpersonal and communicative skills.
- During the project planning and estimating phase, the project manager will learn company costing techniques, company standards and performance measurement techniques.
- The project manager frequently interfaces with senior management during the objective-setting phase, conflict resolution, priority-setting, and status reporting.
- Through successful execution of projects, the project manager can obtain functional management commitment and support.
- Project managers know how to balance values, planning, tradeoffs, and judgment.
- Project direction can change rapidly should changes take place in the external or internal environment.
- In most situations, project managers can show organizational personnel the importance of information feedback and decision support systems.
- Project managers try to develop a climate conducive to the planning and execution of tasks.

Executives believe that the above nine topics provide an individual with company operations knowledge, planning and estimating skills, interpersonal skills, and top management visibility, thus creating a strong background for future strategic planners.

Unfortunately, executives tend to look only at the macro level of project management rather than the micro level. At the macro level, the above four topics are strong driving forces for using project management as a training, selection, and breeding ground for future executives and strategic planners. On the micro level, there are severe limitations and restraining forces that are often overlooked by senior management. These restraining forces must be overcome and will be described in the following sections.

11.1 UNDERSTANDING PROJECT MANAGEMENT

In the simplest possible terms, project management is a management technique or approach designed to accomplish single, unique, or one-of-a-kind objectives by getting work to flow multidirectionally within the corporation. Each project has a time, cost, and performance constraint and must interact either formally or informally with both the internal and external environments.

All corporate resources are either controlled by or report directly to the line managers. The project managers obtain resources through often lengthy and time-consuming negotiations with line managers and, more often than not, end up with less than desired resources. Project managers must rely heavily upon their interpersonal skills and communicative techniques to get the job done.

Project managers are usually given a great deal of responsibility but with very little commensurate authority. Executives tend to delegate authority, if at all, on a project-by-project basis, depending upon the size and nature of the project, the size and nature of the business, the appropriate lifecycle phase, and management's capabilities at all levels of the organization. Because of this, project managers must share their authority, responsibility, and accountability with the line managers. Project planning, execution, and monitoring, therefore, becomes a joint effort between the project and line managers.

Based upon the above description, it should be no surprise to anyone that project management is an excellent approach for the planning, scheduling, execution, and control of strategic projects. One key point needs to be made here: when project management had its birth, the line managers wore two hats—that of a project manager and that of a line manager. As project management matured and projects grew in size, a separate single-hat position for the project manager was created mainly for those large projects that required integration across several functional lines.[1]

For those readers familiar with project management, it must be understood that the role of the project manager is one of staff support for those managers and executives that have the ultimate responsibility for strategic planning and execution. Because of the corporate importance of the strategic planning functions, there is nothing wrong with line managers and executives acting as project managers on strategic projects as long as they can maintain the proper balance between managing the strategic planning/execution effort and their line function responsibility at the same time. However, there may be a strong preference to have people full-time and totally dedicated to the strategic planning function because of its importance.

11.2 LEVELS OF PLANNING

Generally speaking, strategic planning can take place at three levels in the organization, corporate, divisional, and functional.

Corporate planning is geared more toward portfolio planning. At the divisional level, strategic planning is equivalent to business strategy planning, whereas, at the functional level, strategic planning becomes synonymous with strategic programming, a concept which some consider as extremely close to project management.

As the project manager progresses from functional to corporate planning, he usually reports higher in the organization and possesses less authority, because senior personnel wish to be more actively involved in critical decision-making. Furthermore, the individual's motivation may diminish as one proceeds from functional to corporate planning because:

- Project managers are motivated by seeing the results of their efforts in the near term. In strategic planning, the results may not become visible for five to 10 years.
- Project managers are motivated by physically performing the planning themselves. At the corporate level, the individual may find that his actual contribution to the strategic planning process is less than at the functional level.

Steiner and Miner have identified a list of parameters that distinguish strategic from tactical planning. This list has been modified in Table 11-1 to show

Table 11-1. Strategic Versus Tactical (Project Management) Thinking
Source: G. A. Steiner, J. B. Miner, Management Policy and Strategy,
Second Edition, MacMillan Publishers, 1982, pp. 20-21.

Parameter	Strategic Thinking	Tactical (Project Management) Thinking
Level of Conduct	Highest Level	Lowest Levels
Regularity	Continuous	Fixed Time Schedule
Decision-making	Heavily Subjective	Objective
Range of alternatives	Large	Small
Uncertainty	High	Low
Nature of Problems	Unstructured	Structured
Information needs	High	Low
Time Horizon	Long	Short
Details	Few	Broad
Personnel involved	Top	Middle/bottom
Ease of Evaluation	Hard	Easier
Point of View	Corporate	Functional
Importance	High	Less Significant

Adapted from Steiner, G.A. and Miner, J.B., Management Policy and Strategy, 2nd Edition MacMillan Publishers, 1982, pp. 20-21.

the relationship between project management and strategic planning. The table indicates that there should be an intermediate phase between project and strategic planning where the project manager will receive "further education" as to how to cope with such changes and differences. Without this type of understanding, the individual could easily disrupt the organization thinking that project planning and strategic planning are identical.

11.3 MANAGERIAL PRACTICE

Because most projects are of a relatively short-term nature, project managers develop a managerial philosophy based upon the here-and-now approach rather than for the future. The application of the legal, social, economical, political, and technological constraints are considered only for the length of the project, and no further. Table 11-2 indicates the change in managerial practices that should take place from project management to strategic planning.

The obvious conclusion from Table 11-2 is the amount of time and effort placed on the social responsibilities of an organization. Project managers who often disregard social responsibilities for the sake of maximizing project profitability will have to reassess their thinking during strategic planning.

11.4 LEADERSHIP STYLES

Most organizations are either project-driven or nonproject-driven, although some organizations are both. In the project-driven organization, each project exists as a separate entity within the company except for administrative purposes. (This is the result of the project manager having the profit/loss responsibility). In such cases, the project manager has the option of selecting whatever leadership style he sees fit to use, regardless of the leadership style of the executive or to whomever the project managers usually reports. In nonproject-driven organizations, the project managers usually adapt to the leadership style selected by senior management.

Strategic planners interface predominantly with senior personnel rather than with lower level line managers and subordinates. As a result, project managers (especially within project-driven organizations) suddenly find that they have severely limited authority to select their own leadership style and must conform to the executive's image of effective leadership. This may create a rude awakening for project managers who considered themselves as the president of their project.

11.5 LIFECYCLE PHASES

Companies that have mastered project management plan and control all projects through the lifecycle phase concept. (The project lifecycle phase concept appears

Table 11-2. Managerial Practice Changes

Project Management	to	Strategic Planning

- *Operational planning dominates*
- *Human beings are treated as any other resource*

- *Strategic planning dominates*
- *An increased emphasis for the social concerns of the organization such as social accounting, social production, and social measures of performance*

- *Emphasis on quantity and cost per unit*

- *Emphasis on quality as well as quantity*

- *Training is necessary only so far as it relates to the project*

- *Training is a life-long learning experience for employees and should be emphasized and budgeted for, but without sacrificing stockholder interest*

- *Employees are needed only for the life of the project*

- *Employees are needed for the continuous growth of the corporation*

- *Decision-making is centralized around the project manager*

- *Decision-making is decentralized through strategic business units*

- *Decision-making is based upon financial/economic considerations*

- *Decision-making must include social responsibilities as well*

- *Decision-making is based upon risk or well-defined short-term environmental assumptions such as inflation, escalation factors, energy costs and price stability*

- *Decision-making is based upon uncertainty rather than risk*

- *Formal authority may be necessary to get the job accomplished*

- *Job satisfaction and work challenge are strong, long-term driving forces*

- *Formal authority can replace interpersonal skills*

- *Interpersonal skills are needed regardless of authority level*

Table 11-2. (continued)

- *Planning is the extrapolation of past and current trends over the life cycle of the project*

- *Planning involves determining alternates, performing tradeoffs, assessing risk and making recommendations*

- *Tradeoffs are made on time, cost and performance*

- *Tradeoffs are made on time, cost, performance and social responsibility*

- *Planning may be performed solely by project manager*

- *Planning personnel actively involve those responsible for implementation*

- *Project manager develops a formal or informal information/control system for his project only. System may terminate functioning when project ends*

- *Development of both quantitative and qualitative data bases for evaluation of alternatives.*

- *Planning may be informal and on an as-needed basis*

- *Planning is continuous*

- *Contributions to successful planning may not be related to the reward policy*

- *Successful contributions to the planning process are recognized and rewarded*

---

to have evolved from the marketing/product lifecycle phase approach which can be found in almost all marketing texts.) Table 11-3 identifies typical lifecycle phases. The advantages of using the lifecycle phase concept are:

- The planning to be performed and information to be processed can be clearly defined for each phase, although in some cases these phases can overlap.
- Resources can be scheduled for each lifecycle phase.
- Incremental budgets can be allocated.
- Executives have clearly defined milestones, such as at the termination of each phase, so as to best interface with the project.
- Well-defined review meetings are possible at the end of each phase.

Table 11-3. Lifecycle Phase Definitions

ENGINEERING	MANUFACTURING	COMPUTER PROGRAMMING	CONSTRUCTION
• Startup	• Formation	• Conceptual	• Planning, data, gathering and procedures
• Definition	• Buildup	• Planning	
• Main	• Production	• Definition and design	• Studies & basic engineering
• Termination	• Phase-out	• Implementation	• Major review
	• Final Audit	• Conversion	• Detail engineering
			• Detail engineering/Construction overlap
			• Construction
			• Testing and Commissioning

The lifecycle phase concept works well for project management because most projects are of a relatively short time duration with fixed objectives. Environmental considerations are usually such that they have no major impact over the life of most projects. Environmental fluctuations can be corrected through manipulations on direct labor hours and dollars.

Lifecycle phases for strategic planning may be regarded as:

• Strategy formulation/definition.
• Implementation and growth.
• Maturity.
• Decline.
• Redefinition.

The characteristics of strategic planning lifecycle phases include:

• Lengthy time duration of phases (years rather than months).
• Phases can and do overlap.
• Strategic planning objectives can change during each life cycle phase.
• Environmental changes have a serious, active impact on the planning process.

Although the tactical project manager plans and replans for contingencies, the project's objectives are fixed, as is the length of each lifecycle phase. In strategic planning, environmental changes can cause periodic redefinition of objectives as well as lengthening or shortening of lifecycle phases.

Although most project managers are accustomed to replanning, perhaps even on a daily basis, motivation still exists because the project will eventually come to an end, and the project manager will see the fruit of his efforts. In strategic planning, with perhaps continuous redefinition and with lifecycle phases of five to 10 years, the individual may feel frustrated by having to wait so long to see the results. Furthermore, tactical project managers feel "in control" during tactical project lifecycle phases but at the mercy of environmental factors during strategic planning lifecycle phases.

11.6 IDENTIFYING PROJECT/STRATEGIC VARIABLES

Advocates of project management argue that project managers must continuously monitor the external environment in order to develop a well-structured program that can stand up under pressure. Project managers must be able to identify these variables so that an explicit definition of the future posture of the organization can be assessed with regard to the constraints on existing resources. Unfortunately, in the real world, life is somewhat different:

* Project managers monitor the external environment only during initial project planning and, once having identified the variables, assumes that they are fixed over the lifecycle of the project.
* These variables are analyzed with regard to project (not corporate) objectives and functional (not corporate) deployment of resources.
* Emphasis is placed upon the personal values of line rather than senior management.
* Project managers monitor the internal environment moreso than the external environment.

In strategic planning, environmental analysis is much more complex because the individual must plan for the best interest of the company rather than the best interest of the project. Environmental analysis for strategic planning and project management must include:

* Internal Environment
    —Management skills
    —Resources
    —Wage and Salary Levels
    —Government freeze on jobs
    —Minority groups
    —Layoffs
    —Sales forecasts

- External Environment
  - —Legal
  - —Social
  - —Economical
  - —Political
  - —Technological
- Competitive Environment
  - —Industry characteristics
  - —Competitive history
  - —Present competitive activity
  - —Competitive resources
  - —Return on Investment
  - —Market share
  - —Size and variety of product lines

Obviously, the project manager must now employ ''global'' thinking rather than localized thinking. In tactical project management, because of the relatively short duration of the project lifecycle, the project manager begins project planning, immediately assuming that all other variables are known and fixed. During strategic planning, the individual's thought process must be expanded to include the following:

- Identification of company strengths and weaknesses.
- Understanding personal values of top management.
- Identification of opportunities.
- Definition of product market.
- Identification of competitive edge.
- Establishment of overall goals, objectives, standards.
- Identification of necessary resource deployment at corporate level.

Therefore, we can see that tactical project managers may tend to become isolated from the environment, whereas strategic planners must live within it. Proper and current identification of strategic variables requires that strong communications channels be established with senior management, at least moreso than at the tactical project level.

11.7 NEED FOR CEO INVOLVEMENT

Individuals interface with senior management, especially the CEO, during both tactical project management and strategic planning. However, the level of involvement takes on a new dimension in strategic planning. During tactical project management, the project manager interfaces with senior management (not necessarily the CEO) during:

- Initial planning (objective-setting)
- Priority setting
- Conflict resolution
- Project sponsorship

Table 11-4 shows the differences when strategic planning is considered. The conclusions from Table 11-4 are that proper direction is mandatory to start the process and keep personnel on track as well as motivated.

Table 11-4. CEO Involvement

Item	Tactical Planning	Strategic Planning
• Executive endorsement	• Senior management (not necessarily CEO) involvement helpful	• CEO endorsement mandatory
• Objective-setting	• May be delegated to user groups/project manager	• Must begin at executive levels
• Planning initiation	• Delegated to project manager	• CEO must start or endorse process himself
• External variable identification	• May be delegated to project manager	• Executive staff responsibility
• Internal variable identification	• Project manager/department	• Strategic business unit responsibility
• Competitive variable identification	• Project manager responsibility	• Strategic business unit responsibility
• CEO commitment	• Helpful, but not necessary	• Mandatory and must be visible
• Line management commitment	• Obtained through project manager's communicative and interpersonal skills	• Strengthened by CEO's declaration of his position and direction

11.8 THE COMMUNICATIONS PROCESS

Successful project managers are communications experts who try to motivate people by continuously keeping them informed on how their efforts fit into the "big picture." Project managers are trained to bring forth immediately not only good news, but bad news as well. Periodic status reporting is mandatory for corrective action to be taken in a relatively short period.

In strategic planning, there are good reasons for not wanting to articulate the total strategy, especially to lower-level managers and personnel. Such reasons include:

- Lower-level personnel are resistant to change and prefer status quo.
- Lower-level personnel are more profit-oriented for the near-term than capable of visualizing future growth.
- Lower-level personnel are committed to their own line groups and may not dedicate themselves to the strategic planning.

In going from tactical project management to strategic planning, the individual must know when to communicate and when not to. Telling lower-level personnel that the strategic plan is to discontinue a product line, drain cash from a profitable venture, or divest the company of one of its divisions, can create severe morale disruption. Lack of communication may cause the individual to find himself in a position of being an outcast from the "informal" organization.

11.9 FORCE FIELD ANALYSIS

During the past several years, there have been many studies to identify the variables which lead to project success. A paper by Dugan, Thamhain, and Wilemon identified the driving and restraining forces for project success based upon the following definitions:[2]

- A driving force, if existent, will propel a team to successful project performance.
- Restraining forces tend to impede successful project performance.

The core of their paper has been adapted to strategic planning and identified in Table 11-5. Columns 1 and 2 of Table 11-5 show the driving and restraining forces for tactical project management as identified by Dugan, *et.al.* Column 3 represents the authors' observations.

11.10 SUMMARY

There appears to be both strong similarities as well as dissimilarities between tactical project management and strategic planning. Because the similarities

Table 11-5. Driving and Restraining Forces

AREA	DRIVING AND RESTRAINING FORCES	
	PROJECT MANAGEMENT	STRATEGIC PLANNING

• Personal drive, motivation and leadership	• Driving forces
	  • Desire for accomplishment
	  • Interest in project
	  • Group acceptance
	
	  • Work challenge
	  • Common objectives
	
	• Restraining forces
	  • Inexperienced leader
	  • Uncertain roles
	
	  • Lack of technical knowledge
	
	  • Personality problems (especially with lower-level line managers)
		• Driving forces
		  • Desire for accomplishment
		  • Interest in project
		  • Credibility with executives
		  • Work challenge
		  • Realistic objectives
		
		• Restraining forces
		  • Inexperienced planner
		  • Unfamiliar with strategic planning
		  • Lack of knowledge concerning internal, external and competitive variables
		  • Personality problems with senior line managers

• Team Motivation	• Driving forces
	  • Good interpersonal relations with project team
	  • Desire to achieve
	  • Expertise (either technical or as a project manager)
	  • Common goals (i.e., lower-level)
	
	• Restraining forces
	  • Poor team organization
	  • Communication barriers
	  • Poor leadership
		• Driving forces
		  • Good interpersonal relations with senior management
		  • Desire to achieve
		  • Expertise as a planner and decision-maker
		  • Common goals (i.e., upper-level)
		
		• Restraining forces
		  • Poor organization
		
		  • Communication barriers
		  • No direction by senior management

- *Uncertain rewards*

- *Uncertain objectives*

- *Lack of credibility in leader's decision-making ability*
- *Rewards too far down stream*
- *Uncertain rewards*
- *Unclear/unrealistic objectives*

- *Management Support*

- *Driving forces*
  - *Sufficient resources*
  - *Proper priorities*
  - *Authority delegation*

  - *Management interest*

- *Driving forces*
  - *Sufficient resources*
  - *Proper priorities*
  - *Proper CEO involvement*
  - *Management's active involvement*
  - *Knowledge of environmental factors*

- *Restraining forces*
  - *Unclear objectives*

  - *Insufficient resources*
  - *Changing priorities*

  - *Insufficient authority/charter*
  - *Management indifference*

- *Restraining forces*
  - *Unclear/unrealistic objectives*
  - *Insuffficient resources*
  - *Frequently changing priorities*
  - *Lack of CEO involvement*
  - *Lack of senior management commitment*
  - *Management unclear over environmental factors*

- *Functional Support*

- *Driving forces*
  - *Clear goals and priorities*

  - *Proper planning*

  - *Adequate task integrators*

- *Driving forces*
  - *Realistic goals and priorities*
  - *Long-term reward opportunities*

  - *Credibility in planner's skills and decision-making*
  - *Continuous flow of information/feed-back*

Table 11-5. (continued)

AREA	DRIVING AND RESTRAINING FORCES	
	PROJECT MANAGEMENT	STRATEGIC PLANNING
	• Restraining forces • Priority conflicts • Funding restraints • Poor project organization	• Restraining forces • Continuously changing priorities • Overburdened work force • Corporate goals different from functional goals • Lack of visible senior management involvement
• Technical Expertise	• Driving forces • Ability to manage technology • Prior track record • Low risk project	• Driving forces • Credibility as a planner • Credibility as a decision-maker • Prior experience in strategic planning • Knowledge of environmental planning variables
	• Restraining forces • Lack of technical information • Unexpected technical problems • Inability to cope with change	• Restraining forces • Poor understanding of company goals • Poor knowledge of strategic variables • Inability to cope with change • Poor technical credibility with line executives
• Objectives	• Driving forces • Clear goals • Clear expectations/- responsibilities	• Driving forces • Clear goals • Clear expectations/- responsibilities

- *Clear interface rela-*
  tionships

- *Clear specification*

- *Restraining forces*
  - *Conflict over objec-*
    tives
  - *Customer uncer-*
    tainties

- *Active visible invol-*
  vement by the CEO
  and top manage-
  ment

- *Restraining forces*
  - *Conflicts among line*
    executives
  - *Inability to analyze/*
    predict the environ-
    ment
  - *Short-term thinking*
    dominates

H.S. Dugan, H.J. Thamhain, and D.W. Wilemon, "Managing Change in Project Management," Proceedings of the Ninth Annual Seminar Symposium on Project Management, Chicago, October 22-26, 1977, pp. 178-188.

(through the driving forces) appear to outweigh the dissimilarities, consideration must be given to using project management for breeding strategic planners. Emphasis must be placed upon bridging the gaps between tactical project management and strategic planning, perhaps through formal training, additional education, or any other technique which causes the differences to become apparent and solvable.

Some executive support must be evident during the conversion process. In addition, there must be a continuous company commitment to the strategic planning process, regardless of short-term profit and loss. Finally, there must be some sort of incentive system which links successful strategic planning to monetary and nonmonetary rewards, at least to the same degree as would be provided by a tactical project management incentive system.

ENDNOTES—Chapter 11

1. For a more detailed analysis, see Harold Kerzner, *Project Management: A Systems Approach to Planning, Scheduling, and Controlling,* 2nd edition (New York: Van Nostrand Publishers, 1984), Chapters 1, 3.

2. H.S. Dugan, H.J. Thamhain, and D.W. Wilemon, "Managing Change in Project Management," *Proceedings of the Ninth Annual Seminar Symposium on Project Management;* Chicago, October 22-26, 1977, pp. 178-188.

Chapter 12

Developing the Implementation Plan: A Project Management Approach[1]

12.0 INTRODUCTION

Strategic planning cannot be successful unless the implementation plan can be executed. Implementation planning, in general, can best be described as the function of selecting the enterprise's strategic objectives and establishing the policies, procedures, and programs necessary for achieving them. Implementation planning may be described as establishing a predetermined course of action within a forecasted environment. (The execution of a strategic plan can be described as a series of smaller implementation plans with each one assuming a forecasted environment.) The requirements of the strategic plan set the major milestones, and the line managers hope that they can meet them through proper detailed planning. If the line manager cannot commit, because the milestones are perceived as unrealistic, the project manager may have to develop alternatives, which may be to move the milestones or terminate the project. Upper-level management must become involved in the selection of alternatives during the planning stage. Implementation planning is, of course, decision-making, because it involves continuously choosing among alternatives. Planning is a required management function to facilitate the comprehension of complex problems involving interacting factors.

The project manager is the key to successful strategic project planning. It is desirable that the project manager be involved from project conception through execution. Strategic planning must be systematic, flexible, enough to handle unique activities, disciplined through reviews and controls, and capable of accepting multifunctional inputs. Successful strategic project managers realize that strategic project planning is an iterative process and must be performed throughout the life of the project, because the environment is continuously changing.

One of the objectives of strategic project planning is to completely define all work required (possibly through the development of a documented project plan) so that it will be readily identifiable to each project participant. This is necessary because:

- If the task is well understood prior to being performed, much of the work can be preplanned.
- If the task is not understood, then during the actual task execution, more knowledge is learned which, in turn, leads to changes in resources allocations, schedules, and priorities.
- The more uncertain the task, the greater the amount of information that must be processed in order to insure effective performance.

These three facets are important because each project can be different, requiring a variety of different resources that has to be performed under time, cost, and performance constraints and with little margin for error. Without proper implementation planning, strategic programs and projects can start off "behind the eight ball" because of poorly defined requirements during the initial planning phase.

12.1 GENERAL PLANNING

Implementation planning is determining what needs to be done, by whom, and by when, in order to fulfill one's assigned responsibility. There are nine major characteristics of successful planning:

- Objective. Goal, target, or quota to be achieved by a certain time.
- Program. Strategy to be followed and major actions to be taken in order to achieve or exceed objectives.
- Schedule. Plan showing when individual or group activities or accomplishments will be started and/or completed.
- Budget. Planned expenditures required to achieve or exceed objectives.
- Forecast. Projection of what will happen by a certain time.
- Organization. Design of the number and kinds of positions, along with corresponding duties and responsibilities, required to achieve or exceed objectives.
- Policy. General guide for decision making and individual actions.
- Procedure. Detailed method for carrying out a policy.

- Standard. Level of individual or group performance defined as adequate or acceptable.

Several of these characteristics require additional comments. Forecasting what will happen may not be easy, especially if predictions of environmental reactions are required. For example, planning is customarily defined as either strategic, tactical, or operational. Strategic planning is generally five years or more, tactical can be one to five years, and operational is the here and now, six months to one year. Although most implementation projects are operational, they can be considered as strategic especially if spin-offs or follow-up work is promising or if part of a master strategic plan. Forecasting also requires an understanding of strengths and weaknesses as:

- Competitive situation.
- Marketing.
- Research and development.
- Production.
- Finance.
- Personnel.
- Management structure.

If implementation planning is strictly operational, then these factors may be clearly definable. However, if strategic or long-range planning is necessary, then the future economic outlook can vary, say year to year, and replanning must be accomplished at regular intervals because the goals and objectives can change.

The last three characteristics, policies, procedures, and standards, can vary from project to project because of their uniqueness. Each project manager can establish project policies provided that they fall within the broad limits set forth by top management. Project policies must often conform closely to company policies, and are usually similar in nature from project to project. Procedures, on the other hand, can be drastically different from project to project, even if the same activity is performed. For example, the signing off of manufacturing plans may require different signatures on two selected projects even though the same end item is being produced.

Implementation planning varies at each level of the organization. At the individual level, planning is required so that cognitive simulation can be established before taking irrevocable actions. At the working group or functional level, planning must include:

- Agreement on purpose.
- Assignment and acceptance of individual responsibilities.
- Coordination of work activities.

- Increased commitment to group goals.
- Lateral communications.

At the "organizational or project" level, planning must include:

- Recognition and resolution of group conflict of goals.
- Assignment and acceptance of group responsibilities.
- Increased motivation and commitment to organizational goals.
- Vertical and lateral communications.
- Coordination of activities between groups.

12.2 PROJECT PLANNING

Successful project implementation must utilize effective planning techniques. From a systems point of view, management desires a successful plan in order to make effective utilization over several different types of projects being executed at the same time. This requires a comprehensive, systematic plan in which the entire company is considered as one large network subdivided into smaller ones.

The systematic steps identified below begin with the preliminary planning phase, which is the most critical stage for the strategic project manager.

The first step in total program planning and scheduling is understanding the project objectives. These objectives may be to develop expertise in a given area, become competitive, modify an existing facility for later use, or simply to keep key personnel employed. The objectives are generally not independent; they are all interrelated both implicitly and explicitly.

Once the objectives are clearly defined, four questions must be considered:

- What are the major elements of the work required to satisfy the objectives and how are these elements interrelated?
- Which functional divisions will assume responsibility for accomplishment of these objectives and the major element work requirements?
- Are the required corporate and organizational resources available?
- What are the information flow requirements for the project?

If the implementation project is large and complex, then careful planning and analysis must be accomplished by both the direct and indirect labor-charging organizational units. The project organizational structure must be designed to fit the project; work plans and schedules must be established such that efficient and effective allocation of resources can be made; resource costing and accounting systems must be developed; and a management information and reporting system must be established.

Effective total program planning cannot be accomplished unless all of the necessary information becomes available at project initiation. These information requirements which must be developed during the first step are:

- statement of work (SOW).
- project specifications.
- milestone schedule.
- work breakdown structure (WBS).

The statement of work (SOW) is a narrative description of the work to be accomplished. It includes the objectives of the project, a brief description of the work, the funding constraint if one exists, and the specifications and schedule. The schedule is a "gross" schedule and includes such items as the start date, end date, major milestones, and written reports (data items).

Written reports should always be identified so that if functional input is required, the functional manager will know to assign an individual who has writing skills. After all, it is no secret as to who would write the report if the line people did not.

The last major item is the work breakdown structure. The WBS is the breaking down of the statement of work into smaller elements so that better visibility and control will be obtained.

12.3 THE STATEMENT OF WORK

The statement of work (SOW) is a narrative description of the work required for the project. The complexity of the SOW is based upon the desires of top management, the customer and/or the user groups. The major elements of a statement of work include:

- General scope of work.
- Contractor's tasks.
- Contract end items.
- Reference to related studies, documentation, specifications.
- Data requirements.
- Support equipment for contract end items.
- Customer furnished property, facilities, equipment, services.
- Schedule of performance.
- Exhibits, attachments, appendices.

The SOW is prepared by the project office with input from the user groups, because user groups have a tendency to write in such scientific terms that only the user group understands the meaning. Because the project office is usually composed of personnel with writing skills, it is only fitting that the project office prepare the SOW and submit it to the user groups for verification and approval.

12.4 PROJECT SPECIFICATIONS

A specification list may be separately identified or called out as part of the statement of work. Specifications are used for man-hours, equipment, and material estimates. Small changes in a specification can cause large cost overruns.

Another reason for identifying the specifications is to make sure that there are no surprises downstream. The specifications should be the most current revision. It is not uncommon to hire outside agencies to evaluate the technical portion of the plan and to make sure that the proper specifications are being used.

Specifications are, in fact, standards for pricing out work. If specifications either do not yet exist or are not necessary, then work standards should be used for estimating.

12.5 MILESTONE SCHEDULES

Project milestone schedules contain such items as

- Project start date.
- Project end date.
- Other major milestones.
- Data items (deliverables or reports).

Project start and end dates, if known, must be included. Other major milestones such as review meetings, prototype available, procurement, testing, etc., should also be identified. The last topic, data items, is often overlooked. There are two good reasons for preparing a separate schedule for data items. First, the separate schedule will identify to line managers that personnel with writing skills may have to be assigned. Second, data items require direct labor man-hours for writing, typing, editing, proofing, retyping, graphic arts, approval, and reproduction/distribution. Many companies identify on the data item schedules the approximate number of pages per data item, and each data item is priced out at a cost per page, say $200/page. Pricing out data items separately often induces a requirement for fewer reports.

12.6 WORK BREAKDOWN STRUCTURE

The successful accomplishment of corporate objectives requires a plan that defines all effort to be expended, assigns responsibility to a specially identified organizational element, and establishes schedules and budgets for the accomplishment of the work. The preparation of this plan is the responsibility of the project manager, who is assisted by the project team assigned in accordance with project management system directives. The detailed planning is also established in accordance with company budgeting policy before (contractual) efforts are initiated.

In planning a project, the project manager must structure the work into small elements that are:

- Manageable. Specific authority and responsibility can be assigned.
- Independent or with minimum interfacing.
- Integratable. Total package can be seen.
- Measurable in terms of progress.

The first major step in the planning process after project requirements definition is the development of the work breakdown structure (WBS). The work breakdown structure is the single most important element because it provides a common framework from which:

- The total program can be described as a summation of subdivided elements.
- Planning can be performed.
- Costs and budgets can be established.
- Time, cost, performance can be tracked.
- Objectives can be linked to company resources in a logical manner.
- Schedules and status reporting procedures can be established.
- Network construction and control planning can be initiated.
- The responsibility assignments for each element can be established.

The work breakdown structure acts as a vehicle for breaking the work down into smaller elements, thus providing a greater probability that every major and minor activity will be accounted for. Although a variety of work breakdown structures exist, the most common is the six-level indentured structure shown below:

Level	Description
1	Total Program
2	Project
3	Task
4	Subtask
5	Work Package
6	Level of Effort

Level one is the total program and is composed of a set of projects. The summation of the activities and costs associated with each project must equal the total program. Each project, however, can be broken down into tasks, where the summation of all tasks equals the summation of all projects which, in turn, comprises the total program. The reason for this subdivision of effort is simply for ease of control. Project management therefore becomes synonomous with the integration of activities, and the project manager acts as the integrator using the work breakdown structure as the common framework.

If the implementation package runs for three or more years, then the upstream activities must be able to be planned for and estimated at level 5, whereas the downstream activities, say two years from now, might be only at level 2 for the moment.

12.7 ESTABLISH PRELIMINARY LOGIC FLOW

Once the WBS is developed, the project manager must decide upon that level at which he wishes to manage the project. Thus, the second step in effective project planning is for the project manager to prepare a "bubble" or *logic flow* for the desired level of the WBS.

It should be understood that the project manager is normally a generalist rather than an expert and that the logic flow must be approved by the line managers. During later steps, line managers will have the opportunity to scrutinize the logic and either recommend or make changes. The line managers are the true experts and the best people qualified to assess risk in the schedule and logic.

Use of the logic diagram to establish the project plan will permit:

- Analysis of the effect of changes; one change can result in a chain reaction affecting other activities.
- Determination of whether a series of activities are critical and the end schedule date cannot be met.
- Replanning and improving the schedule to compensate for technical problems which cause slippages in the schedule and to make tradeoffs.
- Determine schedule status at a given time and for correlating time, cost and performance.

It must be understood that, as the plan is continuously re-evaluated, environmental conditions may change so that a new logic flow will be necessary. This is particularly true in strategic planning, if we consider a long time horizon.

12.8 LINE MANAGEMENT REVIEW

The third step in the project planning process is each line manager's review of the preliminary planning documents, namely the statement of work, specifications, milestone schedule, and the work breakdown schedule. Detail planning cannot be performed effectively unless the line managers fully understand the requirements for the project.

Once the work breakdown structure and activity schedules are established, the program manager calls a meeting for all organizations, which will be required to submit pricing and scheduling information. It is imperative that all pricing or labor costing representatives be present for the first meeting. During this "kickoff" meeting, the work breakdown structure is described in depth so that each pricing unit manager will know exactly what his responsibilities are during the program. The kickoff meeting also resolves the struggle-for-power positions of several functional managers whose responsibilities may be similar or overlap on certain activities. An example of this would be quality control activities. During the research and development phase of a program, research personnel may be permitted to perform their own quality control efforts, whereas during production activities, the quality control department or division would have overall responsibility. Unfortunately, one meeting is not always sufficient to clarify all problems. Follow-up or status meeting are held, normally with only those parties concerned with the problems that have arisen. Some companies prefer to have all members attend the status meetings so that all personnel will be familiar with the total effort and the associated problems. The advantage of not having all program-related personnel attend at that time is of the essence when pricing out activities. Many functional divisions carry this policy one step further by having a divisional representative together with possibly key department managers or section supervisors as the only attendees to this initial meeting. The divisional representative then assumes all responsibility for assuring that all costing data be submitted on time. This may be beneficial in that the program office need only contact one individual in the division to learn of the activity status, but may become a bottleneck if the representative fails to maintain proper communication between the functional units and the program office, or if the individual simply is unfamiliar with the pricing requirements of the work breakdown structure.

Following the meeting, the project manager must remain available for questions/answers with the line managers. It may take the line managers a week or longer to digest the information. It is not uncommon for the line managers to take exception to some of the information and to request that changes be made, especially in the logic or sequencing of events and activities.

12.9 PRELIMINARY WBS PRICING

In some companies, detail planning cannot begin until management has a "rough" cost for the project. In such cases, the project manager will conduct a "quick and dirty" pricing estimate in order to see if the cost is feasible.

More and more executives are in favor of this fourth step, which is the incremental stage of pricing/estimating. Usually, a "quick and dirty" pricing of the WBS can be performed in a week or so and at a very minimal cost. The alternative to this would be to perform detail pricing/estimating, and this may take months and be very costly.

These costs are then shown to the executives or the project sponsor. If the costs are within reason, then the project manager will be authorized to begin detail planning and estimating.

12.10 DETAIL WBS PRICING

The fifth step is detail WBS pricing, and this is normally the beginning of detail project implementation planning. In this step, the line managers are expected to use the various estimating methods available to them for project estimating. These estimating methods can range from order-of-magnitude analysis to detail estimates.

Projects can range from a feasibility study; through modification of existing facilities; to complete design, procurement, and construction of a large complex. Whatever the project may be, whether large or small, the estimate and type of information desired may differ radically.

The first type of estimate is an *order-of-magnitude* analysis and is made without any detailed engineering data. The order of magnitude analysis may have an accuracy of $\pm$ 35 percent within the scope of the project. This type of estimate may use past experience (not necessarily similar), scale factors, or capacity estimates (i.e., $/# of product or $/KW electricity).

Next, there is the *approximate estimate* (or top-down estimate), which is also made without detailed engineering data, and may be accurate to $\pm$ 15 percent. This type of estimate is prorated from previous projects that are similar in scope and capacity, and may be titled as estimating by analogy, rule of thumb, and indexed cost of similar activities adjusted for capacity and technology. In such a case, the estimator may say that this activity is 50 percent more difficult than a previous (reference) activity and requires 50 percent more time, man-hours, dollars, materials, etc.

The *definitive estimate* is prepared from well-defined engineering data including (as a minimum) vendor quotes, fairly complete plans, specifications, unit prices, and estimate to complete. The definitive estimate is also referred to as detailed estimating and has an accuracy of $\pm$ 5 percent.

Another method for estimating is the use of *learning curves*. Learning curves are graphical representations of repetitive functions in which continuous operations will lead to a reduction in time, resources, and money. The theory behind learning curves is usually applied to manufacturing operations.

Many companies try to standardize their estimating procedures by developing an estimating manual. The estimating manual is then used to price out the effort, perhaps as much as 90 percent. Estimating manuals are usually better estimates than industrial engineering standards, because they include groups of tasks and take into consideration such items as down time, clean-up time, lunch, and breaks.

Estimating manuals, just as the name implies, provide estimates. The real question, of course, is "How good is the estimate?" Most estimating manuals provide accuracy limitations by defining the type of estimates.

Not all companies can use estimating manuals. Estimating manuals work best for repetitive tasks or similar tasks that can use a previous estimate adjusted by a degree of difficulty factor. Activities such as R&D do not lend themselves to the use of estimating manuals other than for benchmark, repetitive laboratory tests. Project managers must make careful consideration on whether or not the estimating manual is a viable approach. The literature abounds with companies that have spent millions trying to develop estimating manuals for situations that just do not lend themselves to the approach.

During competitive bidding, it is important that the type of estimate be consistent with the customer's requirements. For in-house projects the type of estimate can vary over the lifecycle of a project.

- Conceptual stage. Venture guidance or feasibility studies for the evaluation of future work. This is often based upon minimum scope information.
- Planning stage. Estimating for authorization of partial or full funds. These estimates are based upon preliminary design and scope.
- Main stage. Estimating for detailed work.
- Termination stage. Reestimation for major scope changes or variances beyond the authorization range.

The exact method for estimating is the responsibility of the line managers but may be dependent upon the level of the WBS. Many projects are priced out at level 5 of the WBS, but the WBS is managed at level 3. In such a case, some elements may be priced out at level 3 or level 4, rather than level 5. Obviously, the lower the level of the WBS, the more accurate the estimate, but the greater the cost of preparing the estimate.

This activity schedules the development of the work breakdown structure and provides management with two of the three operational tools necessary for the control of a system or project. The development of these two tools is normally the responsibility of the program office, with input from the functional units.

The integration of the functional unit into the project environment or system occurs through the pricing out of the work breakdown structure. The total program costs obtained by pricing out the activities over the scheduled period of performance provides management with the third tool necessary to successfully manage the project. During the pricing activities, the functional units have the option to consult project management for possible changes to the activity schedules and work breakdown structure.

The work breakdown structure and activity schedules are priced out through the lowest pricing units of the company. It is the responsibility of these pricing units, whether they be sections, departments, or divisions, to provide accurate and meaningful cost data (based upon historical standards, if possible). All information is priced out at the lowest level of performance required. Costing information is rolled up to the project level and then one step further to the total program level.

Under ideal conditions, the work required (man-hours), to complete a given task can be based upon historical standards. Unfortunately, for many industries, projects and programs are so diversified that realistic comparisons between previous activities may not be possible. The costing information obtained from each pricing unit, whether or not it is based upon historical standards, should be regarded only as an estimate. How can a company predict the salary structure three years from now? Will the business base (and therefore overhead rates) change over the duration of the program? What will be the cost of raw materials two years from now? The final response to these questions shows that costing data is explicitly related to an environment that cannot be predicted with any high degree of certainty. The systems approach to management, however, provides for a more rapid response to the environment.

Once the cost data are assembled, it must be analyzed for the potential impact on the company resources of people, money, equipment, and facilities. It is only through the total program costs analysis that resource allocations can be analyzed. The resource allocation analysis is performed at all levels of management, ranging from the section supervisor to the vice president and general manager. For most programs, the chief executive must approve final cost data and the allocation of resources.

Proper analysis of the total program costs can provide management (both program and corporate) with a strategic planning model for integration of the current program with other programs in order to obtain a total corporate strategy. Meaningful planning and pricing models include analyses for monthly manloading schedules per department, monthly costs per department, monthly and yearly total program costs, monthly material expenditures, and total program cash-flow and man-hour requirements per month.

Previously, we identified several of the problems that occur at the nodes where the horizontal hierarchy of project management interfaces with the vertical hierarchy of functional management. The pricing out of the work breakdown structure provides the basis for effective and open communication between functional and program management, where both parties have one common goal. After the pricing effort is completed, and the program is initiated, the work breakdown structure still forms the basis of a communicative tool by documenting the performance agreed upon in the pricing effort, as well as establishing the criteria against which performance costs will be measured.

At the completion of the fifth step, the project manager should have detailed costs and schedules for all activities at the desired levels of the WBS. However, it must be noted that the schedules and costs are based upon unlimited resources. Line managers may have approximate start and end dates for their activities but, until exact calendar dates are identified, the line managers will assume that the necessary resources will be available when needed. In later steps, the line managers will be allowed to update their budgets and schedules based upon exact calendar dates and availability of resources.

12.11 REVIEW COSTS WITH THE LINE MANAGERS

In the sixth step, the project manager will review the cost of each WBS element with each of the line managers. The purpose of this review is to make sure that:

- All elements priced out.
- Each department knows respective responsibilities.
- High risk areas identified.
- Costs realistic.

It is often the case that the actual pricing is performed not by the line manager himself, but by one of his personnel. Based upon the confidence that the project manager has in the pricing estimates, the project manager may simply review the estimates with the functional employees rather than with the line manager. In either event, the intent is still to make sure that the line managers are committed to the estimate and the schedule.

12.12 DECIDE UPON THE BASE COST

If the cost, schedule, and logic are realistic, and if the line managers can provide the necessary support and commitment, the project manager must then decide upon the basic course of action. This so-called *base case* is the prime direction for the project, and is the seventh step in the planning process.

The base case approach is selected based upon how well it satisfies the project's strategic objectives and possibly the ease by which downstream tradeoffs can be performed. The parameters considered in selecting the base case include:

- Primary objective. Coordinate activities into one master plan in order to

complete the project in:
- —Best time
- —Least cost
- —Least risk
- Secondary objectives. Studying alternatives:
  - —Develop optimum schedule
  - —Use resources effectively
  - —Communications
  - —Refinement of estimating criteria
  - —Good project control
  - —Ease of revisions/tradeoffs
- Constraints. Ability to satisfy customer/company limitations:
  - —Calendar completion date
  - —Cash or cash flow restrictions
  - —Limited resources
  - —Approvals

12.13 FINALIZATION OF THE COST/SCHEDULE

The eighth step is the finalization of the costs and schedules. The project manager must decide upon the final cost for each element of the WBS and the schedules for each WBS element. Good project managers know that there will always be "fat" built into the budgets and schedules by the line managers. The project manager will never try to remove this cushion from the line managers as long as the program can be sold to senior management or the customer. This step is crucial for the project manager, because the project manager must defend and support his position. If the project manager's defense is weak, senior management may view the project as a high financial risk and project funding may be cancelled.

12.14 SENIOR MANAGEMENT REVIEW

Project execution cannot begin without a review and approval by senior management. This type of review meeting is often called a *pricing review* meeting, where the project manager must justify his costs/schedules as well as any other assumptions made.

Although the pricing of a project is an iterative process, the project manager must still burden himself at several iteration points by developing cost summary reports so that key project decisions can be made during the planning. There are at least two times when detailed pricing summaries are needed: in preparation for the pricing review meeting with management, and at pricing termination. At all other times, it is possible that simple cosmetic surgery can be performed on previous cost summaries, such as perturbations in escalation factors and procurement cost of raw materials. The list identified below shows the typical pricing reports/tables:

- A detailed cost breakdown for each WBS element. If the work is priced out at the task level, then there should be a cost summary sheet for each task, as well as rollup sheets for each project and the total program.
- A total program manpower curve for each department. These manpower curves show how each department has contracted with the project office to supply functional resources. If the department manpower curves contain several "peaks and valleys," then the project manager may have to alter some of his schedules to obtain some degree of manpower smoothing. Functional managers always prefer manpower-smoothed resource allocations.
- A monthly equivalent manpower cost summary. This table normally shows the fully burdened cost for the average departmental employee carried out over the entire period of project performance. If project costs have to be reduced, the project manager performs a parametric study between this table and the manpower curve tables.
- A yearly cost distribution table. This table is broken down by WBS element and shows the yearly (or quarterly) costs that will be required. This table, in essence, is a project cash flow summary per activity.
- A functional cost and hour summary. This table provides top management with an overall description of how many hours and dollars will be spent by each major functional unit, as per division. Top management would use this as part of the forward planning process to make sure that there are sufficient resources available for all projects. This also includes indirect hours and dollars.
- A monthly labor hour and dollar expenditure forecast. This table can be combined with the yearly cost distribution, except that it is broken down by month, not activity or department. In addition, this table normally includes manpower termination liability information for premature cancellation of the project by outside customers.
- A raw material and expenditure forecast. This shows the cash flow for raw materials based upon vendor lead times, payment schedules, commitments, and termination liability.
- Total program termination liability per month. This table shows the customer the monthly costs for the entire program. This is the customer's cash flow, not the contractor's. The difference is that each monthly cost contains the termination liability for man-hours and dollars on labor and raw materials. This table is actually the monthly costs attributed to premature project termination.

These tables are used both by project managers and upper-level executives. The project managers utilize these tables as the basis for project cost control. Top level management utilizes these tables for selecting, approving, and prioritizing projects.

There are three possible outcomes from the pricing review meeting. First, management can cancel the project because the costs are too high. Second, management can ask the project manager to reprice the project using different assumptions and ground rules. Third, management can authorize the project to begin, but the project manager will have at his disposal only, say, 85 percent of the funding requested. This last case is troublesome, because the project manager must reduce the costs by 15 percent. This is usually accomplished by asking (or "begging") the line managers to perform the work in less time.

12.15 IDENTIFY RESOURCE REQUIREMENTS

Step 10 is the beginning of the full detail planning process and begins with the identification of the required resources. During the previous steps, the functional managers performed their planning and estimating activities by assuming unlimited resources. However, once the project is approved by senior management, the line manager's resources are limited.

If senior management has reduced the budget by 15 percent, then the project manager may have to negotiate for above average personnel in order to offset the reduction in man-hours and cost. The worst situation would be for the project manager to have to force the line managers to either remove the padding in their estimates or to accept unreasonable risks.

Identifying the resource requirements includes two additional functions. First, the project manager may find it necessary to prepare job descriptions establishing the qualifications expected of the functional personnel. This task is often difficult to perform, because the project manager may not be the best person qualified to identify the requirements.

The second function is the negotiation of qualified personnel. Again, the project manager may have to rely upon the line manager's expertise. However, the project manager should solicit the line manager's opinion on the capabilities of the people to be assigned and how much supervision will be required.

12.16 LINEAR RESPONSIBILITY CHARTS

Step 11 is the development of the linear responsibility chart, which assigned responsibility of each WBS element to specific people or titles. The ideal situation is for the project manager to work with other managers in deciding upon the exact responsibilities based upon the exact knowledge of who is or will be assigned. Unfortunately, this exact knowledge is not known, and the linear responsibility chart must be periodically updated.

12.17 FINALIZATION OF THE PERT CHART

Step 12 is the finalization of the *PERT chart*. Although a preliminary PERT chart was developed earlier, it was based upon unlimited resources and using standard estimates. The finalized PERT chart contains time durations based upon the actual skills of the assigned employees and their availability.

12.18 DETAILED SCHEDULES AND CHARTS

The scheduling of activities is Step 13 and the first major requirement of the project office after project go-ahead. The project office normally assumes full responsibility for activity scheduling if the activity is not too complex. For large projects, functional management input is required before scheduling can be completed. Depending on project size and contractual requirements, it is not unusual for the project office to maintain, at all times, a project staff member whose responsibility is that of a scheduler. This individual continuously develops and updates activity schedules to provide a means of tracking project work. The resulting information is then supplied to the project office personnel, functional management, team members and, last but not least, presented to the customer or executive.

Activity scheduling is probably the single most important tool for determining how company resources should be integrated so that synergy will be produced. Activity schedules are invaluable for projecting time-phased resource utilization requirements as well as providing a basis for visually tracking performance. Most projects begin with the development of the schedule so that accurate cost estimates can be made. The schedules serve as master plans from which both the customer and management have an up-to-date picture of operations.

Certain guidelines should be followed in preparation of schedules, regardless of the projected use or complexity:

- All major events and dates must be clearly identified. If a statement of work is supplied, then those dates shown on the accompanying schedules must be included. If for any reason the milestone dates cannot be met, then executive management should be notified immediately.
- The exact sequence of work should be defined through a network in which interrelationships between events can be identified.
- Schedules should be directly relatable to the work breakdown structure. If the WBS is developed according to a specific sequence of work, then it becomes an easy task to identify work sequences in schedules using the same numbering system as in the WBS. The minimum requirement should be to show where and when all tasks start and finish.
- All schedules must identify the time constraints and, if possible, should identify those resources required for each event.

Although these four guidelines serve as reference for schedule preparation, they do not define how complex the schedules should be. Before preparing the schedules, three questions should be considered:

- How many events or activities should each network have?
- How much of a detailed technical breakdown should be included?
- Who is the intended audience for this schedule?

Most organizations develop multiple schedules: summary schedules for management and planners, and detailed schedules for the doers and lower level control. The detailed schedules may be strictly for interdepartmental activities. Project management must approve all schedules down through the first three levels of the work breakdown structure. For lower level schedules (detailed interdepartmental) project management may or may not request sign of approval.

12.19 "WHAT-IF" CONSIDERATIONS

Good project managers always play "what-if" games in order to develop alternative courses of action. This is Step 14. The "what-if" considerations begin with a sensitivity analysis to determine the most critical or sensitive elements in the schedule. It is not necessary for the most sensitive elements to fall on the critical path.

Once the contingency plans are developed by the project manager, the information is usually withheld from release to the functional departments for fear that the functional departments easiest way out is often not the best.

12.20 PROGRAM PLAN

Fundamental to the success of any project is documented planning in the form of a program plan. This is Step 15. In an ideal situation, the program office can present the functional manager with a copy of the program plan and simply say, "accomplish it." The concept of the program plan came under severe scrutiny during the 1960s, when the Department of Defense required all contractors to submit detailed planning to such extremes that many organizations were wasting talented people by having them serve as writers instead of doers. Since then, because of the complexity of large programs, requirements imposed on the project plan have been eased.

For large and often complex projects, customers may require a project plan that documents all activities within the project. The project plan then serves as a guideline for the lifetime of the project and may be revised as often as once a month, depending upon the circumstances and the type of project (research and development projects require more revisions to the project plan than manufacturing or construction projects). The project plan provides the following framework:

- Eliminates conflicts between functional managers.
- Eliminates conflicts between functional management and program management.
- Provides a standard communicative tool throughout the lifetime of the project (it should be geared to the work breakdown structure).
- Provides verification that the contractor understands the customer's objectives and requirements.
- Provides a means for identifying inconsistencies in the planning phase.
- Provides a means for early identification of problem areas and risks so that no "surprises occur downstream."
- Contains all of the schedules defined previously as a basis for project analysis and reporting.

The project plan is a standard from which performance can be measured. It serves as a cookbook for the duration of the project by defining for all personnel identified with the project:

- What will be accomplished?
- How will it be accomplished?
- Where will it be accomplished?
- When will it be accomplished?
- Why will it be accomplished?

The answers to these questions force all personnel to take a hard look at:

- Project requirements.
- Project management.
- Project schedules.
- Facility requirements.
- Logistic support.
- Financial support.
- Manpower and organization.

The project plan is more than just a set of instructions. It is an attempt to eliminate crisis by preventing anything from "falling through the cracks." The plan is documented and approved by all parties to determine what data, if any, is missing and the probable resulting effect. As the project matures, the project plan is revised to account for new or missing data.

Finally, project, line, and executive management must analyze other internal and external variables before finalizing the schedules and plans. A partial listing of these variables would include:

- Introduction or acceptance of product in marketplace.
- Present or planned manpower availability.
- Economical constraints of the project.
- Degree of technical difficulty.
- Manpower availability.
- Availability of personnel training.
- Priority of the project.

12.21 SUMMARY

In this chapter, we have presented a project management approach to implementation. The policies, procedures, and programs for achieving corporate strategy and objectives are the essence of implementing the plan. Applying the procedures of project management puts the plan into action.

ENDNOTES—Chapter 12

1. Most of this chapter has been adapted from Harold Kerzner, *Project Management: A Systems Approach to Planning, Scheduling, and Controlling*, 2nd edition (New York: Van Nostrand Publishers, 1984), chapters 11 and 14.

Index

Miner, John B., 21
Mintzberg, Henry, 35
mission, 29, 39, 51
   focus of, 40
models, uses and purposes of, 36
Modigliani, Franco, 111
Mueller, James A., 175, 226, 228
multinational strategies, 342-357
   choosing entry modes for, 354
   choosing target markets for, 349
   designing entry strategies as,
   347
   monitoring and revising entry
   strategy in, 356
   planning model for, 348
   reasons for, 342
   three-stage evolution in, 345
multinational-enterprise stage, 346
multiple market firm, strategic
   planning process and, 31

N

Nason, H.K., 186
natural resources, 42
net profit margin, 110
net working capital, 97
new product development, 156
   classification of, 229
   cumulative expenditures and
   time spent in, 157
   departmental responsibilities in,
   230
   mortality rate for, 157
   success of, 158
non-integrated strategies, 64
nondisclosure agreements, 159

O

objectives, 44, 56, 57, 88
   functional, 46, 47
   operationalizing measurable
   annual, 45
   research and development, 170,
   187
offensive research and
   development, 168, 200
offices, location of, 79
on-the-job-training (OJT), 256
operating cycle, manufacturing
   firm, 96
operating leverage, 105, 107

product lifecycle and, 108
   profitability and, 106
operations costs, 225
options, strategic, 73
order-of-magnitude analysis, 384
organic growth, 238
organizational survival strategies, 1

P

Packard, Davide, 289
patents, 159, 183
peak-load pricing, 141
Pearce and Robinson paradigm, 29
performance outcomes, 48
personal selling, 144
personnel planning, 256, 260
PERT charts, 391
pitfalls in strategic planning, 15
planning
   levels of, 360
   process of, 7
plant utilization, 50, 79
policies, 51
   issues involved in evolution of,
   12
   product, 131
   role of, 12
"Policy as a Field of Management
   Theory," 35
Porter Model, 58
Porter, Michael, 27, 35, 119, 120,
   123, 138
portfolio planning, 68
   classification matrix for, 75
   research and development and,
   158
posturing, 232
pricing strategy, 50, 92, 139, 140
   competitive advantage of, 142
   competitive cycle and, 143
   external environmental factors
   affecting, 140
   methods of determining, 141
prior art, 181
proactive firms, 6
problem children, 70
producibility, 268
   iterative design process
   considerations for, 269
   objectives and designs of, 268
product characteristics, 91

product differentiation, 138
product lifecycle
impact of marketing mix
elements on, 137
operating leverage and, 108
patterns for, 133, 134
research and development and,
167, 169, 174
significance of marketing mix in,
136
strategic planning use of, 135
product marketing, 325
product policy, 131
product-line strategy, 135
product/market evolution
fundamental stages of, 120
sources of distinctive
competence in, 121
production capability, 41
production support, 198
productivity, 50
effective interaction and, 263
factors influencing, 262
international rating of, 262
manufacturing, 162-165
products offered, 41
profitability, 8, 42, 50, 57
components of, 301
effects of operating leverage on,
106
improvement of, 300
profitability ratios, 109, 110
profits, 50
improved chances for, 4
understatement of, 113
project management, 358-374
CEO involvement in, 367
communications in, 369
concept of, 359
developing implementation plan
for, 375-396
driving and restraining forces in,
370
force field analysis in, 369
identifying project/strategic
variables in, 366
leadership styles for, 362
levels of planning in, 360
lifecycle phases in, 362-366
managerial practice in, 362
research and development, 193

strategic thinking vs., 361
project termination, 215
promotion strategy, 92, 143
model for, 145
public relations, 147
publicity, 144
purchase volume, usage group
differences in, 132
push vs. pull strategy, 146

Q

quasi-integrated strategies, 64
Quarterly Financial Report, 97
Quinn, James B., 175, 195, 226,
228

R

rate-of-return pricing, 141
ratio analysis, 112
raw material availability and quality,
83
regular plus extra dividend policy,
111
research and development
research and development
aligning goals and objectives in,
187
benefits of, 162
budgeting for, 154
business objective matrix for,
227
controlling costs of, 218
corporate image in, 174
corporate position of, 196-197
current business and political
factors influencing, 184
effect of market share on, 184
executive involvement in, 185
external environment factors
and, 177
external influences and, 179-184
factor and subfactor ratings for
new products in, 212
factors influencing strategies of,
170
fragmented markets and, 174
function of, 154
governmental constraints on,
160
human behavior and, 161
integration of functional